Advance Reviews

Tarek Fatah has dared to question the received wisdom about the centrality of the Islamic State to the destiny of the universal Muslim community. He shows through painstaking, meticulous research that the sooner the Muslims rid themselves of the deadweight of wasteful and vain centuries of tribal and clannish feuds and sectarian strife in the name of true Islam and the Islamic state the greater will be their chances of getting out of the rut of obscurantism and fanaticism. Like all other civilized religious communities of the world the Muslims too need to adopt secularism and pluralism as an integral part of their social and political orders. I am sure this book will generate much-needed critical discussion on political Islam.

Ishtiaq Ahmed, Ph.D.
Professor of Political Science, University of Stockholm, Sweden.
Visiting Senior Research Fellow at the Institute of South Asian Studies (ISAS), Singapore

Chasing a Mirage should be required reading for the Left in the West who have mistakenly started believing that Islamists represent some sort of anti-imperialism. Tarek Fatah convincingly demonstrates that the Islamist agenda is not only medieval and tribal, it is misogynist and reactionary and has been a serious threat to progressive forces throughout history. The agenda of the Muslim Brotherhood and the Jamaat-e-Islami must never be confused with the struggle for social justice, equality and enlightenment. *Chasing a Mirage* is an extremely valuable contribution to the fight by progressive Muslims against Islamist fascism.

Farooq Tahir
Secretary General
Pakistan Labour Party

In *Chasing a Mirage,* Tarek Fatah takes a unique look at Islamic history, one that may cause some discomfort among the orthodoxy. The book provides an amazing insight into the power struggles that have plagued Muslim society for centuries and how Islam has often been used as a political tool, rather than as a religion. Fatah also addresses internalized racism within the Muslim community and the role it continues to play in conflicts like the one in Darfur. The book is a valuable contribution to the on-going debate within the Muslim community about how it reconciles with modernity.

Senator Mobina Jaffer

Parliament of Canada, Ottawa

Tarek Fatah's is a voice that needs to be heard. Canada needs a healthy, reasoned debate about the issues he is raising, and indeed so does the world. He is never afraid to speak his mind, and he refuses to shrink quietly into the night. The questions he is posing are critical.

Bob Rae
Former Premier of Ontario, Toronto

This book focuses on the internal debate within the Muslim world of today and the rise of political Islam from the viewpoint of a critique of Muslim historiography and hagiography. The author reminds us that the sacralisation of Muslim politics and the canonisation of Islamist political thinking was the direct result of centuries of centralisation of power (both political and representational) at the hands of right-wing Muslim demagogues and ideologues whose own politics can only be described in present-day terms as Fascist and intolerant.

Dr. Farish A. Noor
Centre for Modern Oriental Studies, Berlin; and
Sunan Kalijaga Islamic University, Jogjakarta, Indonesia

Tarek Fatah rightly explains that the decline of the world's Muslims does not come from the absence of a puritanical Islamic state. It is the result of the state in which the Muslims currently find themselves. He also calls for making a distinction between pietistic Muslims and those pursuing power in Islam's name. Some of his views, especially in relation to U.S. policies and the war against terrorism, are bound to generate controversy, and not everyone who agrees with his diagnosis will necessarily agree with his prescription. But Fatah joins the expanding list of Muslim authors challenging Islamism and demanding that Muslims should revert to Islam an essentially spiritual and ethical belief system instead of stretching history to present Islam as a political ideology.

Professor Husain Haqqani
Director of Boston University's Center for International Relations
Co-Chair of the Islam and Democracy Project at Hudson Institute, Washington D.C.

Fatah writes with a startling knowledge of and empathy for his religion and its adherents. He argues with biting intelligence for a genuine and cleansing understanding of Islam's history and how it should be understood in the modern world. His analysis of the difference between a state of Islam and an Islamic state is vitally important. This is the best criticism; based in love.

Michael Coren
Columnist, Toronto Sun

This fascinating work by brave and brilliant Tarek Fatah is simultaneously thought-provoking, instructive and enlightening for laymen and scholars, Muslim and non-Muslim. This wonderful combination of knowledge, wisdom and foresight—a progressive and honest Muslim's cry from his heart—is an invaluable and rare addition to the corpus of Islamic literature in the post-9/11 world, a bold step towards Islamic Reformation and Enlightenment.

Dr. Taj Hashmi
Professor, Asia-Pacific Center for Security Studies, Honolulu

Chasing a Mirage

Chasing a Mirage

The Tragic Illusion of an Islamic State

Tarek Fatah

John Wiley & Sons Canada, Ltd.

Library and Archives Canada Cataloguing in Publication Data

Fatah, Tarek, 1949–
    Chasing a mirage : the tragic illusion of an Islamic state / Tarek Fatah.

Includes bibliographical references and index.

ISBN 978-0-470-84116-7

    1. Islam and state. 2. Islam—21st century. 3. Muslims. 4. Islamic countries—Politics and government. I. Title.

BP163.F38 2008   297.2'72   C2008-900614-3

Production Credits
Cover design: Ian Koo
Interior text design: Natalia Burobina
Typesetters: Thomson Digital
Printer: Friesens

John Wiley & Sons Canada, Ltd.
6045 Freemont Blvd.
Mississauga, Ontario
L5R 4J3

This book is printed with biodegradable vegetable-based inks. Text pages are printed on 551b 100% PCW Hi-Bulk Natural by Friesens Corp., an FSC certified printer.

Printed in Canada

1 2 3 4 5 FP 12 11 10 09 08

For
Benazir Bhutto
and
Daniel Pearl
A Muslim and a Jew,
both victims of terrorism.

"The Taliban are the expression of a modern disease, symptoms of a social cancer which shall destroy Muslim societies if its growth is not arrested and the disease is not eliminated. It is prone to spreading, and the Taliban will be the most deadly communicators of cancer if they remain so organically linked to Pakistan."

—Eqbal Ahmed
Daily *Dawn*, Karachi, 1998

"What do the Islamists offer? A route to a past, which, mercifully for the people of the seventh century, never existed. If the 'Emirate of Afghanistan' is the model for what they want to impose on the world, then the bulk of Muslims would rise up in arms against them. Don't imagine that either Osama [Bin Laden] or Mullah Omar represent the future of Islam . . . Would you want to live under those conditions? Would you tolerate your sister, your mother or the woman you love being hidden from public view and only allowed out shrouded like a corpse?"

—Tariq Ali
Letter to a Young Muslim, April 25, 2002

CONTENTS

Preface

I AM AN INDIAN BORN IN PAKISTAN; a Punjabi born in Islam; an immigrant in Canada with a Muslim consciousness, grounded in a Marxist youth. I am one of Salman Rushdie's many *Midnight's Children*: we were snatched from the cradle of a great civilization and made permanent refugees, sent in search of an oasis that turned out to be a mirage.* I am in pain, a living witness to how dreams of hope and enlightenment can be turned into a nightmare of despair and failure. Promises made to the children of my generation that were never meant to be kept. Today, the result is a Muslim society lost in the sands of Sinai with no Moses to lead us out, held hostage by hateful pretenders of piety. Our problems are further compounded by a collective denial of the fact that the pain we suffer is caused mostly by self-inflicted wounds, and is not entirely the result of some Zionist conspiracy hatched with the West.

I write as a Muslim whose ancestors were Hindu. My religion, Islam, is rooted in Judaism, while my Punjabi culture is tied to that of the Sikhs. Yet I am told by Islamists that without shedding this multifaceted heritage, if not outrightly rejecting it, I cannot be considered a true Muslim.

Of all the ingredients that make up my complex identity, being Canadian has had the most profound effect on my thinking. It is Canada that propels me to swim upstream to imitate with humility the giants who have ventured into uncharted waters before me. Men like Louis-Joseph Papineau, Tommy Douglas, Pierre Trudeau, and Norman Bethune; women like Agnes Macphail, Rosemary Brown and Nellie McClung. For it is only here in Canada that I

---

* In the novel, a group of children are born in that first minute of India and Pakistan's independence from Britain and witness the turmoil resulting from the partition of the sub-continent. These 1001 children have magical abilities; some can read minds while others travel through time and some indulge in witchcraft.

can speak out against the hijacking of my faith and the encroaching spectre of a new Islamo-fascism.

In this book I attempt to draw a distinction between Islamists and Muslims. What Islamists seek and what Muslims desire are two separate objectives, sometimes overlapping, but clearly distinct. While the former seek an "Islamic State," the latter merely desires a "state of Islam." One state requires a theocracy, the other a state of spirituality.

Islam—my religion—offers a universality best reflected in Mecca, Saudi Arabia, where for thousands of years pilgrims have circumambulated the Ka'aba* in the image of planets revolving around the Sun, walking around what they believe is the epicentre of their world. I have sat through many nights perched on the upper floors of the Ka'aba, watching as tens of thousands of people spun rings around the black cube, oblivious that they were mimicking the behaviour of sub-atomic particles of matter. Or perhaps a reflection of the millions of galaxies that swing around an invisible centre, in a whirlpool of limitless emptiness. Men and women have long trodden the sacred ground in a way that symbolizes the endless motion that gives life to this universe. The simple fact that countless fellow humans have walked this path and millions more will do so in the future, makes the Ka'aba a holy place; one's mere presence becoming an act of worship. It is one of the few places in the world where humanity sheds its pomp, class, colour, and comfort to submit. Twice I have done the pilgrimage known as the *hajj*, once emulating my wife's strict conservative Fatimide Shia custom and again, four years later, in my mother's more relaxed Sunni traditions. On both occasions it was the sight of the human multitude, stripped to their bare necessities, that made me recognize the universality of my faith.

Chasing a Mirage is a cry from my heart to my co-religionists, my Muslim sisters and brothers. It is a plea to them to remove their blindfolds, once and for all; to free themselves from the shackles of conformity that have stunted their development for so long. In this book, I try to demonstrate that from the earliest annals of Islamic history, there have been two streams of Islamic practice, both running concurrently and parallel, but in opposite directions, leading to conflicting outcomes. From the moment the Prophet of Islam died in 632 CE, some Muslims took the path of strengthening the state of Islam, while others embarked on the establishment of the Islamic State.

The phrase "state of Islam" defines the condition of a Muslim in how he or she imbibes the values of Islam to govern personal life and uses

---

* *Ka'aba*: Islam's holiest place. It is a cuboidal building inside a mosque.

faith as a moral compass. In contrast, the "Islamic State" is a political entity: a state, caliphate, sultanate, kingdom, or country that uses Islam as a tool to govern society and control its citizenry. At times, these two objectives overlap each other, but most often, they clash. Islamists obsessed with the establishment of the Islamic State have ridden roughshod over Quranic principles and the Prophet's message of equality. However, Muslims who have striven to achieve a state of Islam have invariably stepped away from using Islam to chase political power, opting instead for intellectual and pious pursuits. These were the people responsible for what is glorious about our medieval heritage and Islam's contributions to human civilization.

This book is an appeal to those of my co-religionists who are chasing the mirage of an Islamic State. I hope they can reflect on the futility of their endeavour and instead focus on achieving the state of Islam. Islamists working for the establishment of an Islamic State are headed in the wrong direction. I hope to convince my fellow Muslims that clinging to mythologies of the past is the formula for a fiasco. I would hope they stand up to the merchants of segregation who have fed us with myths and got us addicted to a forced sense of victimhood. Conventional wisdom in the Muslim world dictates that to move forward, we need to link to our past. Fair enough, but in doing so, we have all but given up on the future, labelling modernity itself as the enemy.

This attitude is best reflected in the January 19, 1992, issue of the now-defunct Islamabad newspaper *The Muslim*. It published an editorial cartoon that even today depicts the dilemma facing much of the Muslim world.

If the cartoon reflected the situation of Muslims in South Asia, their Arab cousins were doing no better. Ten years later, in 2002, the United Nations Development Program (UNDP) released a scathing report slamming Arab

The Muslim

countries for oppressing women, subjugating citizens, and failing to provide adequate education.

The report, written by distinguished Arab intellectuals and presented by Rima Khalaf Hunaidi, the former deputy prime minister of Jordan, accused the Arabs of squandering oil wealth and gave them a failing grade on virtually every measurable human index from education to economy, development, and democracy. Hunaidi suggested that only Arabs can address what she called "some very scary signals," and she summed up by concluding: "The three main deficits are freedom, gender and knowledge."

Reaction to the UNDP report was predictable. Soon after it appeared in a Canadian newspaper column titled "Tough Report Says Arab World Stuck in Dark Ages," a prominent Egyptian Canadian responded by accusing the newspaper of running a "racist" headline. Instead of reflecting on the report and worrying about its findings, the writer went on the defensive, making the outlandish claim that "there is more freedom of the press in Egypt today than in Canada." It is this inability to face the truth that has become systemic among Muslim opinion leaders. This attitude is cause for serious concern. For it is far more difficult to acknowledge our mistakes than to blame them on a foreign conspiracy.

This book is aimed at my fellow Muslims with the hope that they will be willing to read and reflect on the challenges we all face. It is an attempt to speak the unspeakable, to wash some dirty linen in public, to say to my brothers and sisters in Islam that we are standing naked in the middle of the town square and the whole world is watching. If we do not cleanse ourselves with truth, the stench of our lies will drive us all mad.

The book is also aimed at the ordinary, well-meaning, yet naive non-Muslims of Europe and North America, who are bewildered as they face a community that seemingly refuses to integrate or assimilate as part of Western society, yet wishes to stay in their midst. Liberal and left-leaning Europeans and North Americans may be troubled with the in-your-face defiance of radical Islamist youth, but it seems they are infatuated by the apparently anti-establishment stance. This book may help these liberals understand that the anti-Americanism of the radical Islamists has little to do with the anti-imperialism of Mark Twain. In fact, the anti-Americanism of the Islamist is not about the United States, but reflects their contempt for the liberal social democratic society we have built and its emphasis on liberty and freedom of the individual itself. My hope is that *Chasing a Mirage* may also reach the neo-conservative proponents of the so-called war on terrorism. I hope to make them realize that their warmongering has been the best thing that happened to the Islamist proponents of a worldwide jihad. The invasion of Iraq was manna from heaven for Al-Qaeda. Bin Laden could not have asked for anything more. I hope that, after reading this book, the conservative Republicans in the United States and their neo-conservative allies in the West will realize that in the battle of ideas, dropping bombs helps the foe, not the friend.

I hope non-Muslims realize that deep inside the soul of all Muslims lives a Rumi, an Averroes, and a Muhammad Ali. Equity and social justice run through every fibre and gene of the Muslim psyche. Poetry, song, and dance are as much a part of our culture as piety, modesty, and charity. Challenging authority, even the existence of God himself, has been part of our heritage, and some Muslims have even lived to tell that tale. For instance, take these lines from 19th-century India's giant Muslim poet Mirza Ghalib (in today's Islamic world, he would be in hiding):

> *Hum ko maaloom hai janat ki haqeeqat lekin,*
> *Dil ke behelane ko Ghalib ye khayaal accha hai.*

[Of course I know there is no such thing as Paradise, but, To fool oneself, one needs such pleasant thoughts Ghalib]

A century earlier, another towering Muslim figure and the foremost name in Urdu poetry, Mir Taqi Mir, had openly embraced all religions, not just Islam:

> *Mir ke deeno mazhab ko poochte kya ho, unne to*
> *Kashka khencha, dehr mey baitha, kab ka tark Islam kiya.*

[Why bother asking of Mir what his creed or religion be? He wears vermillion, sits in the temple, And has long renounced Islam.]

I write in the same tradition. I hope my provocative invocations may trigger a spark, an *iskra*, that may lead us to do a serious self-examination about the direction in which we are heading. Can we end the catastrophic lack of honesty that so many of us have become accustomed to? It is my dream that Muslims, including my naysayers—and trust me, there are plenty of them—will read this book and attempt to answer a few questions in the privacy of their solitudes, when they need not be on the defensive and have no fear of being judged.

The book is an attempt to differentiate between the Islamic State and the state of Islam, and the best way to demonstrate the difference between these two concepts is to note that today, Muslims of Pakistan live in an Islamic State while Muslims of India live in a state of Islam. The 150 million

Muslims of India, despite being deeply religious, are for the better part known to have few links or inclinations towards the goals of international terrorism. On the other hand, the 150 million Muslims of Pakistan have become the recruiting grounds for Al-Qaeda, not just on its own territory, but among its diaspora as well. Muslims need to reflect on this dilemma.

Muslims are told incessantly that true Islam can only prosper under the protection of an "Islamic State," but the facts suggest that nothing could be further from the truth. Muslims living as religious minorities in secular societies—be it in South Africa, India, Canada, the United States, or Britain—are able to speak their minds, live under the rule of law, and get equality of citizenship. On the other hand, Muslims cannot even dare to imagine such rights in present-day Islamic States. And as for as the caliphates of the past, in those that we have come to glorify and mythologize as our golden past, dissent invariably led to death.

The book is aimed also at my Arab brothers and sisters who have suffered at the hands of colonialism, going back to the 15th century. Repeated wars, oppressive dictatorships, and an Islamist upsurge have made things worse. Theirs is a just struggle seriously compromised by an inept leadership that has sold them out more than once. The Arabs were the first Muslims, and the rest of the Muslim world cares deeply for them. However, there is a serious lack of reciprocity in this relationship. Many Arabs approach the subject of Islam as if it were their gift to the rest of the world, not God's gift to humanity. Any critique by non-Arab Muslims of the Arab world's woes is seen as an insult to Arab pride itself and invariably elicits a swift and predictable response—the hurtful charge of working for Israel. It would not be a stretch to say that Arabs today need leadership, not land.

Arabs have much to be proud of. They have contributed more than their share to human civilization, but they also need to recognize that in contemporary times, the plight of the Palestinians has been abused and misused by their leadership for ulterior motives. They also need to fight internalized racism that places darker-coloured fellow Muslims from Africa and Asia on a lower rung of society. Taking "ownership" of Islam as if it were a brand name that didn't have to be practised, but merely protected and projected, has made us lose the very essence of the message of Muhammad. The relationship between Arab and non-Arab must be one of respect and dignified equality, not one of the Arab and his *Mawali.*

---

* *Mawali* (or *Mawala*): A term in Arabic used to address non-Arab Muslims. In the 7th century, the Mawali were considered second class in Arabian society, beneath free tribesmen. It has entered the lexicon of India, where it is used as a derogatory term for someone involved in menial work or a homeless person.

The only Arabs who today vote without fear of reprisal live in Europe and North America, yet the Islamist leaders among them dream of turning these countries into the very Islamic States they fled. A prominent Egyptian-Canadian imam said on a television talk show that he wanted all Canadians to embrace Islam so that Canada could be ruled under sharia law. He defended the death penalty as punishment for men and women who engage in consensual extramarital sex, saying it is not he but God who wants adulterous individuals killed. Another prominent Arab Islamist in the United States was quoted by the *Detroit Free Press* as urging Muslims to "educate non-Muslims about Islam," saying Muslims in the United States have a unique opportunity to spread Islam.

Instead of asking for non-Muslims to convert to Islam, these imams should be telling their Muslim congregations: "You have been lied to for centuries." Muslims need to educate themselves about Islam, not proselytize their religion to non-Muslims. It is time for them to read the truth about Islamic history since the death of Prophet Muhammad. They should stop glorifying the politicization of Islam, a phenomenon that has produced a panorama of tragedies and bloodshed, including a serious blow to the unending Palestinian struggle for an independent and sovereign state alongside Israel.

The rich heritage left behind by Muslim scientists, thinkers, poets, architects, musicians, and dancers, has been *in spite of* the Islamic extremists, not because of them. My book will hopefully offer a challenge to these imams and is an attempt to break their monopoly on the message.

The book is also aimed at Pakistanis who deny their ancient Indian heritage despite the fact that India derives its name from the River Indus, which is in Pakistan. Pakistanis are the custodians of the ancient civilization of Harappa and Mohenjo-Daro, not Madain Saleh in Saudi Arabia or Giza in Egypt. When Pakistanis deny their Indianness, it is equivalent to the French denying their Europeanness. In attempting to forge an identity that defies language, geography, culture, clothing, and cuisine, many Pakistanis, especially the second generation in the West, have become easy pickings for Islamist extremist radicals who fill their empty ethnic vessels with false identities that deny them their own ethnic heritage.

I am hoping that potential recruits from the diaspora of Pakistani youth will realize they are being taken for a ride by the Islamists and are nothing more than gun fodder for the supremacist cults that use Islam as a political tool to further its goals. I hope Pakistanis and their children realize that they are victims of what one of Pakistan's leading historians, Professor K.K. Aziz, called *The Murder of History*. In his book by that name, he reveals that for fifty years Pakistanis have been fed myths disguised as truths.

One of the lies that has been passed on to the youth is the falsehood of their ancestry. Aziz, who has taught at the universities of Cambridge and Heidelberg, wrote:

> Here I may add an interesting footnote to the sociological history of modern Muslim India and Pakistan. Almost every Muslim of any importance claimed, and still claims today, in his autobiography reminiscences, memoirs, journal and bio data, that his ancestors had come from Yemen, Hejaz,* Central Asia, Iran, Ghazni,† or some other foreign territory. In most cases, this is a false claim for its arithmetic reduces the hordes of local converts (to Islam) to an insignificant number. Actually, it is an aftermath and confirmation of Afghan and Mughal exclusiveness. It is also a declaration of disaffiliation from the soil on which the shammers have lived for centuries, and to which in all probability, they have belonged since history began. If all the Siddiquis, Qureshis, Faruqis,‡ ... have foreign origins and their forefathers accompanied the invading armies, or followed them, what happens to the solemn averment that Islam spread peacefully in India? Are we expected to believe that local converts, whose number must have been formidable, were all nincompoops and the wretched of the earth—incapable over long centuries of producing any leaders, thinkers, or scholars?"

This book is not the first to critique what ails Muslim societies. Since 9/11, there has been a flood of writing that offers recipes for a turnaround. The term *Ijtehad* has become the cliché, thrown around at conferences and workshops as the ultimate panacea to "reform" Islam. An entire industry has sprung up around inter-faith dialogue, with the people who are the source of the problem offering cures. It is not just Islamic theology that needs to be re-interpreted; Islamic history needs to be re-read and re-taught without prejudice, without preconceived notions, and above all, without the fear of the fatwa. What the proponents of reformed Islam fail to realize is that there are many ways Islam can be practised. Whether one is ultra-conservative or totally secular in one's approach to Islam should be of no one else's concern. There are numerous sects in Islam, with further sub-sects. In fact, dare I say that it is not Islam that needs to be revised or reformed, but Muslims'

---

* Hejaz: An Ottoman province that briefly became an independent state and was later occupied by neighbouring Nejd in 1925, which incorporated it into present-day Saudi Arabia.

† Ghazni: Present-day Afghanistan.

‡ Arabized last names used by many Indo-Pakistani Muslims to denote their superiority and to distance their ancestries from being Indian.

relationship with their faith that needs to be addressed. This book attempts to show that whenever Muslims have demonstrated a sense of security and confidence in their faith, without wearing it on their sleeves, they have flourished. In contrast, whenever in history they became obsessive about rituals and defensive about their religion, as if it were a brand name that needed protection from competition, they stumbled. And as they became obsessed with religion, they stifled independent thought and individual liberties, seriously damaging their own societies. The debacle of Muslims in 13th-century Iraq, 15th-century Spain and 18th-century India came about when extremists of that time tried to whip society into order. This should have been a lesson for us all, but that was not to be.

Chasing a Mirage is not a textbook on Islamic history. However, it does deal with vignettes of Islamic history that remain hidden from Muslims. The book will show that throughout Islamic history, all attempts to use Islam to justify or validate political power—and there are countless examples—have invariably ended in bloodshed and war.

The book is divided into three sections. Part 1 deals with the politics behind the Islamic State; the three countries that today lay claim to that moniker; and Palestine, where Islamists are trying to create such a state. Part 2 covers Islamic history from the power struggle that developed immediately after the death of the Prophet, through the four caliphates that followed and defined Islam in medieval times. Part 3 deals with contemporary Islamic issues, including jihad, *hijab,* sharia law, and the agenda of Islamists in the West.

In the second part, where I touch on Islamic history, I have limited my critique to the four major periods of Islamic history—the Umayyads of Damascus, the Abbasids of Baghdad, the Andalusians of Spain, and of course, the "Rightly Guided" Caliphs following the death of Prophet Muhammad, may peace be upon him.* (I could have included an analysis of the Turkish Ottomans, the Indian Moghuls, and the Iranian Safavids, but by the time these later empires arose, they had shed all pretence of emulating the Rightly Guided Caliphs, and they governed as classic monarchies.)

Missing from this book is any discussion about the Islam of East Asia and Sub-Saharan Africa, two regions that give Islam its greatest hope of a renaissance. Mauritania and Mali in the west, and Indonesia and Malaysia in the east may appear as the hinterland of Islamdom, but the scholarship and democracy emanating from these regions are cause for hope.

---

* Peace be upon him: A salutation that Muslims say after uttering the name of Muhammad, the Prophet of Islam, as a mark of their respect and love for him. Often abbreviated to PBUH, or SAW (the Arabic phrase is *Sallalahu aleyhi wasallam).*

This book is an unusual critique of the Muslim community in that it does not delve into the specifics of Islamic beliefs and practices or pass theological judgments. However, I do try to focus on the issue of the mixing of Islam and politics, and try to show that since the earliest days of Islam—from the succession of Muhammad—Islam and Muslims have suffered immensely when Islam has been used as a tool to seek or retain power.

Through this book, I hope to convince my co-religionists that we need to inculcate within ourselves the state of Islam and stop chasing an Islamic State. We need to break the literalist chains that confine our understanding of religion and be open to a more reflective attitude towards the divine. Perhaps we need to pay heed to the words of the founder of the Sikh faith, Guru Nanak, who in the 16th century, while addressing his Muslim friends, wrote:

> Make mercy your Mosque,
> Faith your Prayer Mat,
> what is just and lawful your Qu'ran,
> Modesty your Circumcision,
> and civility your Fast.
> So shall you be a Muslim.
> Make right conduct your Ka'aba,
> Truth your Pir,*
> and good deeds your Kalma and prayers.

Tarek Fatah
Toronto, Canada

---

* *Pir.* The Punjabi word for saint.

PART ONE

The Illusion

CHAPTER 1

Politics and Theology of Islamic States

IT WAS JUST AFTER MIDNIGHT on April 4, 1979. Zulfiqar Ali Bhutto, the deposed prime minister of Pakistan, lay on the floor of his dark cell in Rawaloindi jail, awaiting his end. His death sentence had been signed by the Islamist military dictator, General Muhammad Zia-ul-Haq, and the hanging was schedule for 5:00 AM. Wasted by malaria and diarrhoea, the once proud and arrogant leader of Pakistan could do little more than stare at the ceiling, counting his last hours. Suddenly, the silence of the prison night was broken by the thud of marching boots coming towards his dimly lit cell. As the emaciated Bhutto turned towards the iron bars, he saw a colonel and two other army officers stop in front of his cell and unlock the door.

"Come to gloat or watch a murder?" Bhutto sneered at the three men in uniform. The grim-faced colonel wasted no time with pleasantries. He had come with a last-minute offer: should Bhutto sign a confession, admitting that it was he who had authorized the military coup in which General Zia-al-Haq had toppled his government, he would live; otherwise, the gallows awaited him.

Enraged, Bhutto lashed out at the officers. "Shameless bastards. I don't want a life of dishonour, lies. Now get out!"

But the army officers were relentless. They had orders to secure a signed confession from Bhutto, no matter what. One soldier grappled with Bhutto while the other forced a pen into his hand. The colonel barked an order: "Sign it!"

Though weakened by disease and starvation, Bhutto did not go down without a fight. Breaking free from the soldiers' grasp, Bhutto landed a punch on the colonel's face. In the fracas that followed, Bhutto fell, his head striking the wall. He collapsed into unconsciousness. As the officers tried to force him to his feet, they found his body had gone limp. The colonel was in a panic. Dead men don't sign confessions. He summoned the prison doctors, but despite attempts to revive him, the prime minister of Pakistan did not regain consciousness. The Islamic republic of Pakistan, the world's first country to be created in the name of Islam, had just murdered its first elected prime minister. In doing so, its *jihadi* army created a martyr, an adversary, that would haunt the nation for decades.

Bhutto's body was dragged to the gallows, where the hangman was told the prime minister had fainted. The hangman, however, refused to go through with the process, avowing that he was a good Christian and could not hang a person who was already dead. The colonel ordered him to do his work or face the consequences. The noose was placed around Bhutto's neck, his body erect above the platform. From beneath his feet, the trap door opened. Many innocent men have been sent to the gallows, but few have been murdered twice.

Earlier that day Zulfiqar Ali Bhutto had bid his last farewell to wife Nusrat and daughter Benazir. As the mother and daughter walked away from their caged hero, sobbing in each other's arms, Bhutto uttered the last words Benazir would hear from him. "Until we meet again."

The two would meet again in December 2007 when Benazir would be assassinated by a gunman, barely a few kilometres from where her father was murdered in a jail cell.

In killing the Bhuttos, father and daughter, Islamists targeted two politicians who wanted to build a modern social democracy free from Islamic extremism. However, it was not just secular liberal Muslims who were labelled as enemies of the Islamic state. Within a year of the Bhutto murder, Islamists would take over Iran where they would slaughter their own Islamic allies. In another five years, they would strike again, this time in Sudan.

On the morning of Friday, January 18, 1985, a dry northeasterly wind blew lightly across the Khartoum North prison. Sudan was about to hang Mahmoud Muhammad Taha, an author, politician, and brilliant scholar of Islam—and veteran of the struggle to keep his northeast African country free of rigid *sharia* law.* Sudanese dictator Gaafar Nimeiry had signed Taha's

---

* *Sharia* law: Law based on Islam's sacred book, the Quran, which God is believed to have dictated to the Prophet Muhammad and nine other sources, mostly written by men in the 8th and 9th centuries. More on sharia in chapter 11.

death warrant a day earlier, based on a *fatwa* issued by the powerful Saudi cleric Sheikh Abdullah bin Baz.

As the handcuffed and hooded Taha climbed the stairs, thousands of Islamists who had been bussed into the prison jeered him. Members of the *Ikhwan ul Muslimeen* (the Muslim Brotherhood),* who had been instrumental in introducing sharia law into Sudan in August 1983, were in a celebratory mood. Taha had exposed the bankruptcy and un-Islamic nature of the Brotherhood's supremacist ideology, and he would soon be silenced.

Before putting the noose in place, the hangman removed the hood covering Taha's face. Taha surveyed the crowd with a smile. Witnesses say that his eyes were defiant as he faced the executioner and stared at the Islamist mob with no hint of fear. The hood was then slipped over Taha's head once again.

As the guards pulled the noose tight around Taha's neck, the Muslim Brotherhood supporters chanted *"Allah o Akbar, Allah o Akbar."* The trapdoor opened. Taha's body fell through it, wriggled violently but briefly, and then went limp, swaying lifelessly in the gentle breeze at the end of the taut rope. The state of Islam was dead. The Islamic State was alive.

Hanged for being an apostate, Mahmoud Taha (1909–85) was anything but a disbeliever. His arguments against turning Sudan into an Islamic State were rooted in Islamic tradition, the Prophet's sayings, and Quranic teachings. However, as a co-founder of the Sudanese Republican Party in October 1985, he was a rare advocate of liberal reform within Islam and Sudanese society.

Even with his impeccable credentials as an Islamic scholar, he was a thorn in the side of the Muslim Brotherhood and other Islamists in Sudan. In 1971, after conducting a widespread campaign against Sudanese Communists, the Islamists turned their attention towards moderate Muslim groups that could be an obstacle in their agenda to create an Islamic State in Sudan. They started a vilification campaign against moderate Muslims, in particular Taha's Republican Party. In 1972 the Islamist clerics in Sudan obtained a fatwa from Cairo's Al-Azhar University that branded Taha an apostate. In 1975 the Saudis also got involved—the Mecca-based Muslim World League and Sheikh Bin Baz declared Taha to have committed apostasy by opposing sharia law in Sudan.

Several weeks before his hanging, Taha and his group had published a leaflet titled *Hatha aow al-tawafan* (Either This or the Flood)—demanding

---

* Muslim Brotherhood: A political organization founded in 1928 in Egypt with the aim of combating secular Arab nationalism and implementing sharia law.

the repeal of sharia law and a guarantee of democratic civil liberties under which a more enlightened understanding of Islam could be freely debated. It was this demand for enlightenment and civil liberties that led to his lynching in front of a chanting mob of Islamists. The kangaroo court that sentenced him to death concluded its trial in less than three weeks.

What was Mahmoud Muhammad Taha's crime? By any Islamic standards, he was a pious Muslim, living in a state of Islam. However, his "state of Islam" came into conflict with the "Islamic State." Taha was aware of the risks involved in opposing an Islamic State. He knew that in the longer than one-thousand-year history of Islam, Muslim blood had flowed freely any time power-hungry politicians, dictators, kings, or caliphs* had invoked Islam to create a mythical Islamic State. Honourable Muslims like Taha who have stepped in the way of the Islamist agenda have paid with their lives or liberty through the eons. They have been murdered by the state or beheaded by Islamist vigilantes who invoked the good name of Islam and sullied it in the process.

Taha's murder gives us a good understanding of how far today's Islamists will go to silence Muslims who disagree with them. Taha was not a secularist. He wasn't an Arab nationalist like Egypt's Nasser or a Baathist like Iraq's Saddam or a Communist like Syrian parliamentarian Khaled Bagdash. Mahmoud Muhammad Taha of Sudan was an Islamic scholar, a freedom fighter, and a man of the cloth—he was a preacher and an *imam*.† He was a visionary who could have saved the world from the theological disaster that it is headed towards today. His story illustrates the dangers facing Muslims who oppose the Islamist agenda and what I view as Political Islam.

Critiquing Political Islam and commenting on the Sudanese scholar's public hanging, the Arab world's leading leftwing intellectual, Egyptian author Samir Amin, has said: "Mahmood Taha of Sudan was the only Islamic intellectual who attempted to emphasize the element of emancipation in his interpretation of Islam. . . . Taha's execution was not protested by any Islamic group, 'radical' or 'moderate.' Nor was he defended by any of the intellectuals identifying themselves with 'Islamic Renaissance' or even those merely willing to 'dialogue' with such movements. It was not even reported in the Western Media."

Amin is right. In Canada, as well as in the United States and Britain, none of the Muslim organizations or the prolific commentators on "all things

---

* Caliph: Initially the title for the successors of Prophet Muhammad, but later used by medieval Muslim kings.
† *Imam:* One who leads prayers in a mosque.

Muslim" thought it worthwhile to write or protest against the execution of Taha by an Islamist government. Why is this so?

Since the first caliphate in Medina in the 7th century, clerics have continually reminded Muslims that their mission on Earth—to spread Islam—is impossible without the establishment of an Islamic State. Such edicts by caliphs and imams have gathered near-universal acceptance despite the fact that neither the Quran nor the Prophet asked Muslims to establish such a state. In fact, the five pillars of Islam,* which form a Muslim's covenant with the Creator, do not even hint at the creation of an Islamic State.

It is not that early Muslims did not get a chance to establish an Islamic State. Through the centuries, from the time of the Rightly Guided Caliphs (discussed in chapter 7) to the Umayyads and the Abbasids, hundreds of Muslim dynasties have tried their hand at creating this illusive Islamic State, and all have failed in laying the foundations of such an entity. Some rulers demonstrated impeccable personal character and integrity, but as soon as they died, murder and mayhem followed. If the creation of an Islamic State was not possible when Muslims were at their peak of power and intellect, it would be reasonable to conclude that this ambition is not realizable when Muslims are at their weakest and most divorced from education and the sciences.

Yet, in the early 20th century, when most of the Muslim world lay occupied by European powers, the movement for an Islamic State was reborn with a fury that today threatens moderate, liberal, and secular Muslims more than it does the West.

Among the founders of this pan-Islamic revivalist movement recruiting Muslims for a *jihad*† against the West was Abul Ala Maudoodi (d. 1976), the founder of the Jamaat-e-Islami political party in India and Pakistan. In promoting jihad and the Islamic state, Maudoodi divided the world between *Darul Islam* (House of Islam) and *Darul Harb* (House of War). He went as far as to question a Muslim's very faith if he or she did not volunteer for jihad to establish an Islamic state. In his booklet *Call to Jihad,* Maudoodi wrote:

> An independent Islamic state is a prerequisite to enable them [Muslims] to enforce Islamic laws and fashion their lives as ordained by God. And if their independence is lost, what chances there remain for their country

---

* Five pillars of Islam: Belief in the unity of God, performing daily prayers, giving charity based on one's wealth, fasting during the month of Ramadan, and performing the *hajj* pilgrimage once in a lifetime, if one can afford it.

† *Jihad:* Holy war. The word also means waging an internal struggle against oneself. More on jihad in chapter 12.

to exist as *Darul Islam* [House of Islam]? Hence the verdict of the Quran is categorical that a person is totally false in his claims of *iman* [faith] if he seeks the safety of his person and property when the very existence of *Darul Islam* is at stake.

Maudoodi and his Jamaat-e-Islami were not alone. In the Arab world, he was linked to the *Ikhwan al Muslimeen* (Muslim Brotherhood), and other Muslim political parties, which set up networks across the world. The one common objective for all of these political forces was and still is the establishment of an Islamic State, and to deal harshly with anyone deemed to be an obstacle in the way.

THE IDEA OF THE ISLAMIC STATE

To the average non-Muslim, any country with a Muslim majority population is viewed as an "Islamic State." This is only partly true and depends on whose definition of an Islamic State is used. Most Muslims too believe that countries with majority Muslim populations are Islamic countries with a distinct Muslim character. However, this is not how the Islamists see the world. From the perspective of those who follow the doctrine of Wahhabism or Salafi Islam* or even the ruling ayatollahs of Iran, a country can be labelled an Islamic State only if it is governed by the laws of sharia. Thus, neither Turkey nor Indonesia is an Islamic State in the eyes of the Islamists.

Maudoodi, one of the main proponents of an Islamic State in the past century, in his book *Islamic Law and Constitution,* poses the question: "What are the fundamental objects for which Islam advocates the establishment of an Islamic State?" Answering himself, Maudoodi quotes two verses of the Quran, suggesting that they require the establishment of the Islamic State: "Certainly We sent our Messengers with clear arguments, and sent down with them the Book and Balance, so that people may conduct themselves with equity" (57:25), and "These Muslims (who are being permitted to fight) are a people who, should We establish them in the land, will keep up prayer and pay the poor-rate and enjoin good and forbid evil." (22:41).

---

* Wahhabism and (Salafi Islam): At times used interchangeably. Wahhabbism is practised by those who follow the teachings of 18th-century Islamic fanatic Muhammad Ibn Abdul Wahhab. Salafism, on the other hand, is a generic term for Sunni Muslims who view the lives of the first three generations of Muhammad's companions from the 7th and 8th centuries as examples of how Islam should be practiced in the 21st.

Nowhere in these verses of the Quran does God ask or authorize the creation of an Islamic State. Yet, from the same verses, Maudoodi concludes that God commands the creation of such an entity. In the same book, Maudoodi writes that such an Islamic State will "eradicate and crush with full force all those evils from which Islam aims to purge mankind."

In this one sentence Maudoodi reveals the true objective of the Islamists. The urge to "eradicate," "crush," and "purge" lies at the heart of their obsession with an Islamic State. When Sudan hanged Taha, the Islamic State was doing precisely what Maudoodi had predicted. It eradicated, crushed, and purged him. The Quranic injunction to "enjoin good and forbid evil" has been turned upside down by the Islamists who rule Islamic States. They "enjoin evil and forbid good," but they know not what they do.

Polish-born Muhammad Asad (birth name Leopold Weiss) died in 1992 but remains one of the Muslim world's most respected scholars, with works that include commentaries on the Quran and the notion of the Islamic State. When Pakistan was created in 1947, it was this grandson of a Jewish rabbi who was invited to assist in the writing of Pakistan's constitution. The fact that his efforts failed suggest that while the theories and romantic notions about the Islamic State make for interesting academic discourse, in practice they fall short.

Asad wrote that a large part of Muslim history "has evolved under the impetus of a deep-seated longing for the establishment of what has loosely, and often confusedly, [been] conceived of as the 'Islamic State.'" This longing is "very much in evidence among Muslims of our time, and which, is nonetheless, subject to many confusions that have made the achievement of a truly Islamic polity impossible in the past millennium."

Asad's hundred-page treatise on state and government is a valuable account of the Muslim dream of an Islamic State, but also underscores the author's assertion that the task cannot be achieved by looking into the past. In his words, "The past thousand years or so of Muslim history can offer us no guidance in our desire to achieve a polity which would really deserve the epithet 'Islamic.' Nor is the confusion lessened by the influences to which the Muslim world has been subjected in recent times."

In his writing, Asad speaks with the knowledge of history and the contemporary practice of Muslim politicians, especially in Pakistan, where his efforts went nowhere. However, he does not face up to the fact that the very exercise of seeking political power is bound to contradict some of the essential aspects of Islamic principles. Even though he judges the period of the Rightly Guided Caliphs (632-661) as "Islamic," he does not address whether he feels that era is the model for the future Islamic states or not, since civil war and conflict came to define those times.

One of the harshest critics of a return to rigid Islamic rule was Ali Abdel al-Razik of Egypt in the late 1920s, when he campaigned against the revival of the caliphate. In his seminal work published in 1925, *Al-Islam wa usul el-hukum* (Islam and the Fundamentals of Authority), Razik argued against the Islamic State and advocated the separation of religion and civil society, drawing the wrath of the influential Al-Azhar University.* His books were burned and he was declared an apostate for merely suggesting that the state of Islam did not require an Islamic State. His book was published in the aftermath of the collapse of the six-hundred-year-old Ottoman Empire† and the abolition of the caliphate system by Turkey's founding president, secular modernist Mustafa Kemal Ataturk. For the first time since 632 CE, the Muslim world had no central political authority. The caliph's authority had been on the wane since the rise of European imperial power in the 16th century, but the 1925 abolition came as a shock to much of the Muslim world, which was largely living under French, British, and Dutch occupation.

It was in this vacuum of political authority that intellectuals like Egypt's Ali Abdel al-Razik raised difficult issues. Razik questioned the need for the revival of the caliphate and proposed the idea of a nation state where religion would not interfere with the political process.

Razik's opposition to the creation of the Islamic State in the form of a revived caliphate stirred anger among Egypt's orthodox Islamic establishment. Paradoxically, a group of Islamic scholars chaired by Sheikh Muhammad Abul Fadl al-Jizawi, the rector of Al-Azhar, had already issued a statement reluctantly coming to terms with the abolition of the caliphate. They had even criticized Muslims who felt bound by an oath of allegiance to the deposed Ottoman caliph and regarded obedience to him as a religious duty. (The statement reflected the mood on the street, where Arab nationalists were

---

* Al-Azhar University: The leading institution for orthodox Sunni Islam. It started out in the 10th century as an institution of Shia Islam. The Shia founders named it after Fatima al-Zahra, daughter of the Prophet Muhammad. Al-Azhar is the second-oldest operating university in the world after the University of Al Karaouine in Fez, Morocco.

† Ottoman Empire: A caliphate was created in 1300 by an Anatolian Turkish prince, Osman I (1259–1326), in the wake of the destruction by the Mongols of the Arab caliphate in Baghdad in 1258. By 1453 the Ottomans, under Mehmed II, had captured Constantinople (now Istanbul). The Ottoman caliphate ended in 1922 when it was abolished by Ataturk, who proclaimed Turkey as a republic the following year.

already welcoming the weakening of the Turkish-based caliphate and had intensified their campaign to have the caliphate returned to the Arabs.)

Razik's critique, however, went beyond the simple acceptance of a *fait accompli*. He launched a vociferous attack on the centuries-old school of Islamic political thought. In this, he took on not only the orthodox Ulema (Islamic scholars) and Al-Azhar, but also self-styled modernist Egyptians like Rashid Rida, who oscillated between Arab nationalism and Islamic universalism, but never gave up on the Islamic State.

In India, respected intellectual Muhammad Iqbal based his opposition to the revival of the caliphate and the Islamic State on the grounds that it was an obstacle to the modernization of the Muslim world. Razik, however, based his opposition on an Islamic perspective, considering his background as an Islamic scholar and as a former judge of a religious court. He argued that the caliphate or the Islamic State had no basis in either the Quran or the traditions of the Prophet. He rightly argued that the Quran makes no mention of a caliphate and invoked the verse that said, "We have neglected nothing in the Book" (6:38).

As long as Razik restricted his criticism to the caliphate, the orthodoxy was willing to tolerate his views. However, when he challenged the long-established belief that Islam as a religion necessitated the creation of an Islamic government, he crossed a line, leading to years of harassment and ostracization with accusations that he was a communist. Undeterred by the witch hunt, Razik concluded that (1) Government or political authority, as necessary as it might be seen to realize Islamic ideals and obligations, was not the essence of Islam and had nothing to do with the primary principles of the faith; and (2) Islam left Muslims free to choose whatever form of government they felt could solve their day-to-day problems, with civil society minus an official state religion being best able to offer such a solution.

Razik clamoured for the de-politicization of Islam, claiming that the only beneficiaries of the Islamic State were the tyrants who ruled Muslim populations and who were able to silence opposition by getting the Ulema to declare that opposition to their government was opposition to Islam.

In India, Islamists overtook Muhammad Iqbal's legacy and he was appropriated as the "thinker" behind the creation of an Islamic State— Pakistan. Razik, on the other hand, faced a lifetime of harassment from the Egyptian Islamists, who denounced him as a blasphemer.

Across the Mediterranean, Ataturk had been moving slowly towards setting up the republican secular state of Turkey. Months before formally abolishing the caliphate, he said:

> Our prophet has instructed his disciples to convert the nations of the world to Islam; he has not ordered for them to provide for the government of these nations. Never did such an idea pass through his mind. Caliphate means government and administration. . . . The notion of a single Caliph exercising supreme religious authority over all the Muslim people is one which has come out of the books, not reality.

The movement to restore the Ottoman caliphate was strong in India, under the leadership of none other than Indian nationalist Mahatma Gandhi. As in Egypt, Muslims in India were taken aback by the abolition of the centuries-old institution. While many among the seventy-million-strong Indian Muslim community saw the end of the caliphate as a grave setback, intellectuals such as thinker-poet Iqbal supported Ataturk's abolition of the caliphate, suggesting that the Turks had made effective use of the Islamic tradition of *Ijtehad.** The Ottoman caliphate, Iqbal said, had long become a symbol of Muslim statehood in name only, as not even the next-door Iranians accepted the sovereignty of the Ottomans.

Iqbal wrote dismissively of the clerics: "The religious doctors of Islam in Egypt and India, as far as I know, have not yet expressed themselves on this point. Personally, I find the Turkish view is perfectly sound." He went on to defend the separation of religion and state, writing, "The republican form of government is not only thoroughly consistent with the spirit of Islam, but has also become a necessity in view of the new forces that were set free in the world of Islam."

Iqbal further cited two examples of how in early Islam the caliphate had adapted to political realities. First was the abolition of a condition that the caliph had to descend from the Meccan Arab tribe of Quraysh. Iqbal cited the ruling of an 11th-century jurist that, since the Quraysh tribe had experienced a political debacle, ruling the world of Islam no longer required belonging to the Quraysh tribe. The second example involved the historian and philosopher Ibn Khaldun, who in the 15th century declared that since the power of the Quraysh had vanished, the only alternative was to accept the country's most powerful man as the country's imam or caliph. Iqbal concluded from all this that there was no difference between the position of Khaldun, who had realized the hard logic of facts, and the attitude of

---

* *Ijtehad:* Literally, "effort." In an Islamic context, it reflects the intellectual effort of a Muslim to reach independent interpretation of the Quran and the Sunna. (The opposite is *Taqlid,* "imitation.") *Sunna:* rules derived from the Prophet's sayings. *Sunna* is the second-most important source of sharia law after the Quran. It refers also to the customs and habits of the Prophet, including his everyday life practices.

modern Turks, who were also inspired by the realities of their time rather than by medieval laws written under different conditions of life.

Both Iqbal and Razik wrote in the 1920s, but in the early 21st century their words seem to come from the future, not the past. Today, Islamic political thought is moribund and has become more fossilized than it was at the end of the Ottoman caliphate. Today's movement for an Islamic theocracy is structured around the creation of an Islamic State based on the works of Abul Ala Maudoodi and Hassan al-Banna of the Jamaat-e-Islami and the Muslim Brotherhood. Their views remain in sharp contrast to their more urbane and secular contemporaries, as they strove for an Islamic State that rejected the ideas of universalism, instead embracing the self-righteous supremacy of Islam at the expense of the other.

Iqbal was an early convert to Ataturk's republican secularism. In his seminal work *The Reconstruction of Religious Thought in Islam,* Iqbal wrote: "Such is the attitude of the modern Turk, inspired as he is by the realities of experience, and not by the scholastic reasoning of jurists who lived and thought under different conditions of life. To my mind these arguments, if rightly appreciated, indicate the birth of an International ideal, which forming the very essence of Islam, has been hitherto overshadowed or rather displaced by Arabian Imperialism of the earlier centuries in Islam."

Iqbal considered the end of the caliphate as the trigger for a Muslim renaissance. He felt the jolt was necessary for the revival of Islam as an instrument of moral awakening, what he referred to as "the spiritualisation of the heart." When using the term "Arabian Imperialism," Iqbal was probably referring not just to early Umayyad Arab rule over non-Arab Muslim lands, but also to the way non-Arab Muslims had been conditioned to see themselves, their language, cuisine, and culture as inferior to their Arab cousins. He supported the adoption of the Turkish language as a medium of prayer and the Quran by the Young Turks.* He wrote:

> If the aim of religion is the spiritualisation of the heart, then it must penetrate the soul of man, and it can best penetrate the inner man . . . We find that when Muhammad Ibn Tumart—the Mahdi of Muslim Spain—who was Berber by nationality, came to power and established the pontifical rule of the Muwahhidun, he ordered for the sake of the illiterate Berbers that the

---

* Young Turks: A coalition of young Ottoman dissidents who ended the sultanate of the Ottoman Empire in 1908 by forcing Abdulhamid II to reinstitute the 1876 constitution and recall the legislature. The following year they deposed him and began modernizing and industrializing Turkish society. They joined Germany during World War I (1914–18) but, facing defeat, resigned a month before the war ended.

Quran should be translated and read in the Berber language and that the call to prayer should be given in Berber.

The tenuous bond between the Arab and the non-Arab Muslim has, over the centuries, created a love-hate relationship, often one-sided and rarely discussed. While non-Arab Muslims have embraced many facets of Arabian culture and custom, the gesture has rarely been reciprocated. Whether it has been the feeble relationship between the Berbers and Arabs, or the never-ending mutual mistrust between Persians and the Arabs, this chasm has gone largely unnoticed in the Arab world. Iqbal's reference to "Arabian Imperialism" would elicit shock and denunciation from even the most liberal Arab; such is the state of denial.

Canada's late comparative religion scholar Wilfred Cantwell Smith broached the subject of Arabism and Islam. In his book *Islam in Modern History,* he wrote about the "Arab's pride" in the context of "Arab glory and frustration." He maintained that while Arab Muslims are proud of their faith like other non-Arab Muslims, the difference is that "in the Arab's case this pride in Islam is not separate from his national enthusiasm, but infuses it and gives it added point." Thus, while the proponents of an Islamic State in Malaysia or Somalia would consider the adoption of Arab culture and custom as part of their Islamicized identity, the advocates of the Islamic State in Egypt would never even contemplate adopting any Indonesian or Nigerian cultural expression. The dysfunctional nature of this relationship has manifested itself most adversely in South Asia and the Indo-Pakistani Muslim diaspora. Smith, who up to 1946 taught in the then-Indian city of Lahore—now capital of Pakistani Punjab—suggests that in the Arab world, Islamist ideology is not an expression of religiosity, but one of patriotic ownership.

Explaining how race and religion overlap in the Arab-Islam identity while being non-existent in Indo-Islamic or Persian-Islamic distinctiveness, Smith writes, "The synthesis is close: identification, at times unconscious, of Islam and Arabism. On the one hand, an Arab need not be pious or spiritually concerned in order to be proud of Islam's achievements . . . On the other hand, Muslim Arabs have never quite acknowledged, have never fully incorporated into their thinking and especially their feeling, either that a non-Muslim is really a complete Arab, or that a non-Arab is really a complete Muslim."

Few in either the Arab or non-Arab Muslim world have talked about this chasm in the *Ummah** that finds its roots in the tribal and racial supremacy

---

* *Ummah:* An Arabic word meaning a community or a nation, but more specifically, it is commonly used to mean the collective community of Muslims around the world (*ummat al-mu'minin*). In the context of pan-Arabism, the word is used to reflect the whole Arab nation.

that was given legitimacy in early Islam. The abolition of the caliphate was seen by many Muslim modernists as a chance to break free from the past and step into the future.

Iqbal was demolishing centuries-old customs and mythologies that had fossilized Islamic thought. He recognized the window of opportunity that came with the advent of Turkish modernism. He envisaged the Muslim world emulating the Turks by ridding themselves of the shackles of medievalism. What he wrote about the Turks in the 1920s still applies. In obvious admiration of Turkey's leap towards modernity, Iqbal wrote:

> The truth is that among the Muslim nations of today, Turkey alone has shaken off its dogmatic slumber and attained to self-consciousness. She alone has claimed the right of intellectual freedom; she alone has passed from the ideal to the real—a transition that entails keen intellectual and moral struggle. To her the growing complexities of a mobile and broadening life are sure to bring new situations suggesting new points of view, and necessitating fresh interpretations of principles, which are only of an academic interest to people who have never experienced the joy of spiritual expansion. It is, I think, the English thinker Hobbes who makes this acute observation that to have a succession of identical thoughts and feelings is to have no thoughts and feelings at all. Such is the lot of most Muslim countries today. They are mechanically repeating old values, whereas the Turk is on the way to creating new values. He has passed great experiences, which have revealed his deeper self to him. In him, life has begun to move, change, and amplify, giving birth to new desires, bringing new difficulties in suggesting new interpretations. The question which confronts him today, and which is likely to confront other Muslim countries in the near future, is whether the law of Islam is capable of evolution—a question which will require great intellectual effort and is sure to be answered in the affirmative.

History shows that Iqbal's optimism was misplaced. Instead of Muslims taking the lead from him and the Egyptian Abdel Razik, the baton was snatched by Islamists like India's Abul Ala Maudoodi and Egypt's Hassan al-Banna. Today, it is epitomized by the followers of Ayatollah Khomeini and the many shades of Islamist movements across the globe. The model of the contemporary Islamic state they propose is strictly connected to the political movement of Islamist domination.

While Islam clearly aspires to universalism, which is a declared goal of the Quran, the Cairo Declaration on Human Rights in Islam adopted on

August 5, 1990, by forty-five foreign ministers of the Organization of the Islamic Conference, leaves much to be desired. Although successive Islamic declarations on human rights have tried to present themselves as compatible with the principle of universal basic rights, a number of severe contradictions exists between these declarations and Western constitutionalism. The most important difference is the Islamic non-separation of religion from state and societal affairs. According to the Foreword of the Universal Islamic Declaration of Human Rights issued by the Islamic Council in the UK in 1981, Islam is firmly rooted in the belief that God, and God alone, is the Law Giver and the Source of all human rights.

This concept results unavoidably in a blurring of religious and political authority, as happened in the past in the person of the imam or caliph. Hence, although the Young Turk Revolution officially did away with the caliphate in 1924, even in Westernized Morocco, the king is still defined in the constitution as *"Amir al Momineen"* (Ruler of all Muslims). Moreover, the implementation and interpretation of human rights depends on their compatibility with the sharia, which most Islamic countries claim is the only authentic source of interpretation of law. According to Articles 23 and 24 of the Cairo Declaration of Human Rights in Islam adopted in 1990, all rights and freedoms are subject to Islamic sharia, which is the only source of reference. In this framework, human rights lose their unconditional character and their focus on the protection of the individual vis-à-vis any kind of power. The influence of the model is reflected in the constitutions, as well as the legal and political practice of all Muslim states, even the relatively secular ones: King Hassan of Morocco presents himself as a direct descendant of the Prophet. However, the extreme case of domination of religious principles is found in the Iranian Constitution. Its Article 2 stipulates:

The Islamic Republic is a system based on belief in:

- The One God (as stated in the phrase "There is no god except Allah"*), His exclusive sovereignty and right to legislate, and the necessity of submission to His commands;

---

* This translation of the Muslim oath is a new phenomenon that betrays the disingenuous nature of the Islamists. By selectively translating one occurrence of Allah as God and leaving the other in Arabic, the Islamists clearly try to give the impression that, in the eyes of Muslims, "God" and "Allah" are two separate entities. The translation of the Muslim oath *La ilaha Illalah* can be translated in either one of two ways: "There is no god, but God," or "There is no Allah, but Allah." Yet, this is deliberately presented as "There is no god, but Allah."

- Divine revelation and its fundamental role in setting forth the laws;
- The return to God in the Hereafter, and the constructive role of this belief in the course of man's ascent towards God;
- The justice of God in creation and legislation;
- Continuous leadership and perpetual guidance, and its fundamental role in ensuring the uninterrupted process of the revolution of Islam;
- The exalted dignity and value of man, and his freedom coupled with responsibility before God; in which equity, justice, political, economic, social, and cultural independence and national solidarity are secured by recourse to a continuous leadership of the holy persons, possessing necessary qualifications, exercised on the basis of the Quran and the Sunna, upon all of whom be peace.

In the same spirit, the majority of the Arab constitutions declare the sharia as the basis of legislation, or at least consider it as a main source of legislation. This prevents most of the countries that pretend to be Islamic States from living up to the standards set by the 1948 United Nations Declaration of Universal Human Rights. It also legitimizes the notion of racial and religious superiority, and allows for multiple levels of citizenship and widespread and systemic discrimination against racial and religious minorities living within a state's borders. Invariably, the human rights of the weak and dispossessed, the minorities and women, the disabled and the heretics, are trampled upon without the slightest sense of guilt or wrongdoing. Men and women are imprisoned, routinely tortured and often killed, while numbed citizens, fearful of offending Islam, unsure about their own rights, insecure about their own identities, allow these violations to continue. By looking the other way, the intelligentsia and middle classes have become complicit in these crimes. They justify their inaction as patriotism, where they stand in solidarity with the Islamic State, with the misguided idea that those who fight for universal human rights are somehow working for Western imperialism or represent the interests of Judeo-Christian civilization.

This rejection of the universality of human rights is not limited to the elites of the world's fifty-six Islamic countries, but is also widespread among the leaders of traditional Muslim organizations. One would expect them to respect the 1948 UN declaration, if not for its universality, then simply as a matter of self-preservation. But this does not seem to be the case. In December 2006, a Toronto-born Muslim lawyer, who had supported the introduction of sharia law in Ontario's Family Courts, critiqued the UN declaration in *Counterpunch* magazine suggesting the UN Declaration of Human Rights was a "western construct," not truly fit for the Islamic world.

The Islamist contempt for the West is not an expression of anti-imperialism or a reflection of anger against colonialism and its devastating effect. Far from it. Islamists were the United States' handmaidens throughout the Cold War. In fact the Islamist disdain for the West is based almost entirely on their rejection of European enlightenment itself—the Renaissance. Abul ala Maudoodi, in his booklet *The Sick Nations of the Modern Age,* had this to say about the Renaissance:

> In short, this [unfettered freedom] was the pernicious seed that was sown during the European Renaissance and which has grown over the centuries into a massive and deadly tree. Its fruits are sweet, but poisonous; its flowers are attractive but full of thorns; its twigs and branches green and verdant, but are exhaling a deadly breeze, which is imperceptibly poisoning the blood of all mankind. The peoples of the West, who themselves planted this pernicious tree, are now disgusted with it. It has created such serious problems in all aspects of their lives that every attempt to solve them raises countless new difficulties and complications. Any branch that is lopped off is replaced by several thorny branches that turn out to be equally or even more dangerous. . . . Endeavours to solve social problems have led to feminism and birth control. Efforts to eradicate social evils by law have resulted in large-scale law-breaking and crime. In short, an endless crock of troubles has sprung from this pernicious tree of civilisation and culture, making life hell for the peoples of the West.

Maudoodi's critique of the West is shared by Islamists not just in the marketplaces of Damascus and Cairo, but even in Toronto, London, and New York. For the Islamist, it is not the West's imperial ambitions or capitalist greed that offends; it is the West's embrace of "unfettered freedom" and individual liberty that is cause for concern. In short, for the *jihadi,* the problem is Western civilization itself, not what it does. And their solution is to rip out the "pernicious tree" of the Renaissance from its roots and plant in its place a new seed of sharia that will give birth to an Islamic State.

One could say there are two Islams that Muslims have introduced to the world. One, peaceful, spiritual, and deeply respectful of the "other," an Islam that relied on the Quranic expression, "To you your religion, to me mine"—the Islam that has deeply impressed people as they saw the integrity and transparency of Muslims and their commitment to honesty and social justice. It is this Islam that today makes Indonesia the world's largest Muslim nation with 250 million people. No Arab or Turkish armies ever conquered this archipelago. No Moghul emperor sent elephant cavalry to Java. Neither did an Abbasid caliph ever get to see Sumatra. It was not people with noble family lineage who brought Islam to East Asia. It was ordinary traders and deeply spiritual saints who set the example for others to emulate. They did not rely on the supposed authenticity of their Meccan Arab bloodlines, but on the nobility of their behaviour and the character reflected in their actions. Because of them, millions turned to Islam, without relinquishing their language, custom, or culture.

However, parallel to this spiritual Islam, an equally militant stream of puritanism and supremacist philosophy was evolving. It sought statehood, political power, and mastery, not just over the conquered, but over competing Muslim interests as well. At the core of this divergence from spirituality and love of the divine was the notion of racial, tribal, and familial superiority, which gave birth to countless monarchist dynasties, each battling the other, all invoking Islam as their raison d'être. Muhammad would have wept to see how his message was misused to consolidate power and subjugate the population. With political power as the ultimate goal for most dynasties in Islamic history and even present-day regimes, Islam became merely a convenient method to acquire or hold onto authority. Whether it was from the pulpit or the throne, opponents from within the faith were almost invariably declared as enemies of Islam, and killed. Of course, this was not exclusive to Muslim dynasties. Brothers have killed their own siblings to retain power across the world, no matter what their religion. The difference is that while most of humanity has come to recognize the futility of racial and religious states, the Islamists of today present this sordid past as their manifesto of the future.

Today, the only Muslims who are free to practise their faith as they choose and participate in public life as equal citizens without having to validate their tribal, racial, or family lineage live as tiny minorities in secular democracies such as India, South Africa, Canada, and many European countries. Yet, even while seeing the advantages of life under secular civil society, many of them are committed to the establishment of an Islamic State. So deeply ingrained in the Muslim psyche is the idea of replicating the so-called Golden Age of the Rightly Guided Caliphs that few are willing to consider the implications of what they are asking for.

To bolster their case for an Islamic State, proponents of such an entity have tried to present the 7th-century treaty of Prophet Muhammad with the tribes of Medina as the "First Written Constitution in the World." In 1941, Muhammad Hamidullah published the English translation of what is known as the Medina Compact between the immigrants of Mecca, the Quraysh, and the tribes of Medina who were hosting the new arrivals in the city. What was essentially a document outlining the contractual obligations of all the parties in a tribal society was presented as if it were a document that should serve as the foundation of any Islamic constitution in the 20th century. If this "constitution" were truly an Islamic constitution and a model for future generations of Muslims, then it should have been the model of governance in the city of Mecca after its capture by Muhammad in 630 CE. But it was not. Neither was it the basis of the state set up by Abu-Bakr on his ascension as caliph after the Prophet's death in 632 CE. This suggests it was a one-time contract that was not replicated anywhere else even during the lifetime of the Prophet. However, copies of this document, falsely labelled as the First Written Constitution of the World, continue to be published and distributed around the Muslim world.

MUHAMMAD: A HEAD OF STATE OR AN APOSTLE?

Why do so many Muslims aspire to create a political entity without which they feel they cannot put into practice the message of Muhammad? What was the task of Prophet Muhammad? Was he sent to Earth to be the ruler of the Muslim world, their king? Or was he Allah's apostle on Earth, a messenger for all of humanity, who left behind a moral compass to serve as guide for a more ethical, equitable, and just society? Alternatively, was he both a Caesar and a Christ for Muslims?

I have no doubt that the Prophet's message of Islam was for religious unity and that Muslims were meant to be one spiritual body, part of the larger human family. Muhammad was undoubtedly the head of this Muslim Ummah. In order to establish the message of God, he used both his tongue and his spear. And before he died he shared with Muslims the last revelation he had received from God, "Today I have completed your faith for you."

During the twenty-three years that Muhammad shared the message of God—the Quran—with the people of Mecca and Medina, many times he and the people were reminded about the role of Allah's Apostle. A study of these Quranic revelations will help Muslims understand whether Muhammad was meant to be head of a political state or the head of a religious community, or both.

The Egyptian scholar Ali Abd al-Razik in his seminal work, *Al-Islam wa usul el-hukum* (Islam and the Fundamentals of Authority), says the Quran confirms the Prophet had no interest in political sovereignty. He adds that the Prophet's "heaven-appointed work did not go beyond the limits of the delivery of the summons, entirely apart from any thought of rulership." He quotes the following verses from the Quran to prove his point:

- Whoso obeyeth the Apostle, in doing so hath obeyed God, and whoso turneth away from thee: We have not sent thee to be their keeper (chapter 4, Sura al-Nisa, verse 83).
- And your people call it a lie and it is the very truth. Say: I am not placed in charge of you (chapter 6, Sura al-Anaam, verse 66).
- Follow what is revealed to you from your Lord; there is no god but He; and withdraw from the polytheists. And if Allah had pleased, they would not have set up others [with Him] and We have not appointed you a keeper over them, and you are not placed in charge of them (chapter 6, Sura al-Anaam, verses 106–7).
- Say: O people! indeed there has come to you the truth from your Lord, therefore whoever goes aright, he goes aright only for the good of his own soul, and whoever goes astray, he goes astray only to the detriment of it, and I am not a custodian over you (chapter 10, Sura Yunus, verse 108).
- Your Lord is Best Aware of you. If He will, He will have mercy on you, or if He will, He will punish you. We have not sent thee [O Muhammad] as a warden over them (chapter 17, Sura al-Isra, verse 54).
- Surely, We have revealed to you the Book with the truth for the sake of men; so whoever follows the right way, it is for his own soul and whoever errs, he errs only to its detriment; and you are not a custodian over them (chapter 39, Sura al-Zumar, verse 41).
- If then they run away, We have not sent thee as a guard over them. Thy duty is but to convey [the Message] (chapter 42, al-Shura, verse 48).
- Therefore do remind, for you are only a reminder. You are not a watcher over them (chapter 88, Sura al-Ghashiyah, verses 21–24).

If the Prophet was not a guardian over his own Ummah, then he certainly was not sent to become a political leader or a king over a country. The Quran states that "Muhammad is not the father of any man among you, but he is the Apostle of God, and the seal of the prophets: and God knoweth all things" (33:40).

Muslims need to consider the possibility that the state and government created by Abu-Bakr after the death of Muhammad was not the first Islamic State, but rather the first *Arab* State. It encompassed the Arabian Peninsula and gave the Arab people a sense of pride in their accomplishments. It allowed them to contribute to human civilization as other great civilizations had done before them. There is no doubt that because of this first Arab State, which later became the Umayyad dynasty, Islam also spread and flourished. But there is evidence that this state found its legitimacy in Arab identity and Quraysh tribal ancestry. Islamic principles of universalism and equality came second. (This subject and the issues of race and tribe are discussed in detail in chapter 6.) Had it been an Islamic State, the Sindhi and the Berber Muslims would not have been treated as second-class Muslim citizens, forced to pay *Jaziya** just as non-Muslims were required to do.

By turning Islam into a political force, the Arabs were able to surge out from the deserts of Arabia, defeat Byzantium and Persia, conquer Egypt and Spain, and influence events as far away as China and India. However, because Muslims had used religion to justify their politics, they were constricted by the rigidity of their beliefs. They were not able to adapt to the changing world of new enlightenment that was triggered by the invention of the printing press and, much later, the steam engine. The American and French revolutions, as well as the Industrial Revolution in Britain, bypassed the religion-based institutions. The Catholic Church and the sheikhs of Islam could do little more than stand silently as spectators.

While Europe industrialized and developed new political systems, the Islamic world took the opposite direction and crumbled under the weight of medievalism, mythologies, superstitions, and the cries of its own people. The very sciences that Muslims had introduced to Europe came back to haunt them as their clerics declared all scientific endeavour and secular education to be the work of infidels and thus a challenge to the Quran. Unable to compete and facing defeat in most spheres of human endeavour, be it sports or space, Islamists have set as their objective the creation of an Islamic State where they can implement sharia law, something they do not have to borrow from the West.

The cause of the violence that has engulfed the Muslim world is centred on the premise of an Islamic State or a caliphate as the prerequisite for the flourishing of Islam. Among the contemporary opponents of the Islamic State is the brilliant Sudanese-American academic, Professor Abdullahi An-Na'im, who teaches law at Emory University in Atlanta, Georgia. In his classic book, *Toward an Islamic Reformation,* An-Na'im writes about the unrealistic utopian dream of an Islamic State: "The authority of the caliph was supposed to be derived from popular support without any principle and mechanism by which that popular support could have been freely given, restricted, or withdrawn. This is, I maintain, one of the fundamental sources of constitutional problems with the sharia model of an Islamic state."

It is no wonder Muslims like An-Na'im are the prime targets of the Islamic religious right. Islamists consider secular, liberal, progressive, or

---

* *Jaziya:* A tax imposed on non-Muslims by Islamic caliphates.

cultural Muslims and even orthodox Sufis a greater threat than the West. The reason is that Muslims opposed to the Islamist agenda cannot be fooled or charmed in a way naive liberal-left politicians can. In fact, radical jihadis and their Islamist apologists have been targeting fellow Muslims for decades. Their conflict with the West is only recent. Long before Islamists donned anti-imperialist paraphernalia, they were the loyal storm troopers for the United States, targeting left-wing and secular Muslims or anyone who was able to unmask their fascist agenda and links to Saudi-funded Wahhabis. Even today, the primary enemy of the Islamist is the fellow Muslim who is unwilling to surrender to the harsh literalist and supremacist use of Islam as a political tool. The Muslims who stand in the way of the Islamist agenda pay a heavy price for their courage.

The call for an Islamic State gives false hopes to Muslim masses. The followers of Maudoodi and Syed Qutb* are dangling carrots and the promise of heavenly pleasures to mislead the Muslim peoples.

Had the Islamic State been possible, Allah would have brought it about it by now. There were enough men of impeccable character and integrity that had the chance to turn their domains into a genuine Islamic State, but everyone who tried, experienced failure. Perhaps there is a reason why Allah did not mention the creation of such a state in the Quran. Perhaps this is why the Prophet Muhammad talked about the message of Islam reaching the four corners of the earth, but gave no instructions on the creation of the Islamic State. Perhaps he was giving us Muslims a message that we have failed to heed. Perhaps it is time to do just that and walk away from the pursuit of an Islamic State and instead work to create a state of Islam within each one of us.

---

* Syed Qutb (1906–66): An Egyptian Islamist who joined the Muslim Brotherhood in 1952 and dedicated his life to the re-establishment of the caliphate and a pan-Islamic nation based on the sharia law.

CHAPTER 2

Pakistan—Failure of an Islamic State

THE QUESTION was straightforward: "If you had to live in a Muslim country, which of the following would you prefer to live in: Iran, Pakistan, Saudi Arabia, Turkey, or Indonesia?" The Facebook poll may not have been scientific, but the answers from a random sample of five hundred subscribers to the online social networking website revealed how ordinary people view the Muslim world.

Seventy-eight percent of the respondents chose secular Turkey or the relatively liberal nation of Indonesia. The three self-professed Islamic States—Iran, Pakistan, and Saudi Arabia—fared poorly, with Iran ending up as a choice of only 3 percent.

If ever there was a case to be made against the creation of an Islamic State, Saudi Arabia, Iran, and Pakistan provide stellar examples. These three countries claim to be Islamic, yet govern their populations by completely different political systems, woven around conflicting visions of Islam. One thing they have in common is the oppression of their citizens. Scores of Muslim societies have flowered on this globe in the past 1,400 years—from Tartarstan on the banks of the Volga to Senegal in West Africa; from Turkey, which straddles Europe and Asia, to Somalia at the mouth of the Red Sea; and including Chechens and Kosovars, Trinidadians and Fijians. But none matches the zeal with which Iran, Saudi Arabia, and Pakistan mix Islam and politics to crush the human spirit.

Two of these nations sit on oceans of oil, while the third—Pakistan—is a nuclear power. They all inherited a rich civilization and culture. They could have been shining examples of a post-colonial renaissance in Islam, but in their fervour to rule according to their interpretation of sharia, the respective ruling elites have made their countries a disgrace to Islam and the memory of the Prophet Muhammad. As if three such nations were not enough, Iran has been working to create an Islamic State in Palestine.

A closer look at these regions leads off in this chapter, with the author's birthplace, Pakistan, where brave people have risen up successfully against three US-backed military dictatorships, and are now confronting the fourth, forcing General Pervez Musharraf to give up his military command and demanding he resign as president.

Of the fifty-four member states that make up the Organization of Islamic Conference (OIC), only one country was created specifically as an Islamic State: Pakistan.

From its bloody birth in August 1947 to the assassination of Benazir Bhutto in December 2007, Pakistan's history has been one of turmoil, war, and civil strife, interspersed occasionally with odd moments of joy that invariably end in even more sorrow. One such rare event that electrified the nation, came after the elections of February 2008. The late Benazir Bhutto's People's Party and the Muslim League of former prime minister Nawaz Sharif, trounced the mullah-military establishment of Pakistan. But will this verdict carry weight? The will of Pakistanis has always been trampled to make way for the military and the mullahs. In its 60-year history, in every election, Pakistanis have rejected those who invoke Islam as their politics. In the historic 1970 elections, the Islamists won only four seats in the 301-member parliament. However, despite their defeat, they colluded with the military to keep the winning party from power, and were complicit in the genocide that resulted in the death of nearly one million fellow Muslims. Thirty-seven years later, Pakistanis have once more voted overwhelmingly to reject an Islamist future for their country. The disastrous defeat of the pro-Taliban Islamists and the success of secular centre-right and centre-left parties, even in the conservative pushtoon belt bordering Afghanistan, should send a clear message to the mullahs, the military, and the rest of the world: Pakistanis, like most Muslims, do not wish to live under the medieval rule of Islamic extremists. The question is this: is anyone listening?

The movement for the creation of Pakistan as the homeland for India's Muslim minority emerged in the 1930s among Muslim academics, landed aristocracy, and the tiny business community. More than an Islamic State based on Islamic law, the idea was to create a liberal democratic Muslim State (a country where Muslims would be a majority) in northwest India. No less a figure than the great poet-philosopher Muhammad Iqbal was the thinker behind this concept, though it is quite certain he did not visualize Pakistan as a country hostile to India and ethnically cleansed of its Sikh and Hindu populations.

The movement within the region that was to become Pakistan made little progress until the early 1940s. After facing repeated electoral failures, the secular leadership of the Muslim League* started trumpeting the slogan ISLAM IS IN DANGER. It recruited religious scholars to spread fear of the prospect of "Hindu majority rule" once Britain withdrew from the subcontinent.

Thanks to a whipping up of religious frenzy, within five years the dream of one sovereign Indian state was killed and Pakistan was born, divided into two wings—East Pakistan and West Pakistan—separated by 1,600 kilometres of Indian Territory. The Indian population—Hindu, Muslim, Sikh, Christian, Jew, and Zoroastrian—had never seen artificial frontiers, but now found themselves divided into three parts. Mother India was a 5,000-year-old entity when the British severed her limbs and granted the country "independence." In the west, the British sliced Punjab into two parts, leaving a gash so deep that the separated entities today believe they were born that way. In the east, Bengal, the cradle of Indian renaissance, was put on the butcher's block, dividing villages and homes and flooding the Ganges delta with the blood of the sons and daughters of poet-philosophers Rabindranath Tagore and Kazi Nazrul Islam.

The biggest losers in this great game of divide-and-rule were India's Muslims. In the name of Islam, they were divided into three separate parts and cut off from each other. Ironically, this division was done in the name of unity. Today, 150 million of South Asia's Muslims live in Pakistan, another 140 million live in Bangladesh, and 160 million in India, yet the apologists of the 1930–40s Muslim segregationist movement that splintered India's Muslims into three countries celebrate this catastrophe as a victory.

Notwithstanding the tragedies of partition, Pakistan could still have emerged as an example for the rest of the Muslim world. It was born on August 14, 1947, at a time when Muslims around the world were colonized people. The middle classes and intellectuals dreamed of a renaissance that could lead their citizens towards modernity. Pakistan's emergence was supposed to be the spark that would ignite the fires of a new Muslim age of freedom and sovereignty. It was the largest Muslim country, a democracy, multilingual, and multinational. It had the highest mountains in its north,

---

* This would become the governing majority party in Pakistan's first parliament.

the Himalayas. It was watered by the mighty Indus and the Ganges. Its poetry was shaped by 13th-century mystic Rumi and 20th-century Nobel laureate Tagore. Its people spoke such rich and musical languages as Bengali, Punjabi, Pushto, Sindhi and, of course, Urdu. Pakistan was Indian yet linked to Arabia; it had Persia as one neighbour and China as its other. The royal Bengal tiger roamed its Sunderban jungles in the Ganges Delta, while the 5,000-year-old ancient city of Mohenjo-Daro sat gracefully on the banks of the mighty Indus. The waters of the Arabian Sea and the Bay of Bengal lapped its shores. It could have been the essence of all of the above. Instead, Pakistan's elites turned the country into a graveyard of its indigenous culture and languages. History was murdered on the altar of religion and a vibrant democracy was strangled by the egos of authoritarian dictators, both civilian and military.

Pakistan was born as a nation of contradictions. A few days before its inception, founder Muhammad Ali Jinnah, popularly known as the *Quaid-e-Azam* (the great leader), had made a surprisingly bold secular statement. He declared, "You will find that in course of time Hindus* would cease to be Hindus and Muslims would cease to be Muslims, not in the religious sense, because that is the personal faith of each individual, but in the political sense as citizens of the State."

Jinnah's speech raised the hopes of his countrymen, imbibing them with the zeal to create a new Muslim identity, one that would become the envy of the world. Using English (he could not speak any Indian language fluently), he made repeated references to the bitterness of the past and extended a heartfelt appeal to Pakistanis to forget the past and bury the hatchet. He said the future Pakistani would be a citizen with equal rights, privileges, and obligations, irrespective of colour, caste, creed, or community. Religion would have nothing to do with the business of the state; it would merely be a matter of personal faith for the individual.

Within months he would change course and start speaking like a medieval emir, rallying his country to come to the defence of Islam and paving the path for the demise of his own promise. His fine Saville Row suits were discarded and he was repackaged as a pious man in traditional Muslim attire. The Scotch, bacon, and cigar gave way to a "Jinnah cap," and the traditional Indian knee-length coat (the *sherwani*) and trousers (*shalwar*). Within a year the country's first law minister, Jogendra Nath Mandal, a Dalit Hindu, would flee for his life and take refuge in neighbouring India.

---

* It was significant that he failed to mention the Sikhs, because the creation of Pakistan would be a particularly tragic blow to those followers of religious leader Guru Nanak.

Jogendra Nath Mandal (1906-56) was a Bengali politician who belonged to the so-called untouchable Hindus known as Dalits. He was a strong critic of the Indian National Congress, which he saw as dominated by upper-class Hindus, lukewarm in their commitment to secure Dalit political rights. Mandal grew close to the Muslim League's Muhammad Ali Jinnah, and after the partition of India he agreed to serve as Pakistan's first minister for law and labour. However, following the Indo-Pakistani War of 1948, Hindu-Muslim riots in East Pakistan, and the death of Jinnah, he was shunned by cabinet colleagues and was denied access to secret files. When Pakistan's first Prime Minister Liaquat Ali Khan endorsed a proposal to make Islam the official state religion, Mandal realized his days were numbered. After coming under verbal and physical attacks, in October 1950 he fled to Calcutta to take refuge in India. In his letter of resignation, he slammed Jinnah's successors for disregarding the rights and future of minorities.

Jinnah lived for only one year after the birth of the nation, but in that time he set the standard of a top-down administration, adopting the style of Moghul emperors, not democratic leaders. To begin with, Jinnah decided not to become the country's first prime minister, instead choosing to be the Queen's representative to the new country as her first governor general. By any parliamentary standards or tradition, the post of governor general is largely ceremonial, like that of Canada's Michaëlle Jean. It has the all the pomp and ceremony, but little true executive power. However, in the words of British Lord Louis Mountbatten, who oversaw the independence of India and Pakistan, Jinnah was incapable of resisting "pomp, the gaudy ceremonials of the top office of the state for which he had worked so hard."

When Mountbatten tried to explain to Jinnah that, under Pakistan's interim constitution, the governor general was a ceremonial head of state and real power lay with the prime minister, Jinnah told him curtly, "In Pakistan, I will be the Governor-General and the Prime Minister will do what I tell him." And that is how history would record his one year in office.

Jinnah revoked the authority of the Muslim League parliamentary group and chose the country's new prime minister. He also named his prime minister's first cabinet for him, and if that was not enough, as governor general also sat in cabinet. There is no question that Jinnah was an extremely popular leader, and his very word was the law. However, as is the case with all popular benevolent dictators, instead of leaving behind institutions of democracy, he left a trail of authoritarian precedents that are invoked and implemented to the nation's detriment even today.

This begs the question: Was this the model of an Islamic State that 20th-century Muslims had been waiting for? Here was a latter-day caliph ruling in arbitrary fashion under the title of governor general, with no room for opposition and abandoning the commitment to secularism he had made barely a few months beforehand. In the bloodshed that followed partition, Hindus and Sikhs were fleeing Pakistan for India, and millions of Indian Muslims started pouring into Pakistan. When the carnage ended, half a million Hindus, Muslims, and Sikhs would be dead. In another twenty-five years, one million more would die in the Bangladesh war of liberation. Do we need more evidence to make the case that mixing religion and politics is not only a disingenuous political tactic, but its results are catastrophic?

Millions of Hindus left Pakistan after partition. However, the tragedy that befell the Sikhs was far more ominous and deserves special mention.

Just as it is inconceivable to wrest Islam from its Arabian roots, Sikhism is a 15th-century religion that originated in Punjab, and its theology and history are intertwined with the fate of Punjab. Sikhs and Muslims, along with Hindus, lived as neighbours in the same villages and towns of Punjab for centuries.

For Sikhs, the Punjabi cities of Lahore and Gujranwala, Nankana Sahib and Rawalpindi were their hometowns and had shared a history with their gurus. With partition, not only was Punjab divided, but the Sikhs were ethnically cleansed from Pakistan's Punjab. As a result of the creation of the Islamic State of Pakistan, the Sikhs lost absolute access to the following holy sites: Gurdwara Janam Asthan, the birthplace of Guru Nanak, in Nankana Sahib; Gurdwara Panji Sahib in Hasan Abdal; Gurdwara Dera Sahib in Lahore, where the Fifth Guru, Arjun Dev, was killed; Gurudwara Kartarpur Sahib in Kartarpur, where Guru Nanak died; and, of course, the Shrine of Maharaja Ranjit Singh in Lahore.

When the killings and cleansing of 1947 ended, not a single Sikh was visible in Lahore. Of course, Muslims too were chased out of the eastern parts of Punjab, but they were not losing their holy places of Mecca or Medina.

Even though we Muslims despair the occupation of Jerusalem, we still have the comfort of knowing that Muslims still live in and around the Dome of the Rock and the Al-Aqsa Mosque. But what about the Sikhs? To feel their pain, Muslims need to imagine how outraged we would feel if, God forbid, Mecca and Medina were cleansed of all Muslims and fell under the occupation of, say, Ethiopia. So why are we comfortable with Sikhs losing their holy sites? This is an outcome of our mad rush to create an Islamic State carved out of India. How can we Muslims ask for the liberation of Muslim lands while we institutionalize the exclusion and ethnic cleansing of all Sikhs from their holy sites inside an Islamic state? Muslims who cannot empathize with the loss of the Sikhs need to ask themselves why they don't.

Before 1947, Punjabi Muslims did not consider Sikhism as an adversarial faith. After all, from the Muslim perspective, Sikhism was the combination of the teachings of Sufism, which was rooted in Islamic thought and the Bhakti movement, an organic link to Hindu philosophy. It is true that Moghul emperors had been particularly vicious and cruel to the leaders of the Sikh faith, but these Moghuls were not acting as representatives of Islam. Not only that, the Moghuls inflicted even harsher punishments on their fellow Muslims.

With the creation of Pakistan, the Sikhs lost something even more precious than their holy places: diverse subcultural streams. One such stream flourishing in Thal region (Sind Sagar Doab) in what is now Pakistan, near Punjab's border with Sind and Baluchistan, was known as the "Sewa Panthis." The Sewa Panthi tradition flourished in southwest Punjab for nearly twelve generations until 1947. This sect (variously known as Sewa Panthis, Sewa Dassiey, and Addan Shahis), is best symbolized by Bhai Ghaniya, who aided wounded Sikh and Muslim soldiers alike during the Tenth Sikh Guru's wars with Moghuls. Sewa Panthis wore distinctive white robes. They introduced a new dimension to the subcontinental religious philosophies. They believed that *sewa* (helping the needy) was the highest form of spiritual meditation—higher than singing hymns or reciting holy books. The creation of Pakistan dealt a devastating blow to the Sewa Panthis and they never got truly transplanted in the new "East" Punjab. The organic relationship between philosophies and land, indeed, requires native soil for ideas to bloom. Other such sects and *deras* (groups) that made up the composite Sikh faith of the 19th and early 20th centuries included Namdharis, Nirankaris, Radha Soamis, Nirmaley, and Sidhs—all were pushed to the margins, or even out of Sikhism, after the partition.

Sikh leaders were equally complicit in this tragedy. In fact, it was they who demanded partitioning the Punjab. Jinnah did not have a monopoly on short-sightedness and pettiness. On March 8, 1947, the Indian National Congress in its Delhi session adopted a resolution supporting the demand of Sikh fundamentalists for a partition of the Punjab. The congress and its Sikh allies demanded that the departing British separate the predominantly non-Muslim areas of the province from the Muslim areas and create a new province called East Punjab that would be a part of India, not Pakistan.

Chasing Sikhs from their holy places turned into a tragedy for Muslims as well as Sikhs. One cannot separate the various organs of the human body and then expect the organs or the human being to survive. This is one reason why, despite my deep admiration, empathy, and affection for the Sikh community for its contribution to my Punjabi culture, I stay adamantly opposed to a further breakup of India to create a separate Sikh religious state of Khalistan. A better idea would be to have open borders and a free movement of people. This should include the right of return for the children and grandchildren of refugees from both sides.

The tragedy of the division of Punjab is best captured in a moving poem by the first prominent woman Punjabi poet, novelist, and essayist Amrita Pritam, "Ujj akhaan Waris Shah noo" (An Ode to Waris Shah), which she is said to have written while escaping in a train with her family from Pakistan to India.* Pritam wrote:

ujj aakhaN Waris Shah nuuN, kithoN kabraaN vichchoN bol,
tay ujj kitab-e ishq daa koii aglaa varkaa phol
ik roii sii dhii punjaab dii, tuuN likh likh maare vaen,
ujj lakhaaN dhiiaaN rondiaN, tainuN Waris Shah nuN kahen
uTh dardmandaaN diaa dardiaa, uth takk apnaa Punjab
aaj bele lashaaN bichhiaaN te lahu dii bharii Chenab

[Today, I beckon you Waris Shah, speak from inside your grave
And to your book of love, add the next page
Once when a single daughter of Punjab wept, you wrote a wailing saga
Today, a million daughters cry to you, Waris Shah
Rise, O friend of the grieving; rise and see your own Punjab,
Today, fields lined with corpses, and the Chenab flowing with blood.]

In the summer of 1947, one week after swearing in his new prime minister and cabinet, and as Pakistanis were celebrating their first Eid-ul-Fitr holiday after Ramadan, Jinnah broke another sacred principle of democracy. He dismissed the duly elected provincial government in the North West Frontier Province (NWFP), which borders Afghanistan. Dr. Khan Sahib, the chief minister of the province, had a comfortable majority. Jinnah installed his own party as the government, but when it failed to get a vote of confidence, he

---

* Waris Shah: An 18th-century Muslim Punjabi poet who wrote "*Heer and Ranjah,*" the tragic saga of two lovers that became a Punjabi epic.

arranged to have all the dismissed members arrested, creating an artificial majority.

From Pakistan's inception, the people of the NWFP—the Pukhtoons—were treated like the riff-raff of society, and that alienation has left scars. Up until the 1970s this alienation contributed to Pukhtoon nationalism. Later, this sentiment would be tapped by Islamists to create the Pukhtoon Taliban of today.

Nine months after dismissing the NWFP government, Jinnah demonstrated his arbitrary power again. This time he dismissed the government in the province of Sind, which belonged to his own party, the Muslim League. And as if this were not enough, the ailing leader of Pakistan then tried to stage a palace coup inside the provincial government of Punjab. In less than a year of the nation's existence, the man who had created Pakistan as a democratic state for the Muslims of India had gone against the grain of democracy, invoked Islam to bring discipline among those who protested, and mere weeks before he passed away, declared to the country's majority Bengali population that their language was not worthy of being the nation's national language as it was not a "Muslim" language. Before he died, he had sown the seeds of the country's breakup. The so-called language riots that broke out after Jinnah's "Urdu Only" speech were the first step towards the ultimate secession of East Pakistan and the birth of Bangladesh.

After Jinnah's death in 1948, the top-down authoritarian model grew in strength. If the Father of the Nation had set the precedent of arbitrary rule, who would dare stand in the way?

The first test of democracy came in May 1949, during a by-election in the constituency of Tangail in then East Pakistan. To the shock of the ruling Muslim League, the party lost the election to the nascent opposition. Stung by the loss and taking it as a personal insult, Prime Minister Liaquat Ali Khan declared the result null and void and the newly elected member of the constituent assembly was jailed along with numerous other opposition activists. One of those arrested, prominent communist leader Moni Singh, was to spend a total of twenty-two years either in jail or underground. He walked in freedom again only after Pakistan broke up in 1971.

After Jinnah's death, the Islamists swooped in for the kill. Those who had opposed the creation of the country now became its guardians. All hopes of a modern constitution for the country were dashed as Islamists from all over the world converged on Pakistan to mould its fresh clay into their fantasy of a latter-day caliphate. Egyptian Islamist Said Ramadan (whose son Tariq founded the Movement of Swiss Muslims and now advises governments) arrived in Karachi to "Islamicize" Pakistan, as did the Polish convert Muhammad Asad, who took upon himself the task of writing the country's principles of existence.

Living in the fool's paradise of the *Arabian Nights*, the Islamists completely ignored the ground reality and the aspirations of ordinary Pakistanis. Pakistan's indigenous languages were all sidelined and a proposal was floated to make Pakistan's national language Arabic (a language that Pakistanis did not speak).

With Islamists flexing their muscles on one side and a constitutional crisis looming, the new governor general, an ailing former British civil servant by the name of Ghulam Mohammad, upped the ante and outdid Jinnah. In 1952 he fired the prime minister, dismissed the cabinet, and started ruling by decree. By 1954, the country was lurching from one crisis to another, with the ruling party suffering massive defeats across the country in provincial elections. As the country was celebrating the founder's birthday on Christmas Day, 1954, the governor general dissolved the Constituent Assembly. If Governor General Jinnah could dissolve provincial legislatures, surely, his successor argued, he could dissolve the federal legislature.

After this palace coup, there was no going back. In between power struggles, Pakistan had its first taste of martial law following a genocidal campaign launched to exterminate the country's Ahmadiya Muslim sect. All dreams of Pakistan growing into a modern secular democracy, as enunciated by Jinnah in his August 11, 1947, speech, had vanished. By 1953, that vision had dissipated and been all but forgotten as Islamist mobs started hunting down fellow Muslims and killing them in the name of Islam.

When a government inquiry investigating these sectarian killings asked the Islamic clerics and scholars of Pakistan whether they agreed with Jinnah's vision of Pakistan as a secular democracy for Muslims, it reported that everyone had replied no, unhesitatingly. The inquiry quoted the Jamaat-e-Islami as saying that "a State based on this idea [secularism] is the creature of the devil." After months of deliberations, the inquiry produced the now famous "Justice Munir Commission Report to Enquire into the Punjab Disturbances of 1953." The findings were remarkable. Among Pakistan's imams and Islamic scholars, no two agreed on the fundamental definition of either an "Islamic State" or a "Muslim."

The report posed the rhetorical question, "What is then the Islamic State of which everybody talks but nobody thinks?" The *ulama** were divided in their opinions when they were asked to cite some precedent

---

* Religious scholars.

of an Islamic State in Muslim history. Most of them, however, relied on the form of government that had existed during the caliphate from the time of the Prophet's death, 632 CE, to 661 CE, a period of less than thirty years.

The commission captured the contradictions and confusion in the minds of the Islamists as they explained the nature of a future Islamic State. Here is the testimony of one witness, Master Taj-ud-Din Ansari:

Q: Is Khilafat* with you a necessary part of Muslim form of Government?
A: Yes.
Q: Are you, therefore, in favour of having a Khilafat in Pakistan?
A: Yes.
Q: Can there be more than one Khalifa† of the Muslims?
A: No.
Q: Will the Khalifa of Pakistan be the Khalifa of all the Muslims of the world?
A: He should be but cannot be.

The inquiry interviewed hundreds of Islamic scholars in an attempt to find a common definition of the Islamic State, but found it an impossible task. The report concluded:

The question, therefore, whether a person is or is not a Muslim will be of fundamental importance, and it was for this reason that we asked most of the leading *ulama*‡ to give their definition of a Muslim, the point being that if the ulama of the various sects believed the Ahmadis to be *kafirs*,§ they must have been quite clear in their minds not only about the grounds of such belief but also about the definition of a Muslim, because the claim that a certain person or community is not within the pale of Islam implies on the part of the claimant an exact conception of what a Muslim is. The result of this part of the inquiry, however, has been anything but satisfactory, and if considerable confusion exists in the minds of our *ulama* on such a simple matter, one can easily imagine what the differences on more complicated matters will be.

---

* *Khilafat:* Caliphate.
† *Khalifa:* Caliph.
‡ *Ulama:* Variant spelling for Ulema, orthodox scholars.
§ *Kafirs:* Non-Muslims.

After cross-examining Pakistan's leading Islamic scholars, the two justices heading the royal commission wrote in obvious frustration:

> Keeping in view the several definitions given by the *ulama*, need we make any comment except that no two learned divines are agreed on this fundamental. If we attempt our own definition as each learned divine has done and that definition differs from that given by all others, we unanimously go out of the fold of Islam. And if we adopt the definition given by any one of the *ulama*, we remain Muslims according to the view of that *alim*, but *kafirs* according to the definition of every one else.

In conclusion, the Supreme Court-appointed commission to investigate Pakistan's first of many Muslim versus Muslim killings had this to say in its report:

> Pakistan is being taken by the common man, though it is not, as an Islamic State. This belief has been encouraged by the ceaseless clamour for Islam and Islamic State that is being heard from all quarters since the establishment of Pakistan. The phantom of an Islamic State has haunted the Musalman [Muslim] throughout the ages and is a result of the memory of the glorious past when Islam rising like a storm from the least expected quarter of the world—wilds of Arabia—instantly enveloped the world, pulling down from their high pedestal gods who had ruled over man since the creation, uprooting centuries-old institutions and superstitions and supplanting all civilisations that had been built on an enslaved humanity. . . .
>
> It is this brilliant achievement of the Arabian nomads, the like of which the world had never seen before, that makes the Musalman of today live in the past and yearn for the return of the glory that was Islam. He finds himself standing on the crossroads, wrapped in the mantle of the past and with the dead weight of centuries on his back, frustrated and bewildered and hesitant to turn one corner or the other. The freshness and the simplicity of the faith, which gave determination to his mind and spring to his muscle, is now denied to him. He has neither the means nor the ability to conquer and there are no countries to conquer. Little does he understand that the forces which are pitted against him are entirely different from those against which early Islam had to fight, and that on the clues given by his own ancestors' human mind has achieved results which he cannot understand. . . . Nothing but a bold re-orientation of Islam to separate the vital from the lifeless can preserve it as a World Idea and convert the Musalman into a citizen of the present and the future world

from the archaic incongruity that he is today. It is this lack of bold and clear thinking, the inability to understand and take decisions which has brought about in Pakistan a confusion which will persist and repeatedly create situations of the kind we have been inquiring into until our leaders have a clear conception of the goal and of the means to reach it. It requires no imagination to realise that irreconcilables remain irreconcilable even if you believe or wish to the contrary. . . . And as long as we rely on the hammer when a file is needed and press Islam into service to solve situations it was never intended to solve, frustration and disappointment must dog our steps. The sublime faith called Islam will live even if our leaders are not there to enforce it. It lives in the individual, in his soul and outlook, in all his relations with God and men, from the cradle to the grave, and our politicians should understand that if Divine commands cannot make or keep a man a Musalman, their statutes will not.

These words went unheeded. The country's politicians knew the value of Islam as a political weapon and they were not about to surrender the goose that lays the golden egg. Despite Islamists acting as the guardians of the faith, ordinary Pakistanis rejected them in one provincial election after the other, instead voting for centre-left coalitions. The ruling elites kept postponing the national elections even after the adoption of the country's constitution in 1956. A merry-go-round of prime ministers made the country the butt of jokes in next-door India.

The stability of the new Islamic State was secured by its close ties to the US global war on communism. This included a witch hunt of Pakistani leftists, which manifested itself in the torture and murder of Hasan Nasir, Pakistan's most well-known Marxist. Pakistan then joined the anti-communist Central Treaty Organization (CENTO), which put Iran, Turkey, and Pakistan under US command, and South East Asia Treaty Organization (SEATO), which included the United States, Britain, Pakistan, the Philippines, and Thailand. Both were US-led military alliances modelled on the North Atlantic Treaty Organization. The strategic partnership of Britain and the United States put Pakistan in conflict with its Arab friends. When Israel, Britain, and France invaded the Suez Canal in 1956, Pakistan's government shamefully backed the invading armies, instead of Egypt.

After a wasted decade, the date was set for Pakistan's first national elections in March 1959. But there was discomfort in Washington and among Pakistan's ruling elites, as well as the Islamist political parties. By all accounts, it was clear that if a free and fair election were held in March 1959, the centre-left coalition led by the newly established National Awami Party

(NAP) would do very well in both wings of the country. The NAP had come about with the merger of various secular left-wing provincial organizations and the banned Communist Party. It was expected to do very well in East Pakistan, the NWFP, Sind, and Baluchistan, and had the entire Punjabi trade union movement behind it. The problem was that its platform called for Pakistan's withdrawal from both SEATO and CENTO.

By now the Pakistan Armed Forces had developed close relations with the Pentagon, and the CIA established bases in the Pakistani city of Peshawar, where U-2 spy planes that flew regularly over the Soviet Union were based. A victory of the NAP, on its own or in a coalition, was a strategic threat to the United States because the NAP had promised to withdraw Pakistan from all US military pacts. An NAP victory would also have dealt a serious blow to the image of the Islamists of Jamaat-e-Islami as they were unlikely to win a single seat anywhere in the country.*

A few years earlier, the CIA had faced a similar situation in next-door Iran where a left-leaning Muhammad Mossadeqh had won the elections; Mossadeqh was removed in a messy coup. In Pakistan, the pro-US armed forces had learned from the Mossadeqh affair. Of course, domestic politics were also at play. The president of the country, Iskander Mirza, was aware that a new parliament would not have him as the head of state and if elections were held, his days were numbered. The US-backed military and the president acted to pre-empt the victory of the centre-left. On October 7, 1958, a coup took place in Pakistan and the constitution of the country was abrogated, thus cancelling the upcoming election. Here is how Air Marshal Asghar Khan, who was then commander-in-chief of Pakistan's Air Force, wrote about the coup in his 1983 classic, *Generals in Politics*:

> I was summoned by the President at about 9 p.m. on 7 October. When I arrived at the President's House, I found Ayub Khan and a number of other army officers, amongst them Brigadier Yahya Khan present. I was told by Iskander Mirza [the president] that he had decided to abrogate the Constitution; martial law had been declared and the army was moving to take over the government. I had no prior knowledge of such a plan and was told that I should stay there for the next couple of hours presumably until all moves had been completed.

---

* In 1970, when the first national elections were finally held, the Islamist Jamaat-e-Islami won only 4 out of the 301 seats in Pakistan's parliament.

Pakistan's first constitution was in tatters. The next day the chief justice of the country would give his blessing and, in two weeks, another putsch would take place with General Ayub Khan overthrowing the president and, on October 27, 1958, declaring himself as the new president of Pakistan. Democracy died that day in Pakistan and, despite an occasional attempt to resurrect itself, it has been held hostage by the military might of the Pakistan armed forces that have been complemented by the country's mosque establishment.

Needing a semblance of legitimacy, in the spring of 1965, General Khan, who by now had promoted himself to the post of field marshal, rigged an election to hold on to his presidency. This triggered outrage among the people, especially in East Pakistan (now Bangladesh). Students and trade unionists joined lawyers and academics in the streets chanting "*Ayub kutta, hai, hai*" (Ayub the dog, shame, shame).

Fearing a mass uprising, the field marshal (a good friend of US presidents Dwight Eisenhower, John Kennedy, and Lyndon Johnson) dipped into the time-tested tool used by all tyrants: He wrapped himself in the flag. What better way to deflect the wrath of the people than to wage war on the infidel "enemy"—India.

So, in August 1965, he launched Operation Gibraltar, sending thousands of Pakistani troops in civilian clothes deep into Indian-administrated Kashmir. New Delhi retaliated by attacking Pakistan on September 6, resulting in a seventeen-day war that ended in a stalemate.

For a few months, Ayub Khan was a hero. The opposition demonstrators had disappeared, branded as traitors. It seemed that he had succeeded in positioning himself as the saviour and would rule Pakistan for another decade. That didn't happen. Within four years, Khan was gone in a wave of citizens' protests that led to nearly 100,000 people being arrested and hundreds killed.

Among the admirers of the fallen field marshal was a young student at Karachi's St. Patrick's High School. His name was Pervez Musharraf. Like Ayub Khan, he, too, would topple an elected government. And like Ayub Khan, he, too, would be the United States' key ally in the region.

Between the eras of these two army generals, another character emerged who symbolized the alliance of the world Islamist movement and the US war on communism. This was General Muhammad Zia-ul-Haq, the architect of the massacre of Palestinians in Jordan in September 1970, now known as Black September. Zia became the number-one US ally to fight the war against the Soviets in Afghanistan and is largely responsible for the destruction of Pakistan's cultural and historic heritage, turning the country into a sort of a flea market pseudo-Arab state, where even the centuries-old greeting of *"Khuda Hafiz"* was declared un-Islamic and banned.* No other politician or military general has accomplished the mixing of Islamist ideology and service to US regional interests in the way that Zia did, yet he is still the darling of the now anti-US Islamists.

The more recent siege of the Red Mosque of Islamabad in the summer of 2007 best reflects the bankruptcy of the Islamicization of politics in Pakistan and exposed the nexus of the *"Mullah*-Military" complex.†

It's important to know that the Red Mosque was a creation of Pakistan's intelligence services, which used it for decades to recruit armed jihadis. It was US-backed Zia who had allowed the Red Mosque jihadis a free hand in spreading their hateful doctrine of extremism under the name of Islam.

The brothers who led the Red Mosque rebellion—the one who was arrested trying to escape in a burka, as well as the mullah who died in the fighting—worked for Pakistan's intelligence agencies. Their father, too, was an employee of the government and ran the fiefdom in the heart of Islamabad until he was assassinated.

The mullahs and radical jihadis in the Red Mosque were all actors in the game of Pakistani roulette. As long as the mosque remained a visible hotbed of Islamist activity, General Pervez Musharraf could show the West that it needed him to fight terrorism. Just as Ayub Khan was able to convince successive US administrations that, without him, Pakistan would slide into communism, Musharraf convinced George W. Bush that, without him, Pakistan would become one large Red Mosque teeming with jihadis trying to whip the nation into an Islamist nuclear power.

What he fails to disclose, of course, is that the arming of the Red Mosque could not have happened without his government's full knowledge. There's no way that machine guns, rocket launchers, and ammunition could be taken into the heart of Islamabad, next door to government ministries, without arousing the suspicion of the country's omnipresent security agencies.

In the end, Musharraf, like earlier pro-US generals, was caught in his own trap. He could not put the jihadi genie back into the bottle, so he had to kill it. He may have come out as a hero to the White House and to Pakistan's ruling upper-class elites, but history dictates a short-lived romance.

---

* *Khuda Hafiz:* Literally "May God protect you."
† *Mullah:* A Muslim who is learned in the sacred laws and theology of Islam.

Those who wish to stamp out the Islamic extremists and their jihadi foot soldiers must realize that to fight malaria one needs to drain the swamps, not shoot individual mosquitoes. The million men and women who came out to greet former prime minister Benazir Bhutto, when she returned after eight years in self-imposed exile, are a testament to the fact that the people of Pakistan reject Islamic extremism and yearn for a liberal progressive Islam. However, these ordinary Pakistanis face a nexus of well-funded Islamic extremists who have infiltrated the state apparatus, both military and civil. The men who sent suicide bombers in a failed bid to kill Bhutto in October 2007, and who ultimately succeeded in assassinating her two months later, sent a chilling message of fear: any Muslim who dares challenge the jihadis will be eliminated. Benazir Bhutto is dead, but the fight between Islam and Islamists is not over. It will be won by ordinary Muslims only if they stand up to the Islamists, and not be cowed by them or compromise in cowardice.

The experiment of an Islamic State in Pakistan has shown clearly that such an entity is only a medieval dream that cannot live up to the standards of democracy, ethics, universal human rights, and the rule of law—standards we Muslims expect when we choose to live in secular democracies like Canada, France, India, or South Africa. It is time to learn a lesson from the experience of Pakistan and come to the conclusion that the myth of an Islamic State can only serve the interests of Islamists and not its citizens, or Islam, and definitely not its non-Muslim populace.

In 1947, the creation of Pakistan may have thrilled the leadership of the Muslim League and the elites of the Muslim community in India who soon had access to the top jobs in the newly created country. However, for the millions of Muslims who refused to leave India for this supposed paradise, Pakistan became a curse word and a burden that they and their future generations would have to carry through no fault of their own. After partition, Indian Muslims, despite their enormous sacrifices and contributions to Indian culture and civilization, would be seen with suspicion by the Hindu nationalists of the country. The Jan Sanghis of the 1950s and 1960s, the Shiv Sena of today, and elements of the Bharatiya Janata Party (BJP) have spared no occasion to cast doubt on the patriotism of Indian Muslims, at times taunting them to "Go to Pakistan." Jinnah's inflated ego may have created an Islamic State, but it also created a nightmare for other Indian Muslims. It has placed an enormous liability on India's 160 million Muslims. That alone should be reason to declare the creation of an Islamic State carved out of India a burden rather than a blessing for Muslims.

If Muslims have suffered in India at the hands of right-wing Hindu nationalists, the plight of Hindus in Pakistan is far worse and systemically institutionalized. Reporting on Pakistan's dismal human rights record, the Asian Centre for Human Rights highlighted the systemic nature of the problem. In August 2007 it reported that the "Pakistan government in its policies, programs and laws only recognizes religious minorities but not the ethnic, linguistic or racial minorities living in the country." Not that religious minorities fare any better.

The constitution of Pakistan segregates its citizens on the basis of religion, and provides preferential treatment to the Muslims. While Article 2 of the constitution declares Islam "the State religion of Pakistan" and the Quran and Sunna to be "the supreme law and source of guidance for legislation to be administered through laws enacted by the Parliament and Provincial Assemblies, and for policy making by the Government," under Article 41(2) only a Muslim can become president. Further, Article 260 differentiates "Muslim" and "Non-Muslim," thereby facilitating and encouraging discrimination on the basis of religion. This application of the constitution can lead to serious violations of human rights.

The constitution is so glued to providing preferential treatment to the majority Muslims that a Hindu judge had to take his oath of office in the name of Allah. On March 24, 2007, Justice Rana Bhagwandas, while being sworn in as acting chief justice of Pakistan, had to take his oath of office with a Quranic prayer: "May Allah Almighty help and guide me, Ameen." Imagine what would happen if a Muslim judge in India, the United States, or Canada were forced to take the oath on the Bible or the Bhagavad-Gita. You would have the streets full of "outraged" demonstrators across the world. Where were these demonstrators when Justice Bhagwandas was humiliated publicly?

Provisions of the Pakistan Penal Code provide harsh punishment for alleged blasphemy. These blasphemy laws undermine major provisions of the constitution of Pakistan, such as the fundamental right to "profess, practice and propagate his religion" (Article 20); equality before the law and equal protection of law to all citizens (Article 25); and the safeguarding of the "legitimate rights and interests of minorities" (Article 36). If the existing laws were not sufficient to institutionalize second-class status of non-Muslims in Pakistan, the Islamists in Pakistan's parliament in May 2007 introduced *The Apostasy Bill* which seeks, among other things, to provide death sentence to any Muslim converting to other religions and imposes life imprisonment for female apostates.

If Saudi textbooks teach hatred against Jews and Christians, Pakistani school texts and teachings malign Hindus and Hinduism. In fact, in more than one textbook Hindus have been cited as the "enemy of Islam."

It is not just Hindus who suffer in this climate of hate. Ahmadiya Muslims have been declared heretic, and practising their faith in public is considered blasphemous. In 2006, ninety cases of blasphemy were reported. Out of these, only forty-eight were registered with the police, and of these, twenty-seven of the accused were Muslim, ten Christian, and eleven belonged to the Ahmadiya Muslim community. Considering the fact that Christians, Hindus, and Ahmadiya Muslims constitute only slightly more than 4 percent of the total population of Pakistan, they have disproportionately been victims of the blasphemy laws.

The fact that a state which claims to take inspiration from the Quran and the teachings of Muhammad can mistreat its minority citizens while trampling over their rights indicates that Islam is once again being used merely as a tool of power, not as an instrument of faith.

Whether it is the Shiv Mandir (temple) of the Hindus in Karachi that has been turned into a slaughterhouse or the Krishna temple in Lahore, which was demolished to pave the way for construction of a commercial complex, the conspicuous silence of those who invoke Islam as their moral compass has done greater damage to Islam than the so-called conspiracies being hatched in London, New Delhi, and Tel Aviv.

In the summer of 2007, after the Islamists were evicted from the Red Mosque in Islamabad, many Christian families had to flee their homes in North West Frontier Province following a threatening letter sent by Islamic militants asking these Pakistani Christians to convert to Islam within ten days or face dire consequences. Disgraceful conduct by any standards, but despicable if carried out in the name of my religion, Islam.

No community has suffered more at the hands of Pakistan's military and its mullahs than the poor yet dignified people of Baluchistan. I know the Baluch well. As a nineteen-year-old political prisoner in 1970, I spent considerable time in the province in a hilltop jail built by the British in the town of Mach. I was part of the Baluchistan movement that in the late 1960s was seeking recognition of their language and provincial status for their region. I shared my youth with the now-grizzled leaders of the Baluchistan movement. They were the people Pakistan should have been most proud of. They were the people who got nothing but sorrow and suffering in return.

Few Pakistanis are aware of the fact that on August 11, 1947, the British protectorate of Baluchistan declared its independence. Three days later, Pakistan also became an independent nation. But the two states coexisted for less than a year. In March 1948, the Pakistan army took action and seized Baluchistan. Under threat of imprisonment, the traditional Baluch leader, the Khan of Kalat, Mir Ahmed Yar Khan, was pressured to sign a treaty of integration. A civil war started and the ill-equipped Baluch irregulars were no match for Pakistan's army. That is how Baluchistan became part of Pakistan as its biggest province, while a third of it still remains under Iranian jurisdiction. The leader of the Baluch uprising was shot dead along with his colleagues, thus beginning Baluchistan's sad association with Pakistan—soaked in the blood of its leaders. For sixty years now, Baluchistan has been under Pakistani military occupation, resulting in at least two more insurrections by Baluch guerrillas. One was led by the legendary Sheroo Marri, better known as "General Shroff" in the late 1950s. Another erupted in the early 1970s, led by leftist youth cadres and leading Baluch politicians in protest over the dismissal of a duly elected government.

Baluchistan accounts for nearly half of Pakistan's land mass and is immensely rich in natural resources, including oil, gas, coal, copper, and gold. Despite this huge mineral wealth, Baluchistan remains one of the poorest regions of Pakistan. Much of the population is malnourished, illiterate and semi-destitute, living in squalid housing with no electricity or clean drinking water. Would the Prophet Muhammad have permitted such ill treatment of a Muslim people by other Muslims invoking Islam and Allah? And where is the Muslim outcry against these atrocities?

Pakistan is a living testament to the bankrupt idea of an Islamic State. The success of its enterprising and hospitable citizens stands in contrast to the failures of the state. Imagine the possibilities of a Pakistan free from the shackles of its Islamist tormentors.

On the morning of February 18, 2008, when Pakistanis prepared to vote in the much awaited election, the front-page banner headline of the Karachi newspaper *DAWN* summed up the choice before the nation: "Make-Or-Break Vote Today." By late evening, as the results trickled in, the verdict of the people of Pakistan was clear. They had categorically rejected the ideology of the Taliban, snubbed the forces of Jihadi extremism, and sent a message of no confidence against the regime of General Pervez Musharraf. Only time will tell if Islamabad's mullah-military nexus will bow to the will of the Pakistani people.

CHAPTER 3

Saudi Arabia—Sponsor of Islamic States

THERE IS A SAYING among the Arabs that "Nothing good ever came out of Nejd." Nejd is a province in central Saudi Arabia, the heartland of the Saudi royal family and the birthplace of Muhammad Ibn Abdul Wahhab, the 18th-century founder of the extremist Wahhabi cult of Islam. Throughout Islamic history this harsh, barren stretch of land—mostly desert, partly rocky plateau sloping eastward from the mountains of the Hejaz—was a backwater that played no significant role in the politics of the Arabs. The negative image of Nejd matched its harsh climate even during the time of the Prophet, for he is recorded as saying: "I see earthquakes and dissension over there and from there shall arise the horns of Satan." He was asked three times to have God bless Nejd, and all three times he is said to have refused to intercede on their behalf. Like so many of the Prophet's sayings, it is difficult to say if this is an authentic *hadith** or merely the creativity of contemporary naysayers of the royal Ibn Saud† family.

Saudi Arabia, one of only two modern countries named after a person that spring to mind, today claims to be the citadel of Islam, its king carrying the title Guardian of Islam's Two Holy Shrines—the Grand Mosque (known as the Ka'aba) in Mecca and the Prophet's Mosque in Medina. However, Islam is merely the cover under which a single family of 5,000 princes and

---

* *Hadith:* The collection of traditions attributed to the Prophet that include his sayings, acts, and approval or disapproval of things. The hadith were recorded centuries after the death of the Prophet and form a major source of sharia law and moral guidance.
† Ibn Saud: Usual way of referring to the descendants of Muhammad Ibn Saud who in 1748 became the first emir or ruler of Nejd in central Arabia.

princelings rule over conquered territory that is occupied by force and kept under control by means of racism, terror, and torture. Today, because of its oil wealth and unstinted support of the United States, which guarantees Saudi rule over Arabia, the royal family has not only been able to promulgate the harshest and most barren interpretations of Islam, but has also managed to spread this cult ideology across the Muslim world and among the Muslim diaspora in the West. So powerful is its reach among the Muslim world that few Muslims question the legitimacy of the so-called Kingdom of Saudi Arabia. After all, the al-Saud family and their Wahhabi allies until 1924 were rulers only of the "Sultanate of Nejd"—not all of Arabia. Their rule over the holy cities of Mecca and Medina came about only after they had invaded the neighbouring Kingdom of Hejaz in 1924, massacring fellow Muslims as they chased out the Hashemite rulers who had been de facto rulers of Hejaz for centuries. Whether we consider international law or Islamic tradition, the invasion of Hejaz by the Sultanate of Nejd was illegal, immoral, un-Islamic, and unjustified.

Just as Muslims today feel outraged at the US invasion of Iraq, in the 1920s Muslims worldwide were horrified at the invasion of Hejaz by a neighbouring Muslim state. From its founding in 968 until its demise and occupation by the Sultanate of Nejd, the Emirate of Mecca—which controlled most of Hejaz, including the city of Medina—was governed by descendants of Prophet Muhammad through his grandson Hassan ibn Ali, known as the sharif or emir of Mecca. The emirate enjoyed a degree of autonomy under the Abbasids, then the Egyptians, and for a long time the Ottoman Turks. Never had Mecca and Medina been governed or ruled by the Nejdis in all its history, yet today Saudi rule over Islam's holiest places is unquestioned by Muslims. Under what doctrine of Islam would the Ibn Saud clan of Riyadh invade, occupy, and amalgamate the Kingdom of Hejaz in 1925 has never been questioned, let alone explained. If Saudi Arabia today invaded and occupied Bahrain or the United Arab Emirates, would Muslims accept this action as legitimate? When Iraq invaded Kuwait in 1990, Saddam Hussein had a better case for merging Kuwait into Iraq as a province than did Abdel-Aziz al-Saud to invade Hejaz and incorporate that kingdom into his own domain in 1925. And if Nejd had the right to invade Hejaz and merge it into its own territory as a mere province, why would the Saudis object to Saddam Hussein invading Kuwait and merging it into Iraq as a province?

During the First World War, the Ibn Saud of Nejd and the neighbouring sharifs of Hejaz were working with the British to undermine the Ottoman caliphate. The Turks even today consider the so-called British-funded Arab Revolt as a stab in their back by Arab Muslims. In the historic city of Bursa, for example, a wayside coffee-shop attendant expressed anger, in mid-1999 as if the "Arab Revolt" in Hejaz and Nejd had taken place not some eighty years earlier but just yesterday. "How could they do that to fellow Muslims in the name of Islam?" he asked me, as he praised Pakistan but railed against the Arab world.

In 1916, neither Ibn Saud of Nejd nor Sharif Hussein of Hejaz had Islam or Muslims on their minds as they took British gold and guns to kill Turkish troops—fellow members of the Ummah (world Muslims).

Nevertheless, both Nejd and Hejaz behaved as independent entities vying for nation status, based on their tribal allegiances, not Islamic principles. In fact, Ibn Saud of Nejd is even said to have sent the sharif of Hejaz a gift of camels and horses to aid the Hejazi war effort against the Turks. Later that year, Sharif Hussein sent another request to Ibn Saud asking for help in men and materials. His army was harassing the Ottoman Turks and blew up sections of the railway line from Amman to Medina. Ibn Saud's response was that assistance was possible "only if Hussein gave his word to refrain from interfering in Najd." This correspondence from the British Foreign Office archives between two rival Arab leaders of neighbouring states only proves that both recognized each other as valid entities, despite intense rivalry between their rulers. It also demonstrates that far from a commitment to Islam and the Muslim Ummah, the family of Ibn Saud were more interested in the mundane matters of power and territory. The subsequent invasion of Hejaz by Nejd and the permanent occupation is not as far off in the past as some Muslims would like us to believe. The 1925 Saudi invasion was a 20th-century occupation of Islam's two holiest places. It was as much an occupation as the one forty years later, when Israel would occupy Islam's third holy place—East Jerusalem.

But this was not the first time the Wahhabis had invaded and occupied Mecca and Medina. In 1802 they had come down from the barren deserts of Nejd, led by the hordes of fanatic jihadis, and destroyed Mecca and Medina, killing and pillaging in the name of Islam. Today, when Islamist extremists kill innocent civilians and invoke Allah to sanctify their terrorism, they are only following in the footsteps of their 18th-century teacher, Muhammad Ibn Abdul Wahhab (1703-92).

The Saudi royal family and the Wahhabi clerics who provide them intellectual sustenance consider themselves the torchbearers of an authentic Islam, which they feel needs to be established before Muslims can experience a revival. But Wahhabi ideology is a joyless, barren belief, so alien to the human spirit that it is even averse to the sound of music and considers clapping a call to Satan.

Wahhab was born into a religious family in 1703, his father being a *qadi** in the town of Uyaina. At the time the practice of Islam in Arabia was relatively lax and even the pilgrimage of hajj[†] was a time of music, procession, and songs. Sufism was widespread and it was not uncommon for Arabs in Nejd and Hejaz to pray at the tombs of Muslim saints. Married at the age of twelve, the young Wahhab was soon to memorize the Quran and become a preacher of some capacity. The Islam he saw practised around him greatly troubled him. He developed a particular appreciation of the works of Ibn Taymiyah, a scholar of the 13th century who took the opportunity of the vacuum created after the Mongol destruction of the Abbasids to propagate a harsh and extremist interpretation of Islam, suggesting God had punished the Muslims because of their lax attitude towards matters of faith.

Wahhab toured Iran, Egypt, and Kurdistan, and by 1730 was back in Nejd, this time in the town of Huraimala, where his father had settled. He started preaching his austere message to the townspeople, who it seems were a frolicking bunch who were unwilling to tolerate such constant preaching. Seeing the writing on the wall, Wahhab fled. He continued his preaching and in 1744 met a tribal chief, Muhammad Ibn Saud, in the town of Diriya, who took a liking to the radical preacher's message. The two agreed to lead a militant reform movement in the Arabian peninsula—what we know today as "Wahhabi" movement—in the 1740s and 1750s. At its genesis it was known as the *Muwahidun,* referring to those who believed in strict monotheism according to the Islamic doctrine of *Tawhid.*[‡] In addition, Wahhab and Muhammad Ibn Saud's followers called themselves followers of *al-salaf,*[§]" a reference to the early companions of the Prophet Muhammad. While Ibn Saud took on the title of emir of Nejd, to look after matters of state, Wahhab became the community's imam, their religious leader. Soon he would take on the even grander title of *Sheikh ul-Islam.* The Ibn Saud-Wahhab partnership was further consolidated when the imam's daughter was given in marriage to the emir's son.

As the Sheikh ul-Islam Wahhab labelled all Muslims who disagreed with his view of Islam as apostates, which in his eyes justified the declaration of jihad on the neighbouring Arab tribes and towns inside Nejd. This also suited

---

* *Qadi*: A judge of sorts.
† *Hajj*: Pilgrimage to Mecca that is one of the five pillars of the Islamic faith and is obligatory on all Muslims, if they can afford it.
‡ *Tawhid*: The foundation of Islamic belief, asserting the oneness of God. The opposite of *Tawhid* is *Shirk*, which refers to idolatry.
§ *Al-salaf*: Literally, "the predecessors."

the interests of Muhammad Ibn Saud. What were once acts of brigandry would now have the force of Islam behind them. The fiery preacher and the ambitious Arab tribal chief would form a toxic cocktail and within years would spread Wahhabism across Arabia. As town after town fell to the marauding bands of Ibn Saud, the Ottomans in Istanbul and the British East India Company in Calcutta took note of this uprising in the burning sands of Nejd. Wherever the Ibn Saud went, Muslims were asked to submit, or die. The hatred the Wahhabis had for their fellow Sunni Arabs, who followed the more relaxed Hannafi Islam, would pale in comparison to their venom against the Shia Muslims and their shrines.

In 1802, Saud Ibn Saud, grandson of the founder of the dynasty, attacked the Shia holy city of Karbala. The Wahhabis captured the city, destroyed the tomb of Hussain ibn Ali—the grandson of the Prophet, whom the Shia consider their third imam—and carried out a massacre that shocked the conscience of the Muslim world. The slaughter was vividly captured in notes written by witnesses:

> We have recently seen a horrible example of the Wahhabis' cruel fanaticism . . . Now the enormous wealth that has accumulated in the [mosques of Imam Hussain] . . . has been exciting the Wahhabis' avidity for a long time. They have been dreaming permanently of the looting of the town and were so sure of success that their creditors fixed the debt payment to the happy day when their hopes would come true. That day came at last. . . . 12,000 Wahhabis suddenly attacked [the mosque of] Imam Hussain; after seizing more spoils than they had ever seized after their greatest victories they put everything to fire and sword. . . . Old people, women and children—everybody died at the barbarians' sword. Besides, it is said that whenever they saw a pregnant woman, they disembowelled her and left the foetus on the mother's bleeding corpse. Their cruelty could not be satisfied, they did not cease their murders and blood flowed like water. As a result of the bloody catastrophe, more than 4,000 people perished. The Wahhabis carried off their plunder on the backs of 4,000 camels. After the plunder and murders, they destroyed the imam's mausoleum, and converted it into a cloaca of abomination and blood. They inflicted the greatest damage on the minarets and domes, believing that those structures were made of gold bricks.

Before the caliph in Istanbul could react to this act of sacrilege, the Wahhabis turned their attention to Mecca and Medina. In 1804, a Wahhabi army, again led by Saud ibn Saud (who by now had become the emir of Nejd) invaded Hejaz where they spread a reign of terror, killing fellow Muslims, destroying ancient monuments and domed mosques. In Medina, the Wahhabis razed the tomb of the Prophet's daughter Fatima. After occupying the two holiest cities of Islam, the Wahhabis restricted access to them, turning back the pilgrims coming for hajj, declaring the caravans from Syria and Egypt to be idolaters.

The Ottoman caliph first thought that the marauding tribesmen would soon leave with their plunder, but when it became clear that the occupation of Mecca and Medina was permanent, he became alarmed and in 1811 dispatched Muhammad Ali Pasha, the Ottoman ruler of Egypt, to challenge the Wahhabis, who succeeded in re-imposing Ottoman sovereignty in 1815. Abdullah Ibn Saud, the new *emir* of the Ibn Saud clan, was captured and taken to Constantinople in chains. Refusing an invitation by the traditional sheikhs and imams of Sunni Islam in Turkey to debate the merits of their competing interpretations of Islam, Abdullah Ibn Saud was beheaded and his body put on display. In Najaf, Wahhab's grandson was tortured by being forced to listen to music. He, too, was beheaded, and thus ended the first jihadi Islamic State in modern history. Wahhabism and the Salafi movement was dead, but only for now. In less than a century, they would re-emerge.

The teachings of Wahhab were not restricted to Arabia. At the time that Wahhab had joined hands with Ibn Saud, another Muslim scholar in India was witnessing the collapse of the Indian Moghul Empire. Shah Waliullah was born in 1703. At the age of twenty-three, he left India for Arabia to perform the pilgrimage of hajj, and during his two years in Hejaz and Nejd, came into contact with Wahhab and joined forces with him. Waliullah stayed fourteen months in Arabia, and on his return to Delhi in 1732, laid the foundation of what was to become Political Islam in the subcontinent. Wahhab's message had now travelled to India.

Shah Waliullah was more concerned with the political disorder and fading glory of Muslim power, but instead of blaming it on the excesses and extremism of the late emperor Aurangzeb, he blamed it on the lack of Muslim resolve to deal harshly with the Hindu majority of the country. His objective was to re-establish the Islamic cultural hegemony in the Indian subcontinent. Waliullah "grew up watching the Mogul Empire crumble," in the words of Wilfred Cantwell Smith, who continued: "Unlike Ibn abd al-Wahhab, he thought and worked from within one of the passing medieval empires, rather than outside. . . . His political ambition was to restore Muslim power in India more or less on the Mogul pattern. Pure Islam must be re-enacted; a regenerated Muslim society must again be mighty."

Echoing Ibn Abdul Wahhab, Shah Waliullah called for a return of true Islam and, to bolster his credibility, he now claimed to be of Arab origin. Waliullah also supported Wahhab's rigidity on strict compliance with sharia. Rejecting any notion of Indian nationhood or any national boundary for Muslims, Waliullah is best known for his invitation to the Afghan ruler Ahmad Shah Abdali to invade India. In his letter to the Afghan king, he said: "All control of power is with the Hindus because they are the only people who are industrious and adaptable. Riches and prosperity are theirs, while Muslims have nothing but poverty and misery. At this juncture you are the only person who has the initiative, the foresight, the power and capability to defeat the enemy and free the Muslims from the clutches of the infidels. God forbid if their domination continues, Muslims will even forget Islam and become undistinguishable from the non-Muslims."

Heeding the call, Abdali invaded India four times, and even though he defeated the mostly Hindu Maratha armies in the Third Battle of Panipat, he also sacked and burned the city of Lahore, invaded Kashmir, and devastated the Moghul capital of Delhi in 1756, blinding the emperor and killing tens of thousands of Indian Muslims. Abdali's barbarity is remembered to this day. (The Pakistan military has thoughtlessly named one of its nuclear missile systems Abdali, not recognizing that Abdali's primary victims were the Muslims of what is now Pakistan! Shah Waliullah and his Wahhabi teachings led to the destruction of the very Muslim rule he had sought to save.)

After the sacking of Delhi by the Afghans, the Moghul Empire never recovered. It is said that so humiliating was the rape and plunder by the army of Abdali's Taliban-type fanatic warriors, that Muslims of Delhi would not speak about the calamity brought on them by one of their own—Shah Waliullah, the disciple of Muhammad Ibn Abdul Wahhab of Nejd.

One wonders if modern-day Muslims are aware of these atrocities committed on fellow Muslims by the House of Saud, Wahhab, and their disciples? If they are, how then do they justify their oft-repeated claim that in following Islam, they follow a religion of peace? Do they expect the non-Muslim to believe this propaganda when the Saudi flag displays a naked sword under the Muslim oath THERE IS NO GOD BUT GOD, AND MUHAMMAD IS HIS MESSENGER?

In 1901, nearly a century after the first Wahhabis had introduced their austere and barren Islam, Abdel-Aziz al-Saud (1879-1953) led the Ibn Saud back into business by recapturing Riyadh from the then ruling family of the al-Rashid clan. Al-Saud's fanatic Wahhabi soldiers and his dozens of sons soon spread across the Arabian peninsula, taking advantage of the weakened Ottoman caliphate, and were egged on by the British. By 1924, Sultan Abdel-Aziz al-Saud of Nejd had gone on a rampage throughout the peninsula. In invading the emirate of Mecca (which by now was known as the kingdom of Hejaz), they once more carried out a massacre in the town of Taif to send a message to Meccans: Surrender or die. On capturing Mecca and Medina, they started smashing the tombs of Muslim saints and imams. In Medina, as their predecessors had done a century earlier, they destroyed the rebuilt tomb of the Prophet's daughter Fatima in the cemetery of Baqi, also known to Muslims as *Janat-al-Baqi*, the Tree Garden of Heaven. The cemetery had remained a sacred place for centuries until that day in 1925 when Abdel-Aziz al-Saud and his Wahhabi militias destroyed every grave and tomb, bulldozing all evidence of the existence of the Prophet's family. The cemetery had a small house, where it is said Fatima would come to grieve the Prophet's death and retreat from the ill treatment she received at the hands of some of his companions. That home too was razed by the Saudis.

The Wahhabis believed, and still do, that visiting the graves and the shrines of the Prophet and his family is a form of idolatry punishable by death. Not sated by the destruction of the cemetery, the Wahhabis attacked every mosque they came across. An attempt was even made to demolish the Prophet's mosque and his tomb, but the idea was later abandoned.

In 1818 CE, Ottoman Caliph Abdul Majid carried out the reconstruction of all sacred places destroyed by the first Wahabbi invasion, restoring the city to its splendour. Once more the Wahabbis would destroy the rebuilt tombs and gravestones. The cemetery where the Prophet once walked among the graves of his family and friends would never regain its lost glory. Wahhabi zealots took pride in defacing the graves and obliterating all memory and history. Contempt for joy has been the hallmark of all Islamists.

In 1925 these joy-hating zealots became gravediggers and destroyers of history. Today, the same zealots have cast destructive eyes at the Prophet's home in Mecca.

By 1932, Abdel-Aziz al-Saud merged the sultanate of Nejd and the kingdom of Hejaz to become the new kingdom of Saudi Arabia, and crowned himself as monarch. The land where Prophet Muhammad had once walked as a voice of the dispossessed was now ruled by a king.

Muslims today cannot deny the fact that a brutal and oppressive regime rules Saudi Arabia, one that occupies the cities of Mecca and Medina, yet across the world, Saudi-funded organizations ensure that any criticism of the Saudi regime and state is seen as an attack on Islam.

The Saudis can do anything they wish and yet face no scrutiny. Take, for example, the case of the Prophet's 1,400-year-old home in Mecca. The Saudis plan to demolish it. What makes this planned demolition worse is the fact that the home of the Prophet is to make way for a parking lot, two fifty-storey hotel towers and seven thirty-five-storey apartment blocks—a project known as the Jabal Omar Scheme—all within a stone's throw of the Grand Mosque. Had the site been destroyed by non-Muslims or some occupying Western army, the entire Muslim world would have seethed with outrage. But the news of the demolition was met with a deafening silence. By November 2007, not a single Muslim country, no ayatollah, no mufti, no king, not even an American or Canadian imam had dared utter a word in protest. Such is the power of Saudi influence on the Muslim narrative.

Compare this to events in December 1992, when a mob of 150,000 Hindu nationalists attacked a 16th-century mosque in the Indian city of Ayodhya. Within hours the mosque was reduced to rubble, and in the weeks to follow, thousands of Indians died in Hindu–Muslim riots. The Muslim world reacted with outrage. Among the countries that expressed anger at the destruction of the centuries-old Indian mosque by Hindu extremists was Saudi Arabia. In the United States and Canada, imams gave fiery sermons and urged congregations to protest. Although more than a dozen years have passed since the destruction of the mosque, there is still bitterness in the air. Muslims worldwide feel a sense of betrayal and impotence at not being able to control their own destiny and protect their historical religious sites.

The question is this: Why is it that when the Babri mosque in Ayodhya was demolished, hundreds of thousands of Muslims worldwide took to the streets to protest, but when Saudi authorities plan to demolish the home of our beloved Prophet, not a whisper is heard?

Is it because Muslims have become so overwhelmed by the power of the Saudi *riyal* currency that we have lost all courage and self-respect? Or is it because we feel a need to cover up Muslim-on-Muslim violence, Muslim-on-Muslim terror, Muslim-on-Muslim oppression?

In this climate of cowardice, a few giants still stand tall. Sami Angawi is one of them. An eminent Saudi architect, he is a brave man in a country where courage is scarce, leading a one-man campaign to save the home of Muhammad. He told London's *Independent* newspaper: "The house where the Prophet received the word of God is gone and nobody cares . . . this is the end of history in Mecca and Medina and the end of their future."

The cultural massacre of Islamic heritage sites is not a new phenomenon. It is said that in the past two decades, 95 percent of Mecca's thousand-year-old buildings have been demolished. Today, the religious zealots in Saudi Arabia are not alone. Commercial developers have joined hands with them and are making hundreds of millions in profits as they build ugly but lucrative high-rises that are shadowing the Ka'aba (Grand Mosque). Isolated voices in Canada did speak out. The Muslim Canadian Congress (MCC) strongly condemned this outrage and called it a cultural massacre of Muslim heritage for the sake of profit. In a letter to the Saudi ambassador in Ottawa, the MCC demanded an immediate halt to these demolitions and the placing of a moratorium on all future destruction of Muslim heritage sites. The letter said, "The sacred places of Islam, regardless of where they are located, belong to the Muslim community worldwide. The countries where they're located are simply trustees and have no right to destroy them."

Responding to the articles in Toronto's *Globe and Mail* and *The Independent* in 2005, Saudi Prince Turki al-Faisal dismissed the news as "rubbish," saying Saudi Arabia was spending more than $19 billion in preserving and maintaining these two holy sites: "[We are aware] how important the preservation of this heritage is, not just to us but to the millions of Muslims from around the world who visit the two holy mosques every year. It is hardly something we are going to allow to be destroyed."

But as *The Independent* followed up in April 2006, "This rebuttal sits at odds with a series of previously unseen photographs, published today, that document the demolition of key archaeological sites and their replacement with skyscrapers." Daniel Howden of *The Independent* quoted Irfan Ahmed al-Alawi, the chairman of the Islamic Heritage Foundation, which was established to help protect the holy sites, pointing to another outrage. Al'awi told *The Independent* about the case of the grave of Amina bint Wahb, the mother of the Prophet. "It was bulldozed in Abwa and gasoline was poured on it. Even though thousands of petitions throughout the Muslim world were sent, nothing could stop this action."

Howden noted that there were now fewer than twenty structures remaining in Mecca that dated back to the time of the Prophet. He listed lost history as including the house of Khadijah (wife of the Prophet), demolished to make way for public toilets; the house of Abu-Bakr (companion of the Prophet), where there is now a Hilton hotel; the house of Ali-Oraid (a grandson of the Prophet) and the Mosque of abu-Qubais, which is where the king now has a palace in Mecca.

Couldn't newspapers such as the *Al-Ahram* of Cairo or the *Dawn of Karachi* or the *Millet* of Istanbul have reported this act of cultural genocide?

They could have, but they chose not to. It took the London *Independent* to highlight this outrage, but it wasn't sufficient to either anger the worldwide Muslim Ummah or embolden ordinary Muslims in the West to challenge the Saudi-funded mosque establishment.

Mai Yamani, the exiled Saudi author of *The Cradle of Islam*, said it best: "When the Prophet was insulted by Danish cartoonists, thousands of people went into the streets to protest. The sites related to the Prophet are part of their heritage and religion, but we see no concern from Muslims."

How can a country bulldoze the grave of the Prophet's daughter, destroy Muhammad's house, build a public toilet inside the house of the Prophet's wife, and burn the grave of the Apostle's mother, and all in the name of Islam? Imagine the reaction across the Muslim world if the destruction of the Prophet's home had been blamed on a Jewish conspiracy with US help. Why have Muslims accepted such glaring double standards as the norm?

This takes me back to an incident that took place in Saudi Arabia on November 20, 1979. It was a day of immense anticipation, as Muslims around the globe were welcoming the dawn of Islam's new century, the year 1400. But it turned into a day of despair.

It was my thirtieth birthday and as my wife, Nargis, and I started to leave our tiny apartment in Jeddah's impoverished Bani Malik district to go to work, we noticed an unusual silence in the otherwise bustling *souk.** People were talking in whispers; there was a hush on the street, with little traffic. For some time we could not find out what had happened. Newspapers were never delivered, there was no news service on the radio to speak of, and the one TV channel was playing an uninterrupted recitation of the Quran. My gut reaction was that a coup had taken place, but if that was true, why were there no troops on the streets? Just a day earlier, Saudi TV had shown clips about the hostage crisis unfolding in Iran and there were rumours that the Shia on Saudi Arabia's east coast were restive. But nothing had prepared us for what had unfolded in Mecca that morning as Islam's 15th century had dawned.

That day an armed uprising by hundreds of armed jihadi fighters had taken place inside the Ka'aba in the city of Mecca. The jihadis wanted to overthrow the Saudi regime and establish an Islamic caliphate across the world. In fact, they claimed that the much-awaited Mehdi had emerged from hiding and was ready to rule the world and establish true Islam.

The BBC and VOA, our two sources of news, carried on as if nothing had happened. I took time off from work and huddled around my shortwave satellite radio while another colleague used a radio scanner to pick up police

---

* *Souk:* A traditional market in the Arab world.

traffic. By nightfall we realized we were in the eye of a major storm, one that could change the course of history. Fighting had broken out inside the Grand Mosque where about 300 gunmen—Saudis, Pakistanis, Egyptians and, yes, American converts to Islam—were holding 100,000 pilgrims hostage as a gun battle raged through the mosque's 1,000 rooms and in its labyrinths. During the two wars I had lived through in Pakistan, I had not felt fear. But that evening as we sat with a few friends, invited to celebrate my birthday, all of us felt like we were dead men (there were no women) walking.

Rumours were abundant that the imam of the mosque had been beheaded and that the Ka'aba itself had been destroyed, but what followed was reflective of the susceptibility of the Muslim to conspiracy theories. We were told by Saudi friends that it had been a joint Israel–US strike that had destroyed the Ka'aba. Horrified at the thought of repercussions, we did not have to wait long. The next day Ayatollah Khomeini's office had accused the United States and Israel of orchestrating the attack, while newspapers in Pakistan reported that the attack on Mecca was very likely conducted by US paratroopers dropped inside the holy mosque. The result was instantaneous. The US Embassy in Islamabad was attacked and a US corporal was hit by gunfire. The embassy was fire-bombed. Elsewhere, a Christian convent in Rawalpindi was burned down along with the offices of Pan Am and American Express.

For two weeks fighting continued in Mecca, inside the Holy Ka'aba, and the ragtag forerunners of Al-Qaeda could only be defeated when the Saudis asked the French to send their elite commando units who gassed the guerrillas into submission. The Saudis—the jihadi guerrillas as well as the state—violated the most sacred place of Islam, yet the anger was directed not at the Saudis, but at Israel and the United States. If that was all, it wouldn't have been so bad. The fact is, there appears to be not a single reference to this monumental and historic uprising of Mecca in any textbook of history or political science anywhere in the Muslim world.

The Saudis have managed to expunge this catastrophe from all the records. Today, few Muslims are aware of what happened during the two weeks of November and December 1979 as they welcomed Islam's 15th century in a blaze of gunfire and the death of about one thousand innocents inside the Ka'aba.

Is it then a surprise that the Saudis can destroy Prophet Muhammad's house and no Muslim is upset? Unless Muslims demand an end to the monarchy of the Saudis and an accounting of the crimes committed against Islam and Muslims by the children of Ibn Saud and his Wahhabi sheikhs, non-Muslims will not take our cries for justice seriously.

CHAPTER 4

Iran—The Islamic State

"DAROONASH MARDUMANASH ra kushtay, Borunash deegaran ra." This Persian saying best expresses the condition where the outward appearance belies the internal circumstance. Roughly translated the Persian idiom says, "While the view from the outside is alluring, the condition of the inside is cancerous."

Ever since the learned mullahs took power in the wake of the uprising against Muhammad Reza Pahlavi, shah of Iran, in 1979, the outside Muslim world has admired the Islamic Republic's autocratic ruling class as the answer to their sorry state. While millions of fellow Muslims inside Iran suffer tyranny, tens of thousands have died, and millions fled, the view projected to the rest of the world is that Iran is the world's only Islamic State opposing American hegemony and neo-liberalism. It isn't just the beguiled Muslim intelligentsia that is fooled by this performance; the pan-Islamist regime has managed to charm the left in the West. Notwithstanding the regime's contempt for women's equality and its vocal homophobia, many on the left in the West—including Venezuelan President Hugo Chavez—have embraced Iranian President Mahmoud Ahmadinejad, with Tariq Ali going so far as to equate him to Simon Bolivar.[*]

If even leading French intellectuals such as Michel Foucault[†] and Roger Garaudy[‡] could be mesmerized by the mullahs, who could blame ordinary leftists of today for tripping over each other to embrace the permanent

---

[*] Simon Bolivar: Early 19th-century Venezuelan leader who helped South America break free of Spanish rule.

subjugation of the citizenry of Iran under the clerics? These children of the French Revolution were willing to see its upside-down image planted in a far-off Iran.

Foucault had first written about Islamism as a political movement in October 1978, as nationwide strikes were taking place in Iran. In a piece for *Nouvel Observateur*, he downplayed the threat of Ayatollah Khomeini's advocacy of "an Islamic government," noting that "there is an absence of hierarchy in the clergy" and "a dependence (even a financial one) on those who listen to them." He wrote that the clerics had no intention of taking over the state and government: "One thing must be clear. By 'Islamic government' nobody in Iran means a political regime in which the clergy would have a role of supervision or control. . . . It is something very old and also very far into the future, a notion of coming back to what Islam was at the time of the Prophet."

Foucault also defended the Islamists of Iran against accusations that they had a hidden anti-female agenda: "Between men and women there will not be inequality with respect to rights, but difference, since there is a natural difference." Would Foucault or the other European and North American Left, or today's supporters of Chavez and Fidel Castro, advocate this equal-but-separate gender equality in their own families, let alone countries?

Foucault's naivety was underscored on March 8, 1979, when, during an International Women's Day march, Iranian women protested an order that women were to cover their heads with the *chador*. The women were attacked by vigilante Islamist gangs who chanted, "You will cover yourselves or be beaten."

While some of the Left can be accused of faulty judgement, other Islamist forces around the world became mouthpieces for Khomeini and the so-called

---

† Michel Foucault (1926–84) was a left-wing French philosopher and historian best known for his analysis of systems of knowledge through what he referred to as the "archaeology" of knowledge. In the aftermath of French student revolts of 1968, Foucault joined young leftist academics and students in occupying university buildings and fighting with police. In 1979, he made two tours of Iran in support of the new Islamic government established after the revolution.

‡ Roger Garaudy (b. 1913) is a French Marxist philosopher who joined the Communist Party in 1933, but after 1956 he distanced himself from orthodox communism, leading to his expulsion from the party in 1970. Garaudy later relapsed into religiosity, first embracing Catholicism and later Islam in 1982, following the Islamic revolution in Iran.

Islamic revolution. It wasn't typical Shia mosques that were propagating Khomeini as the messiah for all of Islamdom, but rather the orthodox Sunni followers of the Jamaat-e-Islami and the Muslim Brotherhood and their North American networks.

In Toronto *The Crescent International,* a pro-Khomeini paper, declared: "Outside Iran, the experience of the Ikhwan al Muslimoon [Muslim Brotherhood] in Egypt, the Jamaat-e-Islami in Pakistan and the Melli Salamat Party (MSP) in Turkey have clearly demonstrated that participation in secular democracies or military juntas are two pitfalls for the Islamic movement."

Far from being a Shia revival movement, the mullahs of Iran see themselves as the leaders of the worldwide Islamist movement and seek the supremacy of Islam over the world as their ultimate objective. This is reflected in the curriculum of the Iranian school system where Grade 11 students are taught:

> The establishment of Muslim rule is one of the most fundamental and most elementary Islamic goals. Without that entity Islam would be exposed to the danger of elimination and the full implementation of Islam would not be possible. . . . Therefore, the theory of "Islam without rule" is an evident *innovation** which has been propagated by the enemies of Islam in order to push the Muslims away from political power and from the sovereignty over their own destiny and [in order] to expand their own [i.e., the enemies' own] rule and supremacy over Muslim societies. The bitter realities that exist in the Muslim societies are a living testimony to this matter.

Ayatollah Khomeini made no secret about his vision of Islam as the supreme dominating religion on earth. This message to the Muslims of the world by Khomeini, inculcating victimhood and urging martyrdom as a response, is also taught to Grade 11 students in Iran:

> O Muslims of all countries of the world! Since under the foreigners' dominance gradual death has been inflicted on you, you should overcome the fear of death and make use of the existence of the passionate and the martyrdom-seeking youths. . . . I am decisively announcing to the whole world that, if the World Devourers wish to stand against our religion, we will stand against their whole world and will not cease until

---

* *Innovation:* This word has a negative connotation in Islamic lexicon. It is a translation of the Arabic word *bida'a,* which means a deviation from true Islam.

the annihilation of all of them. . . . Even if we are cut to pieces a thousand times, we shall not stop fighting the oppressors.

The 1979 revolution that transformed Iran from an oppressive monarchy under the shah to an Islamic republic under Ayatollah Ruhollah Khomeini is said to have begun in January 1978 with the first major demonstrations, and ended in December 1979 when the new theocratic constitution was imposed. Khomeini became the country's supreme leader, answerable not to the electorate, but to a six-member Council of Guardians, three of whom would be appointed by the supreme leader.

The uprising against the shah of Iran was not a revolt by the clerics alone. In fact, the leading elements in the protests were the trade unions and student bodies. However, the overconfidence of secularists and modernist Muslims, of liberals and leftists in their power and ability to control the revolution was over-matched by the shrewdness of Khomeini, who first won the support of these liberals and leftists when he needed them to overthrow the shah, and then, when the time came, played one against the other until he had eliminated them all in a piecemeal fashion. In fact, one section of Iran's communists, the Tudeh Party, stuck with Khomeini as the clergy and their militias carried out nationwide assassinations of the rank and file of groups such as the *Fidayeen* and the *Mujahideen Khalq*. The left had been warned of just such an event by the visionary leftist thinker Bijan Jazani. Jazani sent out warning signals in his famous book *Tarikh e si salleh* (History of Thirty Years) in the 1960s that if the left did not close its ranks and start organizing the masses, a potential existed for a clerical theocracy headed by the likes of Ayatollah Khomeini who would hijack the movement against the shah's dictatorship.

As much of the Iranian left in 1979 walked around as if they had just stormed the Winter Palace of the Czars and fashioned themselves as the Bolsheviks, alienating their support base by mocking Islam, Ayatollah Khomeini was able to cast himself in the footsteps of the beloved Shia imam Hussain ibn Ali, while portraying the shah as a modern-day version of Hussain's foe, the despised Caliph Yazid. While the Iranian left was suppressed mercilessly by the shah's intelligence arm, SAVAK, the clergy was left alone as they strengthened their links with the ordinary masses, the poor and often conservative peasants, who later became the mullah's shock troops.

The strength of the Iranian urban left was still considerable, and on May Day, 1979, a million men and women packed downtown Tehran in a massive show of strength. But they could not translate this strength into an effective alternative coalition that could respond to the rising threat of the Islamists.

While the Left fought among itself, Khomeini was developing the ideology of the Islamic Republic, the foundation of which was the doctrine of *Velayat-e faqih.** This states that until the appearance of the Shia' "hidden imam"—the Mehdi—society should be governed in the interim by a supreme leader, a leading Islamic jurist best qualified to interpret God's will and the meaning of Islamic law. Under this doctrine, Muslims require guardianship, in the form of rule or supervision. It is this doctrine that accorded Khomeini the title and office of Supreme Leader; all others were subordinate to him.

The Velayat-e faqih established that obeying an Islamic government was actually an expression of obedience to God, ultimately more necessary even than prayer and fasting for Muslims, because without it true Islam would not survive. It was a universal principle, not one confined to Iran. All the world needed and deserved just government (i.e., true Islamic government), and Khomeini regarded the export of the Islamic revolution as imperative.

But this is not what Khomeini was telling the other coalition members of the revolution. To them, he was suggesting that he would play a merely advisory role as a father figure. No less a party than the Iranian communists of the Tudeh Party fell for the ruse, and for quite some time, they betrayed their own leftist partners to assuage the ageing Ayatollah.

To understand the oppressive nature of the Iranian regime, and how it relies on the use of Islam to maintain its grip on power, one needs to study the history of Iran, its constitutional development, and the role that Britain and the United States played in derailing the nation's democratic institutions. In addition, the institution of the Velayat-e faqih needs to be looked at, since this body virtually guarantees that no matter what the people of Iran want, they will not be able to dislodge the Islamic theocracy by democratic means.

The secular liberals and the Left should have been familiar enough with the history of Iran to recognize that until their powers were clipped in the 1920s, the ayatollahs had been an integral part of the ruling classes for centuries and they desperately wanted their privileges restored. It had been King Reza Shah who had removed the mullahs from almost all institutions of power. With the notable exception of Bijan Jazani, who was clear-headed and knew the dangers of the Islamist mullahs, the Left largely ignored the

---

* *Velayat-e faqih*: The Supreme Leader doctrine.

dangers posed by the mosque establishment. After Reza Shah's changes in the 1920s, the clergy were told to restrict their activities to running their mosques and seminaries. Their large land holdings were confiscated. Next door in Turkey, Mustafa Kemal Ataturk was taking his own initiative to end the influence of the imams in matters of the state. So in 1979, as the mullahs entered the corridors of power, it was foolish to not expect them to go for complete control.

The wily and deceiving nature of the *taqqiyah*-focused[*] clergy of Iran was on full display during the great struggle between the elected prime minister, Muhammad Mossadeqh, in 1952–53 and the shah. The role of Khomeini's mentor, Ayatollah Kashani, during this period illustrates the conniving tactics the men in cloaks and black turbans have employed. At the height of the struggle, Kashani, a leading mullah of that time, openly sided with the monarchists, inciting his followers to oppose Prime Minister Mossadeqh, whom he falsely labelled as a communist and atheist lover, echoing the language of the British Oil companies, Britain's MI5, and the US Central Intelligence Agency (CIA). For the ayatollahs, it was not democracy that mattered, it was betting on who would be best for their own power. Not that US imperialism or the Anglo oil companies of the time had any better principles to offer either. Their machinations are well documented in Kermit Roosevelt's book *Counter Coup: The Struggle for the Control of Iran*, and of course, the classic by Stephen Kinzer, *All the Shah's Men*.

Ayatollah Kashani was vocal in opposing the nationalizing of the British companies that controlled Iran's oil productions and declared such moves as un-Islamic. (The contempt the ayatollahs had for Prime Minister Mossadeqh was best reflected in remarks made by Khomeini on his return to Iran in 1979, when he referred to the late Mossadeqh as "that man who was slapped by Islam.")

As a result of the ayatollahs' collaboration with the shah and the CIA-backed coup that overthrew elected Prime Minister Mossadeqh in 1953, relations between the king and clerics were respectful, each refraining from interfering in the other's domain.

Then, in the 1960s, came the "White Revolution" of Muhammad Reza Pahlavi, which included land reforms and laws recognizing women's rights. The mullahs were outraged at suffrage rights proposed for women. In addition,

---

[*] *Taqqiyah*: To conceal or disguise one's beliefs, ideas, feelings, and opinions, when faced with imminent danger. The closest word in English is "dissimulation," a form of deception in which one conceals the truth. Some Muslims assert that taqqiyah is an act of hypocrisy where the act of lying is given religious sanction.

the land reforms hurt the interests of some of the clergy. Khomeini was the first to come out openly in opposition to the new rights being offered by the so-called White Revolution. He claimed that taking land from absentee landlords and giving it to the peasants went against Islam. He labelled the new pieces of lands given to peasants as *ghashi** and urged the peasants to not till them.

The peasants knew better than to listen to the ayatollahs. Thus far, Khomeini had silently tolerated the oppression of the shah and his dictatorial policies, but now that the economic interests of the landed aristocracy—many of them mullahs—were at stake, he rebelled. In addition, the thought of advancement of women in Iran proved to be the straw that broke the camel's back. Khomeini launched a campaign against the shah's regime in 1962 by assailing its new electoral legislation, which gave women the right to vote, as conflicting with Islamic values, and issued a fatwa against the White Revolution. Khomeini was arrested in 1964 and sent into exile.

After his return to Iran in 1979, Khomeini got down to the task of creating a new constitution for the country. Although the constitution committee had revolutionaries of all shades, Khomeini was their leader. He was soon elbowing out the non-clergy, and even though the communists as well as liberals protested, they were in a minority and powerless to change the situation. Many of them, whether secular or religious, did not approve—some didn't even know—of Khomeini's plan to introduce the institution of the Velayat-e faqih, or rule by *marja*.†

The original draft of provisional constitution for the Islamic Republic did not have the provision for the post of Velayat-e faqih or Supreme Leader. So when it was discovered in subsequent drafts, there was vocal protest, both behind doors as well as in the street. In response, Khomeini and his supporters purged their former allies and went ahead with the revised draft of the proposed constitution. Newspapers that protested the closed-door proceedings were attacked, while opposition groups such as the National Democratic Front and Muslim People's Republican Party were banned.

The agenda of the ayatollahs was unfolding according to script. The proposed constitution was amended again to include a Council of Guardians that would have the power to veto legislation passed by parliament (which it often has) as well as deny the right of people deemed "un-Islamic" to run for public office.

---

* *Ghashi*: Usurped land.
† *Marja*: Islamic clerics.

In November 1979, the new constitution of the Islamic Republic was passed by a referendum. Khomeini instituted himself as the Velayat-e faqih— Supreme Leader. All of a sudden a revolution that was supposed to bring in a new age to Iran was turning full circle and heading back to medieval times.

The institution of the Velayat-e faqih and the so-called Council of Guardians became the tools through which the clergy would maintain an iron grip on power. Iran may have a parliament, a president, regular elections, and even the odd riot, but all of that is show and tell—a carefully staged drama where the legislators are mere actors going through their routines. To entertain the masses as well as the outside world, the mullahs occasionally throw in a "liberal" ayatollah, as in Ayatollah Khatami, knowing very well the impact disarming smiles and flowing robes can have the liberal-left-wing in the West. After all, the people who could stage the Iran–Contra Affair and hold back the release of hostages to facilitate the defeat of Jimmy Carter, can put on any show the Western observer or the ordinary innocent non-Iranian pan-Islamist wishes to see.

For the Muslim diaspora in the West that looks upon Iranian ayatollahs as the reincarnation of 12th-century liberator of Jerusalem Saladin, the question is this: How many more fellow Muslims in Iran need to die at the hands of these ayatollahs before you wake up from this fantasy love affair with men in flowing robes, well-groomed beards and trimmed bangs peeping from under their turbans?

In the 1988 massacre of Iranian prisoners, following an uprising by guerrillas of the *Mujahideen-e-khalq*,[*] Khomeini issued an edict to judicial officials asking them to screen every Iranian political prisoner and kill those who would not repent anti-regime activities. Issued shortly after the end of the Iran–Iraq war in July 1988, the fatwa said: "All those who have in the prisons nation-wide, persisted, and continue to persist, in their position of heresy, are considered belligerent and therefore sentenced to execution."

Grand Ayatollah Hossein-Ali Montazeri, who is still held under house arrest by the regime, writes in his memoirs that more than thirty thousand political activists were killed as a result of Khomeini's fatwa. He says that

---

[*] *Mujahideen-e-khalq*: Part of the Mujahideen uprising came about after an incursion into Iran from neighbouring Iraq, where many of the Iranian exiles were based.

children as young as thirteen were hanged during a two-month period of barbaric frenzy.

In June 2001, Christina Lamb, the diplomatic correspondent of London's *Telegraph*, relying on secret documents smuggled out of Iran, reported that because of the large numbers of political prisoners, forklift trucks were used to make it easier for prisoners to be hanged from cranes in groups of six, in half-hourly intervals. Lamb quotes from Montazeri's memoirs, that when 3,800 people had been killed by the end of the first fortnight of executions, he wrote to Khomeini, saying that the killings should stop as they would be seen as a vendetta and spark opposition to the regime. Montazeri wrote to Khomeini, "The execution of several thousand prisoners in a few days will not have positive repercussions and will not be mistake-free."

How can any Muslim defend such oppression and mass murder in the name of Islamic solidarity? Those who fantasize about the revolutionary characteristics of the Iranian revolution and its supposed anti-imperialist posture should imagine walking in the shoes of the 30,000 who were ordered killed by the mullahs in the summer of 1988.

While non-Muslim leaders such as Hugo Chavez and Fidel Castro have embraced the mullahs, almost no one in the Muslim world's latent Left supports them. They can see through the fog of deception that bedevils their comrades in the West. Samir Amin, one of the leading Marxist intellectuals of the Arab and developing world, who now lives in Senegal, made a scathing attack on what he called the "turbaned dictatorship of Iran."

As part of his critique of Political Islam, Amin said: "The system of Political Islam in Iran has reached deadlock ... False comparisons are frequently made between the Islamist parties and the Christian Democratic parties of Europe (i.e., if the Christian Democrats have governed Italy for fifty years, why shouldn't an Islamist party govern Algeria or Egypt?). But once in power, an Islamist government immediately and definitively abolishes any form of legal political opposition."

Notwithstanding Amin's critique, some in the Left continue to romanticize the Islamic Republic as a means to vent their anger against George Bush. They seem to be following in the footsteps of the Soviet Union, which embraced the Iranian mullahs as a way of getting back at the United States.

As the shah fled in 1979, not just Iranians, but people around the developing world, hoped the revolution would bring freedom of speech and the press. It did not. In defending forced closing of opposition newspapers and attacks on opposition protesters by club-wielding vigilantes, Khomeini explained: "The club of the pen and the club of the tongue is the worst of clubs, whose corruption is 100 times greater than other clubs."

More than three million Iranians, Muslims, and non-Muslims have fled Iran in the past two decades. Some of my own friends have walked their way over mountains into Turkey, dodging bullets and living in miserable conditions until they came to Canada. Others fled eastward through Baluchistan and on to Karachi or Lahore to escape the brutality of the Islamic vigilantes. Is this what an Islamic State is all about? Would any of the born-in-Canada or born-in-Britain young Muslims who chant slogans defending the Iranian mullahs care to live a day in Iran? Has any one of them ever thought of applying for immigration to the Islamic Republic? They should try, especially the darker-coloured Indo-Pakistanis or the Somalis. Perhaps the shock of being referred to as *kaka siyaah** by their hosts might make them realize that Iran is not a reflection of Islam and the Prophet's traditions, but an autocracy as vulgar in its self-righteous claim to power as the Saudi royal family.

A country floating on an ocean of oil has managed to increase absolute poverty. Not surprisingly, the poor have risen up in riots, protesting the demolition of their shantytowns and rising food prices. Disabled war veterans have demonstrated against mismanagement of the Foundation of the Disinherited,[†] while ordinary bus drivers and bakery workers have marched in protest only to witness their leaders disappear in the prison system of the Islamic Republic.

For Canadian Muslims, the death in an Iranian prison of Zahra Kazemi should be enough to jolt their consciousness. Unfortunately, it doesn't. The Persian saying about the allure from the outside, while a cancerous poison devours the inside, applies in this case too.

The late Kazemi was an Iranian-Canadian freelance photographer from Montreal, Canada. On June 23, 2003, she was arrested in front of Tehran's infamous Evin prison while taking pictures of demonstrators demanding the freedom of activist students jailed in the prison. Nothing was heard from her until nineteen days later, when Iranian authorities announced the Canadian photographer had died in custody after an accident. They were lying. The fact is that fifty-four-year-old Zahra Kazemi was raped and tortured, and died as a result of beatings to her head that caused a fractured skull.

For me, her murder had a special meaning, though I never met the brave woman. She was my age, my generation. She shared my profession,

---

* *Kaka siyaah*: Darkie or black boy.
† The Foundation of the Disinherited: A charity established by Khomeini ostensibly to use the assets seized from former royal foundations to assist low-income groups. The foundation in time has come to be one of the largest conglomerates in the country, controlling hundreds of expropriated and nationalized factories, trading firms, farms, and apartment and office buildings, as well as two large newspaper chains.

and above all, like me she had reluctantly left an oppressive Muslim society to find a home in Canada. One would have expected her death to galvanize Canada's Muslim organizations into demanding that her killers and rapist be brought to justice and that her body be returned to her son in Montreal. But unlike the 2002 brouhaha over Maher Arar's torture in Syria, Zahra Kazemi's torture and death aroused little passion among the Muslims outside the Iranian-Canadian community. I guess she just didn't fit the bill of the shy Middle Eastern woman in a coy *hijab.* Some even argued that Kazemi was responsible for her own demise.

Although Iran's Islamic Republic insists that her death was accidental, and one Canadian Arab supporter of Hezbollah appeared on television to deny that she was raped, Shahram Azam, a former military staff physician at the jail where she was held, has stated he examined Kazemi's body and observed evidence of rape and torture, including a skull fracture, broken nose, crushed toe, broken fingers, and severe abdominal bruising. But Zahra Kazemi is just one more statistic among the tens of thousands of Iranians who have been killed by the Islamic State of Iran since the 1979 revolution that was stolen by the Iranian clergy, all in the name of defending Islam and fighting the West. To date, her son's demand and that of the Canadian government to have Kazemi's body returned to Canada has been dismissed. Is this the Islamic state that Islamists yearn for? Had they been in a state of Islam, the city's "Islamic" leaders and mosque imams would have staged a permanent vigil outside the Iranian Embassy in Ottawa to demand justice. But, unfortunately, the Islamists of Canada and the West in general have fallen for the romantic allure of the mullahs' shadowboxing with the United States.

One of the little-known facts about Iran is its hidden racial ruling structure. This is reflected in the racial origin of the men who qualify to rule the country as the Velayat-e faqih. The racial character of this position is largely disguised as a religious requirement, making any opposition to it an attack on Islam itself. Few people know that the position of Velayat-e faqih is closed to any Iranian who is *not* of Arab ancestry. For the sons and daughters of the Persian civilization, it would seem that such a restriction would be very difficult to digest. But, apparently, they have. The racial ancestry of Iran's current leaders is also delineated by the colour of turbans they wear. While the turbans of men like Khatami and Khamenie are black,

---

* *Hijab*: The veil that some Muslim women wear over their forehead and hair.

signifying their superior Arab roots, the rest of the clergy—those of Persian ancestry—dare not wear the sacred black turban; they are allowed only to wear white turbans. This ubiquitous and blatant racial division is never the subject of discussion or debate.

The Arab ancestry that is a prerequisite for the job of the Supreme Leader of Iran is not just any Arab ancestry. An applicant for the job would have to prove his roots to the Arabs of Mecca of the 7th century. And not just any Meccan Arabs; he would have to belong to the Meccan Arab tribe of the Quraysh. And not just any Quraysh, but the Hashemite clan of the Quraysh tribe. And not just any member of the Hashemite clan; he would have to find his roots to the Hashemites related to the Prophet himself. And not just any relative of the Prophet, but only those who can prove their lineage to his daughter Fatima and her husband, Ali Ibn abu Talib. These men are known as the *Syeds*. Only an Arab Syed of Iran can rule the country as its supreme leader.

And if the racial nature of the Velayat-e faqih were not enough, racial origin became an issue in the country's first presidential elections when one Jalal-uddin Farsi was disallowed from running for office because his father was born in Afghanistan! I guess Afghan blood sells a bit cheaper in the market of racial hierarchies than Arab blood.

Addressing this bizarre display of racial exclusivity built into the Islamic Republic of Iran, the pro-Khomeini periodical *Crescent International* explained: "In defence of the new Constitution, it has been argued that the office of the President is purely for Iran. The condition of Irani [*sic*] blood and origin does not apply to the highest office, Vilayet-e-Faqih, or to membership of the Islamic Consultative Committee (the Majlis). These it is alleged are institutions of wider relevance to the world of Islam whereas the presidency is a local Irani [*sic*] institution."

While the Quran and Prophet Muhammad talked about the equality of all Muslims, irrespective of race or origin, placing emphasis on meritocracy over skin colour or tribe, racial origin plays a significant role in the destiny of seventy million Iranians. Persia, which once produced Islam's leading intellectuals and thinkers and had a major hand in creating the enlightened period during the Abbasid caliphate, is getting its rich heritage tarnished at the hands of Islamists. The ruling ayatollahs have not only hijacked Islam to cling to power, but they have turned cruel and inhuman punishment into the most visible attribute of the faith.

If this is the democracy that is touted as the essence of an Islamic State, is it any wonder that most Iranians don't wish to have anything to do with Political Islam? When Iran's mullahs camouflage racism as Islamic universalism and trumpet it as the foundation of their Islamic State, they betray the essence of the equality of all human beings enshrined in the 1948 United Nations Declaration of Universal Human Rights.

Not all ayatollahs in Iran agree with the current leadership. In fact, far from being a monolithic institution, the Iranian clergy are quite diverse in their attitudes towards the fundamental question of state and religion and the institution of Velayat-e faqih. It is quite likely that the changes the Iranian people desire in their country may come from within the religious establishment. The religious seminaries of Qom, Iran's holy city, are not like the Sunni *madrassahs* of Pakistan and Saudi Arabia, where students learn by rote and repetition. They are vibrant institutions that house more than fifty thousand students studying Islamic theology. Unlikely as it may sound, it is from Qom that a challenge to the theocratic principles that are the foundation of the current regime, the institution of Velayat-e faqih, may arise.

Shia Muslims consider Prophet Muhammad's son-in-law Ali as their first imam. They believe that he was followed by ten successors who were murdered by Sunni caliphs. Fearing for his life, the twelfth imam went into hiding, leaving behind instructions that he would not return until the end of time. Shia theology dictates that during this period no person can have lawful political authority. For centuries before the Iranian revolution, most Shia clerics maintained that until the emergence of the hidden imam—the Mehdi—men of religion should refrain from political activity.

The new institution of Velayat-e faqih introduced by Khomeini turned this long-standing assumption upside down, causing much debate inside Qom. Some Shia clerics are particularly uncomfortable with the idea that the Velayat-e faqih derives his authority from God and is not accountable to the people.

The most well known among the dissident clerics is Grand Ayatollah Ali Montazeri, a revered cleric who was Khomeini's designated successor before he was put under house arrest for complaining about the mass execution of political prisoners. Another cleric, Hojatoleslam Mohsen Kadivar, has gone as far to say that what the current leaders of Iran are practising today is not Islam. In the 1990s he was jailed when he argued that Iran could not have clerical rule and claim to be a democracy at the same time. He labelled the rule of ruling ayatollahs as clerical despotism, not the freedom Iranians had sought through their 1979 revolution.

Then there is Grand Ayatollah Sistani, an Iranian based in Iraq but with a large following among Shia clerics. Sistani has approved Iraq's post–Saddam Hussein constitution, which gives ultimate authority to elected politicians rather than clerics, a clear detour from the direction set by Khomeini.

Inside Qom, Mofid University is considered a liberal institution. One of its leading teachers is Hojatoleslam Fazel Maybodi. In an interview with a British magazine he said something few would expect from an Iranian theologian—that he did not believe all political ideas should come from within Islam. He went on to suggest a separation between politics and Islam, saying politics is an experimental, man-made activity, and that Islam should respect it.

Men like Grand Ayatollah Ali Montazeri and Maybodi may be few, but as long as even a handful of such Iranian clerics speak their mind, and as long as Iranian women rebel against the oppressive misogyny of the mullahs, there is hope for the Iranian revolution to reach its intended potential, a secular democracy where Iran can again play the historic role it once did. A free and democratic Iran where ayatollahs become the people's moral compass, not their executioners, would trigger a renaissance in the rest of the Muslim world. When that happens, the results of the poll where only 3 percent of the people polled chose to live in Iran, will likely be reversed. Until then we would all have to suffer alongside the brave students and ordinary women and workers who are waging a lonely fight against a murderous regime.

Iran under the ruling ayatollahs is the quintessential Islamic State whose main victims have been the people of Iran; the Persian spirit; and, tragically, the very state of Islam.

CHAPTER 5

Palestine—Future Islamic State?

IT WAS THE FALL OF 1969. Pakistan was under the military government of General Yahya Khan. Troops enforced martial law with an unmistaken discipline. No political activity was permitted, no slogans, no parades, and no literature, especially near airports and military installations. But on that late autumn night at Karachi Airport, a smartly turned-out lieutenant colonel was going to make an exception. "Only for five minutes. Not one second more," he snapped. We were about twenty young men standing impatiently outside the international arrivals terminal, waiting to greet a very special visitor. "You have my word," Comrade B.M. Kutty, the erstwhile activist, told the officer. "We just wish to welcome her to Pakistan." The officer gave a sly wink of approval and shifted into Urdu to say: "Don't get me into trouble. All sorts of demonstrations have been banned."

The picture of Leila Khaled walking out of the terminal door is still etched in my mind. I was, like millions of young boys of Pakistan, in love with her. She smiled as she met with a couple of the more senior Palestinian students among us, Ahmed Shouly and Muhammad Mustafa. I still remember them, especially the red-haired Ahmed Shouly, who had taught me how to sing the "Internationale." "*Falasteen, Falasteen*," we chanted. "Pakistan–Palestine friendship *Zindabad*.*"

We were young and Palestine was younger then. It was our cause, too, and some of us Pakistanis were eager to fight the Israeli occupation. Leila

---

* Zindabad: Long live.

Khaled was an embodiment of the struggle. She looked tiny compared to her pictures, but for us, she was our larger-than-life Greek goddess.

As a pacifist I abhorred physical violence, as did my colleagues, but Khaled's 1969 role in the hijacking of a TWA aircraft to Damascus meant more to us than an act of terrorism. First, she was a Muslim woman smashing all Islamist assumptions and beliefs about the supposed role of women, and second, she exemplified the aspirations of a people under occupation seeking freedom.

The lieutenant colonel stepped forward to hush us up and then told us to leave the premises. It was around midnight and no one was supposed to know Khaled was in town for a secret stopover in Karachi on her way to an unknown destination. The Pakistan military government had consented to her visit, but did not wish to acknowledge her presence or their permission. No other cause brings Pakistanis together like the cause of Palestine. From the far Left to the ultra Right, as far as Palestine was concerned, the nation was one. Not even Kashmir can garner such unanimity.

My connection to Palestine began in 1967, when I first met a Palestinian. It was my first day at the University of Karachi when I bumped into Ahmed Shouly. I was distributing anti-government leaflets on the campus and he took one. It was also his first day at a university in Pakistan. He glanced at the text and asked, "*Inta** Socialist?" I said, "Yes." "*Masha'allah*—me too," he grinned.

From that day on, the Palestinian struggle for a homeland became my struggle, because I felt a bond to a people betrayed by their own leadership, sold out by the Arabs and made to suffer, and worse, be humiliated by their friends more than their enemies. After years of living under Israeli occupation, made strangers in their own home, the Palestinians deserved better.

Earlier that summer, the world around me had crumbled as the Six-Day War woke us to the reality of the hollowed termite-ridden colossus that was the Arab army. My hero, Egypt's Gamal Abdel Nasser, had turned out to be a paper tiger. The Israelis had defeated the Arabs comprehensively. In Karachi old men wept as if they had had a personal calamity. How could tiny Israel defeat 200 million Arabs in twenty countries? We too in Pakistan had just come out of a war, but we had held our adversary, India, to a draw, an "enemy" five times larger than us.

Notwithstanding the conspiracy theories that the United States had helped Israel win the war, deep inside I had a gut feeling that there was something seriously rotten in the kingdom of Arabia. My Palestinian comrades

---

* *Inta*: Arabic for the word "you."

in Karachi would educate me. Brilliant and brave, tough and handsome young men, they filled me with a passion that still burns. They exposed the corrupt monarchies and pseudo-socialists of the Arab world—millionaires mimicking misery, who used the trauma of the Palestinians to further their own agenda. I learned about the Islamists of the Muslim Brotherhood, for whom secular Palestinians were more of a threat than the Israelis, their supposed enemies. The Palestinians in Pakistan would express surprise at the strength of the Pakistani Islamist groups on campus. They were shocked at the strong-arm tactics and bullying methods of the Jamaat-e-Islami toughs; in Jordan and the West Bank, they would tell me, the *Ikhwan* al Muslimeen*, or Muslim Brotherhood, were a fringe element.

Little did they know how the Palestine struggle for nationhood would be hijacked by the Islamists. One could never have imagined then that the most secular, educated, and enlightened people of the Arab world would fall victim to the allure of radical Muslims Syed Qutb and Hassan al-Banna. If, in the 1960s, the Palestinian movement was the cry for freedom of a people, in forty years it would be transformed into the international cause of Islam. Instead of a resistance movement to end the Israeli occupation of Palestinian land, the Islamists turned it into a war to wipe out the Jews. In the 1960s, there was never even a hint of anti-Semitism among the progressive and secular Palestinians. No doubt there was deep bitterness about Israel's occupation, but I never once heard a derogatory remark against Jews. On the other hand, the Islamist discourse was never free of hate and bigotry.

Like a sucker, Palestine shrinks in size every time it is licked. If this trend continues, Palestine will be reduced from a possible nation state to a shrivelled and fragmented Bantustan. We are in danger of turning the dream of a state into a reservation where future tourists will visit quaint villages, admiring Palestinian embroidery and handicrafts while young men and women dance the *dabka* to entertain visitors. Islamists would win; Palestine could be lost—forever.

This must not happen. Today, more than ever before, the challenge to end the Israeli occupation requires that the men and women of Palestine take back ownership of their struggle from the Islamists and their Iranian backers. For if the Palestine resistance is nothing more than an Islamic

---

* *Ikhwan*: Islamist political party born in Egypt, but with branches across the Arab world.

struggle, there is no need for a Palestinian state. Radical Zionists argue there are dozens of Islamic countries—why do we need one more? And if it is an issue of Islam's third holy place, Jerusalem's Al-Aqsa Mosque, from where it is believed Muhammad ascended to the heavens to meet God, then surely our critics could argue, we can get Israeli guarantees for access and jurisdiction. After all, don't we Muslims occupy the birthplaces of the Sikh faith? Have we not eliminated Zoroastrianism almost entirely and control all of its holy places? Are we not in control of vast tracts of Buddhist civilization on the Indus river? If Palestine is merely a struggle to establish an Islamic State, it is a cause that will never gain support outside the Muslim world.

Let Saudi Arabia, the occupier of Mecca and Medina, first treat Palestinians within its borders with some respect and dignity before it talks about the "liberation" of Jerusalem or Al Quds. Let Iran first respect the human rights of its own citizens before lecturing the Israelis about international law and the freedom of Palestine. With friends like Saudi Arabia and Iran, the Palestinians hardly need enemies.

Leila Khaled did not risk her life to read about Palestinian newscasters being threatened with death for not covering their heads. George Habash and Naif Hawatmeh did not dedicate their lives for a Palestine where sharia law would govern. The Christians of Ramallah, Bethlehem, and Jerusalem did not fight for a Palestine only to be told they would be *Dhimmis** in an Islamic Republic modelled like clay by ayatollahs in the Iranian heartland city of Qom. And were literary theorist/activist Edward Said alive today, would the most eloquent voice for Palestine wish to live under sharia law? For the sake of Said, Palestinians must reject the Islamist cause.

When the rock band The Teardrop Explodes produced the love song "Just Like Leila Khaled Said" in the 1980s, they had not anticipated a Palestine where the Hamas education minister would ban a book of folkloric tales because of its "immoral" references to romance.

Svend Robinson was Canada's first openly gay Member of Parliament and the most prominent advocate of Palestine among Canada's politicians. Imagine his shock when we heard the Hamas foreign minister, Mahmoud Zahar, tell CNN that "homosexuals and lesbians, [are] a minority of perverts and the mentally and morally sick." Zahar said that Palestine needed an "Islamic" society because a "secular system allows homosexuality, allows corruption, allows the spread of the loss of natural immunity, like AIDS." Later, Zahar would condemn dancing between men and women.

---

* *Dhimmies*: Non-Muslim citizens of the Islamic State.

What a sad rebuke to North America's most passionate advocate of the Palestinian cause. I once chatted with Svend Robinson after his shoving match with an Israeli soldier near Ramallah, in Palestine. I asked him about Palestine's gay population, and whether it was true that they were increasingly taking refuge inside Israel. He said he was saddened to read about the persecution of gays in Palestinian society, but he hoped better sense would prevail. "One cannot ask for one's human rights and then abuse another minority with a vengeance," he said. "That will be a sad day for Palestine, but we should remember, even in the West, it took decades for our society to accept gay rights. Give them freedom and a sovereign state and I am confident Palestine will emerge as the most progressive Arab society."

Today, more than ever before, Palestinians should view Islamists with deep suspicion, especially the ones in Marxist attire who espouse support for the Islamist Hamas movement while living in the belly of what Islamists view as the Great Satan, unwilling to give up residence or the comforts of the United States. The Palestinian movement cannot be allowed to degenerate into a fad for out-of-luck leftists in search of a cause. Those who hate Israel more than they love Palestine cannot be part of the solution. When these rich armchair anti-imperialists spout on about Palestine, they seem to do so out of an addiction, not a commitment.

Instead of denouncing the medieval nature of Hamas pronouncements, the leftists in the Palestinian diaspora have labelled any critic of the Islamists as an agent of Zionism. They have been even more contemptuous of their fellow Palestinians who do not endorse Hamas and the Muslim Brotherhood's agenda in Gaza and the West Bank, not even sparing the leading icons of the resistance.

The Palestinian poet Mahmoud Darwish is the embodiment of his people's struggle. Yet the Islamists and their Marxist allies would not care to spare even him. His name has been tarnished and dragged through the mud, punished for what one Palestinian commentator says was Darwish's "temerity to remain a secular nationalist and oppose Hamas and other Islamist groups."

Chief among the left-wing Palestinians who have become the US front for Hamas is Joseph Massad, professor at Columbia Univeristy. He has led the vitriol against Darwish. He insinuated that Darwish's loyalties to President Mahmoud Abbas were not sincere, but rather came at a price. Mocking Darwish, the American-Arab professor wrote:

Perhaps Mahmoud Darwish's recent poem in support of the coup [dismissal of the Hamas government by Mahmoud Abbas] published on the front page of the Saudi newspaper *Al-Hayat*, can be explained by the monthly checks he receives from the Fatah-controlled Palestinian Authority, and he is not alone. . . . Those secularists who support dictators and colonizers are mainly interested in living the good life provided to them by the treason of Fatah and its corruption and its theft of the money of the Palestinian people to pamper its leaders and intellectuals.

Another American-Arab academic, As'ad AbuKhalil of California State University, also suggested Darwish had sold out. He wrote mockingly on his blog: "The position of Mahmud Darwish on Oslo became more clear when Arafat bought him an old house in Ramallah, and increased his generosity to him. . . . I expect him [Darwish] to declare [Israeli Prime Minister Ehud] Olmert the 'knight of Zionism' any day now." AbuKhalil sarcastically suggested that Darwish's recent poetry reading in Haifa translated properly would read: "I want Nobel. Please give me Nobel. I really want Nobel. Please give it to me NOW. If you give me Nobel, I will keep repeating that Arabs are in love with Israeli nuclear weapons."

When Palestinian academics in the United States sully the name of Mahmoud Darwish, they reflect their own arrogant self-righteousness, nothing more. The mating of the Islamists and the Marxists can only give birth to an ugly monster. They would dare not give up their privileges to match the sacrifice of Darwish, who, as Hussein Ibish of the American Task Force on Palestine (ATFP) reminds us, has lived in Ramallah under its rigours when he could easily be living in the comfort and security of New York or California if he so chose.

Ibish, one of the most articulate spokespersons for the Palestinian cause in the United States, wrote a stinging rebuke to Hamas supporters in the United States, saying: "These hyperbolic, hyper-personalized and low-blow attacks on Darwish typify the style and substance of the approach to Palestinian politics that has been developed by the leftist and secular defenders of Hamas. It is all about condemning other Palestinians, Arabs and their supporters in the harshest imaginable terms as traitors, quislings, collaborators and prostitutes. It is worth noting that in some contexts these accusations could well constitute an incitement to violence."

Other brave people have stepped forward to denounce Hamas and the Islamist agenda in Palestine. The Syrian poet Adonis has joined a rising tide of intellectuals who have been outspoken against the rise of Islamization of the political discourse in the Arab world and Palestine. In an interview aired on Dubai television in March 2006, Adonis made critical observations about Arab society and the mixing of religion and state.

When asked about his views on democracy in Palestine, which brought Hamas to power, Adonis said he supported it, but opposed establishing any state on the basis of religion, "even if it's done by Hamas." When asked by the interviewer if he would oppose the mixing of religion and politics "even if it liberates Palestine," Adonis remarked, "Yes, because in such a case, it would be my duty to fight this religious state." This was long before the Hamas military takeover of Gaza in June 2007, when its militia committed war crimes by executing in cold blood wounded fighters belonging to the rival Fatah. The religious state Adonis feared in March 2006 had already surfaced by June 2007.

Adonis may have had the courage to speak his mind on Dubai TV, but few of his Arab admirers in North America and Europe have joined him, choosing instead to take the route of "community patriotism" that permits the Islamists free rein while killing the free spirit of Adonis. Painting a rather bleak picture of the Arab world, Adonis also told Dubai TV that Arabs were now in a "phase of extinction, in the sense that we have no creative presence in the world."

When the interviewer interjected, saying Adonis' views were "very dangerous," he ended up making an even harsher prognosis: "The Muslims today—forgive me for saying this—with their accepted interpretation [of the religious text] are the first to destroy Islam, whereas those who criticize the Muslims—the non-believers, the infidels, as they call them—are the ones who perceive in Islam the vitality that could adapt it to life. These infidels serve Islam better than the believers."

Intellectuals like Adonis find themselves immediately ridiculed by the Islamists as, at best, irrelevant and at worst, anti-Islam and thus apostates. A concerted attempt has been made to depict liberal secular Muslims as agents of the United States, working against the Islamic Ummah. Added to that social pressure is, of course, the now-familiar death threat.

Have these sharia-Bolsheviks not read about the origins of the Islamic fundamentalist movement in Palestine? Victor Ostrovsky, the former officer with Israel's Mossad intelligence service, who wrote *The Other Side of Deception*, levels the charge that the Israeli Right had a hand in encouraging Islamic fundamentalism among Palestinians as a way to undermine the Palestine Liberation Organization (PLO). He wrote: "Supporting the radical elements of the Muslim fundamentalism sat well with Mossad's general plan for the region. An Arab world run by fundamentalists would not be a party to any negotiations with the West, thus leaving Israel again as the only democratic, rational country in the region. And if the Mossad could arrange for Hamas . . . to take over the Palestinian streets from the PLO, then the picture would be complete."

It is not just Ostrovsky making this claim. Ziad Abu-Amr of Bir Zeit University, has written about the sudden appearance of Muslim Brotherhood and Hamas hoodlums on campuses trying to elbow out the PLO. When the PLO tried to dialogue with the Islamic fundamentalists, he commented, "The Muslim Brotherhood leadership urged Fatah to purge its ranks of Marxist elements to be aware of the futility of secularism, and to cooperate closely with Islamic groups."

When author Robert Dreyfuss interviewed Philip Wilcox, who headed the US consulate in Jerusalem in the mid-1980s, Wilcox said: "There were persistent rumours that the Israel secret service gave covert support to Hamas, because they were seen as rivals to the PLO."

The PLO and Fatah were aware of this nexus. PLO leader Yasser Arafat accused Hamas and its leader, Sheik Yasin, of acting "with the direct support of reactionary Arab regimes . . . in collusion with Israeli occupation." He told the Italian newspaper *Corriere Della Sera* in 2001: "Hamas is a creation of Israel, which at the time of Prime Minister Shamir, gave them money and more than 700 institutions, among them schools, universities and mosques." Arafat added, "Israeli Prime Minister Yitzak Rabin admitted Israeli support for Hamas to him, in the presence of Egyptian president Hosni Mubarak." Arafat said Rabin described it as a "fatal error."

Not only did Israel have a hand in nurturing the Islamists, it did everything possible to undermine the credibility of Palestine's secular and democratic leadership who had reconciled themselves with the State of Israel. They were willing to build peace, if not friendship, with the Jewish state. When Israel complains that it had no peace partner, it is not true. Israel had ten years to deliver on Oslo, but all it did was build additional settlements, restrict Arafat to his Ramallah compound, and put Fatah leader Marwan Barghouti in prison. Whom did they expect would fill this vacuum? Gandhi?

Israel's intransigence and arrogance has made us all lose ten years and a lot of goodwill on all sides. Jehad Aliweiwi, a former executive director of the Canadian Arab Federation, a supporter of Fatah, who was born in Hebron in the occupied West Bank, told me: "There is an Arabic adage that says 'those who don't possess something cannot give it.' Before Oslo, I, as a Palestinian living in Hebron, could travel anywhere in the West Bank, go to Jerusalem and Nazareth and go to Gaza. Today, as a consequence of Oslo, Gaza is farther away from Hebron than Toronto, despite being less than fifty miles apart. No one can go to Jerusalem. Can you blame Palestinians for now asking for a one-state solution?"

Today the Palestinians are weaker than they have ever been. Their ability to engage in an armed struggle to "liberate" Palestine died the day they were expelled from Lebanon without their arms and scattered to faraway camps, in Tunisia, Sudan, and God knows where. The Arab states looked on as the youth of Palestine wept, and the hearts of their supporters sank in despair. Then, one day, I read in the *Arab News of Jeddah* that a PLO fighter had died helplessly in Sudan after being attacked by a monkey. I wanted the earth to open and swallow me. We were defeated, both from within and without, by the humiliation this fighter suffered by spending his entire life to fight a war only to have his firearm confiscated and so was unable to protect himself from a predatory monkey.

Palestinians need to recognize the dangers of falling for Hamas and its Islamist agenda. If they don't, they will be sacrificing a state of their own to serve the geopolitical interests of Iran in the region. Palestinians need to pay heed to Samir Amin, the Egyptian Marxist who described Islamist parties as "organisations whose aim is the conquest of state power, nothing more, nothing less." Amin said that "wrapping such organisations in the flag of Islam is simple, straightforward opportunism." Amin clarified that Political Islam "is not a 'liberation theology' analogous to what has happened in Latin America. Political Islam is the adversary of liberation theology. It advocates submission, not emancipation." He said that movements like Hamas, which "constitute Political Islam refuse to offer a precise program, contrary to what is customary in political life. For its answer to concrete questions of social and economic life, Political Islam repeats the empty slogan: *Islam is the solution.*"

Still, there is hope. There is the possibility that President Mahmoud Abbas can deliver on a negotiated settlement with the Israeli government. Israel will not disappear and those who convinced us that "Allah will help us push the Jews into the Sea" were lying. Israel has a lot to account for in the damage it has inflicted on the Palestinians. It caused the 1948 "Naqba"—the Catastrophe—but it was not Israel alone. It was politician Nuri as-Said's Iraqis who sold out after secret deals made on the island of Rhodes; it was Jordan's King Abdullah trying to reach backroom deals with Israel's Golda Meier; but above all it was the arrogance and self-righteousness that made us refuse every advantage that came our way, lose every war we fought, and fail to develop a literate, democratic, secular society as an answer to Israel's challenge. The all-or-nothing strategy meant "all" for the monarchs and mullahs, and "nothing" for the Palestinians.

Those who speak in North America of the "one-state" solution, and package their discourse as a well-meaning, well-thought-out plan, fail to understand that this argument is being seen by Israel as another coded strategy for wiping the Jewish state off the map of the Middle East, not by war but by demographics. They should know that Israel will never accept any "one-state" solution. While these North American supporters of Hamas put every possible hurdle in the way of President Mahmoud Abbas, instead of helping him, the lives of ordinary Palestinians continue to be hell on earth. Israel may very well be the devil that it is made out to be in the Arab discourse, but what is our answer to Tel Aviv's challenge?

What Palestinians have going for them is international law, which makes it clear that Israel must put an end to its occupation and dismantle its settlements in occupied territories. UN Security Council Resolutions 242 and 338 provide the basis of a future peace accord. But as long as Iran and the Islamists play the spoiler, no progress can be made. This dispute is not about religion; it is a conflict that pits two people who hold contradictory national visions against one another in a tiny piece of land. Adding a religious dimension to the dispute has weakened the Palestinian position. After all, if the dispute were to be resolved on the basis of divine texts, the Torah provides a far stronger real estate case for Israel than the Quran does for the Palestinians. In fact, by relying on divine texts to make their case, Hamas and its Iranian and Brotherhood backers have foolishly validated Israel's claims not just to the 1967 borders, but to one that includes all of the West Bank. The Palestinian case should not be complicated by questioning Israel's right to exist in safe, secure borders, without the perennial fear of being annihilated as an entity. Rather, Palestinians and their supporters must demand that what Israel desires for itself, that is, security and dignity, should be accorded to Palestinians as well.

One of the most overlooked peace initiatives that was worked out by Palestinians and Israelis was the Geneva Accord announced in December 2003. The accord was the initiative of former Israeli minister of justice Yossi Beilin and the former Palestinian minister of information, Yasser Abed Rabbo.

Both had been official negotiators for their sides, but after the election of Prime Minister Ariel Sharon in February 2001, Beilin and Rabbo continued to meet, in an unofficial capacity. The outcome was a very detailed agreement, which was launched in Geneva on December 1, 2003, and had the blessings of American presidents Jimmy Carter and Bill Clinton, and Poland's Lech Walesa. What politicians could not agree upon, civil society had managed to accomplish. It showed that despite the deep fissures that divide the Palestinian from the Israeli, despite the uneven relationship between the occupier and the occupied, there existed within both Israel and Palestine a group of men and women who could manage to transcend hate and war to continue to desire peace. In the Geneva Accord, both Beilin and Rabbo showed a readiness to cede a part of their dream. With the Israeli peace camp weakened from the failure of Taba, and the rise of Hamas as a result of Fatah's ineptitude and corruption, there was a realization that both sides had to compromise, and they did.

What made the Geneva Accord unique was the fact that it addressed the tough questions up front, including the acceptance of final borders, the issue of Jerusalem, and the question of Palestinian refugees. On the Palestinian side, President Abbas tacitly approved the plan and gave Rabbo his unofficial blessings. However, on the Israeli side, Beilin was not so lucky. In the political posturing of Israel's fluid political scene, few politicians stepped forward to endorse Beilin's fine work. Amos Oz and a few other intellectuals and peace activists in Israel spoke out endorsing the Beilin–Rabbo document, but even the Labour Party refused to endorse it, dismissing Beilin as a lightweight.

The accord, if ever implemented, would have forced the Israeli side to make the sacrifice of accepting Palestinian sovereignty in East Jerusalem. The agreement states that Jewish neighbourhoods of Jerusalem will be under Israeli authority, and that Arab neighbourhoods of Jerusalem will be come under Palestinian sovereignty. In addition, both sides agreed that Palestinian Jerusalemites who currently are permanent residents of Israel shall lose this status upon the transfer of authority to Palestine of those areas in which they reside. The accord also had Israel agreeing to call the Temple Mount the "Esplanade of the Mosques."

If the Israelis were willing to accept East Jerusalem as a capital of Palestine, what they extracted in return was an enormous concession from the Palestinians. The accord called for the Palestinians to renounce their right of return to Israel, restricting them to the territory of the new state of Palestine, and provided for adequate compensation.

The accord asserted the simultaneous existence of a viable Palestinian state and of an Israel with legitimate, secure borders. But it went further. The accord came with a detailed border that traced, almost olive tree to olive tree, the line of partition. With this border, according to the accord, while Israel would demolish most of the settlements, it would retain some settlements currently beyond the Green Line,* as well as Jewish neighbourhoods in East Jerusalem. In return for the annexation of land beyond the 1967 border, Israel would hand over alternative land to the Palestinians, based on a 1:1 ratio. The plan carefully identifies the settlements that must be dismantled, and those near the Green Line or Jerusalem that will be kept for an exchange of an equal amount of territory.

As one commentator said, the Geneva Accord was not a plan of dreamers. It was not a Utopia, rather a concrete plan, precisely negotiated, almost maniacally meticulous.

Unfortunately, the Geneva Accord was lost in the polemics of the dispute. A lesson in political pragmatism, handed out by the two civil societies to their leaders, was wasted with hardliners on both sides mocking the stature of Beilin and Rabbo rather than discussing the merits of their proposal.

The stakes are high for the Palestinians and Israelis. If the Palestinians do not rally behind their president and strengthen his mandate for a peaceful solution, the only place that will bear the name of Palestine will be a town in Texas where parts of the Columbia shuttle fell from space in 2003. And for Israel, the challenge is bigger. If as victors of many wars the Israelis still cannot facilitate the creation of a viable and sovereign Palestinian state with East Jerusalem as its capital, it will always be known as a country that swallowed another state and people. The enmity that this would generate would last for hundreds of generations. At some stage in the future, the Arabs will have regained their ability to stand up for themselves and could make good use of their strategic geopolitical position.

North American Palestinians today are in the unique position to help frame the debate about Palestine as one of the fundamental human rights of a people and the application of international law to resolve the dispute. The challenge is to resist the temptation of portraying Israel as the monster drinking the blood of Palestinians. That tactic has failed every time it has been used, most infamously by Soha Arafat on television in the presence of Hillary Clinton in 1999 (Soha accused Israel of poisoning Palestinian air and water and causing cancer; Hillary then kissed her). It will not fly. It is not rocket science to understand that any message to convince Americans will fail if in that message it is the Americans who are repeatedly told that they are not in control of their own nation, but instead are being manipulated by a Zionist conspiracy. Even if this were true, what good does it serve to

---

* Green Line: Armistice lines that were established between Israel and neighbouring countries after the 1967 Arab–Israeli War.

tell the Americans, in effect, "Now that you know we hate you, when can you start helping us?"

There is no point yelling at Americans while trying to influence their foreign policy. No American will listen to a screaming mob flying Hezbollah and Hamas flags in Dearborn, Michigan, and chanting "Death to America" in unison with Iranian ayatollahs. This is a recipe for disaster, not for an independent and sovereign Palestine.

Palestinians should understand that those who defend terror as a tool against Israeli civilians may appear to be friends to the Palestinian cause, but in fact the consequences of terror do irreparable damage to that cause. On October 22, 2004, when Canadian TV host Michael Coren asked Mohamed Elmasry of the Canadian Islamic Congress if "everyone in Israel . . . irrespective of gender, over the age of eighteen, is a valid target [of terror]," the Egyptian-Canadian cleric replied with an emphatic "yes." Three years later, it was just such a doctrine that led a young Palestinian to enter a Jewish seminary in Jerusalem and slaughter eight students. Did he achieve anything? No. Nothing. And if his nihilistic action was not enough to hurt the Palestinian quest for statehood, the reaction of Hamas supporters, shown celebrating the massacre, ensured the damage was done.

Two articulate and respected Palestinian Americans—Ziad Asali and Hussein Ibish of the American Task Force on Palestine—have developed a strategy that can help the Palestinian cause. But as Ibish says: "Certainly Palestinian-Americans and their allies have to recognize that their traditional approaches have failed. They must also see the poverty and pointlessness of a purely negative agenda of accusations, condemnations and criticism without positive content of any kind. Internal backbiting and mutual recriminations rationalized as 'exposing the traitors and collaborators' is not a strategy for anything constructive."

Bravo. However, as Ibish points out, the romance with Hamas has to end. He writes: "Those liberals and leftists presently inclined to be sympathetic to Hamas need to step back and ask themselves: are we really labouring to support the creation of another theocracy in the Middle East? Would we want to live in such a society? Is that what liberation looks like?"

The late Faiz Ahmad Faiz, Pakistan's revolutionary poet, once lamented the birth of another Islamic State in his now famous "The Dawn of Freedom":

yeh daaGh daaGh ujaalaa, ye shab-gaziidaa sehar
wo intezaar tha jiskaa, ye woh sehar to nahiin

[This scarred, marred brightness, this bitten-by-night dawn
The one that we awaited, surely, this is not that morn]

I hope the birth of Palestine is not as big a disappointment to Faiz as was Pakistan. For Faiz, Palestine was a cause he worked for all his life and he said his best moments were when he edited the journal *Lotus* in Beirut and lived among the Palestinians.

Perhaps the Geneva Accord was dead on arrival. However, the spirit of the accord still lives on and has received the backing of both presidents Clinton and Carter. Forty years after I first fell in love with Palestine, she still eludes my embrace, imprisoned by Israel. To Israel I say: You have all the aces in this game of poker. If you wish your great-grandchildren to live in peace with the offspring of the Palestinians, end the occupation now. I say this as someone who, despite his deep affection and love for Palestine, has an equal admiration of the Jewish people and their enormous contribution to human civilization and their right to a safe, secure state of Israel.

However, the Palestinians too deserve a state, and dignity. Give them back their country. Set free my love so I can embrace her before I die. Let Palestinians walk as free men and women where once the prophets walked. I urge every Israeli to listen to Galilee-born Mahmoud Darwish. They don't need to love him; they only need to recognize his spirit of defiance to know that the Palestinians are not going to disappear. Here he is immortalizing the spirit of his occupied nation:

Record!
I am an Arab
And my identity card is number fifty thousand
I have eight children
And the ninth is coming after a summer
Will you be angry?
Record!
I am an Arab
I have a name without a title
Patient in a country
Where people are enraged . . .

PART TWO

The Genesis

CHAPTER 6

The Prophet is Dead

ISLAM CAME TO FREE HUMANITY from the clutches of the clergy. Instead, the religion of peace has become a prisoner of war, held captive by the very priesthood it came to eliminate. Muslims have been double-duped for centuries—lied to by their leaders and the clerics who supposedly hold the keys to heaven.

The falsehoods Muslims have been force-fed are not only about faith but about early Islamic history. We have been indoctrinated to believe that our faith banned slavery, when the fact is that for 1,400 years we have institutionalized it. We are told that our ancestors gave equality to women, yet we defend the most horrendous treatment of our mothers and daughters. Growing up we were told that all Muslims were equal in the eyes of God, only to find out we were not equal in the eyes of man. We have been programmed to believe that when we invade other countries, it is for their good, but when we are invaded in return, it is wrong. The innumerable glorious achievements of Muslim civilization make us all proud, but remain tainted with countless lies that have been drilled into the minds of each passing generation. When a lie goes unchallenged for over a millennium, it unfortunately attains the legitimacy of gospel truth.

The first falsehood imposed upon Muslims by our clerics concerns the events immediately following the death of Prophet Muhammad in 632 CE. Almost all Muslim scholars, especially contemporary ones, have repeated the legend, without any hesitation, that after the death of Allah's Apostle his successor was "elected" with unanimous consensus at the end of an all-night conference of Muslim elders. In one example, Abul Ala Maudoodi (1903–79), founder of the Jamaat-e-Islami political movement and the intellectual leader of world Political Islam, writes that it was Umar[*] who proposed that Abu-Bakr succeed the Prophet as a spiritual leader.[†] Then "all the people of Medina (who for all practical purposes were representative of the entire country) without any pressure or incentive and out of their love for him, took an oath of allegiance." This version of events is absolutely false, yet few Muslims know that or are willing to discuss it. I intend to.

More than one scholar of Islam has cautioned me to avoid discussion involving the companions of the Prophet. They suggest writing on this subject is inviting danger. The militant terrorist organization *Sepah-e-sahaba* (Soldiers of the Companions) has been created solely with the objective of liquidating those who raise questions about these "companions." This group has assassinated hundreds of Muslims in Pakistan on the charge that they were disrespectful to the Prophet's companions.

The second fable that we Muslims have been forced to swallow since our early childhood is the legend that after the death of the Prophet, an era of universalism and meritocracy emerged in Arabia in which men and women were judged solely on the basis of their piety, and not on the colour of their skin, their race, or tribal ancestry. Again, not true. Within hours of Muhammad's death, tribalism was invoked and racial identity was used to consolidate power and sideline opponents. To this day, the internalized racism that was sanctioned and sanctified in early Islamic history devours the worldwide community of Muslims—the Ummah—like a cancer.

Islamists argue that the period following the passing away of Muhammad was Islam's golden era and that we Muslims need to re-create the caliphate of that time in order to bring the political system it was associated with into today's world. I wish to demonstrate that when Muslims buried the Prophet, they also buried with him many of the universal values of Islam that he had preached. The history of Islam can be described essentially as the history of an unending power struggle, where men have killed each other to claim the mantle of Muhammad. This strife is a painful story that started within hours of the Prophet closing his eyes forever, and needs to be told. I firmly believe the message of the Quran is strong enough to withstand the facts of history. It is my conviction that Muslims are mature and secure in their identities to face the truth. This is that story.

---

[*] Umar: He was to become the second caliph of Islam.
[†] Abu-Bakr: The first caliph of Islam, as the successor to Prophet Muhammad.

Muhammad's death came at a time of great change in human history. Arabia was not the only nation state that was evolving. China had just been reunified in 589 CE, leading to the Tang dynasty (618–907 CE), which historians mark as a high point in Chinese civilization. It was the image of this China that Muhammad had invoked when urging his fellow Arabs to seek knowledge. Across the oceans, in India, the Gupta Empire had reached phenomenal heights in science, mathematics, astronomy, and philosophy, inventing the concepts of zero and infinity along with the symbols of the numbers from one to nine. These were later adopted by the Arabs through trade and became known as Arabic numerals. It is these numerals, developed by Hindu mathematicians, that adorn the pages of every Quran in the Muslim world. This was the globalized world into which Muhammad the internationalist had pushed the tribal pastoral Arabs.

At the crossroads of human civilizations, Arabia and the Muslims found themselves being propelled into the role of shaping the future. On its northern borders, the Arabs found themselves caught between the two dominant powers of the world, the Byzantines and the Persians. While Muhammad was still young and working on the caravans of his wife Khadijah, the Sixth Byzantine–Persian War broke out when between Eastern Rome and the New Persian Empire in 603, both superpowers of the day contending for the control of western Asia. In 627, while Muhammad was consolidating Muslim successes against his naysayers in the Arabian Peninsula, Byzantine Emperor Heraclius defeated the Persian army and regained Asia Minor, Syria, Jerusalem, and Egypt. In Persia, Kavadh II sued for peace with the Byzantines and handed back Armenia, Byzantine Mesopotamia, Syria, Palestine, and Egypt. Weakened by the wars against its western enemies, Persia fell into further chaos when, in 628, Khusrau Parvez II, the new ruler of Persia, was murdered by his son. Within decades, both the Byzantines and Persians, exhausted by centuries of warfare, would be defeated by the new power emerging from Arabia.

Muhammad died on Monday, June 8, 632 CE. It is said that he breathed his last as the searing heat of the midday summer sun beat down on the city of Medina. Exactly where he breathed his last is disputed, however: his wife Aisha said he died in her lap; his son-in-law and trusted lieutenant, the poet/philosopher/warrior Ali ibn Abu Talib, said Muhammad died resting on his shoulder; both accounts could be true, according to some sources.

But with such conflicting versions of Muhammad's last moments, it was no coincidence that Ali and Aisha would fight Islam's first civil war against each other, in the Iraqi city of Basra, only twenty-four years after the Prophet's death.

Muhammad left behind no explicit instructions of what was to be done once his people were without him, and within hours of his death, a power struggle ensued that remains unresolved even today and has, over a millennium, cost the lives of countless Muslims. By the time the sun set on Medina on the day of his death, grief and mourning had given way to intense arguments and a deepening division. Politics had overtaken piety, and tribalism had resurfaced. Men who were of upstanding character and known for their goodwill, who are still revered by the billion Muslims of the 21st century, succumbed to the temptation of invoking noble ancestries as the basis of their claims to leadership of the nascent Muslim Ummah. Barely two months after the Prophet proclaimed that all Muslims were equal, irrespective of their tribal or racial origin—that black and white, Arab or non-Arab, had no superiority over one another—his followers were laying claim to leadership based primarily on their tribal lineage, while denying power to others simply based on where they were born.

Muslims today are deeply conscious of this troubling aspect of their history, but few dare discuss it in public. Although the Quran enjoins Muslims to speak the truth without fear, even if it hurts themselves or their families, it is taboo to speak the truth about the battle over succession that started among the Prophet's companions even before he was given a burial.

The competing narratives of the sad events that unfolded that hot summer day in June 632 are delivered in partisan sermons in front of captive congregations, but never in an open discourse free of fear or reprisal. For anyone who asks tough questions or suggests that all Muslims can learn from this, that politics should be kept out of religion, vilification awaits, and a possibility of the frightening stigma of apostasy. The punishment for apostasy is death.

Muhammad would have been traumatized to see that immediately after his death his companions started feuding over power, at times with swords unsheathed, and even threatened to burn down his beloved daughter Fatima's home. Their intentions were noble, their character was impeccable, and their integrity unquestionable: they wanted to preserve the infant community and protect its frontiers from enemies of Islam. But their methods and tactics were badly flawed. The legacy of this early debacle is such that even today, power is rarely handed over in the Muslim world without bloodshed.

In not defining a political model under which Muslims could govern themselves, the Prophet in his wisdom may very well have left it open to his followers to develop governance according to the socio-economic conditions they lived in. After all, even though it was the Prophet who had himself authored the Medina Compact, which established the rules of governance in the city state of Medina, he did not implement a similar agreement in Mecca when he returned at the head of the conquering Muslim army. If time, geography, and demographics could dictate different governing systems in different cities in the lifetime of Muhammad, the question arises: Why should Muslims of today search for a model of an Islamic State that is rooted in the past? If such a model existed, why didn't the Prophet apply the Charter of the Medina Compact to Mecca? Is the concept of an Islamic State a mirage? Are we being asked to chase one? Yes, on both accounts.

How Muslims should govern and who should govern them were the questions that tore the community apart after Muhammad's death. The same questions still define the conflict that pits Muslim against Muslim today. Nearly 1,400 years later, the problem remains unresolved.

But while Muslims may still be distraught at the early conflicts in Islam, few, especially among the Islamist leadership, are willing to acknowledge that the differences of opinion among the early Muslims were not over the state of Islam, but the Islamic State. There was virtually no argument among the protagonists about the principles of the new religion that was attracting thousands to its fold every day. There was near unanimity among his companions and followers over the call for "submission" only to the Creator alone. But within hours of his demise, the clarion call of the Quran for the equality of all human beings was forgotten. Rival groups jostled for power, brokered and manoeuvred, setting the pattern for the manner in which politics is practised even today in the Arab world.

This is a subject few Muslims are willing to discuss or analyze in a frank and open debate. Historical depictions of these conflicts are written from a partisan perspective where one or the other party to the conflict is blamed for the tragedies that unfolded. Few Muslim historians have addressed the cause of the chasm that appeared among the leaders of the Muslim community so soon after the death of the Prophet.

One such historian was the late Iranian scholar Ali Dashti. According to him, early Islamic conflicts happened because "ambition for the leadership replaced zeal for the religion as the pivotal motive." Dashti's blunt assessment and frank analysis of the power struggles that engulfed early Islam resulted in his book *Twenty-Three Years* being banned in Iran under the rule of both the shah and Ayatollah Khomeini. The author was imprisoned, tortured, and eventually exiled. Dashti wrote: "The study of the history of Islam shows it to be a sequence of struggles for power in which the contestants treated the religion as the means, not as an end. . . . The further the Prophet's death receded into the past, the greater became the tendency to treat the religion as a means, rather than as an end in itself—to use it as an instrument of seizure of the leadership and the rulership."

Today, the tendency to use religion as an instrument of political power is reflected in the competing visions of Islam offered by Saudi Arabia and Iran. Final authority in both countries has been wrested from ordinary citizens and preserved for the king in Saudi Arabia and the Supreme Leader in Iran. In Iran, this leader is supposedly accountable only to God, but in actuality, he is accountable to himself alone.

The Prophet knew his last days in this world were at hand. He had been ill for some time and was preparing his followers for the moment when he would no longer be among them. The Muslims of the time included the tribes of Arabia; the freed African slaves; the immigrants from Persia, Yemen and Abyssinia; the women who were newly empowered by the message of Islam; and the landless and the poor, who were being treated with justice and equality for the first time in their lives. They had smashed the symbols of servitude, separation, and superstition. They had arisen with a zeal and fervour the Arabs had never before known.

Two months earlier, during his last journey to Mecca for the hajj pilgrimage, Muhammad had spoken about the completion of his mission on Earth. Addressing pilgrims, Muhammad said: "Hear me O people, for I know not if ever I shall meet you in this place after this year." These were not the last words of Muhammad, but it was to be his last formal speech. As tens of thousands stood in rapt attention, Muhammad made stirring remarks that still resonate today as the defining spirit of the Muslim community, even among those who adhere to Islam merely as a culture, not a religion. "Neither inflict, nor suffer inequity," he said, spelling out the principles of social justice in a world where teeming millions believed it was their destiny to suffer inequity.

Muhammad declared that everyone was equal before God, without distinction of social class or racial origin: "O people, your Lord is one, and your ancestor is [also] one. You are all descendants from Adam and Eve who was born of earth. The noblest of you all, in the sight of God, is the most devout. God is knowing and all wise [Quran sura 49:13]. An Arab is superior to a non-Arab in nothing, but devotion."

The spirit of equality and rejection of ethnic or racial superiority had been explicitly revealed to Muhammad in an earlier revelation: "O mankind!

We created you from a single (pair) of a male and a female, and made you into nations and tribes, that ye may know each other (not that ye may despise each other). Verily the most honoured of you in the sight of Allah is (he who is) the most righteous of you. And Allah has full knowledge and is well acquainted (with all things)."

Multiculturalism and anti-racism emerged in North America and Europe as stepping stones towards equality as late as the 20th century. But here was the Prophet of Islam sowing the seeds of racial equality in the 7th century. Muhammad came to a world where identity was primarily based on race and being on the wrong side of the racial divide would mean a life sentence into servitude, if not slavery. Tragically, the words of the Quran and these anti-racist teachings of Muhammad were metaphorically paved over within hours of his death.

Later that day, while returning from the plains of Arafat, Muhammad again addressed the hajj pilgrims, reciting aloud the last revelation he had received from God through the Archangel Gabriel. That verse completed the Quran, a book whose words would change the course of human history—triggering a fountain of knowledge at one time, but today providing intellectual sustenance to Islamic extremists. This last revelation was a profound end to the process that started twenty-three years earlier on the day the archangel is said to have woken Muhammad from his meditation in a cave and commanded him to "Read"—the first word of the Quran.

Muhammad had been on a long journey of tribulations and triumphs. Arabia had changed dramatically in the two decades since that lonely dark night in the cave. Now, when Muhammad was about to unveil the final words of the Quran, scribes rushed to hear him, bringing writing materials of parchment, bones, and leaves. His companions, some say 100,000 strong, gathered around, clinging to his every word as he recited the final verse of the Quran: "This day have I perfected your religion for you, completed my favor upon you, and have chosen for you Islam as your religion."

Within decades of Muhammad's death, God's instructions that the Prophet had perfected and completed Islam would be conveniently interpreted by scholars serving caliphs as the means to allow additions to Islam. Sultans and caliphs would add layer after layer to the Islam that God had said he perfected in his last revelation to Muhammad. To this day, Muslims are subject to laws God never authorized either in the Quran or through his messenger, Prophet Muhammad. The stoning of women, the killing of gays and lesbians, the concept of royalty, the Velayat-e faqih, and tons of new concepts were added to the faith of Islam by one ruler after another, invoking religion to pursue political power and luring the Ummah towards an Islamic State that has not yet been consecrated after 1,400 years of waiting.

If Muslims are to understand why our political systems have failed, or why asking for a political framework modelled on the pattern set by the Rightly Guided Caliphs of Islam is a recipe for failure, then the account of what happened in 632 needs to be revisited. Islamists who demand the introduction of an Islamic political system based on 7th-century political manoeuvrings are neither willing to analyze the imperfect processes that led to bloodshed, nor are they ready to concede that the bloodshed that occurred was a result of political ambitions. The first dynasty of Islam, the Umayyads of Damascus, arose only after the blood of Muhammad's own family had been shed, but generation after generation of Muslims has been conditioned to look the other way. Any discussion about the role of the early caliphs is considered as bordering on blasphemy. The stature of the early caliphs and the companions of the Prophet has been raised from their being mere mortals to that of being at par with the Apostle of Allah and thus beyond reproach or criticism, no matter how devastating the consequences of their actions.

If the political system introduced during the Golden Period of Islam by the four Rightly Guided Caliphs resulted in the assassination of three of them, triggered civil wars, led to secessionist conflict, and caused the slaughter of the Prophet's family—who were left starving and thirsty on the plains of Karbala in Iraq—surely that system cannot be seen today as the model for tomorrow. If at all there is something from that time in history that Muslims need to emulate, it is the personal character of Muhammad's companions. The integrity and the transparency of their lives, as well as their aversion to pomp and show, could shame many of the Muslim leaders. Their truthfulness and humility are what all Muslims need to embrace. These were men who died leaving little inheritance for their families, such was their creed of social justice and equity. But the political system they created, and then got killed implementing, is best left as a subject for historians to discuss, rather than offering it as a recipe to resolve the ailing condition of the Muslim world.

Perhaps the Prophet could foresee the turmoil that his death would trigger and he talked about this in his last stroll in Medina before illness and an excruciating headache took their toll. A few nights before he passed away forever, Muhammad ventured to the cemetery of Baqi on the outskirts of Medina. (This is where his son Ibrahim, his daughter Ruqqaiya, and many of his companions lay buried; this too is the location of the house that his daughter Fatima would later visit to grieve Muhammad's death.) Only Abu Muwayhibah, a man the Prophet had freed from slavery, accompanied him. As the two men reached the cemetery, Muwayhibah quotes Muhammad as saying: "Peace be unto you, O people of the graves. Happy are you, for you are much better off than men here. Dissensions have come like waves of darkness, one after another, the last being worst than the first."

Husayn Haykal, the Egyptian biographer of the Prophet, used a different translation: "Peace be upon you who are in these graves. Blessed are you in your present state to which you have emerged from the state in which the people live on earth. Subversive attacks are falling one after another like waves of darkness, each worse than the previous ones."

The prophetic prediction of "dissensions" was already unfolding as the Apostle of Allah trudged back home. No one dared ask him whom he had chosen as his successor. Abd Allah bin Muslim Ibn Qutaybah, an Andalusian historian of the 9th century, reports that Abdullah ibn al-Abbas, the Prophet's cousin, met Ali as the Prophet lay dying and said: "The Prophet is about to die! Go, therefore and ask him if this affair [that is, the caliphate] shall be ours, that he may declare it. But if it belongs to someone else, then he may at least enjoin kindness towards us."

The historian then reports that Ibn Abbas went to Umar and Abu-Bakr and asked if the Prophet had left any instructions regarding his succession. Both said that they knew nothing about any such instructions. On hearing this, Ibn Abbas returned to Ali and said: "'Stretch out your hand that I may pledge allegiance (ba'yah) to you . . . Your own relatives will then offer their ba'yah and all the people will follow suit.' Ali, displaying caution, and his desire for consensus, asked, 'Will anyone quarrel with us concerning this matter?'"

The next day the Prophet suffered a headache that left him in a painful condition. Even as he lay perspiring in the stifling heat of the Arabian summer, the dissension that he had predicted was surfacing among his trusted troops and their commanders.

Muhammad, the visionary and statesman, even in his dying days was carefully moulding a new people out of the clay of Arab tribal traditions. On May 26, 632, just days before he slipped into the illness from which he would not recover, Muhammad had authorized the last of his many military campaigns. This time he ordered a three-thousand-strong expeditionary force to attack the frontier of the Byzantine Empire in an area near the Syria–Jordan border of today. A few years earlier, in the battle at Mu'ta, Muhammad's adopted son Zayd had died fighting the Byzantines and the Prophet wanted to respond appropriately to the enemy.

However, his choice of the man to lead the expedition became a source of much dissent. Muhammad broke all tradition and chose a young Black African man, barely twenty years old, promoting him over many senior and experienced commanders. There were murmurs of dissent, with many Muslims reluctant to fight under the command of Osama bin Zayd, openly expressing their unhappiness with the Prophet's decision.

Muhammad is said to have personally prepared a ceremonial flagpole, with his own hands, and given it to young Osama. The camp was then erected at Jorf, five kilometres from Medina on the route to Syria. He ordered all his followers at Medina to join it at once, not excepting even the renowned companions. It is said that only Ali, his trusted lieutenant and son-in-law, was required by him to remain with him at Medina, and was exempted · from going.

About a week after Muhammad had summoned the men to the Syrian expedition under Osama, he perceived that the progress to join the camp at Jorf was slow and poor, so he once again addressed the people to join the Syrian expedition. Muhammad was daily becoming more ill and the expedition weighed upon his mind.

The two groups within the young Muslim community were the *Muhajirun* (the Meccans) and the Ansar (the Medinans). Veterans from both camps were unhappy at being superseded by the young man who was the son of a Black slave from Ethiopia, and openly expressed their reluctance to fight under his command. The grumblings angered the ailing Muhammad, who got up from his bed and, despite a high fever and a throbbing headache, asked his wives Aisha and Hafsah to help him take a bath. The two bathed him with water to cool his fever, dressed him up and bandaged his head to ease his throbbing headache. They then helped him walk to the mosque, where he went to the pulpit and addressed the congregation. Upset at the dissension among the ranks over selection of the young Osama, the Prophet told the congregation: "O people, dispatch Osama's troops, for though you question his leadership and the leadership of his father before him, yet he is worthy of this command, even as his father was worthy of it." He declared from the pulpit that this discontent was a form of disobedience and that Osama bin Zayd was the best choice. "Carry out the expedition to the Syrian border," he ordered.

It is only after his reprimand that people hastened to the camp to join Osama's army. However, despite the Prophet's direct order to move towards Syria, the army remained camped on the outskirts of Medina. The refusal to follow a direct order of the Prophet was unprecedented. It was indicative of things to come, though, as the power struggle would unfold.

According to the Shia historians, there was more to the dissent than just the age or the race of the young Osama. Knowing that Muhammad's end was near, some of the companions were reluctant to leave Medina at such a critical time, fearful that, if they absented themselves, Ali ibn Abu Talib might become the uncontested successor to Muhammad. Shia scholars conclude that since Muhammad was aware he was about to die, he aimed at keeping Ali and his family in Medina, while keeping all others away from the city, so that Ali could establish himself as the Prophet's successor in a smooth transfer of power.

However, this does not explain why the Prophet would ask his father-in-law, Abu-Bakr, ultimately his successor, to lead the prayers in his absence. Speaking to the congregation, Muhammad said, "Look to these doors which open into the mosque, and close them all save those which lead to the house of Abu-Bakr, because I have known no better companion than he." He later asked Abu-Bakr to lead the prayers in his place, a task many saw as the Prophet's nod to Abu-Bakr being his successor.

Suffice to say that as his end neared, every decision Muhammad took, every word he spoke, was seen and interpreted in the context of his succession. Ali was his closest companion, and confidant, with whom he had the closest bond. Muhammad had described Ali in glowing terms. At one time he said, "I am the city of knowledge and Ali is the key to that city." Then, addressing pilgrims who were accompanying him back to Medina after his last hajj in Mecca, Muhammad told the congregation while he rested at a small lake called Ghadir-e-Khumm:* "O my people! Allah is my guardian (*Mawla*) and I am guardian of the faithful and I have superior right on and control over their lives. And this Ali is the guardian of all those for whom I am a guardian. O Allah! Love him who loves him and hate him who hates him."

These words of the Prophet have been invoked over centuries to validate the historical claims of the Shia over Sunnis and vice versa. Irrespective of their claims, the divide in Islam is over politics, not piety. The question that remains unanswered is why the Prophet did not clearly earmark his successor or the system that would determine the leadership of his community in the future. Or could we deduce from his silence that he foresaw the dissension and division that would tear apart Muslims and become their destiny through history, despite their immense contributions to human civilization. Perhaps the Prophet never wanted to see Islam rise as a political power, but as a movement of social justice and unadulterated monotheism for all of humanity, not just

---

* Most Sunni scholars contest the authenticity of the Prophet's speech at Ghadir-e-Khumm, which no longer exists.

Muslims. After all, the Quran describes God as *Rab ul alameen* (Lord of all humanity), not *Rab ul Muslimeen* (Lord of all Muslims). Among his last words recorded by chronicler Ibn Ishaq is the profound statement, "I have allowed only what the Quran allows and I have forbidden only what the Quran forbids." A profound statement that if taken to its logical extreme would nullify so much of the dogma that has turned Muslims into an ossified people unable to break out of the mythologies that encase them in a stranglehold.

What if Muhammad did want to dictate his last will and testimony, but was prevented from doing so during his illness? A credible account of just such an incident is recounted by the late French historian Maxime Rodinson, whose book *Muhammad* was described by the late literary critic Edward Said as "a major contemporary Occidental work on the Prophet, and is essential reading." Iranian dissident Ali Dashti too recounts this episode from Muhammad's last hours in his book *Twenty-Three Years*.

Here is how narrators have detailed the events of the day when Muhammad wanted to write or dictate his will, but was not allowed to. Ali Dashti writes:

> Later he awoke and, in evident awareness of death's approach, said to those around him, "Bring me an inkwell and the sheet, so that I may write something (or cause something to be written) for you. After that, you will not err in future." Regrettably, this last request of the prophet was not carried out. Those present were at first astonished, and then began arguing amongst themselves . . . Umar insisted against bringing the paper saying, "His fever is too severe. You have the Quran. God's book is sufficient for us."

Maxine Rodinson gives a slightly abridged account of what happened:

> After a time he [Muhammad] became delirious. He apparently asked materials to write a document, which should keep the faithful from error. Those present were much perplexed at this, wondering whether they ought to trust the abstractedness of a sick man. Supposing that the new text happened to contradict the Quran; surely it would sow the seeds of dissension and dismay? Ought they to obey him when he was not in his right mind? They argued so noisily that he gave up the idea and signed to them to go away.

In the account by Husayn Haykal, after Muhammad angrily asked the people to leave, his uncle al-Abbas felt concerned that the people would lose something important if they did not hasten to bring writing materials. However, Umar "held firmly to his judgment, which he based on God's own estimate of His Holy Book—in this scripture we have left nothing out."

Before long, Prophet Muhammad had passed away. (According to Aisha's version of events, Muhammad raised his eyes, stared at the ceiling, said a prayer, and then passed on forever.) As the wailing of the women reached a pitch, a crowd gathered outside the house and in the courtyard. Chroniclers say there was a sense of panic and fright among the people. Neither Muhammad nor his companions had ever suggested that the Prophet was immortal, but still Muslims found themselves in unchartered territory. Suddenly, the man who had pulled them out of their pagan past, made them reject all that they had treasured and thrust them into a position of strength against the then-superpowers of the world—Persia, Byzantium, Egypt, and Abyssinia—was no more. Who would lead them? What would become of them?

Frightened and in a state of shock, the people of the Oasis left their daily chores and rushed to the house of Muhammad. In this pandemonium, the man who had earlier stopped Muhammad from dictating his last will and testament was in a complete state of denial. Upon hearing the news and hardly believing it, Umar had returned quickly to the Prophet's quarters. There, he went straight to Muhammad's bed and looked at his face. While the women were wailing and beating their chests, Umar perceived the Prophet as being in a coma, from which he believed he would soon emerge. When a colleague tried to convince him of Muhammad's death, Umar said to him in anger, "You lie."

He then went to the mosque and started proclaiming at the top of his voice that Muhammad had absented himself but would return. He threatened to cut off the arms and legs of anyone who perpetuated false rumours of the Prophet's death.

At the mosque, the community was stupefied. They knew that the Prophet had died, but here was Umar, one of his closest companions, violently insisting otherwise. By now, Abu-Bakr had heard the news and had returned to Medina. He first went to see Muhammad, paid his respects to the departed Apostle, covered his face, and then entered the mosque where Umar was still speaking to the congregation. Abu-Bakr tried to calm Umar down.

After failing to persuade Umar to quieten, Abu-Bakr took the unusual step of standing up and motioning the people to walk away from Umar's tirade. He then spoke to the people and made a profound speech that made a clear distinction between God and his Messenger. Abu-Bakr reminded them that Muhammad had warned them repeatedly that they must not honour him in the same way as the Christians honoured Jesus. He was a mere mortal like themselves. "Oh men, if anyone worships Muhammad, Muhammad is dead. If anyone worships God, God is alive, immortal." He then quoted the words that had been revealed to Muhammad after the battle of Uhud (fought on March 22, 625 CE), when rumour had spread that the Prophet had been killed and panic ensued:

> Muhammad is only a messenger;
> and many a messenger has gone before him.
> So what if he dies or is killed!
> Will you turn your back and go away in haste?
> But he who turns back and goes away in haste
> will do no harm to God.
> But God will reward those
> who give thanks (and are grateful).

The audience listened in stunned silence. The stirring speech by Abu-Bakr and his recitation of the Quranic verse put an end to the histrionics of Umar, the chroniclers say. As he listened to Abu-Bakr, it finally dawned on Umar that the Prophet was gone forever, never to return. His knees buckled and the mighty warrior collapsed to the ground, fury making way for fear, a silence replacing the sermon. Order was restored. However, this chaotic incident, resulting from the histrionics of Umar, would pale in significance compared to what was to unfold in the coming hours and days.

The tussle that was about to unfold that fateful Monday in June 632 would cause such a serious wound to the Muslim psyche that even today it remains unhealed. The scars etched on the very consciousness of the Muslim soul are hidden only to those who willfully choose to deny the existence of such blemishes, and of course, the vast majority of the Ummah who are blissfully ignorant of the sad side of their heritage and thus refuse to or cannot learn the lessons. However, when these wounds do open up every few years, thousands die. In 2006 alone, more than thirty thousand Iraqis died as Sunni and Shia Arabs killed each other in a gory display of hatred that goes back to the power struggles that unfolded after the death of the Prophet of Islam.

The last prophecy of Muhammad—that "dissensions" would come like waves of darkness, one after the other and getting worse each time—was about to unfold.

As the people started to leave the mosque of Muhammad, the paths were separate. The men of Medina, known as the Ansar, including the tribes of Khazraj and Aws, headed towards the courtyard of the clan of Banu Saidah—the Saqifah—to gather around its ailing leader, Saad bin Ubadah, to plan and strategize the future leadership of the Muslim community and their own role in its future. The Meccans—the Quraysh—on the other hand gathered in and around Abu-Bakr's home with Umar taking the lead in asserting that only one of them—the Meccans—should succeed the Prophet.

Incredible as it may sound, lost in this politicking were the people closest to Muhammad, his family—the Banu Hashim clan. While the Quraysh of Mecca and the Ansar of Medina started their jostling for power, the family of Muhammad, with the Prophet's son-in-law Ali ibn Abu Talib as their leader, withdrew to his home to take care of the more mundane task of preparing for the burial of the Apostle. Led by Ali, this small group included Ibn al-Abbas*; the son of the Prophet's adopted son Osama; as well as a few trusted members of the Quraysh tribe, such as Zubayr and Talha.

There are fascinating, and at times, varying accounts of what transpired that day, but one thing is clear: the debate between the leaders of the Meccans and the tribal chiefs of Medina was acrimonious and went late into the night. Sadly, God's Messenger was the last thing on the minds of his followers. In the disturbing words of historian Maxime Rodinson, "as night fell, everyone had forgotten the body still lying in Aisha's little hut."

One member of Muhammad's family was to suffer particularly great hardship: in the days after losing her father, Fatima would also lose the property her father had left for her as an inheritance, and later her husband Ali would be murdered, her older son Hassan poisoned, and, in the great tragedy that hangs over all Islamic history, Fatima's younger son Hussain would be beheaded and others of her family massacred by fellow Muslims. To this day millions of Muslims mourn the tragedies that befell the daughter of the Prophet, and while so many mutter endless platitudes about the equality bestowed on women by Islam, they cannot explain how the one woman who deserved justice was denied. Fatima was the Muslim Joan of Arc and she was left to burn on the stake as men squabbled with each other for the power they still seek, and which eludes them like a desert mirage.

Fatima's shadow looms over us Muslims, not letting us escape the transgressions our ancestors committed. Not until Muslims acknowledge and accept responsibility, not until they face the truth and shed hypocrisy,

---

* Ibn al-Abbas' descendants would go on to form the Abbasid dynasty, which would rule the empire from 750 until the Mongol invasion of 1258.

will they be able to face themselves in the mirror every morning. How could we have done what we did to the family of the Prophet? We claim to adore him, yet we refuse to accept the grave injustice committed against the person he loved most—his daughter.

If there is a trait that has defined Muslim behaviour when it comes to seeking power, it was set into motion in the burning sands surrounding the oasis of Medina the day the Apostle died. It is indeed a miracle that Muslims came out of that fateful power struggle as a community and survived as a force to reckon with.

The tribal chiefs of Medina collected under tents in the courtyard of Saad bin Ubadah (better known today as the Saqifah Banu Saidah) to decide on the future of the Muslims and who should exercise authority over the community. There was widespread agreement among them that the successor to Muhammad must be from the Ansar, the tribe of Medina who had offered sanctuary to the Apostle when his enemies wanted to kill him. The Medina Arabs also formed the overwhelming majority of the Muslim community and as such they felt it was their right to govern, now that the Prophet had died.

The Medinian deliberations were not held in secret. Soon word got out to the Meccan immigrants who were assembled in Abu-Bakr's home. Umar realized that if the Quraysh of Mecca did not make a move quickly, the game was over for them. He urged Abu-Bakr to go with him to the Saqifah and confront the machinations of the tribal chiefs of Medina. Abu-Bakr, who had just averted a serious conflict inside the Prophet's mosque, agreed, and the two of them, along with their followers hurried to where the Medina meeting was taking place. An unanswered question remains: why did Umar and Abu-Bakr not take other Meccan companions of the Prophet with them to the meeting of the Medina Arabs? After all, Ali, Uthman, Talha, Zubayr, Saad bin Abu Waqqas—all very prominent members of the Meccan faction—were close by.

As they entered the hall, they heard the ailing leader of the group, Saad bin Ubadah,* urging the people of Medina to lay claim to the leadership of the Muslims. "Strengthen your hold on this affair, for you have the rightful claim to it . . ."

Another man from Medina, seeing Umar and Abu-Bakr entering the tent, stood up and addressed them: "We are the Ansar, the Helpers of God and the army of Islam. You, the Emigrants [from Mecca] are only a brigade in

---

* Saad bin Ubadah: One of the Prophet's closest companions, and the first Muslim in Medina. It was Saad who had prepared the arrangements for the Prophet to escape to Medina.

the army. Nonetheless, a group of you have gone to the extreme of seeking to deprive us of our natural leadership and to deny our rights."

The speaker continued to glorify the people of Medina, while paying polite tribute to his guests, the Quraysh of Mecca. The speeches enraged Umar. It is reported that he was "ready to put an end to this situation once and for all by the sword." Once more the cool head of Abu-Bakr prevailed as he restrained Umar and stood up to address the gathering.

In a stunning invocation of tribal primacy and the nobility of family lineage that went contrary to the Quran as well as the Prophet's last speech, Abu-Bakr argued that the next leader of the Muslims should come from the Quraysh tribe of Mecca. He said they were the first to embrace Islam, and because of their noble lineage among the Arabs, deserved to succeed Muhammad. He told the people of Medina gathered in the courtyard: "The Muhajirun (Meccan Arabs) are the first people on earth to worship God truly, and the first to accept faith in God and His Messenger. . . . No man would dispute their right except a wrongdoer. We are therefore the chiefs (Umara) and you (the people of Medina) are the subordinates (Wuzura)."

Abu-Bakr went further, telling the gathering: "The Arabs do not and will not recognize any sovereignty unless it belongs to the tribe of Quraysh. The princes shall be from among us, whereas your group (people of Medina) will furnish the viziers."

The historian Tabari has a slightly different rendering of Abu-Bakr's speech from that above, but in that version too, it is clear that Abu-Bakr was clearly pointing out to the supposedly divinely ordained superiority of the Meccan Quraysh Arab tribe over all other Muslims, including the Medinans. Abu-Bakr extolled the virtues of the Arabs of Medina, but emphasized to his hosts that despite their high status, they should recognize the Meccan Arabs as the "leaders" and consider themselves as no more than the "helpers." He then warned them that "only a wrongdoer would dispute" what he had said.

As the discussion heated up, the claim of racial superiority of the Meccan Arabs angered the audience. One of them, a veteran of many battles, stood up and proposed a dramatic new solution: shared sovereignty. The men of Medina pursued their proposal of a dual succession to Prophet Muhammad, while rejecting the notion of Meccan tribal superiority.

Umar rejected the idea of two concurrent successors, insisting that since Prophet Muhammad was from the tribe of the Quraysh, only they had the right to succeed him. He said: "Alas no two men can hold equal power together by God. The Arabs would never agree to such an authority over them when the Prophet is of another people. But they would not refuse to delegate the management of their affairs to those among whom prophethood appears, that is the Quraysh."

The back-and-forth arguments continued with both parties refusing to give in. What is remarkable about the episode is that none of the chroniclers mention any side invoking the Quran as a guiding principle to settle the dispute. After all, the Quran states quite explicitly (chapter 49, verse 13) the equality of all humans: "O mankind! We created you from a single (pair) of a male and a female, and made you into nations and tribes, that ye may know each other (not that ye may despise each other). Verily the most honoured of you in the sight of Allah is (he who is) the most righteous of you. And Allah has full knowledge and is well acquainted (with all things)."

One fear that the people of Medina voiced, that a man from neither camp might seize office, came to fruition within forty years when Caliph Muawiyah* usurped power and founded the first Muslim dynasty—the Umayyads. During his life, the Prophet had preached about the essence of humanity, the equality of all people, irrespective of their racial and tribal origin, but as the sun set on Medina that evening, no one was asking the question, What would Prophet Muhammad have done?

Seeing no solution in sight as the night wore on, Abu-Bakr changed the subject and reminded the people of Medina of their own rivalries. In a brilliant tactic, Abu-Bakr tried to pit the two tribes of Medina—the Khazraj and the Aws—against each other. He posed the hypothetical question: "If the men of Khazraj were to show their ambitions concerning this affair, the men of the Aws would not fall behind. Likewise, were the men of the Aws to seek it, those of the Khazraj would surely do the same. There are, moreover, between these two tribes, deaths and injuries that can never be healed. If therefore any man of either of you were to bellow out his claim to this office, he would place himself between the two jaws of a lion: to be chewed up by his Quraysh opponent or wounded by his rival of the Ansar."

The tactic worked. The two tribes of Medina that had been brought together as one by Muhammad's message of Islam were that night again divided among themselves, debating who among them deserved to rule, if not the Meccan Quraysh. This would not be the first time the policy of divide and rule would succeed, and it would not be the last time it would be used. As the solidarity of the men of Medina crumbled, Abu-Bakr, sensing victory, held up the hands of Umar and another Meccan, Abu Ubaydah bin Jarrah. "Either one of these two men of the Quraysh is acceptable to us as leader of the Muslim community," he said. "Choose whomsoever you please."

---

* Muawiyah: Founded the Umayyad dynasty of Islam after defeating caliph Hassan, who had succeeded his father Ali, the fourth caliph.

Amid the confusion and bickering, a prominent notable of the Aws tribe of Medina broke ranks and walked over to Abu-Bakr. Soon more followed, and in the mayhem, Umar took his sword in one hand and raising the hand of Abu-Bakr in the other, he declared: "O Abu-Bakr, stretch forth your hand and I will give you my oath of fealty. Did not the Prophet himself command you to lead the Muslims in prayer? You, therefore, are his successor. We elect you to this position."

The men of Medina were soon rushing to pledge their allegiance to Abu-Bakr, lest their loyalties be questioned later. The ageing leader of the two tribes of Medina, Saad bin Ubadah, in whose courtyard this drama was unfolding, is said to have found himself nearly trampled by his own followers as he fell over from his bed to the floor. This was the man who had introduced Islam to the people of Medina. One historian reports Umar cursing the old man, "Kill Sa'ad, may God kill Sa'ad." Umar then stepped on Saad bin Ubadah's head, saying, "I intend to tread on you until your head is dislocated." At this, Saad bin Ubadah grabbed Umar's beard, and said, "By God, if you remove a single hair from it, you'll return with no front teeth in your mouth." Abu-Bakr intervened and urged Umar to relent and not harm Saad. The leader of the Medina Arabs was carried away to his home, where he stayed for many days, deeply disillusioned at the turn of events and the way he had been mistreated. For days, he was pressured to give his oath of allegiance to Abu-Bakr, but like Ali ibn Abu Talib, Saad bin Ubadah refused to do so.

It must have been heartbreaking for Saad to be treated with such disrespect and ingratitude. As he lay on the floor, he must have remembered the endless days of torture he had to undergo in the prison of the Meccan pagans who had captured him and wanted to extract from him information about who else was aiding Muhammad in Medina. At that time, the Prophet and his handful of followers lived isolated on a street of Mecca, boycotted by the city's Quraysh Arab tribe and Saad and his group were secretly arranging to smuggle out the Apostle to safety in Medina.

Liyakat Takim, professor of Islamic Studies at the University of Denver, in his book *The Heirs of the Prophet*, suggests that during the debate on the succession of the Prophet, his companions reverted to practices that had been current among pagan Arab tribes before the advent of Islam. He writes: "Pre-Islamic mode of authority surfaced immediately after Muhammad's death when some of his followers invoked an erstwhile tribal procedure for the selection of a chief. The convening of the tribal council and the selection of Abu-Bakr as the first caliph to succeed the Prophet was incipience of the routinization of charisma. At the same time, it was the first manifestation of the re-emergence of the pre-Islamic polity."

Takim, a Canadian of Tanzanian descent, believes that the re-emergence of pagan Arab tribal norms continued after Abu-Bakr became the first successor to Muhammad. During Umar's caliphate, for example, "Islam came to be identified with the Arabs. He tried to keep non-Arab Muslims out of Arabia, especially from Medina."

While the scramble for power and resulting ascension of Abu-Bakr took place, the family of the Prophet was closeted inside his home, cut off from the power brokering at Saqifah. But at Saqifah, the gathering scattered in despair. Some men swore allegiance to Abu-Bakr, while others just walked away in disillusionment. At his public ceremony in the Prophet's Mosque in Medina, Abu-Bakr gave a stirring speech, saying:

> I am appointed to govern you, although I'm not the best of you. If I act well, you must take me, and if I act unjustly, you must correct me. Truth is faithfulness and falsehood is treachery. No nation has failed to fight for Allah, Allah has punished it with abasement; nor has wickedness become widespread without ever sending calamity. Obey me as long as I obey Allah and his Prophet. But should I rebel against Allah, and his Prophet you will owe me no obedience. Rise to your prayers and may Allah have mercy on you.

While Muslims would like to believe that the ascension of Abu-Bakr was the result of an election that came about after vigorous debate and consultations, the fact is that not a single member of the Prophet's family, the Banu Hashim clan, was consulted. Nor was there any input from the tens of thousand of Muslims who lived in Mecca, or the Bedouin tribes in the desert hinterland. Needless to say, not a single woman, not even the wives or the daughter of the Prophet, had any say in the question of who was now to lead the Muslims. By declaring that only Arabs belonging to the Meccan Quraysh tribe could fill the seat of the caliph, Abu-Bakr set the seal of authority on the theory of tribal and racial supremacy of the Arab over the non-Arab for many centuries to come.

It was not until nearly four hundred years later that Abu-Bakr's namesake, a jurist by the name of Qadi Abu-Bakr Baqillani (d. 1013), would declare that belonging to the Quraysh tribe was not a prerequisite to becoming the caliph. Another four hundred years would pass before the great Ibn Khaldun would demolish the idea of Arab ancestry and tribal lineage to the Quraysh as a prerequisite for occupying the seat of the caliph. For eight hundred years after the Prophet died, only the sons of one Arab tribe dominated, while all other Muslims, especially non-Arabs, were considered second class.

Despite the fact that there is ample historical evidence about the doctrine used to keep non-Arabs out of power for centuries, most Arab commentators and Islamic historians are oblivious of the impact of this ruling by Abu-Bakr. Of course, the Shia also dispute the validity of Abu-Bakr's ascension, but their theory of succession is even narrower and more restricted than that of the Sunni. The Shia also believe that only a person of Arab descent can claim leadership of the Muslim community, the person they refer to as their imam. However, in their doctrine, this Arab cannot be just any Arab, but must prove to be a direct descendant of the Prophet's family from his daughter Fatima. Is it any surprise the Supreme Leaders of Iran have all been men claiming to have Arab ancestry, not Persian?

Complete denial over the events that led to the nomination of Abu-Bakr as caliph is so pervasive that schoolbooks and even college history books state as fact that Abu-Bakr was unanimously elected by the Muslim community. The belief that Quraysh Arabs are superior is hardly ever challenged.

One example of how the theory of Arab Quraysh superiority is maintained even today can be found in the booklet *Islam and the Race Question*. This publication, authorized by UNESCO, was written in 1970 by Abdul Aziz Kamil, the then-Egyptian minister of religious and charitable institutions. On the qualities required for a Muslim to be a candidate for the position of caliph, Kamil writes:

> Islamic scholars have discussed the qualities required in a caliph who would govern the affairs of Moslems. They were: learning, justice, competence, and sound sense and organs—since these affect both a man's judgment and his actions; opinions differed, however, regarding the fifth condition, which was that he had to be related to the tribe of Quraysh. The last condition rested on a *unanimous agreement* [emphasis mine] reached by the Companions at a meeting which took place on the day following the Prophet's death.

Kamil accepts uncritically the myth that Abu-Bakr was elected, and that the election was unanimous. He also manages to get UNESCO to validate the myth. He fails to mention that Muhammad had never set a condition that Muslim leaders should be from the Quraysh. Kamil does not acknowledge that this condition was contrary to the Quran's teachings on equality before God, and thus could not be valid as practice within Islam.

⌘

After Abu-Bakr assumed power, tension between the Ansar of Medina and the Quraysh of Mecca showed signs of subsiding. (Many of the Ansar had given allegiance, with only the ailing Saad bin Ubadah refusing to acknowledge Abu-Bakr's caliphate.) However, in the home of the Prophet, resentment simmered among the Banu Hashim, who sat grieving around his body. Snubbed by the rest of the Quraysh, seething with anger, they took an unprecedented step: they buried the body of Muhammad right within his own house. They allowed no one else to attend the funeral. Maxime Rodinson writes: "Ali, Abbas, and their friends seem to have been anxious to avoid such a ceremony in which Abu-Bakr, leading the funeral procession would appear as the Prophet's appointed successor." It had been expected that the Prophet would be buried at the Baqi cemetery, alongside his son Ibrahim, his daughter Ruqqaiya, and many of his companions. Even Aisha, dearly loved by Muhammad, who was the daughter of Abu-Bakr, is said to have learned of the preparations only when she heard Ali and his Uncle Abbas digging the grave in the middle of the night.

The dispute over succession had been resolved between the Ansar and the Quraysh. However, Muhammad's son-in-law, Ali, disputed the legitimacy of Abu-Bakr as the successor of Muhammad for many months. He and Fatima withdrew themselves from the public arena, not opposing Abu-Bakr, but more significantly refusing to give their allegiance to the new caliph. It was not as if Ali had not made attempts to challenge the authority of Abu-Bakr. On the Tuesday night after burying Muhammad, Ali along with Fatima is reported to have approached the tribal leaders of Medina, seeking their support in his dispute with Abu-Bakr. The men of Medina, having already tasted a meltdown on their own turf, did not wish to prolong the crisis tearing at the heart of the young Muslim nation. They told Ali that had he come to the Saqifah before Abu-Bakr and Umar came, the Ansar would certainly have pledged allegiance to him.

Ali's response reflected his frustration with the entire political process. He argued, "Should I have left the Messenger of God in his house unburied and gone to quarrel with men over his authority?" Fatima, in equal distress, added, "Abu al-Hasan [Ali] did only what he should have done. But God will bring them [that is Abu-Bakr and Umar] to account for what they did."

Having failed to win the support of the Medinian leaders, Ali and the rest of Muhammad's family went back to Fatima's house. The next day Umar and a group of Meccans surrounded the house and threatened to set it on fire if the people inside did not come out and pledge allegiance to Abu-Bakr.

There are various versions of what happened next. In one, Umar at some stage went in and brought out Ali by force. Defiant in spirit, Ali refused to be cowed, asking Umar, "What if I do not give allegiance?" To which Umar replied, "We would cut off your head." Ali retorted, "You would then have killed the brother of the Messenger of God."

Umar's response, if correctly reported, must have devastated Ali. "That you are the servant of God, yes we agree, but that you are brother of the Messenger of God, no, we do not," said Umar. Ali must have been enraged, but is said to have turned the other cheek and demonstrated a calmness that later became his defining trait.

In another, more tragic, version of the events at Fatima and Ali's home—a version that is dismissed by Sunni Muslims as untrue—when Ali refused to come out of the house, Umar ibn al-Khattab and his men broke down the door, throwing Fatima to the floor. Abi'l-Hasan Ali Bin Husain Masudi, as quoted in the book *Peshawar Nights*, says that Fatima, who was pregnant at the time, was so severely crushed behind the door that she had a miscarriage.

A few days later, Umar's men again came to Ali's house. This time they detained and dragged Ali before Abu-Bakr, where he again refused to submit to the new caliph.

It would take six more months and the death of his beloved wife, Fatima, before Ali would succumb to pressure and give his allegiance to Abu-Bakr. He was being treated as a social outcast and without Fatima, he was a very lonely man.

Fatima had died a heartbroken and deeply disillusioned woman. The daughter of the Prophet never spoke to Abu-Bakr after he took away her father's inheritance, the garden of Fadak. She never forgave Abu-Bakr for what she thought was rightfully hers, bequeathed to her during the Prophet's lifetime. When Ali and Fatima went to Abu-Bakr to demand that he return the garden of Fadak to its rightful owner, Abu-Bakr told the young couple, "I did hear the Messenger of God say, 'We prophets do not give any inheritance. Anything we leave behind must remain as public charity.'"

Fatima must have been dumbfounded. Neither Ali nor Fatima, the closest to the Prophet, had ever heard the Prophet say what Abu-Bakr was suggesting he had heard the Prophet say.

The disinheritance of the daughter of the Prophet of Islam would set the precedent of treating women as second-class Muslims. The trend towards full gender equality that Muhammad had initiated was halted soon after his death. If the daughter of the Prophet of Islam could be deprived of her inheritance, what are the chances of the millions of daughters who are denied their just inheritances to this day by families invoking Islamic laws? If Fatima could be cheated and humiliated, is it any wonder that Muslim women in the 21st century find their path to respect and dignity strewn with obstacles justified by religious laws? We treat these laws as if they came from the Quran itself, when in fact they were created centuries after the death of the Prophet.

True to their nature, Ali and Fatima walked away from this encounter in a mood of resigned disappointment. Fatima never forgave Abu-Bakr. Even though Ali had given up his claim to the leadership of the Muslim community, and yielded to Abu-Bakr, he remained bitter about the injustices he and Fatima had suffered. The historian Masudi reports Ali telling Abu-Bakr in one exchange, "You have defrauded us of our right and did not heed it."

There is much to be said in defence of Abu-Bakr. The embryonic community of Muslims was vulnerable, and he restrained the more aggressive Umar, intervening on the side of caution, bringing calm to dangerous and explosive situations. During the two years Abu-Bakr served as caliph, he was forced to put down scores of revolts. Despite the criticism that has been levelled against him, it is clear that during his reign he demonstrated extremely high standards of character and personal integrity. He did not seek personal wealth. He consulted his followers before making decisions—not only the ruling elite, but also the common people and the poor. For that era in history, it was a remarkable time of democratic rule.

Even in the matter of Ali and Fatima, there is evidence that Abu-Bakr was cognizant of the hurt he had caused and genuinely regretted the turn of events. Historian Tabari quotes Abu-Bakr as saying to one of his companions on the eve of his reign: "I wish I had not searched the house of Fatima, daughter of the Messenger of God, or allowed men to enter it, even if it was shut for the purpose of inciting war . . . I wish I had asked the Messenger of God who should take care of this charge after him."

Was there a reason for Muhammad's silence on the issue of who would hold power after his death? Could it be that the Prophet wanted no one to succeed him? The final revelation of the Quran, the last words he received from God, had been a specific instruction to Muhammad and the Muslims: "Today I have completed your religion for you." Nowhere in the Quran does God suggest that an Islamic government be set up after Muhammad's death. Nowhere does Muhammad, in all of the hadith, or his collected sayings, speak of an Islamic State.

Eventually the dust settled in the succession struggles, but they would resurface repeatedly. This first encounter left a mark on the politics of the Arabs forever. Tribalism and racial identities of the pre-Islamic times triumphed over principles of meritocracy and universalism preached by Muhammad and as ordained by the Quran. Once it was settled that Quraysh Arabs deserved to rule over the Ansar Arabs because of the former's nobility and tribal superiority, there was no stopping the argument that the Arabs were superior to the Persians, the Africans, and the Indians. The pre-Islamic traditions of Arab tribalism and family lineage to this day affect Arab attitudes of superiority towards each other and, of course, their non-Arab co-religionists.

The Iranian scholar Ali Dashti writes that before the advent of Islam, the Arabs used to boast about the superiority of the tribe, clan, or genealogy over those of others. Their claims to superiority were not based on virtues and graces, but on prowess in killing, plundering, and abducting other men's women. The teachings of Islam negated this concept and made piety the measure of a person's merit. Unfortunately, the new standard was not long maintained in practice—to be precise, until 644, with the death of Umar, who became second caliph of Islam after Abu-Bakr named him as his successor. During the reign of the third caliph, Uthman,* nepotism prevailed over piety. Devout men such as Abu Dharr Ghaffari† were thrust aside, and members of the caliph's clan, such as Muawiyah, were appointed to governorships. Later, under the Umayyad dynasty (661–750), the great Islamic principle of nobility through piety was simply ignored. Tribal pride was still of supreme importance, but now the setting was broader. Men from the barren deserts of Arabia had conquered vast territories. According to Dashti, "The conquest . . . intoxicated the Arabs with pride." It seemed clear to them that they were superior and the conquered nations were inferior. Dashti writes that the Umayyads despised the non-Arabs under their rule and even those who converted to Islam did not enjoy the equality of rights enshrined in Islamic law.

Muslims around the world are told incessantly by Islamists that they need to look back to the era of the first four caliphs of Islam as the model for their political aspirations for the future. However, submitted to even a cursory scrutiny, the era reveals an incompatibility with the standards of today's secular democratic civil societies, where citizenship is based on human created laws, not divine texts and specific race, religion, tribe, or clan. Yet clerics feed this myth and make millions of young Muslims chase the mirage our ancestors have been pursuing for a millennium without success.

In the 21st century, we Muslims have a choice. Either we can emulate the great Muslim scientists and philosophers, such as Averroes and Kindi, Avicenna and Khaldun, or we can follow the orthodoxy that labelled these giants as apostates. In making that choice, we need to be aware that we sacrifice the state of Islam when we chase the elusive mirage of an Islamic State.

---

* Uthman: The third caliph of Islam, selected by a council of six peers named by Umar, who was murdered.
† Abu Dharr Ghaffari: A companion of the Prophet, better known for his advocacy of the poor and sometimes referred to as the first Muslim socialist.

CHAPTER 7

Medina—The Politics of the Rightly Guided Caliphs

ISLAMISTS—MUSLIMS WHO BELIEVE in Islam as a political creed, not just a religion—are unanimous in their conviction that the way Muslims governed themselves during the reign of the first four caliphs of Islam provides a clear model, if not a blueprint, for a 21st-century Islamic State.

Sunni Muslims consider this period of about thirty years as the only time when Islam was ever fully established as ordained by the Quran and in accordance with the teachings of the Prophet. Some refer to it as the Golden Age of Islam. Historians refer to the first four caliphs who succeeded Muhammad—Abu-Bakr (d. 634), Umar (d. 644), Uthman (d. 656), and Ali (d. 661)—as the Rightly Guided Caliphs (*Khulafah al-rashidun*). Sunni Muslims hold all four in the highest esteem, but Shia Muslims consider the first three as essentially usurpers of the caliphate. They believe that Ali, who eventually became the fourth caliph, should have been chosen to lead the Muslim community immediately after the death of Muhammad.

Abul Ala Maudoodi, one of the leading ideologues of the world Islamist movement, writes: "The period of the 'Right-going' Caliphate . . . was a luminous tower towards which the learned and the pious of all succeeding ages have been looking back as symbolic of the religious, moral, political, and social orders of Islam *par excellence.*"

Jamal Badawi, a leading Canadian Islamist who sits on the boards of a number of Muslim organizations that support the concept of introducing sharia law in Canada, also states that the period of the first four caliphs was the model for all times. Writing for the *IslamOnLine.com* web magazine, Badawi says: "Unfortunately, the complete and perfect model of an Islamic political system does not exist today. But this does not mean that it is a utopian system that exists only in theory. It existed in a complete and perfect form during the lifetime of Prophet Muhammad (peace be upon him), and during the reign of the first four Rightly Guided Caliphs."

Despite the turmoil and tragedy of the power struggle that followed the death of Muhammad, it is clear that a change had occurred which was remarkable for that time and place in history. Instead of power automatically moving to the next of kin or immediate family, some degree of discussion and debate took place and power was passed to a person outside the Prophet's bloodline. The Meccan Arabs invoked tribal supremacy over the Medina Arabs at the outset, but all four Rightly Guided Caliphs rejected hereditary succession. Even though Ali laid claim to succession as his right, being the cousin of the Prophet, he demonstrated statesman-like leadership, working closely with the three men who were chosen to be caliph before him. Even on his deathbed, he refused to name his son Hassan as his successor.

There is much for Muslims to be proud of in that the first and second caliphs, Abu-Bakr and Umar, ruled the fledgling community of Muslims with impeccable character, integrity, and transparency. Even today, they are held as role models for Muslims in their personal behaviour, humility, and commitment to social justice. The nepotism and vanity that would characterize subsequent Muslim rule could be contrasted with the frugality and aversion to wealth of these two companions of Muhammad, also known as the "two elders" (*shaykhayn*).

Like the Prophet, they did not govern with a political model of process and statehood, nor did they leave such a model when they died. They relied on arbitrary decisions, replicating the tribal customs that had governed Arab society for ages. Their reigns were marked by rebellion and conflict, yet they succeeded in consolidating the community and rule over Arabia from Medina.

Abu-Bakr and Umar were followed by Uthman and Ali, whose mutual distrust led to much bloodshed and caused permanent fissures in the community. For centuries, those wounds have remained unhealed and unattended, becoming permanent sores on the Muslim body, festering wounds that continue to bleed, sapping the strength of a people trapped in the past.

We Muslims may consider the Rightly Guided Caliphs as symbols of piety and impeccable character, and want all of humanity to emulate their humility and transparency. But the political processes they adopted cannot be seen as the prototype for today's Muslims to follow. Muslims can ill afford to look back at that time to map out their political future in the 21st century. This is not simply a question of comparing the 7th century with the 21st, or pitting pre-medieval Arabia versus post-industrial West. It is putting the three-decade period of the four caliphs under scrutiny and asking questions that need to be raised.

Did the political process that was adopted to choose a successor to Muhammad reflect his teachings and the Quran? Can the political system of the first four caliphs be taken as a panacea for the ills of today's Muslims?

In raising these issues, my intention is not to show disrespect towards these companions of the Prophet, but to demonstrate that they were mere mortals, rising to the challenges of their time, facing the uncertainties resulting from the loss of the Prophet, who left no direction to them as to how power should be transferred after his death. Their piety as Muslims was beyond reproach, but their quest for power and their reliance on tribal and family lineage to acquire and retain control was not aligned or empathetic with the message of universality and equality that is promulgated in the Quran, according to my understanding.

Muslims have a right to ask why they should have any obligation to adopt, as an article of faith, the political structures and institutions created *after* the death of Muhammad. After all, God makes it clear in his last revelation to Muhammad that "Today I have completed your faith for you." A system devised by mere mortals (even though they were the companions of the Prophet), and one that failed to last beyond three decades and that created permanent divisions in the global Muslim community, should never be presented as the cornerstone of Islam. In fact, every single Muslim dynasty in 1,400 years since the death of Ali has rejected the political processes adopted by the Rightly Guided Caliphs.

In the past century, especially since the Second World War, dramatic changes have come about in how the world views racial and religious exclusivity. The equality of citizenship, irrespective of race and religion, is being embraced by societies as varied as India and Canada, making the notion of adopting the blueprint of the Rightly Guided Caliphs as an alternative to secular democracy simply untenable. The fact that secular democratic societies like India and Canada take away the power of the clergy to determine public policy is a frightening thought for Islamists and their radical jihadi allies. This explains the resurgence of propaganda and cult-like following for radical organizations such as the Hezb-al-Tahreer, the Ikhwan, and the Jamaat-e-Islami, and their followers in the United States and Canada.

While the rest of the world has been confronting issues of race and racism, the political leaders and intelligentsia of the Muslim world have failed to do so. What began as the superiority of the Meccan Arab over the Medinan Arab has evolved into systemic racism against the Black African, the Persian, and the Indian. Even in the 1700s, when the Ottoman, Moghul, and Safavid empires in the Muslim world wielded power, Muslims found little fault in systemic racism. Earlier Islamic dynasties were complicit in the slave trade, with no less an Islamic scholar and historian than Ibn Khaldun writing in 1377 that "the Negro nations are, as a rule, submissive to slavery, because (Negroes) have little that is (essentially) human and possess attributes that are quite similar to those of dumb animals."

This attitude about "Negro nations" espoused by one of the greatest Muslim scholars did not arise in isolation. It is the direct result of revisionism of the meaning of the Quran that introduced a hierarchy among Muslims of different races. Today, when the *Janjaweed** militia hunt down and massacre Darfuri Muslims in Sudan, their action stems from centuries of ingrained belief in the racial and tribal superiority of the Arab over the darker Black African.

When ideologue Abul Ala Maudoodi writes in glowing terms about the time of the first four Muslim caliphs, many Muslims disagree with his proposition—not out of disrespect for the Prophet's companions, but simply as an assertion that there can be no place in civic society for systemic discrimination based on race and religion.

Ibn Khaldun's comparison of Black Africans to "dumb animals" was similar to the reaction of Arabs in the Iraqi province of Kufa during the reign of Umar. The caliph appointed Ammar bin Yasir as governor of the newly conquered province, but was compelled to withdraw the appointment because Yasir was Black and the people would not tolerate being governed by a man they referred to as "slave with a mutilated ear." Could the residents of Kufa be blamed for their racism when race, family, and tribal lineage had already been invoked to justify denying the caliphate to the Medinan Saad

---

* *Janjaweed*: A blanket term used to describe mostly militiamen who are primarily members of nomadic "Arab" tribes fighting Darfur's settled "African" farmers, who are darker-skinned. Despite the Arab origin, the term *Janjaweed* is derived from the Persian word, jang, "war," and jangawee, "warrior," but has a connotation of "a devil on a horse."

bin Ubadah?* Once the Quraysh Arabs were defined as the chosen people, the slippery slope of racism led Muslims to its logical extreme—racism directed against African Blacks.

ABU-BAKR AL-SIDDIK—THE CALIPH OF THE MESSENGER OF ALLAH

Muhammad was the Messenger of God, the Apostle of Allah. However, what title would befit his successor, his father-in-law, Abu-Bakr Al-Siddik, who had taken over the reins of power? He was the caliph in that he was a vice-regent or deputy, but was he the "Caliph of God" or the "Caliph of the Apostle of God"? The distinction between the two titles may seem trivial, but the choice made by Abu-Bakr is profound and significant in our understanding of the nature of his rule.

Some of his supporters felt that he should refer to himself as the Caliph of God. They felt the caliphate of Abu-Bakr was a continuation of the Prophet's mission and, as such, he was the Caliph of God.

To this day, many Muslims continue to misunderstand the position of Abu-Bakr in Islamic history and assign near divinity to him. To his credit, Abu-Bakr rejected the title and said, "I am not the caliph of God, but the Caliph of the Apostle of God." However, his acceptance of the fact that he was merely vice-regent of the Prophet, not acting as a representative of God, did not stop some of his followers showing him the same kind of reverence and obedience that they had shown to the Prophet Muhammad. Abu-Bakr in his speech to Muslims after taking command as the caliph had said, "O People, I have been given authority over you; yet, I am not the best of you. If I do good, assist me, but if I err, then you must set me straight."

Having said that, he did not hesitate in ordering the Arab tribes in the hinterland of Arabia to submit to his rule or face him in battle. And many a battle he had to fight, as large numbers of Arabs refused to accept his authority. While some Arab tribes reneged on their acceptance of Islam, others switched loyalties to men who claimed to be new prophets.

Thus, any critique of Abu-Bakr's decisions as a caliph is considered an act of blasphemy worthy of the death penalty. It was for this reason that any refusal to submit to Abu-Bakr was seen as a rejection of Islam itself.

---

* The Night of Saqifah mentioned in chapter 6.

This led to what Muslim historians and theologians refer to as the Apostasy or *Ridda* Wars* against those who were accused of abandoning their faith in Islam. Ostensibly, these wars were fought to confront those who had forsaken Islam, but the facts indicate otherwise. There is no doubt that many Arab tribes reneged on their pacts with Muhammad and were ready to abandon the faith. But there is evidence that others did not go against Islam, but simply refused to give their oath of allegiance to Abu-Bakr. The latter, while staying within the Islamic fold, disputed the process by which Abu-Bakr had taken command. They rejected the notion that only the Arabs of Mecca had the right to be leaders of the Muslims.

Others believed that the rightful successor of Muhammad was not Abu-Bakr, but Muhammad's cousin and son-in-law, Ali. They felt that since they had not been consulted and were not involved in the decision reached at Saqifah, they were under no obligation to accept the new caliph's authority. These Arab tribes also claimed they found nothing in the Quran or the sayings of the Prophet that would give legitimacy to the establishment of the new caliphate.

Some tribes refused to pay their annual charity, *zakat,* to the tax collectors sent by the caliphate. They maintained that in their understanding of Islam, the alms tax was an individual's act of charity to the poor and needy, not a money grab by Abu-Bakr's tax collectors. Notwithstanding the fact that many of these tribes remained faithful to Islam, they were bracketed alongside those who had actually abandoned their faith and were unfairly declared apostates, deserving of the severest punishment—death by beheading—a practice that has broad acceptance among Islamists even today.

To this day, all five major schools of Islamic jurisprudence agree that a Muslim who abandons Islam must be executed. This despite the fact the Quran does not sanction the death penalty upon Muslims who abandon Islam. The Quran states that God despises apostasy, but the apostate is threatened with punishment in the next world only. Yet scores of Abu-Bakr's opponents were put to death during these early conflicts, and Islamic scholars have used these killings as a precedent to justify the death penalty against any Muslim found guilty of apostasy.

The Apostasy or Ridda Wars were primarily about politics, not religion. They were conducted to ward off the danger of the first Arab state disintegrating. There is no doubt that had Abu-Bakr not taken swift action to put down the many rebellions and those who refused to submit and pay

---

* *Ridda* means secession; commonly defined as the rejection of Islam in word or deed by a person who has been a Muslim.

allegiance to him, the new state would have crumbled. Central Arabia was in the hands of Musaylima, a tribal chieftain and self-proclaimed prophet. Other tribes in Oman, Yemen, Bahrain, and Mahra remained Muslim but broke ties with Abu-Bakr.

In terms of practical politics, Abu-Bakr had no alternative. Any ruler of a fledgling state would have followed similar policies. But his actions were not derived from Quranic principles. The Quran explicitly rules out the use of force to compel people to accept Islam: "There is no compulsion and coercion in matters of religion." If refusal to offer allegiance was a punishable crime, then many companions of the Prophet were equally guilty of the same. Saad bin Ubadah and Ali were the most prominent among the dissidents, yet their punishment was a social boycott, not death. Both faced violence and threats, but were not harmed physically. Abu-Bakr's lieutenant Umar surrounded Ali's house and threatened to burn it down, for example.

Ali lived to tell the truth. Others in the hinterland were less fortunate. One incident recorded by most historians is the confrontation between Abu-Bakr's general, Khaled ibn Walid, who belonged to the Meccan Quraysh tribe, and Malik ibn Nuwairah of the Banu Yarbu tribe near the Persian frontiers of Arabia. Malik was a companion of the Prophet who had been asked by Muhammad a few months before his death to collect the zakat from among his tribe. On hearing of the Prophet's death, Malik returned the tax monies that had been collected to his tribe, as he refused to recognize Abu-Bakr as the new caliph. Infuriated, Abu-Bakr ordered Khaled to track down the dissident. The clash ended in the defeat of the rebel tribe. When the two men came face to face, Malik told Khaled ibn Walid that while he continued to be a Muslim, he would not accept Abu-Bakr as the new caliph. The disagreement between the two was not about religion; it was clearly a political dispute between two Muslims over tax collection. The Quran had exhorted Muslims to settle their conflicts by reconciliation, not violence, as they were brothers in faith. Notwithstanding these injunctions, Khaled ordered the rebel to be beheaded. Malik's head was struck off and later used by Khaled as support for a cooking pot.

The cold-blooded beheading of Malik ibn Nuwairah horrified even the passionate Umar, who told Abu-Bakr that Khaled should be punished for killing a Muslim; Abu-Bakr responded by suggesting Khaled had made a mistake.

The clash between Malik and Khaled is perhaps the earliest incident in Islamic history of a political dispute being turned into a religious conflict and a declaration of apostasy—a death sentence. Umar, despite his reputation as a volatile person, prone to getting excited easily, differed with Abu-Bakr on conducting the Apostasy Wars. He challenged Abu-Bakr: "How can you fight against these men, since the Apostle of God said, 'I was commanded to fight against men until they say, There is no god, but God, and whosoever says that, protects from me his property and his life, except what is due from him, and his account with God'?"

To this day Muslims are defensive when it is suggested that Islam was spread by the sword. The fact is that Islam was spread by both the sword and word of mouth. Justifying the Apostasy Wars on one hand and denying the role of military might in the expansion of the frontiers of the first Arab state is a difficult juggling act. Of course, it is true that no Arab armies ever conquered Java, Sumatra, or the Malay Peninsula, and that Bengal became Muslim without even sharing a contiguous border with any other Muslim state. Islam did spread through peaceful means in some parts of the world, but it is dishonest to suggest that the sword had no part to play in the expansion from the towns of Medina and Mecca to the inner sanctums of Byzantine and Persian empires.

The Saudi flag displays the Muslim oath, the *Kalima*,* written in Arabic script. Under the words, the Saudis proudly flaunt a sword. By putting the sword and the Muslim oath next to each other, the Saudi flag is reflective of how some Muslims have themselves tarnished Islam with the symbol of war and killing. Muslims need to stop apologizing for the murderous acts of our co-religionists, even such exalted personalities as Khaled ibn Walid. We need to accept the fact that these men may have lived among the Prophet, but they were mere men, and like all of us, susceptible to errors in judgement; men who could not remain unaffected or resist the dynamics of political power and negative influence of military might.

Muslims need to study the Apostasy Wars as a subject of history, not religion. Only by separating the divine from the secular will we be able to live up to the Quranic invocation to "Cover not Truth with falsehood, nor conceal the Truth when ye know (what it is)." By mixing early Islamic history with Islamic theology and keeping all contentious issues outside the fold of public debate, we have ensured that our thought processes remain fossilized in the era of the medieval discourse rather than flourish in the unique freedoms of civic society.

We can learn a great deal about the socio-economic nature of the conflict by studying the genealogies of the two factions: the tribes who supported Abu-Bakr in the Apostasy Wars and those who opposed him.

---

* *Kalima*: the Muslim oath taken on becoming a Muslim—*La 'ilaa-ha 'il-lal-laa-hu mu-ham-ma-dur ra-soo-lul-laah* (There is no god but God and Muhammad is his Messenger).

Abu-Bakr's injunction that the Quraysh Arabs of Mecca were divinely ordained to rule over all Arabs was a powerful concession to his own tribe. The Quraysh rallied to his side and used this new authority to ensure their supremacy over the rest of Arabia. The Quraysh saw the benefit of subjugating the rest of the population under their rule as it secured for them the lucrative caravan trade routes and prominent positions in the new state. Abu-Bakr, on the other hand, could rely on the Quraysh—especially the Banu Ummaya clan—to back him as he struggled to win legitimacy as Caliph of the Apostle of Allah. The title, which would change with each new caliph succeeding Abu-Bakr, mixed the authority of religious leadership of the Muslims with that of the state administration. This mixing would lead to much confusion and many injustices in the coming centuries. Sultans and kings invoked religious authority to rule in the footsteps of Abu-Bakr, but had neither his wisdom nor his religious knowledge. Abu-Bakr had been the Prophet's earliest companion, a person of piety, patience, and clarity. Those who invoked the institution created by him merely imitated the title, not his humility and piety.

The Ridda Wars under Caliph Abu-Bakr may have consolidated the infant Muslim community and established the first Arab state, but they also laid the ground rules for many future tragedies where Muslims killed fellow Muslims. Abu-Bakr himself said, "If I do good, assist me, but if I err, then you must set me straight." So why should we hesitate to say that the model of governance that resulted in the killing of innocent Muslims is not what Muslims should be asked to emulate? Undoubtedly, at the time of Abu-Bakr, most states and dynasties in the region were governed by the might of the sword and a lack of accountability to the ordinary citizen, but surely this is not the way we Muslims wish to live in the 21st century.

Muslim rulers had claimed to be Caliphs of God because, they said, if God had not willed them to rule, they would not be ruling. This is at best fallacious. The manipulation of religion and politics made it possible for future monarchs to issue proclamations as if they were divine injunctions. The trend set by the early caliphate allowed future sultans and caliphs to "use religion as a breastplate to protect their throne and to ward off those who rebelled against them . . . they gave the people to understand that obedience to the Imams is . . . obedience to God and disobedience to them [is] disobedience to God."

The title given to the institution of caliph underwent embellishment as tyrants took over. One version was "Caliph of God upon His Earth, His Shadow which was spread out over his servants. Praise by God and Exalted above that which they associated with Him."

The sultans and caliphs who held power in the past, and the tyrant kings, ayatollahs, and generals who rule Muslim countries today, have all merged politics and Islam to justify their oppression. Only a few countries—including Indonesia, Malaysia, Turkey, Senegal, and Mali—have escaped this toxic cocktail.

From the *madrassahs** of Pakistan to the campus of Al-Azhar University in Cairo, the caliphate has become attached to the study of Islam itself. The kings, generals, and religious leaders have always disguised their despotic rule as a practice of Islam. They have ensured that even today the worldwide Muslim community's political mindset is mired in 7th-century thinking.

Earlier in our history, a tradition of dissent existed. Scholars such as Abu Hanifa, Imam Shafi, Imam Hanbal, Bukhari, and Taymiyah all had conflicts with the state authority of the caliph. Today, however, despots have trampled on their Muslim subjects, forbidding them to investigate the science of governance and politics. In the name of Islam, they have deceived Muslims, creating a stagnant pool of subservience. As a result, the Muslim no longer sees any source of authority in politics beyond religion, even in matters that are purely executive and entirely secular. Political thinking is paralyzed. The religion of Islam did result in the creation of the caliphate, but the caliphate is not an ingredient of the faith. Whether one lives as an Inuit Muslim in the Arctic with not a single other Muslim in sight or in the heart of Mecca alongside millions of fellow Muslims, Islam does not differentiate between the two and certainly does not obligate the Inuit to create a caliphate on Baffin Island.

The Prophet's daughter Fatima found out about the personal dangers of dissent back in the 7th century, when Abu-Bakr confiscated her property, which meant that Ali's ability, as well as her own, to mount any serious challenge to the authority of the Quraysh was hampered by their lack of resources. In contrast, the Prophet's wife Aisha—Abu-Bakr's daughter—along with his other wives were given their share of the property and were awarded handsome stipends.

For Fatima, the shock of having to live under virtual house arrest, boycotted by the ruling elites, must have taken a heavy toll, and she died within six months of her father's passing away. With Fatima gone and finding himself ever more isolated, Ali sued for peace with Abu-Bakr, inviting the caliph for what turned out to be a tearful reconciliation between the two giants of early Islam. At the afternoon prayer, Abu-Bakr paid tribute to Ali and the latter offered a public allegiance to the Caliph of the Prophet of Allah. With Ali's submission to Abu-Bakr, the social boycott of the family of

---

* *Madrassahs*: Schools.

Muhammad—the Banu Hashim—ended, and at least on the surface there was a period of amity between the various factions of the early Muslims. Ali had given allegiance to Abu-Bakr, but at no time did he give his approval to the process adopted to select Abu-Bakr. He maintained that the Prophet had selected him as his successor and he hoped to succeed Abu-Bakr when the ageing caliph died. That was not to be.

Abu-Bakr's two-year reign consolidated the community and brought some degree of reconciliation among feuding factions. One aspect of his rule that left an indelible mark for all time was his refusal to benefit personally from the wealth that was accumulating in the state coffers. We are told that he took three *dirhams* a day as a salary—a trivial amount—only because he had to give up his thriving trade business on becoming caliph. He lived a life of humility and ensured that wealth acquired through war booty was divided equally among the community. In his will, he asked that a date palm that he owned be sold to pay his debt to the state treasury. Abu-Bakr's allowance was a pittance compared to the 4,000 dirhams a year paid to soldiers of the early caliphate.

Unlike the Prophet, Abu-Bakr addressed the question of succession during his lifetime. If Ali had any hope that the caliph would correct the wrongs done on the Night of Saqifah, he was rudely disappointed. While at Saqifah, there had been at least a semblance of a debate and the succession of Abu-Bakr was not carried out by proclamation, this time there was no public consultation. It is reported that Abu-Bakr consulted with two companions, Uthman and Abd al-Rahman bin Awf, and they arbitrarily decided that Umar would be the next caliph.

Because of the Apostasy Wars, the Meccan aristocracy—many of them very recent converts to Islam—were firmly in charge as generals in the armies and owed their success and wealth to Abu-Bakr. By announcing Umar as his successor, Abu-Bakr pre-empted any serious challenge by them. In Medina, Umar was in undisputed control, and the only other serious contender, the general Khaled ibn Walid, was away in Syria fighting the Byzantines.

Once more Ali had to submit to the reality of politics. Again, the caliphate had eluded him. In announcing his successor, Abu-Bakr made mention of the competing interests, but emphasized his confidence in Umar. He assured the others that the wealth that was pouring in from the newly conquered territories would not abate. He said:

> I have entrusted your affairs to him (Umar) whom I feel is the best of you.
> Each of you is inflamed with anger by that, for each wants the succession
> to be his instead. You have seen that the world has opened up. When it

opens up, it continues to come on until you adopt curtains of silk and pillows of silk brocade, and are pained to lie on *adhari*[*] wool, as anyone of you (now) is pained to sleep on thorns. By God, that anyone of you be brought forth to have his head chopped off, for (something) other than the penalty for a mortal sin, could be better for him than plunging into the depths of this life. You will be the first to lead people astray tomorrow, so that you will turn them from the way to the right and left. O guide of the way, it is either the light of dawn or evil!

UMAR BIN AL-KHATTAB—THE COMMANDER OF THE FAITHFUL

In August 634, two years and three months after the death of Muhammad, Abu-Bakr, the Caliph of the Apostle of Allah, died. The new caliph: Umar bin al-Khattab. The caliph soon dispensed with the cumbersome title of the Caliph of the Caliph of the Apostle of Allah, opting for a new title that would be used by Muslim leaders for centuries. He referred to himself as the *Amir ul Momineen,* the Commander of the Faithful.

As the Amir ul Momineen, Umar would in fact be the first to become head of state of the emerging empire. As the ruler, he instituted a number of crucial reforms, including the fixing of the Islamic calendar to date state records and transactions. His rule is also known for institutionalizing the concept of *sabiqa,* or precedence, to determine various levels of citizenship based on when and where a person or their family had converted to Islam, and *shura,* the concept of consultation.

A true political genius, Umar was a passionate man whose rule set the stamp on much of political thought in the coming decades and centuries. He recognized very early on that the warring tribes of Arabia led by the merchant class of the Meccan Quraysh had seen unprecedented wealth during their raids into neighbouring territories. The Ridda Wars had taken tribal raiding parties and turned them into larger army groups. Any suspension in military enterprise would result in a restive population that had just tasted the luxuries of silk curtains and pillows and thousands of dirhams for each soldier. While Abu-Bakr had fought wars to save the state, Umar's expeditions were largely expansionary, and within ten years he had defeated both the Byzantines and the Persians. With each conquest, unimaginable riches were coming into the

---

[*] *Adhari*: From Azerbaijan.

state treasury and Umar was faced with a dilemma: how to distribute this wealth. Until now, a strict form of equality had prevailed among the early Muslims. Everything captured as war booty was distributed equally among the Muslim population. However, the Arab state was no longer limited to a few tribes around Medina and Mecca. The Muslim population was not a few thousand, but in the hundreds of thousands and increasing every day, with non-Arabs joining the ranks of the faithful.

Ali insisted that the example of Muhammad be followed strictly and all wealth acquired be shared by the entire population. However, Umar had the foresight to see the need for a state treasury and state records. He adopted the Byzantine administrative model he had discovered in Damascus; moving away from the example of Muhammad and his predecessor, Abu-Bakr, and dismissing the advice of Ali, he laid the foundation of a state administration and a sort of ministry of finance and revenue. He also instituted the first regular army of full-time paid soldiers. Was Umar violating the principles of Islam by abandoning a practice set by Muhammad himself? The fact that he did demonstrates that the practice of politics and statecraft were not determined solely by Quranic principles, but good faith, expediency, and the pragmatism of day-to-day management. With regard to the Sunna—the practice of the Prophet's examples—these too were shown to have been changed when the issue of wealth distribution was addressed.

It may not have been his intention, but the formula Umar developed for distribution of wealth set the foundation of entitlements that were not based on merit, but rather on family lineage, race, and tribe. Umar insisted that Muslims who had fought against Muhammad could not be seen as equal to Muslims who had fought on the side of the Prophet. Thus, he awarded the highest stipends to Muhammad's earliest companions who fled with him to Medina from Mecca and fought alongside him in the Battle of Badr—on a sliding scale, with the least paid to Muslims who converted to Islam only after the fall of Mecca. Without doubt, Muslims believe that in the eyes of God, the most deserving were the earliest companions, but could a financial value be attached to one's submission to Allah and acceptance of Islam? In the eyes of Umar, this differentiation was valid. Others felt this was contrary to the teachings of the Quran; Ali, despite the fact that he was given the highest share of the booty and stipend, suggested the distribution be equal. But while Ali was applying the teachings of Muhammad and the Quran, Umar could possibly have been seeing this as a matter of statecraft and management.

The policy of *sabiqa*—determining people's level of piety based on a sliding scale of when they accepted Islam—when applied to their share in war booty, would in future generations lead to further entrenching of unequal citizenship rights in Muslim lands. What Umar conceived as a hierarchy of respect and honour among the Prophet's companions would soon become the basis of institutional discrimination that still vibrates in the Muslim psyche. It is no wonder that so many Indian Muslims, who have roots going back to the Indus Valley civilization of 2500 BCE, attach last names such as Qureshi, Siddiqui, and Hashmi to establish their superior family lineage and to distance themselves from their own Indian ancestry. Others add the title Syed before their first names to establish their direct lineage with the Prophet.

In the sixth year of Umar's domain in 640, the region was hit by a drought. Crop failures resulted in widespread famine, hunger, and severe shortages. Umar decided to dip into the state coffers and offer government help to all the citizens affected. However, he tied the distribution of famine relief to the same principles he had applied to the allotment of war booty—a sliding scale of preference based on when a person had accepted Islam, as well as their racial and tribal origin. Members of the Meccan Quraysh tribe were given more than other Arabs of Mecca; all of the Meccan Arabs were given preference over the Arabs of Medina—the Ansar. Even among the Medina Arabs, he created two levels: the Aws tribesman received more than members of the Khazraj tribe. Then he placed all Arabs over non-Arabs; and all free men over slaves or non-Arab Muslims, who were referred to as *Mawali* or clients.

Umar's intentions were clearly made in good faith because he kept his own family at the bottom of this hierarchy, refusing to increase his stipend. When Ali, Uthman, Talha, and al-Zubayr went to him with the suggestion that he should increase his salary in view of his needs as head of state, Umar reacted angrily, totally rejecting any personal benefits for himself or his family. He said to his wife: "Tell them on my behalf that the Messenger of God was frugal, put the surplus in its proper place, and contented himself with the bare necessities. By God, I am also frugal."

Indeed, the hallmark of Umar's ten-year rule was the huge amounts of wealth pouring into the hands of the Umayyad elites of Mecca on one hand, and the marked contrast of Umar's frugal lifestyle. It is said that in his last year as caliph, Umar realized that by setting a sliding scale of benefits, based not on equality but on family lineage and tribe, he had deviated from the example of the Prophet. The historian al-Yaqubi records Umar as saying: "I had sought to placate people by preferring some of them over others. But if I live this year, I will observe equality among all people and will not prefer any person over another. I will follow the example of the Messenger of God and Abu-Bakr."

But that was not to be. Before he could rectify this erroneous hierarchy of Muslims, he died. What he created in good faith, as a reward for the early acceptance of some Muslims, would become an institutional justification for discrimination by one group of Muslims over another. It entrenched tribalism within a community that was created to enjoin equality, and his decree made it possible for the Meccan Arabs of the Banu Ummayah to turn Islamdom into a royal dynasty of kings for the next hundred years.

However, Umar's most defining political contribution was his creation of the *Shura* or Consultative Council to determine a successor. He could have followed precedence, but chose to reject Abu-Bakr's model for succession. Whereas Abu-Bakr had appointed his successor unilaterally during his lifetime, Umar did not wish to take this responsibility on himself. Perhaps this was one more way of keeping Ali ibn Abu Talib out of contention. Ali, who had been a patient contender for the high office of caliph, would find disappointment yet again. Once more, the excuse made was that the Meccan aristocracy would not permit someone from the Banu Hashim clan of the Prophet to be their leader. Instead, Ali was one of the six men assigned the task of selecting from among themselves the next man to lead the Muslims. Ali must have seen through this ploy, but went along with the process to ensure rifts in the community did not boil over.

Within a dozen years of the Prophet's death, the rules of succession would be altered three times, some say to suit predetermined outcomes. Yet Islamists around the world have no hesitation in pointing to this era as their template for the political institutions of the elusive Islamic State they seek. At Saqifah bani Saida, there was a near free-for-all leading to a near stampede when people gave public allegiances to Abu-Bakr. On his deathbed, Abu-Bakr side-stepped any such public consultation and appointed Umar. And when it came time for Umar to hand over power, he created an entirely new institution to render a successor, an institution that would never be called upon again in any caliphate anywhere in Islamic history, not even by his immediate successor, Uthman, who too would fall to an assassin's dagger.

Compared to other empires at the time, Umar's Shura Council may very well have been a revolutionary idea, where the ruler disqualified his own son as his heir and appointed six notables of the community to select from among themselves one as his heir. Umar's Shura Council did not survive in Islamic history, but another tradition that began in his era would stay with Muslim rulers for centuries. It was the way he would depart from this world—murdered in a mosque. In fact, all the remaining caliphs referred to as the Rightly Guided Caliphs would meet the same fate, dying by the knife of an assassin.

Umar had successfully laid the foundations of the state, borrowing heavily from the Byzantine and Persian models, including their record keeping, bureaucracy, a salaried full-time army, and generally a very high standard of transparency in governance.

During Umar's reign, the Islamic empire saw phenomenal growth. Mesopotamia and parts of Persia were taken from the Sassanids, while Egypt, Palestine, Syria, North Africa, and Armenia were taken from the Byzantines. Many of these conquests resulted from fierce battles fought by Arab armies on both the western and eastern fronts.

The one triumph that Muslims consider as Umar's crowning glory is the 637 defeat of the Byzantines in Jerusalem and its capture by the Muslim army. Muslims lost Jerusalem to the Crusaders in 1099, but the Kurdish warrior-king Saladin won it back ninety years later. Muslims lost Jerusalem again in 1967 to the Israelis. Many still dream of another Saladin to get just a part of the city back in Muslim hands, but if there is a Kurd warrior worthy of stepping in Saladin's shoes, he would be too busy fighting for his own people's freedom from other occupying Muslims—the Iranians, the Turks, and the Arabs.

Umar also introduced punishments that had no sanction in the Quran. Despite the fact that the Quran did not permit stoning to death as a punishment for adultery, Umar introduced it, suggesting that the Prophet had sanctioned it. He is quoted as having said: "Stoning is a duty laid down in Allah's Book for married men and women who commit adultery when proof is established, or if there is pregnancy, or a confession."

The fact that the Quran has no such prescription of a death penalty is lost on many Muslims. Few dare to intervene as, even today, Muslims are stoned to death by fellow Muslims. Islam is invoked to carry out this horrendous, cruel, and inhuman punishment. Stoning to death as a punishment is based on the Judaic texts, but today, this act defines the brutality of Islamist governments, not the Jewish state. The stoning-to-death regime gets further legitimacy from a saying by Muhammad's young widow, Aisha: "When the verses 'Rajm' [Stoning] and ayah 'Rezah Kabir' descended, they were written on a piece of paper and kept under my pillow. Following the demise of Prophet Muhammad, a goat ate the piece of paper while we were mourning."

It is astonishing that the absence of a death sentence for adulterers in the Quran would be blamed on a goat eating God's revelation. Yet this fable has gone unchallenged and scores have died in Iran based on a saying by Aisha, a woman for whom, ironically, the Shia Iranian clerics have no love lost.

Introducing stoning to death as a punishment for adulterers was not the only change Umar introduced in Islam. Another radical change was taking away the right of Muslim men to have temporary contract wives, a practice called *muta'a* that is still alive and well in Iran and among Shia Muslims. The Prophet had sanctioned the practice, and when Umar banned it, Tabari reports that there were murmurs of protest. A man approached Umar and asked him about the banning of temporary marriage. Umar replied: "The messenger of God permitted it at a time of necessity. Then people regained their life of comfort. I do not know any Muslim who has practised this or has gone back to it. Now, anyone who wishes to can marry for a handful of dates and separate after three nights. You're right."

Introducing the death penalty for adultery and abolishing the concept of temporary marriage were dramatic departures from established Islamic laws and customs. On one hand, this demonstrates the fact that even in very early Islam, few things were carved in stone other than the belief in the oneness of God and allegiance to Muhammad as his Messenger. However, it also showed that Umar was a decisive leader who took risks and swift measures to resolve issues; measures that were based on pragmatism, not restricted by ideological constraints.

However, where Umar failed was his inability to eliminate the mutual distrust and division that was plaguing the Muslims due to internal distrust and suspicion among the various clans, tribes, and political factions.

A month before he was murdered, Umar is said to have been told by his informers that Ali and his friends were plotting to assert the right of the Prophet's family, the Banu Hashim, over the caliphate. This prompted him to make his famous address where he reasserted the right of the Quraysh tribe to hold the office. He talked again about the night of Saqifah banu Saidah and denounced any attempt of any family to demand the exclusive right to rule, a clear shot across the bow of Ali to desist from asserting his claim as the rightful successor of the Prophet.

Within months of this speech, the matter of his succession would come to a head. Chroniclers report that in early November 644, as Umar prepared to lead the morning prayers, a Quraysh dignitary's Persian slave who had converted from Christianity crept through the rows in the congregation, pulled out a dagger with two blades that had its haft in the middle, and stabbed Umar six times, inflicting a mortal wound below the caliph's navel. The disgruntled slave, Abu Lu' lua, had had an altercation with Umar a few days earlier over his treatment by his master, al-Mughira bin Shu'ba. The caliph had dismissed his complaint, and this was probably what had triggered the assassination.

However, there were immediate claims by Umar's son Ubayd Allah and his sister Hafsa that the Persian slave had not acted on his own but that he was part of a wider conspiracy. Ubayd Allah first avenged his father by fatally stabbing the slave and then proceeded to kill the leading Persian in the community, al-Hurmuzan, who served as an adviser to Umar. Not satisfied, Ubayd Allah then proceeded to kill the assassin's daughter and then murdered a Christian Arab, a mathematics teacher by the name of Jufayna, who had nothing to do with the incident at all. These killings were based solely on unsubstantiated rumours that all three—the slave, the mathematics teacher, and the Persian adviser—had been seen with the murder weapon a day earlier.

After this rampage, Ubayd Allah threatened to kill all the foreign prisoners in Medina, along with unnamed members of the Medina Arabs and some from Mecca. Before he could carry out his threat, Umar's son was apprehended.

The scholar Wilfred Madelung speculates in his book *The Succession to Muhammad* that it is not unlikely, given Umar's recent warnings against Ali and his clan's ambitions, that Ubayd Allah also had Ali ibn Abu Talib in mind as one of his targets. The actions of Ubayd Allah reflected not just the anger of a son, but also the fact that Muslims were not seen as one cohesive Ummah, even at that time of the so-called golden era. Arab superiority in Islam, institutionalized after the death of Muhammad, had seeped into the narrative of these early Muslims. The fact that a Muslim Persian of the rank of adviser to the caliph would be murdered, purely based on his common ethnicity with the Persian Christian slave, should have rung some alarm bells among the Muslims. This was not what the Quran had revealed, nor was it part of the Prophet's teachings. Collective punishment based on ethnicity and religion was emerging, yet nothing was done to stamp it out. Despite Ali's demand that Ubayd Allah face justice for committing murder, the new caliph, Uthman, pardoned him. Once more Ali seemed to be standing up for Islamic injunctions while his opponents relied on Arab tribal custom.

In fact, even as Umar lay dying, mortally wounded, he invoked the superiority of the Arabs over non-Arabs. While instructing the six-member council to select a new caliph, he told them, "I commend to the caliph after my death the Arabs—for they are the very substance of Islam—for what is their due for alms be taken and assigned to their poor."

This is not the only reference in the chronicles about Umar referring to Arabs as the chosen Muslims. Tabari writes that Umar bin al-Khattab used to say that there were four matters connected to Islam that he would never neglect: (1) what he called the "strength in God's wealth" and not having any of it for his own family; (2) the welfare of the emigrants of Mecca who accompanied Muhammad in taking refuge in Medina; (3) the people of Medina who opened their city for Muhammad and the fleeing emigrants; and (4) "The Bedouins, who are the original Arabs and the mainstay of Islam."

Clearly, a hierarchy among Muslims was being established, not for reasons of piety or principles of faith, but for the purposes of politics, power, and the sharing of wealth and war booty, including slaves and concubines. By referring to Arabs as the "mainstay of Islam" or "the very substance of Islam," Umar was sanctifying ethnic hierarchies among Muslims, which the Umayyad dynasty would institutionalize.

The effect of such words was compounded by Umar's rulings that forbade the marrying of Arab Muslim women to Persian Muslim men, while permitting such marriages if the genders were reversed. Non-Arab Muslims were discouraged from settling down in Medina. Even if one were to give Umar the benefit of doubt and assume that he might not have intended to position Arabs as superior to Persians, Africans, or Indians, that is how his words were interpreted. Through the centuries and even today, this concept of superiority has defined and soured relationships among Islam's many ethnic communities, rendering the claims of a common Ummah as nothing more than a hollow slogan.

How can present-day Islamists reconcile with the notion of Arab superiority over non-Arabs, and then offer this inequity as a template for a 21st-century Islamic State? This is a question few Muslims dare to ask, and even fewer risk looking for an answer. The reason for this wall of silence is that the mere offence of questioning the decisions of any companion of the Prophet has been deemed a sin.

The *Uprightness of all Sahaba* is a Sunni doctrine. In accordance with this, it is a sin to curse or criticize any of the companions of Muhammad, making it an act of apostasy. One Sunni scholar states:

> Someone who speaks ill of the Companions of the Messenger of Allah (peace and blessings be upon him, his family, and companions) has innovation (bid'a) in matters of belief, and is going against the way of Ahl al-Sunna in this matter. Speaking ill of the Companions of the Prophet (peace and blessings be upon him) is a dangerous sign, and it is feared that such a person may have other methodological variances—intellectual or nafsanic [spiritual]—from the way of mainstream traditional Islamic scholarship.

Such statements make it impossible to critique any of the rulings made after the death of Muhammad, even if these rulings contradict the Quran.

While Muhammad died emphasizing the equality of all Muslims, his caliphs could not resist the temptation of falling back to tribalism and invoking the pagan Arab tradition of family lineage, instead of the Quranic injunction of merit, as a measure of human quality.

Uthman bin Affan—The Caliph of Allah

Abu-Bakr and Umar may have made tactical errors in how they proceeded to establish the Islamic state, but there is no question that they regarded the caliphate as a responsibility to be met selflessly, taking no material gain for themselves or their families. In fact, Umar made a determined effort to ensure that neither his son nor any other member of his family would succeed him or have any say in the choice of his successor. However, when Umar died, the caliphate turned into a kingdom; nepotism and hereditary rule would become established and any pretence to merit would be done away with forever.

The Islamist scholar Abul Ala Maudoodi, even though he described the period of the Rightly Guided Caliphs as "a luminous tower," has criticized Uthman's leadership qualities, blaming him for permitting ignorance to creep back among Muslims.

He writes that after the Prophet died, two "great leaders of Islam"—Abu-Bakr and Umar—carried on with his mission successfully. Then Uthman became leader, and after the initial stage of his leadership:

> Two important factors weakened the Caliphate. First, the fast expanding Islamic State brought in new problems every day, thus adding to the pressure of work and responsibilities of the Caliph; and second . . . Uthman, who had been elected to shoulder the heavy burden of Caliphate, did not possess the qualities of leadership to the extent his fore-runners had been endowed with. Consequently, "Ignorance" found its way into the Islamic social system during his Caliphate.

Shortly before his death Umar appointed a six-member Shura Council comprising Ali, Uthman, Abd al-Rahman bin Awf, Saad bin Waqqas, al-Zubayr bin al-Awwam, and Talha bin Abd Allah. He asked them to retreat for three days and not come out until they had reached a decision as to who among them would be the next caliph. This was a unique institution created by Umar and reflected his political genius as a statesman who was not afraid of treading uncharted waters. It is said that he personally favoured Ali, but did not appoint him because he did not want to set a precedent. The historian Baladhuri reports that Umar told his son Abd Allah, "If they choose for the caliphate the bald one (Ali), he would lead them on the right course." His son asked, "What prevents you from appointing him, O Commander of the Faithful?" Umar answered, "I will not burden both the alive and dead."

If the selection of Abu-Bakr was an all-night squabble, the selection for the successor of Umar began on a sour note with heated arguments, so loud that the dying Umar asked them to stop the wrangling and postpone the discussions until after his death. "All of you stop this! When I am dead, hold your consultations for three days. Let Suhayb lead the people into prayers. Before the fourth day comes you should have your commander from among you."

That evening Umar passed away and was buried alongside the Prophet and Abu-Bakr. Even at the funeral, the historian Tabari reports, there was tension. As Ali and Uthman came forward to lift the body from opposite ends, Abd al-Rahman exclaimed, "How eager you both are to get hold of the caliphate." After the burial and prayers, the council met, but could not come to any conclusion. Supporters of Ali were upset that he agreed to sit on the council, as they felt its composition ensured that Uthman would be selected, not Ali. His uncle, al Abbas, warned Ali that the outcome was a foregone conclusion. Uthman would be the next caliph, and by joining the council, Ali was putting a stamp of approval on his own exclusion, once again. But Ali replied, "I do not like dissension in the family."

Three days later, the council was still deadlocked between Ali and Uthman, with Abd al-Rahman bin Awf as the arbiter. In the end, it came down to a simple question put to both contenders. Reminiscent of the Night of Saqifah, Abd al-Rahman asked both Ali and Uthman to appear before a larger group of notables from among the Meccan as well as Medinan Arabs. As expected, verbal feuding broke out between the Umayyads, who were supporters of Uthman, and the Hashemite backers of Ali. In the end, Abd al-Rahman brought it down to one question. He would give allegiance to the one who would promise to follow in the example of Abu-Bakr and Umar, in addition to the Quran and the Prophet. While Uthman agreed immediately, chroniclers report that Ali refused, arguing rightly that there was no need to follow the example of Abu-Bakr and Umar if one followed the Quran and the Prophet's example.

Abd al-Rahman bin Awf refused to listen to Ali's protestations, stepped up to Uthman and gave his allegiance. The third caliph of Islam had been selected. For the third time in a row, Ali ibn Abu Talib, who believed he had been promised the caliphate by Muhammad himself, had to suffer humiliation. For the third time, Ali demonstrated immense character and resolve, swallowed his pride, and took the oath to serve under Uthman. However, this time the fissures created by the continued humiliation of Ali would rupture into the open. For the first time in Islam's short history, two political parties would emerge: the Party of Uthman (Shia Uthman) and the Party of Ali (Shia Ali).

Uthman's ascension as caliph would become the foundation stone of the Umayyad dynasty, a dynasty that would ironically place some of Muhammad's bitterest opponents at the helm of Islam's first kingdom. While Muhammad's own family would have to run and hide for their lives to escape persecution, his former archenemies and their progeny would rule in his name. Ironically, the same pagan tribe that persecuted Muhammad during Islam's infancy would, in Islam's ascendancy, harass his progeny—of course, this time as Muslims, not as pagans.

If there was any indication of things to come, it was in the title that Uthman chose for himself: "Caliph of Allah." With this decision, Uthman clearly violated the promise he had made to Abd al-Rahman bin Awf that he would follow the example of Abu-Bakr and Umar. His next symbolic step was even more daring. While Abu-Bakr and Umar would sit a step lower than where Muhammad had sat on the steps of the *Mimbar* or pulpit, out of respect for the Apostle of Allah, Uthman decided to sit at the same level as the Prophet. When some people in the congregation objected and asked why he was elevating himself to the status of the Prophet and not following Umar's example, Uthman scoffed at them and is quoted as saying, "Umar had prepared the gesture for me." This symbolic step was deeply troubling to many Muslims and the historian Yaqubi quotes one man in the congregation saying, "Today evil was born."

From the outset, Uthman's decision to elevate himself as the *Khalifat Allah*, Caliph of God, and to sit higher in stature than his two predecessors, created rifts in the community. There were rumblings; those who had been miffed by the third consecutive blocking of Ali and the Prophet's family from the caliphate galvanized into what history would come to know as the Shia Ali. Sunni Muslims are reluctant to delve into a discussion about Uthman, but his twelve-year rule was marked by intrigue, nepotism, and rebellion. A pious man himself, known for his kindness and generosity, Uthman was an ageing figure, who simply could not stop his own family members and tribal associates of the Umayyad clan from amassing immense wealth. Whereas Abu-Bakr and Umar were symbols of frugality and humility, Uthman can perhaps be better described as Islam's first monarch. Uthman was no longer the deputy to the Messenger of God in the footsteps of Abu-Bakr and Umar. He was ruling by the grace of God himself. The title "Caliph of God" became the standard title for all Umayyad caliphs, in clear violation of Islamic spirit, and with no justification or validity.

Despite taking on an inflated title, Uthman's first letters to his governors and army commanders were nevertheless reflective of his mild-mannered and kind personality. He wrote to them:

> God has commanded the Imans to be shepherds. He did not direct them to be the tax collectors . . . But your imams are assuredly on the verge of becoming tax collectors rather than shepherds. If they turn out thus then modesty of manners, integrity and faith will be at an end. Verily, the most just conduct is for you to examine the affairs and obligations of the Muslims. So that you may give them what is properly theirs and take from them what they owe.

However, in practice, Uthman's ostentatious lifestyle encouraged others in the elite to flaunt their wealth, and for the first time in Islam's brief history, inequity and disparity between rich and poor became visible. In response to rumblings from among the populace, including some of the companions of the Prophet, Uthman justified his actions by saying, "Abu-Bakr and Umar decided with regard to this public wealth to observe frugality towards themselves and their families. But I have decided to be generous towards my next of kin." He is on record as the first caliph to invoke the Quran to stifle opposition, quoting the sura that says, "O you who believe, obey God and the Prophet and those in authority among you," and warning his detractors that opposition to a caliph was going against the teachings of the Quran itself. For centuries, tyrants in Muslim lands would invoke the same verse of the Quran to stifle opposition and to sentence rebels to prison, exile, and, at times, beheading.

Nepotism under Uthman reached levels where even those among his clan who had fought against Muhammad and had never accepted Islam were rehabilitated. One of Uthman's uncles, a man named al-Hakam, had been banished by the Prophet from the city of Mecca to Taif. Muhammad, Abu-Bakr, and Umar did not rescind this expulsion, but as soon as Uthman took power, he lifted the ban on al-Hakam, claiming that Muhammad had in fact promised to pardon the man. He then allocated al-Hakam's son one-fifth of all revenue generated from the new provinces in Africa. There are numerous recorded incidents of impropriety involving state treasuries and the allocation of tax revenue to family and clan members. The son, Marwan, would later become one of the Umayyad caliphs.

Resentment against Uthman's arbitrary rule deeply embarrassed Abd al-Rahman bin Awf, who had enabled the crowning of the caliph. Abd al-Rahman is said to have confronted Uthman, and after the two had a heated exchange, the disappointed kingmaker walked out, promising to never speak to the caliph again. Years later, when Abd al-Rahman was on his deathbed, it is reported that he refused to speak to Uthman when the caliph came to inquire about his health. In fact, Abd al-Rahman bin Awf was so bitter that he left instructions that on his death Uthman not be allowed to lead his funeral prayers.

It is said that, for the first half of his rule, Uthman was given the benefit of doubt, but in later years, there were public displays of division, some taking place in the Prophet's mosque itself. Chroniclers have written about shouting between Muhammad's wife Aisha and Uthman. The incident relates to Uthman's refusal to apply the maximum punishment to his half-brother, al-Walid, who had been caught leading the morning prayers in Kufa in a state of drunkenness.

The dissension among the Muslims against the nepotism and elitism of Uthman's relatives and family led to two of Muhammad's companions openly demanding that the caliph return to the austerity of his predecessors. Ammar bin Yasir and Abu Dharr al-Ghaffari challenged Uthman quite openly. In fact, Ammar bin Yasir carried an open letter signed by dozens of prominent Muslims urging Uthman to mend his ways. The reaction was swift. Ammar was severely beaten by family members of the caliph and left unconscious on the doorsteps of the Prophet's mosque.

Abu Dharr al-Ghaffari, who is still revered by Muslims as the voice of the poor, and often invoked by Muslim Marxists as their source of inspiration, was even more vocal and public in his criticism of Uthman and his governor in Syria, Muawiyah. It is reported that Abu Dharr would stand outside the Prophet's mosque every day and speak to large groups, extolling the virtues of Prophet Muhammad and his family while attacking and exposing the scandals of nepotism and corruption in the Uthman administration.

One incident in Medina triggered particular outrage. Uthman placed his cousin al Harith bin al-Hakam in charge of the Medina market, allowing him to impose a private tax on all the shops and stalls. Al Harith, using his clout as a member of the inner circle in power, imposed a monopoly on all imported goods and then sold them at exorbitant markups to the traders, a practice still widespread among the merchant classes of Saudi Arabia.

Abu Dharr would have none of this profiteering, but he did not restrict his actions to mere protest. He laid the foundations of the first political party in Islam, the Shia Ali. Abu Dharr preached solidarity with Ali and exhorted Muslims to bring the family of the Prophet into the caliphate to restore the dignity of Islam, which he felt was being seriously compromised by the Umayyad clan of Mecca and the close family of Uthman.

Infuriated by this open challenge thrown by Abu Dharr and his unrelenting daily criticism at the doors of the Prophet's mosque, Uthman clamped down on dissent and had Abu Dharr exiled to Syria under the watchful eye of Muawiyah, another relative whom he had appointed as governor of the rich province. Exile did not deter Abu Dharr, who became a thorn in the side of the governor, reprimanding him for living the ostentatious lifestyle of a king and reminding him of the Prophet's message of equality and justice. By now, the Umayyad grip on the state was near complete, but widespread dissent against it was brewing below the surface. Abu Dharr was too respected a person to be silenced, and his exhortations against the wealthy elites was "setting the poor aflame" according to Tabari. Unable to silence him, Muawiyah sent the rabble-rousing activist back to Medina. Strapped on a camel without a saddle, Abu Dharr arrived in Medina, in pain and distress, where he had a face-to-face meeting with Uthman. Not much came from this meeting and Abu Dharr was exiled again, this time to a remote place in the desert known as al Rabadhah, where the aging rebel was to live out his last years in isolation.

It was not just Abu Dharr who was outraged. People across the state were either openly rebelling against the family members of Uthman appointed as governors, or were deeply upset at the injustices being committed in the name of the caliph by his relatives. Uthman's response was to use force and invoke his position as an imam to silence opposition. Those who did not obey were sent into exile, and most of these were supporters of Ali. In the meantime, power was shifting to Damascus, where Muawiyah was building an almost independent and parallel state, having seized the immense captured wealth of the Byzantines.

As the situation became more and more grave, Uthman invited all his governors to Medina to consult on a course of action. The governors were all his hand-picked family members, and they were part of the problem, not the solution. After the meeting, Uthman met privately with Muawiyah, who suggested that either Uthman expel all his opponents from Medina or allow him to behead Ali, Talha, and al-Zubayr, to put an end to the leadership of the rebels. When Uthman rejected this outrageous proposition, Muawiyah is said to have warned the caliph, "If you do not kill them, they shall kill you."

The first act of rebellion occurred after the Egyptians, unhappy over the appointment of a new governor, came to Medina with a list of demands. After much negotiation and mediation by Ali, Uthman decided to reverse his decision and restore the original governor. This action could have quelled the revolt, but when the Egyptians intercepted a messenger from Uthman, they were shocked to read that instead of sending instructions to the governor that he should resign, Uthman had asked him to behead some of the Egyptian rebels. Some say this message was a forgery, the work of Uthman's cousin Marwan. However, the revelation that Uthman had not kept his word inflamed the Egyptians, who came back to Medina, this time besieging Uthman's home demanding that he either abdicate or die. There are many versions of the forty-day siege, and how it climaxed in the tragic murder of Uthman, but few wish to discuss the implications or the reasons of this bloodbath.

My purpose here is not to delve into the various narratives about who killed the third caliph of Islam, or who was instrumental behind the scenes. My question to Islamists, who portray this period as a golden age of Islam, is this: What aspect of this power struggle, the gory murders and punishments, exiles and palace coups, do they feel is relevant for Muslims in the 21st century? If this was the best of Muslim traditions, why would we wish to emulate them?

Long before the siege, senior companions of the Prophet were exchanging messages across Arabia, openly calling for the removal of Uthman. Volumes have been written about the intrigues and conspiracies that became the order of the day in Uthman's last years. Some of the texts are a downright embarrassing read for Muslims. Were these power-hungry men, owners of slaves and concubines, who grabbed state lands for themselves and dipped greedily into the state treasury, those who set the standards by which Muslims should measure themselves today? How did we come to a situation where men who openly defied the Quranic injunction of equality are thought to be above criticism? And how come the one man who did represent all the qualities of piety, wisdom, integrity, courage, and patience found it so difficult to get acceptance from his peers in the "best" period of Islam? This man was Ali and he too could not put an end to the bloodshed and political machinations that started on the fateful Night of Saqifah and that continue even today to cause bloodshed on the streets of Gaza, Karachi, Baghdad, and Algiers. Unfortunately, Muslims continue to be taught that the blame for their failures lies not within themselves, but elsewhere. An example of such teachings is found in the three-volume *History of Islam* published in

Saudi Arabia by Darussalam. In addressing the turmoil that followed the murder of Uthman, the book blames the unrest on the *Munafiqeen** and "Jews posing as Muslims."

ALI IBN ABU TALIB—THE TRUSTEE OF THE MESSENGER

On Saturday, June 18, 656 CE, after being denied what he believed was his rightful place as head of the Muslim community—the Ummah—for twenty-four years, Ali ibn Abu Talib took office as the fourth caliph of Islam. In a public ceremony at the Prophet's mosque in Medina, rebels from Egypt and Iraq and ordinary citizens of Medina who had participated in the siege and murder of Uthman came one by one and to give their pledges of allegiance to Ali. The succession, though, was not as smooth as most Muslims have come to believe.

The rebels from Kufa and Basra, who had listened to Ali and had not participated in the violence, clearly backed Ali. However, most of the Egyptian rebels wanted Talha to be the next caliph. Hitherto a strong ally of Ali, Talha—along with al-Zubayr—was not ready to endorse Ali, and there were private negotiations between the parties. It is reported that while the people of Medina were solidly behind Ali, the Meccan Quraysh wanted to arrange a Shura Council to discuss the matter. The Umayyads, who dominated the Quraysh tribe, were stunned by the assassination of Uthman, whom they considered one of their own. They were reluctant to see Ali become caliph. However, they were aware of his immense popularity among the ordinary citizens, particularly among the rebels from Kufa, whose leader, al-Ashtar, was leading Ali's bid. The Quraysh attempt to create an obstacle in the way of Ali never materialized.

Both Talha and al-Zubayr also gave their pledges to Ali, though later they would claim that these were given under duress. According to the chroniclers, however, Ali did not force anyone to submit to his rule. He was the first of the caliphs to have had his ascension validated in a mass meeting without coercion or threats. But many Meccans refused to support the new caliph, some having left the city during the siege and others starting to move to Mecca the day after Ali became caliph.

---

* *Munafiqeen*: Arabic for those who are accused of abandoning Islam. The word *apostate* is the closest translation. Islamists insist that the word *munafiqeen* be translated as "hypocrites."

Ali had barely taken command when plans were set in motion to overthrow him. Before he could consolidate his control over the administration, or address the widespread discontent that had led to the overthrow of Uthman, he had to deal with a mutiny from an unlikely source. So far, the division among Muslims had been the Party of Ali on one side and those who were known as the Party of Uthman—the Shia Ali versus the Shia Uthman. However, there was now a three-way split. While the Umayyad supporters of the murdered Caliph Uthman were still smarting from their loss, there emerged among the rest of the Quraysh a group that wanted to go back to the governing example set by Abu-Bakr and Umar, which Uthman had rejected with his ostentatious style, and which had never been accepted as legitimate by Ali. There was another triangular tangle: the three major cities of Islam—Medina, Mecca, and Damascus—became hotbeds of competing alliances, all vying to wrest power from each other. The disputes had nothing to do with piety, religiosity, or one's conviction in the Quran, but were purely about power and the control of the Islamic State, clearly at cost to the state of Islam.

Some of Ali's detractors headed north to Damascus to join Muawiyah, while others went south to Mecca. Aisha, who was already on her way to Mecca when Uthman was killed, was joined there by Talha and al-Zubayr. The two former comrades of Ali, who had only recently pledged their allegiance, abandoned him, and on reaching Mecca, formed a triad with Aisha aimed at toppling Ali. The scene was set for Islam's first civil war. The pretext used to justify a revolt against Ali was his refusal to punish the murderers of Uthman. The fact that it was Talha himself who had been the main force behind the rebellion against Uthman, made his call for avenging Uthman's murder seem hypocritical. As Aisha, al-Zubayr, and Talha plotted in Mecca, Ali had his hands full dealing with the regional, governors appointed by the late Uthman, all of them his close family members.

Driven by a sense of social justice rather than political pragmatism, Ali made a crucial error in staking out his priorities: instead of first consolidating his power, and unmindful of the conspiracy being hatched in Mecca, Ali opened a new front by dismissing all the regional governors and appointing his own trusted men. He was advised by close confidants not to take such a bold step so early in his term, and to let the Umayyad governors develop a sense of security in their regions. However, Ali would have none of that. He was determined to put the concepts of merit and piety above that of tribe and family. He rejected the notion of the superiority of the Meccan Arabs over other Muslims, and now that he was the caliph, he was in no mood to compromise.

Ali's cousin and close confidant, Abd Allah ibn Abbas, pleaded with Ali to back off and wait. He warned Ai that if the caliph moved immediately against the Umayyad governors, he would be accused of having been involved in the conspiracy to murder Uthman. Ali's intransigence would cost him dearly. While he clung to the spirit of Islam that he had inherited from Muhammad and the Quran, the Muslim community around him had other ideas. In thirty years, the companions of Muhammad had moved on to become the elite in society. Uthman had given them a taste of wealth and power, which they preferred over the wisdom and piety Ali was offering. His unbridled zeal for austerity and integrity, and refusal to compromise caused two of his closest allies—Talha and al-Zubayr—to defect.

Both wanted a share in the power structure as well as wealth. When Ali appointed Talha as the governor of Yemen and al-Zubayr as the governor of Bahrain, the two insisted that mere governorships were not enough and they should be rewarded with money from the state treasury. Ali could have compromised, but he refused, and indignantly rescinded both their appointments as governors. The two promptly but discreetly broke their alliance with Ali and proceeded towards Mecca, ostensibly to perform the *umra** pilgrimage, but in reality to team up with the Quraysh to overthrow Ali.

One of Ali's first moves was highly symbolic. As the new governor of Egypt, he chose Qays bin Saad bin Ubadah—the son of the late Medina tribal chief Saad bin Ubadah, who had been ill-treated by Umar and whose claim to be leader of the Muslims had been dismissed by Abu-Bakr since he was not an Arab from Mecca. By honouring the son of Saad bin Ubadah, Ali seemed to be rectifying what he thought had been an injustice committed against the very people who had given Muhammad refuge when he escaped from Mecca. However, to the Quraysh of Mecca the appointment was a rebuke to their superiority and cause for alarm. If this was an indication of how the future would unfold under Ali, the Meccans saw their privileged position being challenged.

In the Quraysh stronghold of Mecca, Ali's nominee for the governorship, Khalid bin al As, was rejected as the entire city rallied in rebellion against Ali. A young man snatched the letter of appointment carrying Ali's seal, chewed it up, and threw it to the floor as an act of defiance. Mecca was in open revolt and Ali's old nemesis, Aisha, was the flag-bearer of the rebellion. Ali was falsely accused of being responsible for the murder of Uthman and fiery

---

* *Umra*: The "little" pilgrimage that, unlike the full-fledged *hajj* pilgrimage, is not compulsory for a Muslim.

speeches were being made denouncing the caliph. Old enmities surfaced; these allowed enemies of Muhammad who had converted to Islam only after the fall of Mecca to come out of the woodwork and revel in war poetry against Ali. The same men of the Quraysh who had mocked and harassed Muhammad during his early days in Mecca were now back attacking Ali.

A war council was set up in Mecca headed by Talha and al-Zubayr, with Aisha as the figurehead to lead the Meccan Arabs in revolt against Ali. They at first considered attacking Medina directly, but realized that they did not have the troops they needed to go to war against the people of Medina, who were already mobilizing behind Ali. Aisha knew that to defeat Ali in battle, she needed men and money. One of the Meccan notables, Ya'la bin Umayyah, stepped forward with a donation of 400,000 dirhams (about $16,000), horses, camels for seventy warriors, and a promise to obtain more manpower and resources from Basra. In mid-October, nine hundred Meccan Quraysh men, led by Aisha on a camel with Talha and al-Zubayr as her deputies, set off from Mecca towards Basra. It is reported that by the time the army reached Basra their strength was close to three thousand men, all eager to avenge the death of Uthman, whom they were told had been murdered by Ali.

Sunni theologians and contemporary Islamists have tried to portray Aisha as the gullible victim of machinations by Talha and al-Zubayr. However, a reading of the medieval chronicles reveals that far from being an innocent bystander, Aisha was a strong-willed woman who played a crucial role in inciting people with her fiery speeches, and who sought revenge against Ali, whom she had disliked all her life. Aisha's dislike of Ali went back to an incident in which Aisha had been accused of impropriety with her slave Safwan. The incident happened when Aisha was travelling with her husband Muhammad in a caravan. After an overnight stay, Aisha says she left camp early in the morning to search for her lost necklace. By the time she returned, the caravan had broken camp and had left without her. Later that day, the main body of the caravan realized that Aisha and a slave were missing. Rescue parties were dispatched and found her with Safwan, who said he too had come to look for the lost young woman.

The two rejoined the caravan, where rumours were rife that Aisha must have been having an affair with Safwan. Many of Muhammad's companions, including Ali, urged Muhammad to divorce Aisha. Muhammad then stated that he had received a revelation from God directing that adultery be proven by four eyewitnesses, rather than simply inferred from opportunity. The revelation in the Quran (24:11) condemned the rumour-mongers with the words: "Lo! they who spread the slander are a gang among you. Deem it not a bad thing for you; nay, it is good for you." Because Ali had urged

Muhammad to divorce Aisha, she never forgave him and the two never had any semblance of a working relationship after the incident. The irony is that the two individuals that Muhammad loved most hated each other and would end up waging Islam's first civil war.

During the last days of Uthman, Aisha had urged people to rise up against the ageing caliph, but when the crisis was coming to a head, she went away to perform the hajj pilgrimage. It was on her way back, during a stopover in the town of Sirif, that she heard of the mayhem that had led to Uthman's death. Aisha had been hoping that Talha would succeed Uthman, but when she was told that contrary to her expectations, the people had chosen Ali, she is said to have screamed: "By Allah. Would that the sky were overturned if the command has decided in favour of your leader (Ali). Take me back. Take me back (to Mecca). By Allah, Uthman has been killed unjustly, and I will seek revenge for his blood."

Aisha returned to Mecca from where she was to organize the rebellion against Ali by way of Basra. Aisha's army was able to take control over Basra, but it was unable to win over the entire population. In the meantime, Ali had been informed of the rebel advance towards Basra and decided to take the fight to them, rather than risk an attack on Medina. He is said to have started with a small detachment of seven hundred horsemen, with messengers dispatched to Kufa to look for additional troops. In Kufa, Ali's comrades, including his son Hassan, staged a coup against the governor and expelled him from his palace. After the governor's dismissal, Hassan and others were able to muster six to seven thousand soldiers from different tribes of Kufa, who joined Ali's contingent on the outskirts of Basra.

As the two armies faced each other, Ali sent an appeal to the citizens of Basra, pleading with them not to take up arms against the caliph or get involved in a fight that was not theirs. The ploy worked and it is said at least three thousand men crossed over to the caliph's side, tipping the balance in his favour. The two armies stood facing each other for three days. A tent was erected in the no-man's land where Ali, Talha, and al-Zubayr met for lengthy discussions, trying to resolve the conflict without bloodshed, to no avail.

On December 8, 656, at around noon, the two armies clashed. This, the first civil war in Islam, would set the precedent for many more that would ravage Islamdom over the years. The battle lasted into the evening sunset, with hundreds of men dying in hand-to-hand conflict. The leader of Aisha's army, al-Zubayr, greatly depressed at the thought of fighting his childhood friend Ali, is said to have abandoned the fight and tried to make his escape. However, he was apprehended by men loyal to Ali, who after beheading this companion of the Prophet, delivered his head to a saddened Ali. In the battle, Talha too was wounded and bled to death. With her two commanders dead, Aisha lost the battle, but she sat on her camel, spurring her partisans to keep fighting, resulting in the senseless slaughter of many pious and brave Muslims. In the end, Aisha's camel was brought down by a spear and she quietly surrendered. With bodies all around them, Ali approached Aisha and harshly reminded her of the devastation she had caused. Defeated, the "Mother of the Faithful" humbly surrendered to the caliph. "You have won the reign, so pardon with goodness," she pleaded.

Ali guaranteed her safety and asked that she be escorted to Basra and then to Medina, where Aisha spent her last days. The lowest estimates of the battle casualties in Islam's first civil war put 2,500 slain in Aisha's camp, while 500 died in Ali's army. Other estimates put the combined death toll at above 10,000, but this seems to be an exaggerated figure. Ali had won the battle, but the war was not yet over. The Muslim blood on the sands of Iraq had not yet dried when dark clouds started gathering over Syria.

Ali had put down the uprising of the Meccan aristocracy, but the victory came at a great cost to his credibility and moral authority. It seriously diminished the institution of the caliphate, which never recovered from this wound.

The next challenge to Ali came from Muawiyah, the governor of Syria, who mocked the caliph by refusing to dignify his demands with a reply. Ali demanded that Muawiyah pledge his allegiance and accept Ali's authority as caliph, but to no avail. After receiving repeated summons, Muawiyah poked fun at Ali by sending him a blank piece of paper. As if the insult were not enough, Muawiyah's emissary conveyed an undisguised threat, informing Ali that sixty thousand elders in Damascus were waiting to avenge the murder of Uthman, and that they held Ali directly responsible for the late caliph's death.

Realizing that the centre of gravity of the new Muslim empire had shifted away from Medina and Mecca towards the newly conquered Byzantine and Persian territories, Ali decided to shift his capital to Iraq, in the town of Kufa. The population in this garrison town was loyal to Ali and he felt it was better placed strategically to respond to the challenge from Damascus.

Seven months had passed since Ali had taken over as caliph, yet there had been no relations established between him and the governor of Syria. While Muawiyah was gathering strength in Damascus and creating a state within a state, showering tribal chiefs with money from state coffers, Ali was alienating the Arab elites by adhering to the strict ethical codes of the Quran. During his twelve-year reign, Uthman had used the state treasury to buy favours and please his entourage. When Ali put a stop to this practice he offended many, including his own brother Aqil, who defected to Muawiyah. In Damascus, Ali's brother was showered with wealth in a show of defiance to Ali's authority. Muawiyah was also able to win the backing of Amr bin al-Aws with a promise that, if Ali were defeated, Amr would be appointed governor of Egypt. While Muawiyah continued with his horse-trading, Ali was confident in the legitimacy of his caliphate and the righteousness of his cause.

As negotiations continued, it was clear that Muawiyah had no interest in submitting himself to the rule of Ali. He proposed that, while Ali was free to have his domain over Iraq, Persia and Hejaz (Mecca and Medina), he—Muawiyah—should be allowed to rule over his domains in Syria and Egypt. Clearly the concept of two leaders of the Muslim community, parallel yet equal, first proposed at Saqifah on the night after Muhammad's death, had raised its head again. The unnatural concept of a single Islamic State for all Muslims was cracking. Ethnicity, culture, regionalism, and custom, along with the greed generated by the allure of political power, were clashing with religion. The vibrant city civilizations conquered and adopted from the Byzantines were rejecting the Bedouin pastures of Arabia. While Muawiyah was awash in wealth and had a regimented Syrian army at his command, Ali was constrained by his austerity measures and had a larger, but less disciplined, ragtag group of Bedouin warriors behind him.

As negotiations failed, Ali decided to face Muawiyah in battle. In April 657, he led an army across the Mesopotamian desert, and after crossing the River Euphrates at Ridda, faced Muawiya's forces that were camped at Siffin. After brief skirmishes where both armies were able to get access to the river for their water supplies, a lull in the fighting ensued. Letters were exchanged between Ali and Muawiyah, which make for some fascinating reading into the mindsets of the two. While Muawiyah feigned a false sense of outrage at the assassination of Uthman, blaming Ali for the murder, Ali mocked his opponent's gambit as nothing more than the greed of a man obsessed with clinging to power. As the negotiations continued, Ali suffered a public relations setback: his emissary defected to Muawiyah.

Daily skirmishes continued between the two sides during the months of May and June until the Islamic New Year—the month of Muharram—came on June 18 and both sides agreed to a truce for thirty days. On the last day of Muharram of the 37th year in the Muslim calendar, Ali ordered his army to prepare for battle against the Syrians.

In customary Arab tradition, one-on-one duels took place for a week. On Wednesday, July 26, as the sand simmered under the harsh Siffin sun, all-out clashes broke out. The slaughter continued for four days, with thousands of Muslims dying at the hands of their fellow Muslims. A senseless meat grinder soaked the desert soil with the blood of those who believed God was on their side. During a brief respite in the battle, Ali proposed a dramatic solution. He suggested that Muawiyah step forward and that the two should have a duel. Whoever was left standing after the sword fight would be the caliph and both armies would give their pledge of allegiance to him.

Some of the Syrians backed the idea, but Muawiyah, the chess player and the backroom deal maker, withdrew behind his lines to avoid the duel. Muawiyah was fighting to keep his crown, while Ali was inspired by his commitment to his faith and his duty to God. Obviously, the possibility of death in battle was not an option for Muawiyah. After all, he and his father had made compromises and converted to Islam only when faced with defeat at the hands of Muhammad in Mecca.

Muawiyah's cowardice had a demoralizing effect on the confidence of his troops. As the fury of battle resumed on the Saturday, the stalemate of static battle lines gave way and the tide shifted towards Ali's cavalry. By noon, sensing impending defeat, Amr bin al-Aws advised Muawiyah to adopt a tactic that might give his army some relief. They ordered their soldiers to attach copies of the Quran on top of their lances and chant, "Let the Quran settle the conflict."

The ruse worked. Seeing the Quran, many in Ali's army refused to engage the enemy for fear of offending God. There was widespread confusion and discord in the caliph's army, and the momentum they had gained that day slipped away from them. Ali exhorted his troops to keep fighting and not to fall for the gimmickry. He warned them that Muawiyah and his men were not men of religion, but hungry for power. His words were not enough. Soon he faced rebellion within his own ranks as some of his allies—the Kharijites, who would in the end murder him—threatened to kill him if he was not willing to permit a truce based on the Holy Quran.

Muawiyah's cunning won him the day. Ali had to accept the offer of arbitration, despite the fact that he was on the verge of victory. The tradition of invoking the Quran as an arbiter is still used in the Islamic world, especially as a means to derail a debate or to avoid discussing the merits of the case. Muawiya's ruse has continued to provide a cover for tyrants throughout Islamic history. After all, who would like to be seen as opposing the Quran?

On August 2, 657, a ceasefire agreement was signed by Ali and Muawiyah. Both agreed to submit to whatever decision the arbiters from both sides would agree on. The ceasefire agreement itself caused serious dissension in the ranks of Ali's armies with the Kharijites rejecting any notion of arbitration, raising the slogan NO JUDGEMENT, BUT GOD'S.

The two arbiters chosen reflected Ali's flaw in managing the affairs of his group. While Muawiyah appointed Amr bin al-Aws, an astute politician who had already made a deal with Muawiyah and had engineered the ploy of introducing the Quran into the battle, Ali's representative was Abu Musa al-Ashari, who was a decent man but could hardly have matched the cunning of Amr. In fact, a month earlier, Abu Musa had opposed Ali during the Battle of the Camel. Ali's first choice as arbiter had been Ibn Abbas, but he could not bring his fractious bunch of tribals to accept his recommendation and he ultimately agreed to appoint Abu Musa instead.

The arbiters spent weeks in negotiation, but could not come to any agreement. In the end, after much wrangling, they agreed they would announce an agreement that each side would reject both Ali and Muawiyah. They would then ask the people to select someone who was independent of the conflict and neutral in his preference. It was agreed that the two arbiters would make this as a joint announcement, asking Muawiyah and Ali to step down. However, Muawiyah's representative Amr had a trick up his sleeve. He had devised a strategy that would turn the agreement against Ali.

Abu Musa spoke first and announced that Ali would step down as caliph. However, when it came time for Amr to speak, instead of announcing his decision asking Muawiyah to step down, he stood up and emphasized that since Abu Musa had deposed Ali, he was confirming Muawiyah as the next caliph.

The chroniclers report that, stunned by this public deception, Abu Musa was enraged and exchanged heated words with his co-arbiter, accusing him of betrayal and treachery. But it was too late. The damage was done and the rest is history.

Ali's caliphate would limp on for another few years. After failing to defeat Muawiyah, he had lost considerable credibility. In the end, the great warrior was murdered. It was not his enemies who killed him, but his allies.

The man who came to epitomize self-sacrifice and religious integrity, equality, piety, and austerity would fall victim to the very people he had rallied to his side. Was he lacking in leadership qualities what he possessed in courage? Ali would die in a Shakespearean tragedy, murdered by religious zealots who felt he had compromised and not lived up to the slogan NO JUDGEMENT, BUT GOD'S. Ali, the man Shia Muslims claim the Prophet himself had chosen as his heir, was done in by the very Muslims who swore an oath to serve him.

On the morning of Friday, January 26, 661, which was the 17th day of Ramadan of the 40th year in the Islamic calendar, as Ali entered the mosque to lead the prayers, he was met by his assassin, who struck the caliph on the back of his head with a poisoned sword. As Ali fell to the ground, the killer, who belonged to the Islamic extremist sect of Kharijites, yelled at the fallen caliph, "Authority belongs to God, Ali, not to you," referring to the arbitration agreement Ali had signed with Muawiyah. Thus ended the so-called golden era of Islam.

There is no questioning Ali's courage and piety, but what about his political acumen? Why was it that he would not let Muawiyah secede as an independent and parallel Muslim entity in Syria, considering the fact that he could not even muster his own supporters to rally around him?

Abu-Bakr had faced a similar revolt against his authority. The ageing caliph had acted in a far more determined manner, labelling all the dissenters as apostates, worthy of death. Ali knew that Abu-Bakr's actions amounted to high-handedness and were drastic. However, Abu-Bakr acted decisively and succeeded, whereas Ali dithered, faltered, and failed.

A comparison of these two stalwarts of Islam is a classic study of the interplay of politics and religion. To govern, Abu-Bakr employed politics over faith and prevailed. Ali, on the other hand, emphasized faith over politics, and failed. A study of both men's Islamic practices should inspire Muslims, but their political ambitions and practices should jolt us from our slumber. Tragically, most Muslims have chosen to pay no heed to the mountain of evidence. The blood of tens of thousands of Muslims murdered and killed by fellow Muslims in the first decades of Islam cries out to us, "Stop chasing the mirage of an Islamic State, men better than you tried and failed. What makes you think you can accomplish what Abu-Bakr, Umar, Uthman and Ali couldn't?" How many more Muslims have to die in search of an oasis that does not exist? But the voices of the dead are drowned in the howling sandstorms of the deserts of Arabia, whose thirst for Muslim blood is matched only by its ability to blind the Muslim Ummah.

There is still time. We Muslims can learn from the sacrifices and mistakes of our ancestors and move towards a better and brighter future, free of violence and mayhem. We can end the thankless and impossible task of creating an Islamic State that no one wishes to live in, and instead strive for a state of Islam within ourselves. We could also learn from one of the descendants of Ali and Fatima, the imam of the Ismaili Shia Muslims, Prince Karim Agha Khan.

Most Muslims condemn the Agha Khan and his followers as non-Muslims. However, he leads his followers in a progressive and dynamic manner, reconciling Islam and modernity with grace and composure that has won him and his community the affection and respect of the entire world. One may differ with his followers' secretive and at times cult-like devotion to their leader, but one must give credit where it is due. To the Agha Khan and his followers, called the Ismaili Muslims, faith is a guide to action, not to be worn on their sleeves. It resides in their hearts. They aspire to no Islamic State, yet live in a state of Islam.

Once upon a time, the Ismaili Muslims too ruled over a caliphate, the Fatimides in Egypt. For centuries after they were defeated, they too craved for a return to their past. However, with the advent of the modern nation state in the 19th and 20th centuries, the Ismailis reconciled with modernity. Today, whether she or he is in Tanzania or Trinidad, India or Indiana, the Ismaili Muslim is at home and at peace.

Can the rest of us emulate the metamorphosis of the Ismaili Muslims from a medieval people to modern thriving community? We need not embrace their theological or religious beliefs, but surely we can learn from their successful reconciliation of Islam with contemporary civilization? They established the 9th-century Fatimide dynasty in Egypt; founded the Al-Azhar University; were expelled from their homeland by their Sunni detractors, dispersed and scattered across Yemen, India, and Persia; faced discrimination and harassment wherever they went; and yet managed to be the most literate, urbanized, charitable, socially cohesive, and upwardly mobile people among the Muslims of the 21st century.

The rest of us Muslims can, of course, continue to label each other as non-believers and apostates. We can hate modernity itself, be envious of human joy, bury our heads in the Arabian sands, and let the bloodthirsty desert have the last laugh.

CHAPTER 8

Damascus—
Islam's Arab Empire

AFTER THE DEATH OF ALI, the fifth caliph of Islam was sworn in. However, so short was his reign that few Muslims even acknowledge his time in office. The distortion of history taught in the Muslim world is so thorough that the Prophet's grandson Hassan bin Ali is mentioned as a caliph only in passing.

While Shia Muslims use the story of Caliph Hassan to validate their narrative of injustice and victimhood, Sunni historians either bypass Hassan's caliphate completely or depict him as a weakling who surrendered his claim to the caliphate in exchange for the patronage and wealth offered by Muawiyah, the Syrian governor. At best, Hassan is eulogized as a peace-loving, saintly figure who gave up his throne in the larger interest of the Muslim community.

Yet others use Hassan's abandonment of the caliphate to justify the Sunni doctrine, which bars descendants of the Prophet's family from assuming the political leadership of the Muslims. In this regard, Akbar Najeebabadi's *The History of Islam*, published in Saudi Arabia and supervised by an American Islamic publishing house in Chicago, is an interesting read. The book suggests that Hassan's father, Ali, should not have become the fourth caliph of Islam: "Had there been a non-Hashemite as caliph instead of Ali bin Abi Talib [Hassan's father], he would have gotten more help from the Arab tribes. Had Ali bin Abi Talib himself not been caliph he would have done better in opposing Muawiyah and crushing Banu Umayyah and would have found himself more powerful and effective in establishing the caliphate of one who was not a Hashemite."

The book then goes on to back up the Sunni doctrine by quoting remarks attributed to Hassan as he lay on his deathbed. Apparently Hassan told his younger brother Hussain: "When Ali ibn Abi Talib (Hassan's father) became caliph after the Prophet's death, swords came out of their sheaths and this issue remained unsettled and now I know it full well that Prophethood and the Caliphate cannot co-exist in our family."

Clearly, the Saudi publishers are trying to validate Sunni doctrines instead of conducting a critical analysis of historical events. The Saudi version of Islamic history does not acknowledge Hassan as the fifth caliph of Islam. Historians agree that after the death of Ali in January 661, his elder son Hassan took oath as the caliph and was acclaimed by the people of Kufa, the capital city of the caliphate. He also received allegiance from the governors of Hejaz and Yemen. Obviously, Muawiyah did not accept Hassan's claim, just as he had rejected Ali's claim. Hassan's caliphate continued until eight months later, when in August he made a deal with Muawiyah, abandoned Kufa, and withdrew to Medina for a life of retirement.

However, the year 661 was not as uneventful as Sunni Muslim historians would have us Muslims believe. Any scrutiny of that year will open the eyes of contemporary Muslims to the dangers of mixing religion and politics. Of course, this is not what Islamists want Muslims to know, and hence the blatant lies that pass as scholarly studies emanating from Saudi Arabia.

The night after Ali died by an assassin's dagger, Hassan announced the sad news at the main mosque in Kufa. Choked by tears, Hassan informed the community that his father had left behind no gold or silver, nor any property other than 700 dirhams (about three dollars). In fact, true to the tradition of Muhammad, Ali had not even nominated his successor, although he had made it known that he believed the leadership of the Muslims should always remain in the family of the Prophet.

Hassan had barely ended his tearful speech when Yemeni governor Ubayd Allah bin al-Abbas, who had fled to Kufa in the face of an assault by Muawiyah's army, stood up and summoned the people to take an oath of allegiance to Hassan as the next caliph. One by one, the notables of Kufa stepped forward and swore their allegiance to the new caliph. Like his father, Hassan was taking over as "Commander of the Faithful" in extremely troubled times.

Ali had been murdered while he was in the midst of preparing a war against Muawiyah, an effort that was not bearing much fruit. Nevertheless, the semblance of an army had been mobilized by Hassan's father and was awaiting orders to march on Damascus. Perhaps the pacifist in Hassan and the recognition of his lack of military strength dissuaded him from launching the attack. For nearly two months, the troops stayed camped around Kufa, with no orders, wondering why the caliph hesitated. Hassan was not even giving fiery speeches to sustain the morale of his loyal soldiers, who were accustomed to his father's legendary oratory.

On the other side, Muawiyah was biding his time. His general, Busr bin Abi Artah, had just returned from a bloody attack in the heartland of Islam—Medina and Mecca—where he had slaughtered children and earned a reputation as a brutal killer who tolerated no dissent. Busr entered Medina and Mecca unopposed and forced the population to switch their loyalties from Ali to Muawiyah, which they did. They knew the consequences of refusal. Basr had destroyed the homes of anyone refusing to submit, and ordered the beheading of the children.

Hassan had been at his father's side when news of Muawiyah's assault on Mecca and Medina came. The governors of these cities had barely escaped with their lives. The governor of Yemen, the man who first gave allegiance to Hassan and would later betray him, lost both his sons to the butchery of Basr. Hassan was aware of the forces arrayed against him. He may have been a patient pacifist, but his reluctance to launch an attack reflected the fact that he was a realist as well. However, his inaction came at a price. His troops became restive and the population felt the new caliph did not have his heart set on either battle or governance. While the extremist Kharijites derided him for cowardice, his uncle and ally in Basra, Abd Allah bin al-Abbas, wrote to him urging him to take some decisive action or risk losing the support of the people.

Encouraged by support from Ibn Abbas and after a careful assessment of his tactical and strategic position, Hassan wrote to Muawiyah, who had appointed himself as a parallel caliph, demanding that he step down and offer allegiance to Hassan. In the letter, signed as "Commander of the Faithful," Hassan mocked the pedigree of Muawiyah, reminding him that he and his father had converted to Islam only after the fall of Mecca and when the two were left with no choice. Hassan's letter contained a thinly veiled threat of military action if Muawiyah refused to give his oath of allegiance.

Muawiyah was accustomed to this game of diplomatic dare. He had outmanoeuvred Ali and was about to use a different tactic on Hassan. Instead of the harshness that had been his manner in confronting Ali, Muawiyah invoked his age, experience, and ability as an administrator, suggesting that Hassan's inexperience would give the enemies of Islam an advantage. Then he threw in the carrot: Withdraw your claim to the caliphate and you will be rewarded by a rich pension and immense land holdings of your choice, he said.

Hassan received the letter but failed to respond. Interpreting this lack of response as a sign of weakness, Muawiyah dropped any pretence of civility and sent a second letter, a sort of "cease and desist" notice, but not without enticement. This time Muawiyah promised to name Hassan as his successor and the next caliph.

Hassan responded by dismissing Muawiyah's demands and rejecting reconciliation based on offerings of land, wealth, and future succession. Once more, men of Islam, companions of the Prophet, were gearing up for bloodshed—not to resolve some theological dispute, but to claim their right to sit on the throne.

Sensing the weakness of his opponent and informed by spies of dissension in Hassan's ranks, Syrian Governor Muawiyah attacked. Leading sixty thousand men, Muawiyah marched to meet the army of Hassan. This time the battle lines were clearly defined along geographical lines: the Syrians were advancing on the Iraqis.

In Kufa, as Hassan heard of the approaching enemy, he addressed the people, urging them to prepare for jihad. He dispatched his messengers to the regional governors, asking them to rally their troops and join him in the war camp at al-Nukhayla. The response to Hassan's appeal is said to have been less than overwhelming. Apparently, unknown to him, some of the governors were already on the payroll of Muawiyah.

Nevertheless, tens of thousands of loyal soldiers answered the caliph's call and began to gather at the war camp. Here, Hassan was to follow in the footsteps of his father and make a wrong choice by appointing Ubayd Allah bin Abbas as the commander of his main army instead of the more trusted and warlike Qays bin Saad. Both father and son were betrayed by the men they appointed as their representatives: Ali's deputy, Abu Musa, at best made an error in judgement, but Hassan's choice as general defected to the other side.

Ubayd Allah, who had deserted his command in Yemen, led the troops up the Euphrates until he reached the Iraqi city of Fallujah (known today as the hotbed of resistance against US occupying troops). A second column of troops was led by Hassan. The next morning the caliph delivered a sermon during which, instead of rousing his troops and urging them to show valour, he spoke of his desire for peace. He said he hoped no harm or evil would fall on anyone. His soldiers were puzzled. Was the caliph giving up without a fight? After exhorting them to rise up in jihad, was he getting cold feet?

Chroniclers describe unrest, which soon broke into pandemonium and open rebellion. His pavilion was attacked by his own troops, who started looting and even pulled off his tunic. The caliph had to escape on his horse, surrounded by servants and some loyal guards. In the mayhem, one of the

Kharijites got near the caliph and attacked him with an axe, causing a gash on Hassan's thigh. The wounded caliph, Commander of the Faithful, was carried away while his would-be assassin was seized and immediately beaten to death, his head crushed by a stone.

As the grandson of the Prophet was nursing his wound, Muawiyah—the son of Abu Sufyan, the Prophet's lifelong enemy—was advancing with his disciplined Syrian army, offering amnesty to each town and tribe until he came face to face with Hassan's twelve-thousand-strong advance guard led by Ubayd Allah.

A brilliant politician, Muawiyah sent a message to Hassan's army commanders saying that their caliph, Hassan, had sued for peace and was willing to sign a truce. When this ruse failed, Muawiyah sent a private emissary to Ubayd Allah, the commander of Hassan's army, with an offer of a million dirhams if he switched sides; half of it up front and the other half on return to Kufa.

Ubayd Allah had sworn an oath of allegiance on the Quran to serve Hassan. His two young sons had been murdered by Muawiyah's army in Yemen. Yet, for a million dirhams, he sold his soul. Rarely in military history has the general of an opposing army been bought in this manner. Hassan, like his father, had placed his trust in the wrong man. At best, Ali and Hassan were extremely poor judges of character, despite being men of exemplary personal character themselves.

All was lost for Hassan—and he knew it. After two days of skirmishes, he accepted the truce offered by Muawiyah on the condition that all his supporters would be given amnesty. Muawiyah sweetened the deal with one million dirhams ($40,000) and all the tax revenue from the agricultural lands of Fasa and Darabjird. The truce was signed, and Hassan and his family withdrew to a life of retirement in Medina.

What historians describe as the "Year of the Community" to signal the end of the strife within the Muslim community is misguided to say the least. In the years to come, much more blood would flow, including that of Hassan's younger brother, Hussain, and with him almost the entire family of the Prophet. In addition, as if the brutal killing of the Prophet's family at the hands of fellow Muslims were not enough, the Holy Ka'aba in Mecca—the House of God and the first mosque of Islam—was reduced to ashes.

Of course, most Muslims are unaware of these tragedies or have been taught their history from an uncritical propagandist approach. The textbooks being distributed by Saudi Arabia in Canada, the United States, and Europe, best represent the spin that Muslim historians have put on these tragic times. *The History of Islam* suggests that the civil war between Muawiyah and Ali was divinely ordained and that the resulting mayhem was actually good for Muslims: "Had these differences not appeared and had Amir Muawiyah and Ali bin Abi Talib not fought with each other, we would have been deprived of a major and essential part of the Islamic Shariah. But why did it start taking place? Allah Himself is the Protector of this religion and He Himself makes provision for its safety. He decreed that that there would be differences between Ali and Amir Muawiyah and the opportunities that followed."

MUAWIYAH: THE FIRST KING OF THE ARABS

One of the ironies of Islamic history is that the men who tormented Muhammad most in his efforts to introduce Islam (and monotheism) to the pagan Arabs would rise to inherit his faith and rule in his name.

Islamist author Abul Ala Maudoodi describes Muawiyah's caliphate as a "tyrant kingdom," and his ascension to the position of caliph as a "counter revolution" that passed power into "impious hands." Muawiyah's father, Abu Sufyan, and Prophet Muhammad were related: their great-grandfathers were brothers. Yet the two clans—the Banu Hashim of Muhammad and the Banu Umayyah of Abu Sufyan—were competitors, often at loggerheads with each other. It is this rivalry that would define the Muslim conflict, which began with the death of the Prophet and has continued for centuries.

Abu Sufyan was one of the most powerful and respected men in Mecca. He viewed Muhammad as a threat to Mecca's social order, a man aiming for political power who was challenging the traditional polytheism of the Quraysh gods, one of which was "Allah." It was Abu Sufyan who initiated several acts of persecution to dissuade Meccans from converting to Islam. After Muhammad migrated to Medina in 622, it was Abu Sufyan who led the pagan Arabs of the Quraysh tribe to war against the nascent Muslim community in Medina. This resulted in the Battle of Badr, which ended in a historic victory for the vastly outnumbered Muslims. However, this was not the end of Abu Sufyan's campaign against Islam and the Prophet. Subsequently, he was the military leader in two campaigns against Muslims, but failed to defeat Muhammad. Eventually the Muslims and the pagans would agree to an armistice, the Treaty of Hudaybiyya in 628, which held for only two years.

In 630, Muhammad assembled an army of approximately ten thousand men and marched towards Mecca. Seeing that defeat was inevitable, Abu Sufyan and his son Muawiyah converted to Islam. In a display of magnanimity, the Prophet embraced his lifelong enemies as his companions in Islam, declaring Abu Sufyan's home a sanctuary. He is said to have made this declaration after conquering Mecca: "Whoever enters the house of Abu Sufyan shall be secure; whoever remains in his own house shall also be secure."

Although Muhammad had forgiven and embraced his clan enemies, the rivalries remained. Many considered the conversion of Abu Sufyan and Muawiyah as a grudging acceptance in the face of defeat.

When Muhammad died in 632, Abu Sufyan was in charge of the southern province of Najran. Upon hearing that Abu-Bakr had been confirmed as the Prophet's successor, he was incensed and offered his help to Muhammad's cousin and son-in-law, Ali, to rise up against the new caliph. But Ali rejected his support, accusing Abu Sufyan of having nothing but animosity towards Islam. In another irony, while Abu Sufyan was willing to submit to Ali, his son Muawiyah would refuse to do so.

The Umayyads further degraded the status of non-Arab Muslims—Persians, Indians, and Africans—a process that had unfortunately begun during Umar's time, but was the only possible outcome of the policy of Meccan Arab superiority that had brought Abu-Bakr to power. Professor Liyakat Takim of the University of Denver writes:

> When the Umayyads were in power between 661 and 750, political leadership was restricted to the Umayyad clan. Arab Muslims were granted honorific status relegating, in the process, non-Arabs to a status of second-class citizens. Despite the Quranic injunction on egalitarianism, Arab sense of pride in Arab identity reasserted itself soon after the Prophet's death. Non-Arab converts to Islam, whatever their previous social status, were treated as second-class citizens (*Mawali*).

The evidence of overt racism and discrimination against non-Arab Muslims by the Umayyads is also detailed in the writings of the Islamist theologian Abul Ala Maudoodi. Analyzing how the institution of the caliphate was turned into a family dynasty by the Umayyads, Maudoodi in his exhaustive book *Khilafat o malookiat* (Caliphate and Monarchy), writes:

> Right from the start, the Umayyad government took on the colours of an Arab government in which the equality of Arabs and non-Arabs was negated. In clear violation of Islamic principles, the Arab rulers imposed *Jazia** on non-Arab Muslims. . . . Non-Arab Muslims felt that they were the slaves of the Arabs . . . During the times of Hajjaj bin Yussuf, non-Arabs were barred from leading prayers.

---

* *Jazia*: The poll tax non-Muslims living in a Muslim country are supposed to pay in lieu of protection provided by the state and for exemption from serving in the army. Under the Umayyads, this tax was also imposed on non-Arab Muslims.

The Arab nature of the first ninety years of the caliphate was most noticeable on its two frontiers—Spain in the west and India in the east. In Spain, which Muslims started to occupy in 711, the Berber Muslims of North Africa far outnumbered the Arabs among the conquerors. However, the Arabs enjoyed a privileged status, and every non-Arab who converted to Islam had to become a client (*mawla*) of an Arab, or another convert already endowed with such an Arab patron. Once Spain had been conquered, the Berber African Muslims staged a rebellion in 739 in North Africa, then defeated the Syrian army that the Umayyad caliph sent to quell the revolt.

In India, where Umayyad armies occupied Sind on the west bank of the River Indus, there are accounts of Sindhi Muslim converts being asked to pay jazia, the tax imposed on non-Muslims. During the reign of Caliph Yazid bin Abdul Malik, Arab Muslim rule on the west bank of the Indus co-existed with Sindhi Muslim rule on the east bank of the river. But in about 723, a large Umayyad army was sent up the river Indus and demanded that the native Muslim ruler Jaysinh start paying the non-Muslim tax. He refused. The Umayyad army, under al Junaid, then crossed the river, and after a long naval battle captured and executed the Sindhi Muslim ruler, declaring him an apostate. With the Sindhi kingdom annexed, the brother of the slain Jaysinh wanted to go to Damascus to complain to the caliph about the unfair treatment of Sindhi Muslims at the hands of the Arabs. Al Junaid captured the brother and had him executed as well.

Islam and Muslims had arrived in India long before the Umayyad army invaded Sind. Some descendants of the Prophet's family had taken refuge in Sind, escaping the wrath of the Umayyad Caliph Yazid, while others had settled in the coastal towns of Mekran, Gujarat, and Malabar in the south, coming in peace as traders from Oman and Yemen. However, the Umayyad raids into Sind caused massive social upheaval and resulted in tens of thousands of Indians being taken into slavery and marched off to Iraq. The first enslavement of Indians took place during the permanent occupation of towns on the Mekran coast of Baluchistan during the reign of Muawiyah—the first Umayyad caliph.

The 9th-century Persian historian Ahmad Ibn Yahya al-Baladhuri writes in his book *Kitab futuh al-buldan* (*The Origins of the Islamic State*) that when Sind was invaded by Muhammad bin Qassim, the prisoners taken were given a choice of death or slavery. There is mention of sixty thousand captives made slaves in the city of Rur, among whom were "thirty ladies of royal blood," while thirty thousand were taken in Brahamanbad, and another six thousand in Multan. One-fifth of the slaves and booty were set apart for the caliph's treasury and dispatched to Damascus, while the rest were scattered among the "army of Islam." Qassim collected gold and silver wherever he could find it. In Multan, he is said to have taken away the gold idol of the main Hindu temple along with the treasures of gold and jewels found in the captured fort. Chroniclers write that Qassim brought back "120,000,000 dirhams [nearly five million dollars]."

One may question the legitimacy of Muawiyah as the sixth caliph of Islam and the tactics he used to hold on to his power base in Syria, but even his most ardent critics admit to his role as a competent administrator and founder of the first Arab dynasty, the Umayyads.

Muawiyah knew he lacked the support of the influential religious circles, and this may be why he transformed the caliphate from a faith-based administration into an Arab tribal aristocracy. He is also credited with having created a postal service and a bureau of registry. As Islamic zeal was not his driving force, Muawiyah had a tolerant policy toward non-Muslims, mainly Christians. Knowing the anger that bubbled just below the surface in neighbouring Iraq, Muawiyah was generous in bribing tribal leaders to guarantee internal stability.

During his twenty-year reign as caliph, Muawiyah resumed the conquests of neighbouring territories, which had come to a halt during the time of Uthman and Ali. To the east, his armies conquered Khorasan in Persia and used it as a base for raids across the Oxus River into Central Asia. To the west, Muawiyah's governor in Egypt sent an expedition under the famous conqueror Uqba ibn Nafi against North Africa, penetrating Byzantine defences as far west as Algeria. However, the prize he most coveted eluded him. Muawiyah had his eyes on Constantinople (Istanbul today). He launched two unsuccessful attacks against the capital of the Byzantine Empire. His son Yazid led the first, and the second attack took the form of a naval campaign fought intermittently from 674 to 680. Both attempts failed. Eight hundred years would pass before a Muslim army would finally conquer Constantinople.

Despite clear historical evidence that Muawiyah's right to the caliphate was doubtful and had no religious support, the claim that he was God's deputy on earth, *Khalifa Allah,* has found widespread acceptance among contemporary Muslims who would rather take the easy path of blind faith than invest time to study for themselves the legitimacy of Muawiyah's claim.

Critical analysis often stumbles against the obstacles of sectarian thinking. If one is Shia, the starting point is one of unbridled hostility towards any opponent of Ali. If one is Sunni, any doubt as to Muawiyah's legitimacy is utter heresy.

In fact, great attempts have been made to position Muawiyah as having been divinely chosen by Allah to be a future King of Islam. Akbar Najeebabadi's *The History of Islam* is just one example. In one passage, while extolling the piety of Muawiyah, the writer describes a scandal surrounding Muawiyah's mother, Hind, who is suspected of having an affair.* Her husband beats her up and throws her out of his house. To settle the matter, the estranged husband and wife are taken to a fortune teller, who not only verifies Hind's chastity but also predicts the birth of a king. He tells her: "You have neither done a bad deed nor committed adultery and you will give birth to a king whose name will be Muawiyah."

What is the author suggesting? Should Muslims believe in the prediction of a pagan soothsayer as a way of validating the right of a king to rule Islamdom in the name of Allah? The absurdity of this argument is lost on Sunni Muslims who believe the story without question.

Numerous sayings of the Prophet have made their way to us in which the Archangel Gabriel tells Muhammad about the special position of Muawiyah. Aisha Bewly, a British Muslim author, writes in her book *Muawiyah*:

> It is reported that Abu Hurayra said that the Messenger of Allah, may Allah bless him and grant peace, said "Jibril came to me and said, 'O Muhammad, Allah has entrusted me with the protection of His revelation, with your protection, and with the protection of Muawiyah b. Abi Sufyan.'"

Bewly then suggests that Muhammad elevated Muawiyah to the level of Abu-Bakr and Umar because of his trustworthiness. The confidence which the Messenger of Allah, may Allah bless him and grant him peace, had in him (Muawiyah) is shown in another story recounted by al-Tabarani and al-Bazaar. This was an occasion when the Prophet consulted Abu-Bakr and Umar regarding a certain matter. They were unable to give a suitable suggestion. The Prophet then sent for Muawiyah saying: "Consult Muawiyah in your affairs since he is trustworthy and reliable."

The fact that this quote was written down more than two hundred years after the Prophet's death, by Sunni theologians who had no love for the Shia, should be enough to question its validity.

The Muslim blood spilt during his reign was due to Muawiyah's fixation with the Islamic State, not the state of Islam. Muawiyah had defeated both Ali and Hassan; he was secure on his throne in Damascus,

---

* The author does not give the year of this incident, but it was before the birth of Muawiyah or the advent of Islam.

revelling in the splendour of the Byzantines he had embraced, but his obsession with Ali would not go. The governor of Syria, who had appointed himself "Caliph of Allah," just could not let go of the guilt that plagued his conscience.

This obsession over Ali manifested itself in a sad tradition that continued for six decades in the ninety-year Umayyad dynasty. At every sermon in Friday prayers, throughout the empire, imams were instructed to curse Ali and his progeny—the grandsons of the Prophet as well as his daughter, Ali's wife Fatima. Cursing Ali became a regular part of Islamic prayer. The curse was also incorporated into the hajj pilgrimage, where on the last day Muslims stood on the plains of Arafat. Of course, none of this is mentioned in contemporary Islamic literature pouring out of Saudi Arabia, Pakistan, and Egypt.

The tradition of the cursing of Ali was instituted by no less a figure than Muawiyah. The cursing was intended to provoke Ali's supporters, who still formed the bulk of the population in Iraq. According to the historian Tabari, in October 661, when appointing a new governor in Kufa, Muawiyah gave him specific instructions: "Do not refrain from abusing Ali and criticizing him, nor from asking God's mercy upon Uthman and His forgiveness for him. Continue to shame the companions of Ali, keep them at a distance and don't listen to them."

While many Sunni scholars deny Tabari's version of history, Jamaat-e-Islami founder Abul Ala Maudoodi agrees with him. In his book *Khilafat o malookiat* (*The Caliphate and Monarchy*), Maudoodi writes, "One other deeply disliked innovation that was introduced during the reign of Muawiyah by himself and by his orders to all his governors, was the instruction that in sermons from the pulpit, Ali should be reviled and insulted."

Maudoodi writes that even the mosque of the Prophet was not spared. Right in front of the grave of the Prophet and in the presence of Ali's sons and grandchildren, Ali was cursed and the Prophet's relatives were vilified.

Ten years after the cursing of Ali had become part of the Friday sermon, Ali's supporters continued to resist peacefully and protested the public slander of the Prophet's progeny. In 670, when a new governor was appointed in Kufa, a minor incident triggered a major hunt for opponents of Muawiyah. The new governor, Ziyad, ordered the arrest of a number of supporters of Ali, accusing them of having rebelled against the authority of the caliph and thus an infidelity towards Allah. The men were rounded up, and after a series of show trials that included hearings before Muawiyah himself, they were given a choice to either curse Ali publicly or face death. Of the eight men, six preferred death and were beheaded as apostates. Thus began the tradition that allowed successive caliphs and sultans to kill their opponents by accusing them of apostasy against Allah. After all, the caliph was not merely a king; he was Khalifat Allah, God's very own deputy on earth.

Muslims today find it difficult to believe that the man who they feel established the first viable Muslim kingdom would have authorized the institutional curse as part of every sermon in every mosque in his domain and that this should continue as part of the annual hajj pilgrimage. However, this is the bitter pill I am asking Muslims to swallow. The actions of those who ruled after the death of the Prophet do not provide even a semblance of what we require in the 21st century. Unless we let go of the past as the model of our future, we are bound to repeat it. Young Muslims in the West, enamoured by the call of the Islamists to revert to the so-called purity of the Golden Age of Islam, need to ask their mentors, "How can a king who made the cursing of Ali and the Prophet's family as part of the hajj ritual be considered Islamic?"

This brings us to the question of the legitimacy of the Umayyads as an Islamic caliphate. What right did they have to rule over Muslim lands and where did they derive their power?

There is no doubt that by championing themselves as people seeking justice for the murder of Uthman, they catered to one faction of the Meccan Arabs and pitted them against Ali and the Banu Hashim. They based their right to rule on the ascension of Caliph Uthman. The murdered caliph was after all selected by a six-member consultative body, the Shura. Muawiyah and the Umayyads falsely invoked the grief over Uthman's death and appropriated the dead caliph's legitimacy as their own God-given right to power. Nothing could be further from the teachings of the Quran and the example of Muhammad, yet no one dared question Muawiyah's right to refer to himself as God's vice-regent on Earth. Every Umayyad caliph was also referred to as a man of "unsurpassed merit" (*al afdal*) and the "best man alive" (*khayr al-nas*). The Umayyads saw their rule as having been decreed by God, for if Allah had not wanted them as caliphs, they argued, the Umayyads would not be the caliphs. (This philosophy of determinism was opposed by the movement of rationalist Muslims, who believed in free will. They emerged in Basra during the 720s, and are known as the Mutazalites.)

However, it seems determinism was widely accepted among the population, even among the opponents of the Umayyads. In fact, when a group of revolutionaries from Khurasan (in present-day Iran) finally toppled the Umayyad dynasty in a bloodbath, they too justified the takeover as God's will. If God had not willed it, how they could have overthrown the powerful Umayyads, they argued. Today, a similar determinism guides Islamists, but only when it suits them. How else can they explain the continuous uninterrupted success of the West after the 15th century and the collapse of Muslim scholarship after our expulsion from Spain? This determinism is at the core of the Islamist discomfort with Europe and the European reliance on reason and rational thought as the basis of any discourse.

Back in Damascus, the palace intrigues and conspiracies continued amid the complexities of tribal loyalties conflicting with marital relationships. Muawiyah played a brilliant game to ensure stability of his regime while firmly stamping out dissent. Sensing the end of his forty-year reign, Muawiyah manipulated the transfer of power to his son Yazid, but not through the Consultative Council, the institution he had promised to respect. The principle of restricting the caliphate from among the Meccan Arabs—the Quraysh—had now been further restricted. Muawiyah decreed that the caliph could only be a member of the Banu Umayya clan. From there it was narrowed down to the sub-clan of Abu Sufyan, the family of Muawiyah's father. Thus, in Muawiyah's eyes, it was Yazid who should succeed him as God's representative on Earth, even though the young prince was neither a man of "unsurpassed merit" nor the "best man alive."

A connoisseur of fine wine, Yazid was too feeble to have won the caliphate on his own might, so the father had to make a living will. But before that, some obstacles had to be removed. First, he began to eliminate the other contenders. Abd Rahman, the son of Khalid ibn Walid, was poisoned. Then, Muawiyah summarily fired Marwan as the governor of Medina, replacing him with his own nephew, al-Walid bin Utba bin Abu Sufyan. This led to a serious rift within the family. Curses wrapped in poisonous verse flew across the royal chambers, as contenders to the throne shed all pretence of respecting the Islamic ethics of Muhammad and hurled Quranic verses and the sayings of Muhammad to support their arguments. To this day, the Quran and the sayings of the Prophet have been used by seekers of power, more as tools to make them appear as authentic Muslims than as their moral compass. The master politician was about to die, but before he left, he ensured that the notables and citizenry would swear allegiance to Yazid as the next caliph.

On April 28, 680, the first king of Islam died. A few days later, Yazid bin Muawiyah, the first Crown Prince of Islam, took over as Caliph of Allah and Commander of the Faithful. Yazid would soon preside over Islam's darkest period, its third civil war. The struggle for power would leave a permanent gash in the Muslim psyche, a festering wound that bleeds in the streets of Baghdad even today. Yazid also earned the unique distinction of being the most despised man in all of Islam.

Muawiyah's legacy does include two decades of stability and military expansion; he is rightly credited for laying the foundations of governance that facilitated the spread of the Islamic empire. However, Muawiyah will be best remembered for placing on the throne of Damascus—in the name of Islam and Allah—his son Yazid, who would preside over the slaughter of the Prophet Muhammad's family.

CALIPH YAZID—CALIPH OF ALLAH AND THE MURDERER OF HUSSAIN

Yazid's first act as caliph after inheriting the throne was not merely to consolidate his power, but to eliminate any possible challenge from disgruntled contenders. He wrote a secret letter to the governor of Medina, his cousin al-Walid, on a parchment that historian Tabari describes as the "size of a rat's ear," ordering him to "Seize Hussain (bin Ali), Abdullah bin Umar and Abdullah bin al-Zubayr to give oath of allegiance. Act so fiercely that they have no chance to do anything before giving oath of allegiance. Peace be with you."

All three had refused to obey Muawiyah when he selected Yazid as his successor and ordered the oath-of-allegiance ceremony be held to seal the unilateral appointment. Hussain and Abdullah were sons of deceased caliphs (Ali ibn Abu Talib and Umar bin al-Khattab, respectively), while Abdullah bin al-Zubayr's father had been appointed to the Shura that elected Uthman. All three felt they had a more substantial claim to the caliphate than Yazid, but only Hussain and Abdullah bin al-Zubayr would defy Yazid in parallel challenges to his authority.

Hussain and Ibn al-Zubayr were ordered to present themselves to the governor. They were not yet aware of the death of Muawiyah, but were astute enough to recognize that something was out of the ordinary. Hussain took precautions, alerting his supporters before going to see the governor, but Ibn al-Zubayr refused to do so and, sensing danger, prepared to escape from the city.

Al-Walid ordered Hussain to submit to Yazid. To strengthen his position, the new governor had now aligned himself with Marwan, the person he had deposed. Hussain stalled for time and suggested he preferred to offer his oath of allegiance in public, not in private. This would have to wait for the next day. Tabari reports that although al-Walid fell for the ruse, Marwan wanted Hussain arrested on the spot and beheaded for refusing to accept Yazid as the new Caliph of Allah. In the end, it was agreed that the next day there would be a public oath of allegiance.

That night, however, Abdullah Ibn al-Zubayr escaped in the darkness of the night with his brother, family, and loyal friends to take refuge in Mecca. Infuriated by his failure to pressure Ibn al-Zubayr into submission, al-Walid turned his attention towards Hussain, demanding an immediate oath of allegiance to the new caliph. Hussain promised to consider the request the next day, but as soon as the sun set, Hussain too fled Medina, hoping to find safety in Mecca.

In a strange twist of fate, the grandson of Muhammad was retracing the footsteps of his illustrious grandfather, only in reverse. The Prophet had escaped the oppression in Mecca to find refuge in Medina; his grandson Hussain was being forced by Yazid, al-Walid, and Marwan to find safe haven in Mecca. While Muhammad's night flight had been to find a place where he could establish a state of Islam, sixty years later his grandson was fleeing the grip of the very Islamic State that Muhammad's followers had created in the name of Islam.

Early historians differ as to what followed. However, it appears that after reaching Mecca, it was Abdullah Ibn al-Zubayr who was able to marshal the support of the townspeople, not Hussain. This is reflected in the fact that from Damascus, Caliph Yazid ordered Abdullah's estranged brother Amr to lead an attack on Mecca and to bring back his rebellious brother, but not Hussain. Setting brother against brother for a battle inside the House of God in Mecca in the name of Islam did not arouse much opposition. Tabari reports, though, that Marwan bin al-Hakam did warn the new governor of Medina, Amr bin Said,* against the attack: "Do not attack Mecca. Fear God and do not violate the sanctity of the House of God. Leave Ibn al-Zubayr alone. He has grown into an obstinate old man of over sixty years of age. By God! If you do not kill him, he will surely die."

However, Amr agreed to lead the attack against his brother. He would not let such trivial matters as piety stand in the way of good old-fashioned revenge and bloodshed. Amr ibn al-Zubayr retorted: "By God! Let us fight

---

* After Abdullah ibn al-Zubayr and Hussain escaped, Yazid dismissed al-Walid as the governor and replaced him with Amr bin Said.

against him [his brother Abdullah ibn al-Zubayr], and let us attack him in the heart of the Ka'aba, and let those who hate it, hate it."

The attack of brother against brother took place in Mecca along two fronts. The Meccans rallied around Abdullah and defeated the army sent from Medina. Amr was captured and imprisoned, later succumbing to a public lashing. Abdullah ibn al-Zubayr not only survived this attack, but also would go on to declare himself a caliph of Islam based in Mecca. His victory and counter-caliphate made him a serious threat to the caliphate in Damascus. Again, Islamic history taught at schools does not recognize Abdullah ibn al-Zubayr as a caliph, this despite the fact that he ruled the heartland of Islam and administered a more pristine form of Islam than his enemies in Damascus.

Little is known about what role, if any, Hussain played in that battle. There are references that Ibn al-Zubayr and Hussain met every two days inside the Ka'aba, but there is no evidence that the two were working together. In fact, if Ibn al-Zubayr had any claim to becoming the caliph, he knew that Hussain would have a more legitimate entitlement. It seems Hussain was biding his time, trying to connect with his own power base in Kufa and the rest of Iraq, where the population was still refusing to accept the Umayyad kings as authentic "Caliphs of Allah." They were still smarting from the intrigue and injustice inflicted on Ali and later on his son Hassan by Muawiyah and the Syrians. Little did they know the worst was yet to come.

On Muawiyah's death, few in Iraq and Kufa had submitted to his son Yazid's authority. As long as the Kufans were leaderless, Yazid had little to worry about. But when news of Hussain's flight from Medina to Mecca reached them, the notables of Kufa met to chart their future. A letter was written on behalf of the Shia Ali, addressed to Hussain and asking him to come to Kufa to lead the challenge to Yazid. The letter said: "Praise be to God who has broken your enemy, the obstinate tyrant who had leapt upon his community, stripped it of its authority, plundered its *fay* [booty from conquered lands], seized control of it without its consent. . . . There is no imam over us. Therefore come, so God may unite us in truth through you."

More than fifty-three other letters arrived in Mecca, some pleading that Hussain take direct action, others speaking in innuendo. One said: "The janab has grown green, the fruit has ripened, the waters have overflowed. Therefore, if you want, come to an army that has been gathered for you. Peace be to you." The word "peace" had already acquired the status of a meaningless cliché.

Hussain was unsure about the veracity of these invitations and wanted an independent assessment of the situation. Was there a genuine groundswell of support for him in Kufa or was he being lured into a trap? Hussain assigned his cousin Muslim bin Aqil to pay a visit to Kufa and ascertain if the people were "united and committed." He instructed his cousin to let him know in a speedy fashion if it was worth his while to challenge Yazid and lead the Shia into battle.

Amid the intrigue of double agents and Yazid's spies, Muslim bin Aqil reached Kufa to discover widespread discontent among the citizens. Within days, he had the commitment of more than twelve thousand men who swore to fight Yazid if Hussain were to come and lead them. Yazid was aware of the development. He had recently appointed a ruthless new governor in the city whose spies reported back on every move Muslim made. In the meantime, buoyed by the strong support he received, Muslim bin Aqil wrote back to Hussain, urging him to make the move to Kufa, where an army waited for him to lead: "The trusted early messenger does not lie to his own people. Eighteen thousand of the Kufans have given oath of allegiance to you. Hurry and come when my letter reaches you. All the people are with you. None of them has any regard or desire for the clan of Muawiyah. Peace be with you."

On receiving this letter, Hussain and his entire family—including women and children—packed up in Mecca and began their journey towards Kufa. The camel train carrying the family of the Prophet moved at a snail's pace through the desert, and when it reached Kufa the situation there had changed completely. Ubayd Allah, the new governor, had entered the city, and through large sums of money and a network of spies, had found out the safe houses where Muslim ibn Aqil was staying. First, Hani bin Urwah, who was hosting the visitor from Mecca, was lured into a trap, arrested, beaten up, and imprisoned in the governor's compound. Within hours, the governor's compound was surrounded by four thousand of the eighteen thousand men who had signed up to join Hussain's army. A day-long mêlée ensued, with Ubayd Allah under siege inside his compound and the mob outside demanding the release of Hani. But by the evening, Ubayd Allah's spies had spread the rumour that the feared Syrian army of Yazid was on its way to relieve the besieged governor, and dire consequences awaited anyone found on the streets. The crowd started dispersing. By nightfall, Muslim bin Aqil was all alone, abandoned by his closest friends, with not even a room to sleep in. Fear, money, manipulation, intrigue, lies, and, above all, cowardice had played a bigger role than the promise of being led by the grandson of the Prophet.

The next day, Muslim bin Aqil was betrayed by the very family who had given him sanctuary. He was led away on a mule, begging for his life so that he could send a message to Hussain not to come. He was led to the governor, humiliated, beaten, tortured, and killed. Muslim bin Aqil's humiliation and death were a prelude to what followed—the slaughter of the Prophet's progeny in the name of Islam. Both Muslim and Hani were beheaded, their bodies thrown into the meat market of the town and dragged through the streets in a scene that would be repeated throughout Islamic history.

Whether it was the bodies of the Iraqi royal family dragged through the streets of Baghdad in the 1950s communist coup, or the mutilated corpses of Pakistani UN soldiers being dragged around in Mogadishu by Somali warlords in the 1990s, the precedent of this brutality was set in Kufa in 680. A golden age? My foot.

Four days later, Hussain received a message from Kufa, letting him know that the tide had turned and the people of Kufa had abandoned their support for him. He was warned, "the hearts of the people are with you, but their swords are with the Banu Umayyah." Instead of turning back, Hussain invoked a vision he had in which Prophet Muhammad had ordered him to do what he was doing irrespective of the outcome. Other reports say Hussain intended to return, but was persuaded otherwise by the brothers of the slain Muslim bin Aqil who sought revenge. "By God! We will not go back until we have taken our vengeance or have tasted the death that our brother tasted," they said, urging Hussain to continue with his mission.

Should he have turned back? Was it suicidal for him to continue towards Kufa, knowing that the townsfolk had abandoned him? These questions are lost today in the polemics of the Shia–Sunni divide. However, what ensued was a bloodbath that has cursed Muslims for more than 1,400 years. When Hussain and his family arrived in Kufa, the Syrian army, forty thousand strong, surrounded them, ordering him to submit to Caliph Yazid. Hussain refused, declaring, "Death will come to you before that." Cut off from water and food, the small band of men fought to the last, until Hussain himself was beheaded. The women wailed and beat themselves in agony. Muslims had slaughtered the family of Muhammad and that too in the name of the "Caliph of Allah." The beheaded bodies of the progeny of Muhammad were buried in Karbala, but the heads were placed on pikes and distributed among the various tribes as reward for their loyalty to the Umayyad caliphate.

Is this what my religion of peace does to its followers? Have we Muslims reconciled with the crime of killing Muhammad's grandson and his great-grandsons? Can we absolve ourselves of the responsibility of this crime if we have not yet stopped the killing of those who are considered "bad Muslims"? Why on earth are Islamists calling these bloody and chilling massacres a "golden age" to which all humanity should revert? And why are Muslims not standing up to the lies and saying without fear, "We do not wish to go back to the times of Karbala, or the Apostate Wars, or the War of Siffin or the War of the Camel, or the thousands of Muslim versus Muslim wars that have drenched the deserts of the Muslim empires"?

And to those who say this was not the Golden Age of Islam, I ask, if not, then please share with me when exactly did such an age occur? After all, the great expansion of the Islamic empire that still sends a quiver of pride up the spines of young Muslim men took place during the Umayyad dynasty, the nearly one hundred years of expansion when Islam governed lands as far apart as Spain and China. What is forgotten is the fact that this monarchy was built on the foundations of murder, intrigue, lies, brutality, all epitomized by the bloody events of Karbala. Can a state structured around the massacre of Prophet Muhammad's own family be considered an Islamic State?

Like today, most of the energies of the Umayyad State—which Professor Khalid Yahya Blankinship of Temple University, Pennsylvania, calls the "Jihad State"—were expended fighting fellow Muslims. Following the murder of Hussain, the other contender to the throne, Ibn al-Zubayr, stayed in Mecca, declaring himself as the new caliph. He challenged the authority of Damascus and extended his rule to Mecca, Medina, and Basra.

In 683, Yazid dispatched an army to subdue al-Zubayr, but while his army suppressed the Medinian opposition in battle, the siege of Mecca led to the destruction of the Ka'aba or Grand Mosque (it was badly damaged in a fire). It is difficult to imagine the savagery of Muslims who would set fire to the Ka'aba, yet this sad event did occur and is part of our history.

Tabari reports that the Umayyad army plundered Medina for three days before turning on Mecca. As battles raged around the vicinity of the Holy Ka'aba, the Umayyad army started bombarding the house of God with stones and wood, setting it aflame. The man in charge of the bombardment is said to have recited, "A ballista with which we bombard the pillars of the mosque is like a raging stallion camel."

Yazid died while the siege of Mecca was still in progress. On his death, the Umayyad army returned to Damascus, leaving Ibn al-Zubayr in control of Mecca as the caliph. It became still more obvious that the state had become a monarchy when Yazid was succeeded by his son Muawiyah II (683–84).

But within a short time, two new factions developed within the ruling elites of Damascus: those supporting Ibn al-Zubayr, who was now firmly in charge in Mecca, and those backing Marwan, who had been deposed as governor of Medina by Yazid's father. Another battle ensued and the army of Marwan triumphed at a battle at Marj Rahit, near Damascus, in 684, and Marwan was successful in deposing Muawiyah II.

The new caliph in Damascus had a controversial past. Marwan ibn al-Hakam's (623–85) ascension pointed to a shift in the lineage of the Umayyad dynasty from descendants of Abu Sufyan to those of Hakam, both of whom were grandsons of Umayyah (for whom the Umayyad dynasty is named). Hakam was also a first cousin to the third caliph, Uthman. When the Prophet conquered Mecca, he ordered both Marwan and his father, Hakam ibn al-Aas, into exile, saying they should never return to Mecca as a punishment for the pain they had inflicted on him and other early Muslims.

Despite this expulsion, which was honoured by both caliphs Abu-Bakr and Umar, the third caliph, Uthman, lifted the exile and made both father and son prominent in his administration. This was a dramatic violation of Muhammad's explicit instructions. The enemies of Islam were now the kingmakers. Nepotism and tribal loyalties had overtaken any semblance of Islamic ethics, values, or rule of law.

Marwan exploited his relationship with Uthman. He was appointed governor of Medina until Muawiyah removed him to ensure his own son's ascension would go unchallenged. On becoming caliph in Damascus, Marwan became obsessed with removing Ibn al-Zubayr, the caliph in Mecca. After all, had al-Walid listened to his advice, Hussain and Ibn al-Zubayr would have been captured in Medina before they made good their escape to Mecca.

One needs to place oneself in those times to recognize the challenge faced by Marwan. Most of the Islamic world recognized Ibn al-Zubayr as the Caliph of Islam—not the Syrian Marwan, who was known to have a suspect pedigree. Marwan did recapture Egypt for the Umayyads, but could not displace his rival in Mecca, the heart of Islam. Marwan died in 685, having reigned for only nine months and failing to undermine either the credibility or the legitimacy of Caliph Ibn al-Zubayr.

Ibn al-Zubayr's caliphate commanded the respect of many Muslims, not just because he was in control of Mecca and Medina, but also because he was thought to have been the first child born after the Prophet and his companions settled in Medina. He was a young companion of the Apostle and his father had been a member of the first Shura appointed by Umar to select his successor. Unlike Marwan and later his son Abd al Malik, Ibn al-Zubayr's family credentials as Muslim were never suspect. Contemporary Islamic textbooks do not refer to him as an authentic caliph, but the fact of the matter is he ruled Hejaz, Egypt, and Iraq as "Commander of the Faithful" for nine years, until his death in Mecca in October 692 at the hands of Abd al-Malik's army. In fact, it was not until the death of Ibn al-Zubayr that the

Umayyads finally ruled over the entire Muslim world and then, too, faced one rebellion after another.

When Abd al-Malik (685–705) inherited the Umayyad throne from his father, any pretence of the Shura system of selection had been abandoned. The pristine form of Islam practised during the times of the Prophet, and to some degree by Abu-Bakr and Umar, was in the distant past. For many ordinary Muslims, the bloody struggles for power are forgotten or glossed over. The facts, however, do not support the notion of a peaceful empire facing minor opposition from within.

While the competing caliphates of Damascus and Mecca fought for the control of the lands, hearts, and minds of the Muslims, another group arose in Iraq. Led by a Shia named Al-Mukhtar, they revolted, hoping to win the caliphate for Muhammad ibn al-Hanafiyah, another son of Ali. Al-Mukhtar fought against the Umayyads in 686, defeating them near Mosul, and against Ibn al-Zubayr in 687, who crushed the revolt and brought Iraq under his rule.

So fractured was the Muslim Ummah in the late 7th century that the Damascus Umayyads started discouraging their subjects from going on the hajj pilgrimage. It is said that while in Mecca, the Syrian pilgrims would be influenced by the oratory of Caliph Ibn al-Zubayr and give their oath of allegiance to the Meccan caliph. Abd al-Malik feared that returning pilgrims would challenge his political as well as religious authority. Many historians report that Abd al-Malik was so frustrated by his inability to capture Mecca and to lead the hajj that he built the Dome of the Rock in Jerusalem as an alternative to the Ka'aba in Mecca. Before Abd al-Malik, there is no record of Muslims going to pilgrimage to Jerusalem, but after he built the Dome of the Rock, this site became a venue for Syrians to visit instead of Mecca and Medina.

The historian al-Yakubi, in his classic *Tarikh al-Yakoobi*, writes:

Abd al-Malik prevented the people of Sham [Syria] from the hajj and this is because Ibn al-Zubayr was taking the pledge of allegiance from the pilgrims. When Abd al-Malik had found out about this, he prevented them from setting out to Makkah [Mecca]. But the people protested and said, "Do you prevent us from doing the pilgrimage to the Sacred House of Allah while it is a duty from Allah upon us?" He said: "Here is Ibn Shihabuddin al-Zuhri narrating to you that the Messenger of Allah said: 'The caravans should not be set out except for three mosques, the Sacred Mosque, my present Mosque and the Mosque of Jerusalem,' [which] stands for the Sacred Mosque for you. And here is the Rock on [which] it is narrated that the Prophet set his foot before ascending to the heavens, it stands for the Ka'aba." Then he built a Dome on the Rock, suspended silk curtains on it and appointed servants for it. And told the people to revolve around it like they revolve around the Ka'aba and so it was during the rule of Bani Umayyah.

Other historians suggest Abd al-Malik decreed that pilgrimage to the Jerusalem mosque was equivalent to the obligatory circumambulation (*tawaf*) around the Ka'aba as ordained in Islamic law. Al-Malik then asked the theologian al-Zuhri to justify this politically motivated reform of religious life. Al-Zuhri then recalled a saying of the Prophet that there are three mosques to which people may make pilgrimages: those in Mecca, Medina, and Jerusalem.

Professor Chase Robinson of Oxford University in his book on Abd al-Malik touches on this subject of the Dome on the Rock. Citing the 9th-century historian al-Waqidi, he writes: "The reason for its construction was that Ibn al-Zubayr had then control of Mecca and, during the Pilgrimage season, he used to catalogue the vices of the Marwanid family, and to summon (the people) to pay homage to him (as caliph). He was so eloquent, and so the people inclined towards him. Abd al-Malik, therefore, prevented the people from performing the Pilgrimage."

No matter what his intentions were, the Dome of the Rock by any standards was not just a majestic building, but also a grand statement, giving Islam's presence in Palestine permanence. Built during his rule, the mosque has immortalized the name of Abd al-Malik. Until then, the rest of the population, which was overwhelmingly Christian or Jewish, had thought of the Muslim presence as transitory. Caliph Abd al-Malik is also credited with the enforcement of Arabic as a language of the empire and the consolidation of the dynasty during his twenty-year reign. Four of Abd al-Malik's sons would inherit his throne: Al-Walid I (705–15), Suleiman (715–17), Yazid II (720–24) and the youngest, Hisham (724–43).

Hisham's reign saw the end of the Islamic military expansion and the collapse of the Umayyad dynasty. When the dynasty fell, the entire royal family was hunted down and killed except for one of Hisham's grandsons. The Umayyads, who had overseen the massacre of the Prophet's family and chased it across the empire, from India to Egypt, were now running for their lives. This time even the dead were not spared. Graves of Umayyad nobles were dug out and the bodies desecrated. Only one of the Umayyads was spared—Caliph Umar ibn Abd al-Aziz. Umar was a nephew of Abd al-Malik; however, unlike previous Umayyad caliphs, he was not a hereditary successor, but was appointed. Not only was this man seen as a symbol of piety and humility during his short three-year rule, but he is credited with the end of institutional discrimination against non-Arabs, especially the Persians, Indians, and North Africans. Umar also ended the practice of cursing the family of the Prophet as part of the Friday prayer sermons and also during the hajj sermon delivered on the Plains of Arafat outside Mecca. He is the only one of the Umayyad caliphs who earned the title of Rightly Guided Caliph, joining the illustrious company of Islam's first four caliphs.

The Umayyad caliphate fits the "Jihad State" label. Territorial expansion was adopted as an act of worship and a duty of every Muslim. The Umayyads also institutionalized the domination of Arabs, particularly their own families, over newly converted Muslims, the Mawalis. In the words of British Islamic scholar G.R. Hawting, the Umayyads regarded Islam "as the property of the conquering aristocracy." If there was one constant theme running through the ninety-year dynasty, it was one of rebellion. From the murder in 656 of Uthman in Medina (who for all historical purposes can be recognized as the founder of the Umayyad kingdom), to the last rebellion by the descendents of the Prophet's uncle, Abbas, the Umayyad story is one of war and turmoil, intrigue, and murder.

The mutiny that finally overthrew the Umayyad caliphate was known as the Hashimiyya—the word refers specifically to Abu Hashim, a grandson of Ali. The uprising was in some ways a continuation of the failed revolt led by Al-Mukhtar, who had led the Shias against Caliph Yazid, claiming to be representing Muhammad ibn al-Hanafiyah. The revolt had been in preparation since 719 in Khurasan, in Persia, and was based primarily among the non-Arab population. By 747, the movement had gained enough strength to emerge as an open revolt carried out under the sign of a black flag. Within a year, all of Khurasan as well as Kufa fell to the mutineers. In January of 750, Abu al-Abbas, the leader of the rebels, faced off against Caliph Marwan II at the Battle of Zab in Iraq.

The Umayyad army was soundly defeated and the last caliph of the dynasty had to flee for his life, relentlessly pursued by the soldiers of Abu al-Abbas, who was soon to crown himself as the new Caliph of Islam. Every member of the Umayyads would be killed, except for one grandson of Caliph Hashim, Abd al-Rahman, who escaped to Spain where he would lay the foundations of the second Umayyad dynasty, an amazing period of Islamic history (see Chapter 9). Spain and Iraq were like two jewels that would tantalize the rest of the world from the 9th to the 12th centuries. The competing dynasties of Spain, under the Umayyads, and Iraq, under the Abbasides, complemented each other in culture, art, music, dance, philosophy, and fine wines, and even erotica and sexuality. Persia enriched Islam with its ancient culture, paintings, vivid colours, and magnificent heritage, while Spain provided fertile soil for Islam to create a civilization unmatched by any in that day and age, with glamorous cities and citadels that glittered with lights, romance, knowledge, and pluralism, which laid the foundations of the Renaissance itself.

In Damascus in the year 750, the slaughter of the Umayyads continued unabated. The new Abbaside caliph ordered that every member of the royal family be killed. Marwan II, who had escaped Damascus and taken refuge in Egypt, was discovered in his hiding place and put to death. Another nephew of his had a hand and foot chopped off, and in that mutilated state he was put on a donkey with his face blackened, and paraded in humiliation throughout Syria with a herald announcing his arrival, "Behold, Aban, son of Muawiyah, the most renowned cavalier of the House of Omayya." The agony of this man ended only after he was no use to his tormentors and was beheaded.

Soon, Damascus was no longer the seat of the caliphate. Baghdad would be born on the shores of the Tigris and the most glorious part of Muslim civilization would bloom. The new caliph, Abu al-Abbas as-Saffah, would of course invoke his lineage to the Quraysh of Mecca and the Prophet's clan of the Banu Hashim. His full name tells the story—Abu al-Abbas Abdu'llah as-Saffah ibn Muhammad ibn Ali ibn Abdullah ibn Abbas ibn Mutalib ibn Hashim.

At last, after waiting in the wings for a hundred years—on many occasions in prison cellars, at other times slaughtered or hunted down—the Banu Hashim were finally in command of Islamdom. The Abbasid caliphate these men created would provide the scene for many of the tales of the *Arabian Nights*. (More on that kingdom, which enriched my childhood with dreams of flying carpets and exotic palaces, in chapter 10.) Its Arabian caliphs would embrace the best of Persian intellect, surround themselves with the might of the Turkish soldiery, and dazzle the world by creating a scintillating society that still fascinates even the harshest critics of Islam and Muslims.

CHAPTER 9

Cordoba—Islam's European Venture

IN HER BOOK *THE END OF DAYS*, Canadian writer Erna Paris paints an almost blissful picture of what she suggests was the world's first multicultural and multi-religious state. Paris describes 10th-century Muslim Spain as a society where people of all faiths and races thrived in relative harmony, but which collapsed within a few hundred years under the weight of external aggression and internal decay. From a Muslim's perspective, her book could very well have been titled "The Best of Days." The paradise on earth that Muslim Spaniards created would eventually disintegrate and disappear without trace, unable to face up to the fundamentalist onslaught of the Catholic as well as Islamist puritans of the day. But, introducing that paradise to her readers, Paris writes:

> The rich synthesis of learning and culture nurtured in Muslim Spain produced a remarkable era of science, philosophy, philology, biblical commentary and literature; and the intellectual activity that characterised this civilisation would have a profound effect on the rest of Europe. . . . The intellectual artistic and cultural brilliance of Arab Spain was a harvest of an open cross-fertilisation, unimpeded, a religious rejection.

This Spanish paradise was centred around the city of Cordoba—the largest city in western Europe at the time—and governed much of Spain's southerly Iberian Peninsula. Paris notes that the Spanish Visigoth* Christian

---

* Visigoth: A Germanic tribe who were converted to Christianity in the 4th century, and became Catholics in the late 6th century after moving to Spain where they established the Visigothic kingdom that survived until it was overrun by North African Muslims in 711.

clergy in northern Spain were morally disgusted by the Moorish society. From their orthodox standpoint, she writes, "the very idea of pluralism was perceived as a threat. God spoke in one voice, for if other sounds were heard, the certainty of a single universal and true religion would be open to question."

If this is the Golden Age of Islam that contemporary Political Islam beckons young Muslim men and women to, perhaps it has some justification. But is this in fact the situation today's Islamists are trying to recreate? Both the Spanish Muslim Empire and its parallel caliphate in distant Baghdad were centres of art, intellect, dance, music, architecture, medicine, engineering, and science; however, they both buckled because they failed to create viable political institutions, the absence of which led to power struggles and endless bloodshed.

Erna Paris is not alone in her fascination with the creative and brilliant society that flourished under the Muslim rulers of Spain. Anyone who ventures to study 9th- to 11th-century Spain almost inevitably speaks of the magnificence of its civilization. However, they also conclude that in contrast to the Muslim success in arts, literature, philosophy, and architecture, Muslims were less successful as politicians, and the entire period was marked by internecine rivalries leading to Muslim versus Muslim wars in Iberia that destroyed whatever they had accomplished. In fact, the majesty of the Cordoban caliphate known to Muslims as *Qurtaba* was destroyed not by Christians, but by fellow Muslims, the Almoravides, a tribe from North Africa.

While the Almoravides destroyed the caliphate of Cordoba, the culture of openness survived. The invaders assimilated and soon adopted the lifestyle of the conquered, finding Spanish civilization irresistible. Even though the caliphate had splintered into a number of small Arab kingdoms, each one rivalled the other in magnificence and they continued to sponsor philosophy, poetry, and science. The reprieve was short-lived. At the end of the 12th century, Spain was again invaded from Africa, this time by yet another fanatical Muslim group, the Almohads. The damage these fanatic Muslims did to Muslim culture and civilization was enormous, but it was their ruthlessness towards non-Muslims that devastated the multicultural and multi-religious society. Jews and Christians were given a choice: convert to Islam or move to the Christian territories in the north. In the words of Erna Paris, "The arrival of the Almohads marked the end of an era. The bright light of Cordoba flickered and went out like a dying star, never to shine again."

By 1492, as Columbus was sailing into the Atlantic sunset in search of India, the last of the Muslims and Jews were being expelled from Spain, bringing an end to the Islamic era that had begun in 711. The rot in Muslim Spain had set in a long time before the forced exodus of Jews and Muslims from Iberia in the 15th century. The brilliant African philosopher Ibn Khaldun, who lived in Spain in the mid 1300s and served as ambassador of the Sultan of Granada to Peter "the Cruel" of Castile in 1363, was able to develop an almost mathematical formula explaining the rise and fall of civilizations after he studied this particular decline. (If Ibn Khaldun was the epitome of Andalusian* intellect and scholarship, he was also the foreteller of its impending doom. More on him later.)

Islam's venture into Europe began one dark April night in the year 711 CE, on the northern shores of Africa.

The man leading this sea-borne invasion of Spain was Tariq ibn Ziyad, a Berber† who was the Umayyad governor of the North African province of Tangiers. Tariq's daring raid across the seas separating Europe and Africa brought him to the southern tip of a narrow peninsula jutting from the Spanish mainland. The rocky cliffs below which Tariq and his seven thousand troops landed still carry his name—Gibraltar, a mispronunciation of the phrase *Jabal al Tariq* (Tariq's Mountain).

To put this in some historical context, in the year that Tariq's army landed in Spain, another young Umayyad general, Muhammad bin Qasim, was landing his troops in India, on the coast of Sind (present-day Pakistan). Sitting in Damascus, presiding over this huge empire, was Umayyad Caliph al-Walid. Never had a king presided over an empire that extended from India in the east to Spain in the west.

Muslim historians maintain that the invasion of Spain was triggered by internal divisions within Spain's ruling Christian aristocracy. They suggest that a disgruntled member of the ruling Visigoth royalty was so miffed at King Rodrigo that he invited the Muslims to come and help him overthrow the monarch. It could also be argued that the Muslim armies of the Umayyad caliphate, comprising the African Berbers and the Syrian Arabs in their westward expansion, had reached the shores of the Atlantic, and the only way they could continue their military conquest—the source of much-needed revenue—was across the Mediterranean, into Spain. To the south lay the

---

* Andalusia: The most southerly part of Spain, but also the name by which medieval Muslims called Spain.
† Berber: An indigenous people of North Africa.

vast sands of the impregnable Sahara. Attempts to move south towards the fabled Wangara had ended in failure with the Muslims losing twenty thousand soldiers among the sand dunes.

Both stories could be correct, but the fact remains that Tariq ibn Ziyad's intentions were clear. There was no going back to Africa. According to the 17th-century Moroccan historian Al-Makkari, after landing in Spain, Tariq ibn Ziyad ordered the burning of all his boats, thus eliminating any possibility of retreat. Then, addressing his troops he said, "Ye Muslims whither can you flee? The sea is behind you and the enemy is before you. By Allah only your courage and patience can now help you."

Within months of landing in Spain, Tariq's army had swept through the countryside, and on July 19, 711, he came face to face with King Rodrigo. Despite superior numerical strength, the Visigoth king was defeated at the Battle of Guadalete. This victory over the Christian army lends credence to the theory that Tariq's invasion was helped by internal dissent and rivalry among the Spaniards. The defeat of Rodrigo was thorough, and the king's body was never found as his army scattered. Soon Tariq entered the city of Toledo, the capital of the Visigoth kingdom, where he joined the few remaining Christian residents in celebrating the Christmas of 711.

It would take the Christian north another three hundred years to wrest Toledo from the Muslim conquerors. Among the residents of Toledo who embraced their new Muslim rulers were the city's persecuted Jews. After being marginalized and oppressed for centuries, Spain's Jews were pleasantly surprised to find that the new rulers allowed them freedom of worship and recognized them as "people of the book." In the centuries to come, Muslim–Jewish relations would flourish; epitomized by two 12th-century Spanish philosophers: Averroes the Muslim and Maimonides the Jew.*

The Berber army, enthused with the zeal of new converts to Islam, was successful beyond the expectation of either the caliph in Damascus or his trusted Arab governor in Africa, Musa bin Nusayr. Worried about Berbers exercising exclusive control over Spain, Musa bin Nusayr recruited a new army of eighteen thousand, mostly Arabs. He led this army into Spain, attacking and conquering the cities and castles that Tariq had bypassed. By mid-714 he had reached Toledo and joined forces with Tariq. The two jostled for power, resulting in an inevitable rivalry. But before matters could get out of hand, the careers of Tariq ibn Ziyad and Musa bin Nusayr came to a hasty end: both men were summoned to appear before Caliph al-Walid in Damascus, never to return.

---

* Muslims know Averroes as Ibn Rushd and Maimonides as Ibn-Maimon.

Caliph al-Walid, it seems, was wary of successful generals in the Muslim hinterland. At the time he was recalling Tariq, he had also ordered his general in India, Muhammad bin Qasim, to be sent back—in a sack.

What followed in Spain over the next seven centuries was an era of enlightenment, culture, architecture, and learning in a secular society that became a beacon of progress for the rest of the world. Notwithstanding the accompanying power struggles, civil wars, and palace coups, Muslim Spain is where scholars from around the world would go, where huge libraries were built, where street lighting and running water were first introduced. It was all possible because of the relaxed attitude adopted by the early Muslim rulers, which was in sharp contrast to the jihadism of the Umayyads and the puritanism of Islamic extremists such as the Kharijites. It was not as if these puritan Islamists had disappeared, but they remained on the margins and even when they succeeded, they could not dislodge the deep roots of pluralism, intellect, and culture that had seeped into the foundations of medieval Spanish Muslim society.

To illustrate the constant religious challenges faced by the Andalusian civilization, one needs to see it through the experience of Averroes and Maimonides. These two men were contemporaries who faced the wrath of their own orthodox co-religionists.

The world of 12th-century Muslim Spain was a haven for social assimilation of not just Jews and Muslims, but also Andalusian Christians— better known as the *Mozarabs*—who were not forced to leave their faith. It was a time of secular pursuits, and the challenging of traditional interpretation of divine texts was not uncommon. Averroes was at the forefront of those who saw the need for applying reason to understand human society and the role of religion. Greek works were already arriving in Spain as early as the 9th century. The writings of Aristotle were being read afresh, leading to the widespread acceptance of rationalism, rather than divine texts, as the basis of judging the merits of an argument. This posed a serious threat to the official authorities of all three religions in Spain. As long as Averroes adopted Greek science, mathematics, and medicine, the imams were unconcerned, but as soon as he ventured into applying critical analysis to Islam, he drew their fury.

For example, Averroes challenged the literalism practised by the clerics. He suggested that philosophers were best able to understand properly the allegorical passages in the Quran on the basis of their logical training and that there was no religious stipulation requiring such passages to be interpreted literally.

The imams in Averroes' home city of Cordoba immediately denounced him as an apostate deserving of the death penalty. There was widespread anger among the mosque establishment, and clerics publicly burned many of Averroes' books. If the Islamic establishment was angry with Averroes, the Catholic Church was even more indignant. As his books on philosophy and rationalism crossed the borders of Spain into Christian Europe, he was considered a threat and labelled as a heathen. The Church reviled Averroes for centuries. It matched, if not outdid, its Islamic counterparts in declaring the philosopher a threat to faith itself.

The Church did not spare the Christian intellectuals in Andalusia, who were also involved in the movement to bring reason and rationalism into public life. In fact, the Church considered any Christian working with Muslims and Jews as a traitor.

On the Jewish side, Moses Maimonides drew the ire of the orthodox rabbis of the time. Here was another philosopher challenging the status quo. A close friend of Averroes, Maimonides shared his Muslim colleague's approach to reconciling religion with reason. In one of his classic contributions, Maimonides—considered in some quarters to be the greatest Jewish philosopher ever—wrote, "If one has the means to provide either the [Sabbath] lamp for one's household or the Chanukah lamp, then the household lamp takes precedence because it contributes to domestic peace."

His approach to Judaism caused a spilt in the Jewish community of Andalusia. The orthodoxy fought back and the great man's books were also burned in public. It seemed all three religions were afraid of rationalist ideas. (It is a pity, but they still are.) These rational thinkers—secularists who reconciled religion with reason—were too far ahead of their time. Their works would affect and change Europe many hundred years later, but in the 12th century, even the enlightened climate created by Muslim rulers of Spain was not sufficient to protect, let alone sustain, the flame of reason lit in the darkness of Europe. That light was snuffed out by the twin attacks from Muslim and Christian orthodoxy. Both Averroes and Maimonides lived during the time when the Islamic fanatics, the Almohads, conquered Cordoba and imposed a very harsh regime on the hitherto tolerant society. Some argue this was the end of Muslim rule in Spain, brought upon by zealots who acted as God's warriors to protect Islam and ended up contributing to the wiping out of Islam in Spain.

In the end, it was as much the Islamist hatred for the pluralistic secular society that contributed to the downfall of Muslims in Spain as it was the

Catholic contempt for Islamic enlightenment. Both Islamic and Christian fundamentalists contributed to the destruction of the world's first multicultural, multi-religious society, leading to an ethnic cleansing of the Iberian peninsula of all Jews and Muslims in a closing act that Erna Paris aptly labels *The End of Days*.

As the curtain fell on seven centuries of Muslim presence in Spain, it was only replicating a catastrophe that had earlier befallen Islamdom's eastern caliphate in Baghdad, where the Mongols and Tartars too destroyed Muslim culture by burning books and turning the Tigris black with the ink and ash of scorched handwritten manuscripts.

Tariq Ali, the Pakistani novelist now settled in Britain, has brilliantly captured the fall of Muslim Spain to the Christian north in his bestselling novel *Shadows of the Pomegranate Tree*. The following passage encapsulates the mood of surrender and defeat in a manner that few classic historical renderings of the tragedy have been able to. The scene is set in the city of Grenada (*Gharnata* to Muslims), seven years after it had fallen to the Christian armies:

On the first day of December in the year 1499, Christian soldiers under the command of five knight commanders entered the 195 libraries of the city and a dozen mansions where some of the better known private collections were housed. Everything written in Arabic was confiscated. . . .

Ximenes de Cisneros had always believed that the heathen could only be eliminated as a force if their culture was completely erased. This meant the systemic destruction of all books. Oral traditions would survive for a while, till the Inquisition plucked away the offending tongues. If not himself, then someone else would have to organise this necessary bonfire—somebody who understood that the future had to be secured through firmness and discipline and not through love and education as those imbecile Dominicans endlessly proclaimed. What have they ever achieved? . . . A soldier had been posted just in front of the prelate's window. Ximenes stared at him and nodded, the signal was passed to the torch-bearers and the fire was lit. For half a second there was total silence.

Then a loud wail rent the December night, followed by the cries: "There is only one Allah, and he is Allah and Muhammad is his prophet." . . . The fire was rising higher and higher. The sky itself seemed to have become a flaming abyss, a spectrum of sparks that floated in the air as the delicately coloured calligraphy burnt itself out. It was as if the stars were raining down their sorrow. Slowly, in a daze the crowd began to walk away. till a beggar stripped himself bare, and began to climb onto the fire. "What is the point of life without our books of learning?" he cried through scorching lungs. "They must pay, they will pay for what they have done to us today." He fainted. The flames enveloped him.

Even today, Muslims shed tears at the great loss. Many, like the beggar, have flung themselves into the fire of the flames that still consume our books, but few have dared to ask the question: Were we responsible for our own doom?

Compared to the carnage that accompanied the rise of the first Muslim dynasty in Syria and Iraq, Islamic rule in Spain was benign. Nevertheless, civil wars, assassinations, and palace coups were not uncommon. In fact, the very first transfer of power in the newly occupied areas of Spain ended with the beheading of the emir (ruler). When Musa bin Nusayr was recalled to Damascus, he appointed his son Abd al-Aziz as his successor. The young man immediately married King Rodrigo's widow in an attempt to mollify a skeptical populace, and wore the late king's crown, which had been presented to him by his new queen. This outraged some Muslim clerics. Within a month, the young wannabe king was killed for committing the blasphemy of adopting a European custom. Suffice to say, no Muslim king ever wore a crown again. Eventually, the shah of Iran mimicked royalty with a crown, but his end was no better than that of Abd al-Aziz bin Musa bin Nusayr of Andalusia.

For about three decades after Tariq's eventful landing on the beaches of Spain, relative peace allowed the country's new leaders to consolidate their rule while maintaining a loose attachment to the caliph in Damascus. Two unique factors were at work.

For one thing, the elite in Andalusia—unlike the situation in other domains of the Islamic empire—were completely autonomous. This suited the new gentry, who had no particular desire to part with a fifth of the war booty and send it to the caliph, as was supposed to happen under Islamic law. The other factor was the mixed ethnicity of the occupiers. Most of them were Berbers from across the Strait of Gibraltar, but there were also Arabs, themselves divided by their Yemeni or Syrian–Hijazi ancestries. While Umayyad rulers in Damascus were facing challenges from fellow Muslims in India and Persia, another sort of trouble was brewing on the Atlantic coast: tensions between the Berbers and Arabs would lead to civil war.

After the defeat of the Muslims in Poitiers, France, at the hands of Frankish leader Charles Martel ("The Hammer") in October 732, Muslim expansion into Europe was halted. The wars of booty that had so far allowed the new rulers of Andalusia to maintain an economy and reward their troops could no longer be sustained. With the end of expansion, the Andalusian emirs had to learn to live from finite resources: the revenue generated by taxation. This led to tension among the notables, and as is often the case, the new adjustments required of a changed economy resulted in the development of ethnic fissures between the Berbers and Arabs.

Andalusia may have been autonomous, but what happened in the rest of the Umayyad caliphate would have a trickle-down effect on the new frontier of Islam. With the end of expansion, there was also a drop in revenue for the Umayyad governors in North Africa. The newly conquered Copts and Berbers there were encouraged to convert to Islam under the caliphate of Umar bin Abd al-Aziz (682–720), and so revenue to Damascus, which was collected from the taxation of non-Muslims, fell dramatically. Hitherto, the Umayyad caliphs had restricted the conversion of non-Arabs to Islam. The Umayyad caliphate, after all, was essentially an Arab empire, Islamic only in name. But when Caliph Umar* was informed about the drop in revenue, and advised to halt the conversion of non-Muslims to Islam, he is reported to have said: "I shall rejoice if all the *Zimmies* [non-Muslims] become Muslims, for God sent His Prophet to be an apostle, not a tax-collector."

On the eastern front, when the governor of Khurasan in Persia complained the people were converting to Islam, merely to avoid the *jazia* non-Muslim poll tax, and that he had knowledge that the converts were not circumcised, Caliph Umar bin Abd al-Aziz wrote to him: "God sent Mohammad to call men to the true Faith, and not to circumcise them."

Caliph Umar may have been right, but his decision did little to reverse the drop in revenue. More money was badly needed to sustain the Syrian army and keep a grip on the empire by rewarding the new nobility that was replacing the Persian and Byzantine aristocracy. This problem was most acute in Egypt, where military expansion had ended at the Atlantic in the west, France in the north, and the Sahara Desert in the south.

To generate revenue, Umayyad governor Ubayd Allah bin Habhab of Egypt resorted to a clumsy and racist policy: he decreed that all non-Arab converts to Islam, in particular Berbers, would be considered non-Muslim. Their privileges as Muslims were withdrawn and they were told to start

---

* Caliph Umar: Not to be confused with Umar (581–644), the second caliph of Islam.

paying the jazia tax that was obligatory for non-Muslims. As in India, this policy of creating a two-tiered hierarchy based entirely on race proved disastrous. The Berbers in North Africa rose up in arms.

In 740, while the Umayyad Arab army was in Sicily on an expedition against the Byzantines, a devout man named Maisara led the Berbers in an attack on the city of Tangiers. The city collapsed within days, with the Berbers not only killing the Arab governor, but massacring the city's entire Arab population, down to the last child. From there the revolt of the Berbers spread rapidly, and within a short period, all of North Africa west of Egypt had seceded from Umayyad control, with the Berbers electing their own caliph. By the time news reached Damascus, the cream of the Syrian cavalry had been wiped out.

In Egypt, the Arab population was furious at the defeat of its legendary army, and deposed Governor Ubayd Allah. In Damascus, Caliph Hashim was stunned. Part of his empire extending from the Nile to the Atlantic had slipped out of his hands. The defeat was particularly stinging because the Arabs had been defeated by a people they considered inferior. How could the darker-skinned Berbers defeat the forces of, supposedly, God's deputy on Earth? He is reported to have declared: "By Allah, I will show them what the wrath of an Arab of the old stamp is! I will send against them an army such as they have never seen; its van will be upon them before the rear has left Damascus."

Twenty-seven thousand fresh Syrian recruits under the command of General Kulthum and his deputy Balj were dispatched to the African front with permission to "behead all that fell into his hands and to pillage every captured town."

The Syrians were in for a nasty surprise. Before they could even reach the Berber army that was west of the Nile, they ran into resistance in the Arab cities of Egypt, where they were treated as invaders, not allies. By mid-741, huge battles were being fought between the Berbers and the Arab armies, with the Berbers inflicting massive defeat on the invading force. Muslims were spilling Muslim blood across North Africa. In the end, Balj and what remained of his army were trapped, unable to retreat back to Egypt. So he fled towards Spain. On reaching the Moroccan coastline, he conquered the coastal town of Ceuta, and he and his troops barricaded themselves there. The Berbers laid a prolonged siege to the town, resulting in near-famine conditions. In Spain, a new emir, the ninety-year-old Abd al-Malik, had just taken over. Balj sent pleading letters to him, invoking Arab solidarity and honour, begging for relief and sanctuary.

While Abd al-Malik was an Arab from Medina, Balj represented the Syrians from Damascus. Abd al-Malik was old enough to remember the humiliation the Umayyad of Damascus had inflicted on Medina and his people. There was little love lost between the two, but the time-tested "enemy of my enemy" principle worked in favour of Balj. Abd al-Malik was also facing a restive Berber population who were deeply offended by their second-class treatment at the hands of the ruling Arab nobility. The Iberian Peninsula had been conquered by the Berbers under Tariq, but the plum positions and the best of lands had been awarded to the Arabs who came with Musa bin Nusayr after the wars had ended. Because Berber rebellion was festering in Spain as well, Abd al-Malik had no choice but to rescue the Umayyad army trapped inside Ceuta and bring them over to the Spanish mainland where he recruited them into his own army to put down the Berber revolt in his own backyard.

Balj, however, turned out to be the proverbial camel that kicked the Arab from the tent. No sooner had the Berber revolt ended than Balj and his men reneged on their contract to leave Spain. Instead, they attacked the emir's palace in Cordoba, expelled him, and inserted Balj as the new emir. Abd al-Malik, who had rescued the Umayyads from Ceuta, would die a horrible death: on September 20, 741, he was dragged through the streets and beaten with clubs, then swords were plunged through his heart. The old man's corpse was placed on a cross atop a bridge, with a dog crucified on his left hand and a pig on his right. So brutal was the treatment of the old man from Medina that the Arab population of Cordoba fell upon each other. On one side were the Arabs of Medina and on the other the Umayyads under Balj. Once more, the hundred-year-old wound inflicted on the people of Medina on the night of the Saqifah Banu Saad was reopened. Another Muslim from Medina had met a horrific death at the hands of the Umayyads.

Abd al-Malik's humiliating death led to a major war between the two Arab groups in Spain. The men from Medina, the long-established Arabs in Spain, were known as the *Baladiyun* (of the country), while the new Arabs who had arrived with Balj were known as the *Shaamiyun* (the Syrians). Al-Malik's sons rallied an army that attacked Cordoba in an attempt to dislodge the Syrians, and even though Balj was killed in the battle, they failed to enter the fortified city and were defeated decisively.

To avenge the death of their leader Balj, the Syrians rounded up all their prisoners and auctioned them as slaves. To inflict the ultimate insult, the slaves were not sold to the highest bidder, but to the lowest. In one case, when a Syrian placed a bid of ten pieces of gold for one of the Baladiyun prisoners, the next bid was a dog, then a goat. Muslims were selling fellow Muslims as slaves in exchange for dogs and goats, all in the name of Islam, and with the intention of establishing the increasingly elusive Islamic State.

The wars between various factions continued intermittently in Spain and with the collapse of the Umayyad dynasty in Damascus, Andalusia was now on its own, cut off from the caliphate.

Enter Abd al-Rahman bin Muawiyah, grandson of Caliph Hashim and the only surviving member of the royalty after the massacres of the Umayyads in Damascus by the new rulers of Islam, the Abbasids.

Abd al-Rahman's mother was a Berber, which meant he had links in North Africa, so he fled there with a few of his servants, including a Mawali (non-Arab Muslim convert) named Badr who would later become his right-hand man in Spain. His first attempt was to reach *Al-Afriqiyah*, today's Tunisia, but the governor there refused to allow him inside the city, fearing he would take over. Not finding a place to settle, the fugitive Umayyad prince sent Badr to Spain with instructions to investigate the possibilities. Badr was able to make arrangements with non-Arab Spanish Muslims in southern Spain, and in the fall of 755, after being on the run for five years, Abd al-Rahman crossed the Strait of Gibraltar. He set up his command post in the homes of the few relatives of Badr and Spanish converts who had welcomed him.

Meanwhile, word spread fast among the troops in Cordoba that the grandson of the great Caliph Hashim had arrived in Spain. Among the elite of the city, there was panic.

From this tiny base, Abd al-Rahman was able to raise an army comprising mostly disgruntled Yemeni settlers and non-Arab Muslims who fell outside the tribal power structures of Cordoban society. In the winter of 755–56, diplomacy as well as armed skirmishes continued between the Umayyad prince and the ruler of Cordoba, Yusuf al-Fihri, and another challenger, al-Sumayl.

As summer approached, Abd al-Rahman had outmanoeuvred his opponents and defeated them in battle. On Friday, May 14, 756, Abd al-Rahman entered the gates of Cordoba and headed to the city's mosque, where he would be proclaimed emir of Andalusia. The second Umayyad dynasty was born and within a year of his ascension to power, the new emir would cut off all formal links with the Abbasid caliphate and sermons in all mosques of Spain would no longer be required to acknowledge the names of the Abbasid caliphate. In effect, Andalusia had seceded from the caliphate and embarked on its own journey.

This had happened once before in Mecca as well as in Kufa, but on those occasions, the secession had been brutally put down. In the case of

Andalusia, Caliph Al-Mansur in Damascus made one half-hearted attempt to assert his authority. He sent an Abbasid army to land in Portugal and attack Andalusia from the west, but when the severed head of the candidate for emir was returned to him, embalmed in a case, the message was clear: the Umayyads in Andalusia were too far away to enable the Abbasids in Damascus to exert their authority.

The Abbasids would never again attempt to assert their authority over the breakaway province, and a new political structure was born in Islam—the concept of multiple Islamic States. Both Andalusia and Iraq claimed to be the rightful representation of Islam. Over the course of years, many dynasties would be born and lay claim to be the rightful caliphate, but never again would all of Islamdom be governed by a single caliph or a unified caliphate. Of course, it is completely lost on contemporary Islamists that for nearly all of Islam's 1,400-year history no caliphate or Islamic State has been able to be sustained without bloodshed and war. Today's Islamists demand the implementation of Islamic sharia law in Canada, Britain, and Europe, but they are either oblivious to the fact that no Islamic State, not even Andalusia, has ever been able to implement it, or they are deceiving their followers into chasing this mirage.

Abd al-Rahman bin Muawiyah governed Andalusia for thirty-three years, fighting off rivals and putting down rebellions in all corners of the state. The dynasty that he established would last another three hundred years and, despite the continuation of strife and civil wars, would become the envy of the rest of Europe. Abd al-Rahman I never took on the mantle of caliph, instead being content with the title of emir. His son Hisham and five more of his successors would also be known as emirs; this, however, would change during the reign of his namesake, Abd al-Rahman III, who in 929 assumed the title of Caliph and Commander of the Faithful.

Professor Hugh Kennedy at the University of St. Andrews in Scotland refers to the reign of Caliph Abdal-Rahman III as "The Golden Age of the Umayyad Caliphate," and describes this caliph as a man of authority as well as compassion. Caliph Abd al-Rahman III is said to have been a cosmopolitan man with a deep understanding of the mutli-religious nature of his kingdom. He was of mixed ancestry, of European as well as Arab heritage. His mother, Muzna, was a Frank, and his grandmother, Iniga, was the daughter of King Fortun Garces of Navarre in northern Spain. However, this mixed heritage did not dilute his commitment to Islam. It made him respectful of the religious beliefs of others. In fact, he was the first of the Spanish Muslim monarchs who invoked jihad as an instrument of expansion. While architecture, literature, music, and other intellectual pursuits thrived during his reign, he was never free of constant civil strife in his domain. In fact, his predecessors had at one time reduced the domain of Andalusia to the limits of the city of Cordoba. The first caliph of Spain pursued an eight-year war against the separatist Muslims and then, after consolidating his regime, waged a seven-year campaign against Christian kingdoms in the north that had never reconciled with the loss of the peninsula.

By the time the last of the Spanish caliphs, Hisham III, came to power, the dynasty set up by Abd al-Rahman I was collapsing. Despite the high level of their civilization and the achievements of their great intellectuals, these Muslims failed, as have other Muslims, to develop political institutions that could withstand the dynamics of power, the exercise of authority, and the accommodation of political opposition. Assassination and overthrowing the caliph were standard procedures.

In 1031, Hisham III was dethroned and the caliphate broke up into a number of separate small Muslim states, each with its own emir, if not caliph, and each with competing claims of ancestral or tribal authority and purity. The competing Muslim states in the Iberian Peninsula—at one time numbering twenty-nine—fought among themselves, with changing loyalties and shifting fortunes, but one could not prevail over another. In the meantime, the Christian advance from the north had begun, with armies slowly reclaiming lands they had lost three hundred years earlier.

In 1085 Toledo, the historic Visigoth capital that had fallen to Tariq ibn Ziyad, was recaptured by Alfonso VI after its Muslim ruler, the self-styled Emir Kadir, had abandoned the city in the face of a citizen's revolt and switched sides to aid Alfonso. After the Christian armies retook Toledo, it became the capital of New Castile. In the absence of unified Muslim leadership, the feuding emirates in Spain had no stomach to take back Toledo. This centre of Hebrew and Arabic literature was lost forever to the Muslims. However, the culture of pluralism and intellectual excellence that Muslims had introduced in their three-hundred-year rule in Toledo did not disappear entirely. The city became home to El Greco, and in subsequent years was known for its tolerance of the Jews and Muslims who chose to remain when the Muslim armies withdrew. In 1230, Toledo became the capital of the united kingdom of Castilla and León.

The defeat of the Muslims in Toledo in 1085 and its capture by the Christian armies not only marked the end of Muslim advances into Europe, but proved to be an immense morale booster to Christendom, which had seen its borders shrink in the face of Muslim advances. When the Muslims failed to take back Toledo, a fresh sense of strength was resurgent across Europe. The beleaguered papacy that had hitherto been unable to help the Christians now seemed more willing to take leadership in defending the faith and the territory of Europe itself.

Up to the end of the first millennium, Christians had been facing one humiliation after another, not just in Spain, but also in the Holy Land. In 1009, Fatimid* caliph al-Hakim bin Amr Allah ordered the Church of the Holy Sepulchre destroyed. There arose a genuine fear and anger in European capitals. Christianity itself was in danger. Even though the caliph's successor in 1039 made an attempt to repair relations by permitting the Byzantine Empire to rebuild the Church, tremendous damage had been done to Muslim–Christian relations in Palestine. Little trust existed between the Fatimid caliphate and the European Christian kings. Tales of persecution, at times highly exaggerated, spread across Europe. News that some Christian pilgrim had been take prisoner in Jerusalem added to the widespread anger against Muslims.

The weak link in the Muslim empire was Spain, where the caliphate had splintered into multiple emirates with no coherent leadership or command. As the Spanish Muslims split into warring factions, Pope Alexander II in 1063 gave a papal blessing to the Spanish Christians, encouraging them to drive the Muslims back into Africa. The Pope granted a papal standard to the Christian forces (the *vexillum sancti Petri*); he promised an "indulgence" to all Christians who died fighting the Muslims. Following the Pope's action in Spain, pleas came in from the Byzantine Emperors in Constantinople, who now faced the new threat of Seljuk Turks. In 1074, a request for help came from Byzantine Emperor Michael VII to Pope Gregory VII, and in 1095, from Emperor Alexius I Comnenus to Pope Urban II.

On Tuesday, November 27, 1095, Pope Urban II stood on a platform in the French city of Clermont, where he issued his historic call for a crusade to take back Jerusalem and the Church of the Holy Sepulchre from the hands of the Muslims. Like the radical jihadi imams of 21st-century Islam, Pope Urban urged Christians to stop their murderous wars against each other and to unite to end the "occupation of Palestine." Like the jihadis who promise paradise to suicide bombers, Pope Urban promised Christian soldiers who died fighting the "infidels" remission from whatever time the Christian had

---

* Fatimids: A dynasty that broke away from the Baghdad Abbasids and was the only Shia Muslim caliphate in Islamic history, created by descendants of the Prophet through his daughter Fatima.

been sentenced to serve in purgatory and an absolution from all his sins. If he were to survive, the European soldier was promised protection against temporal punishment for any sins he might commit. Thus began the Crusades as Christian volunteer soldiers headed east to liberate Jerusalem, while others joined the *Reconquista** in Spain.

Islamdom faced an attack from Europe on two sides. After the fall of Toledo in 1085, Andalusia ceased to exist as a viable contiguous territorial unit and was forever vulnerable to attacks. From the 11th century onwards, Andalusia survived as a loose confederation of warring Muslim Bantustans, each vying for supremacy by invoking tribal lineage and Islam as the justification for their authority. The Muslim ruler of Toledo who joined forces with the Christian "enemy" was not the only one. Muslims have many times been betrayed by treacherous leaders. In 1099 Jerusalem too fell to the Christian crusaders and that defeat too was possible only because of the complicity of members of the Muslim elite who sided with the invaders to spite their Muslim opponents.

After Toledo, Saragossa was taken in 1115 by a Christian army and in 1147 Lisbon fell to Alfonso I of Portugal. As the Christian armies inched southward, the petty emirs of the dozen *Taifa* kingdoms in Andalusia were panicking. Their very survival was at stake. A plea went out to the Berber kingdoms in Morocco and West Africa, and the Almoravides rulers responded. They sent an army to Spain which pushed the Christians back to Leon. The Andalusians were saved from the Christian onslaught, but had to pay a price. The hardy Berbers were in no mood to go back to their tribal existence in Africa. The succulent pleasures of high culture, fertile land, and the beautiful women and architecture were enough to make them decide to stay. Bilj had come to seek refuge but refused to leave, and the Almoravides did the same. But their puritan ultra-conservative Islam disrupted Andalusian society. Radical Islam was unknown to the Andalusians, but their Almoravides rescuers imposed the harshness of the deserts and mountains of Morocco on the lush valleys and flowing hills of Spain. They ruled Muslim Spain for only forty years. By 1145, Muslim Spain was again mired in internecine wars. The rival tribal states not only fought over land, but enticed poets and artists from each other's domains to adorn their courts and indulge their taste of high culture.

With the Christian threat still looming from the north, in 1146 Andalusia was now invaded from the south by the Almohads, who had only recently routed the Almoravides in Marrakesh, ending their rule with a massacre.

---

* *Reconquista*: Wars in which the Christians drove the Muslims out of Spain and Portugal.

The Almohads turned out to be like the Taliban of today. Their armies saved Andalusia from total collapse, but they systematically started destroying all vestiges of culture that their fanaticism found offensive. For the first time since Tariq had landed at Gibraltar, all non-Muslims were ordered to convert to Islam. Andalusian civilization now faced a twin threat: Christians in the north and Islamic extremists from the south. The two would fight each other in the coming decades and Andalusia would shrink to a vassal state, owing its existence to foreigners.

The Almohads could have dealt the Reconquista a lasting blow, but the advancing Muslims failed to capitalize on their advantage. In 1195, the Almohads decisively defeated the army of Alfonso VIII of Castile at Alarcos, but did not press on to retake Toledo or any of the cities that had been lost in the previous century. The Almohad caliph, apparently more concerned with his Moroccan domains, retired to North Africa. This allowed the Christian armies to regroup.

It was not until 1211 that the Almohads launched another offensive. This time the fractious Christian powers had united with the support of the Pope. Led by Alfonso VIII, the Christians inflicted a major defeat on the Almohad army at Las Navas de Tolosa in July 1212. Alfonso VIII and the combined armies of León, Castile, Aragon, Navarra, and Portugal, completely surprised the Almohad forces. The Christians had found a secret route through a mountain pass and attacked the Muslims from the rear. Caught unprepared, 100,000 Muslim soldiers were slain and Almohad Caliph Muhammad al-Nasir fled to Africa. After this defeat, Muslim nobleman Yusuf bin Nasir negotiated with the Christians and withdrew all Muslim forces to the state of Granada. Thus began the Nasrid dynasty in 1232, the last Muslim kingdom in Spain.

Ferdinand III, king of the now united Spanish provinces of Castile and León, resumed the Christian advance. Cordoba fell in 1236, Majorca in 1230, Valencia in 1236, Seville in 1248, and Algarve by 1250. Muslim Spain was now confined to the kingdom of Granada, in the southern mountains from Algeciras to Almería. A slow, lingering death had begun, but it would take another 250 years before the last Muslims were expelled from Iberia and Islam was driven out of Spain.

With the advance of Christian forces in Spain came the spectre of the Inquisition. Like the Crusades, the Inquisition had its origin in the papacy. In 1208, in the wake of the defeat of the Crusaders by Saladin,* the Catholic

---

* *Saladin*: Known to Muslims as Salah al-Din Ayyubi (1138-93) he was a Kurd who conquered Egypt in 1169 and in 1171 ended the Fatimid caliphate to found his own Ayyubid dynasty.

Church turned its attention towards European Christians, which it felt were not adhering to the official doctrine.

Pope Innocent III launched the Albigensian Crusade, this time not against infidels, but against a sect of Christians in the south of France, the Cathari. Also known as the Albigenses, the Cathari Christians were quite hostile to the Pope and the Roman Catholic Church. What bothered the Vatican authorities was their belief in reincarnation and practices that mirrored Hinduism and the Zoroastrian faith. They were labelled as heretics.

Between fifteen thousand and twenty thousand Christian soldiers responded to the Pope's call, and this army invaded a region where a large percentage of the population was Cathari. The army of zealots was led by the fanatic papal legate Arnald-Amaury. When asked how to distinguish between the devout Catholics and the heretic Catharis, the papal legate replied in one of the most infamous quotes from Christian history. Abbot Arnald-Amaury is said to have declared: "Kill them all. God will recognise His own." In the massacre that followed, twenty thousand Christians were slaughtered by fellow Christians in the name of Christianity. The massacres continued for forty years. The last surviving Catharis fled to Catalonia in Spain and the Inquisition was born.

As Muslims continued to recede south, the Inquisition was first instituted in Aragon in 1238, but with little of the ferocity of the Inquisition in France. Castille, León, and Portugal did not introduce the Inquisition until 1376. The real horror of the Christian Inquisition became apparent as the Muslim empire shrunk to the edge of Spain in Granada. As the Muslims fell back, the relative pluralism that Jews, Christians, and Muslims had maintained over centuries gave way to mass murder in the name of God. In February 1481, outside the borders of the Kingdom of Granada, six Christians were burned alive at the stake. In Seville, a city once known for its music, dance, and high culture, 288 people were burned alive, while hundreds more were sentenced to life imprisonment. When the last Muslim kingdom fell to the Spanish Christian forces, the Inquisition imposed a new order: all Muslim and Jews were forced to convert to Catholicism, leave Spain, or face death. There is a spot on the outskirts of Granada where the last Muslim king is said to have stopped and wept, and was scorned by his mother for his tears.

In the last few decades, Muslim tourists from around the world have started visiting the spot overlooking Granada. They wonder how a civilization as rich as the Andalusia could have come to such a disastrous end. However, few Muslims are willing to conduct a critical analysis of our failures. The answers are usually to blame the traitors—and there were many—and to suggest that these defeats and elsewhere were the result of God punishing Muslims for not leading our lives in a literalist and puritanical form. Few have contemplated the misuse of Islam and the invocation of tribalism and familial lineages, and the absence of political institutions as the reasons for the decay.

At the core of every Muslim failure lies the question of succession and the ethereal undefined entity that every sultan and caliph postured to establish—the Islamic State and its governance under the laws of sharia. Muslim Spain, as well as all Muslim empires, failed to agree on the question of rightful succession. The absence of any laws, divine or otherwise, with regard to succession, has led to bloodshed among Muslims on a scale greater than any such discord or conflict with Christians, Hindus, or Jews. The issue of succession and the incessant and obsessive urge to establish the Islamic State has made the Muslim Ummah a prisoner of its own delusion. The pursuit of puritanism, whether by the Almohads of Marrakesh or by Emperor Aurangzeb of Moghul India, has had only one outcome—disaster.

No one has better captured the futility of the Muslim obsession with the need for establishing a caliphate or an Islamic State than Taj al-Din Abu al-Shahrastani, the 12th-century Muslim historian from Turkmenistan (1086-1153), who said: "Never was there an Islamic issue which brought about more bloodshed than the caliphate." Hundreds of years after al-Sharastani uttered those words, Muslim blood would continue to spill, as it does today, as each new breed of Islamist seeks power, but camouflages its greed by hiding under the cover of Islam.

The system of seniority to determine succession that Muslims had inherited from the Arab tribes did not last long and soon was replaced by the hereditary system. Had this new system been adopted, the problem of determining succession would not have led to the perpetual cycle of bloodshed. After all, monarchs across all empires had followed this system from time immemorial. However, in the case of the early Arab Muslims, although the system of hereditary succession was adopted, they also retained some sort of a parallel tribal seniority system. The pretense of honouring a tribal code as well as paying lip service to consensus ensured that no succession was truly smooth. Of the fourteen Umayyad caliphs, only four were followed by their sons.

In Spain, the Umayyads opted for the hereditary system for succession, but instead of making the eldest son succeed his father, they threw in the concept of the "most fitting." This variable was so subjective that every prince and his mother thought they were the most fitting. Invariably, after the death of every Spanish Muslim emir or caliph, a power struggle would erupt. Who would be the arbiter of which prince was the fittest of them all? Blood lineage was so mixed in Spain that blue-eyed blond princes with Castilian mothers would be hard-pressed to compete with the Meccan Quraysh heritage of their stepbrothers who had "more authentic" lineage, and skin colour to prove it.

The one factor few scholars have dealt with is the role of the harems and numerous wives of the ruling monarchs. These harems resulted in at times a dozen competing Crown princes competing for one throne. The Christian kings, too, may have had access to multiple sexual partners, but their Catholicism ensured that they had one queen and thus fewer pretenders to their respective thrones. In addition, the European model of succession was that the eldest son had the right of first refusal, and he seldom refused.

The harems of the sultans added a complex dimension to the politics of the palace. Competing wives, not to mention concubines, promoted their sons with jealous ambitions. The fear that their offspring would be passed over for another wife's prince ensured a constant background of intrigue and drama. And whenever a prince was crowned, the dejected and the rejected would bicker in family feuds that would make the new ruler weaker and unable to govern effectively until after he had put down his brothers, his stepbrothers, their uncles, and, of course, the many stepmothers. Added to this practice was the general acceptance of warring and raiding in tribal Arab tradition, dating back to pre-Islamic time. Al-Qutami, an early Umayyad poet, aptly described this behaviour: "Our business is to make raids on our neighbour and our own brother, in case we find none to raid, but a brother."

Even when Granada was surrounded by Christian opponents (and only the sea on the east harboured no enmity), the ruling Nasrid dynasty failed to consolidate its rule or to bring some semblance of unity. A study of the last three sultans who ruled Granada during the years 1461 to 1491 illustrates why the absence of stable political institutions and the adoption of 7th-century Arabian tribal culture in 15th-century Spain led to the disappearance of al-Andalus. Which begs the question: If 7th-century prescriptions failed to cure 15th-century Muslim ailments, how will this treatment cure the 21st-century Ummah?

Up to the end of Umayyad rule in the 12th century, Andalusia was more Arab than Islamic. Of course, the sultans were Muslim, believers in the true sense, but religiosity did not govern their discourse—it merely provided them the legitimacy as rulers. This era provided a safe space for secular thought and respect for intellectuals and the intelligentsia who were not part of the palace intrigues. However, after the interventions of the North African Almoravides and Almohads, the culture of the land had become increasingly less tolerant and more hardline Islamic in nature. With this incursion in the 13th century, Andalusia became restricted to the southeast corner of Spain in the emirate of Grenada.

The caliph or emir rarely shared any power, either as a secular head or as the religious leader. The absolute control of the monarch meant that if the ruler was weak, so was the entire country, and if he was incompetent, the fortunes of the entire population would suffer. There were no checks and balances, and this led to the chronic instability that has hovered over Islamdom's politics since the death of the Prophet. Ironically, Islamists present this chaos as a panacea to Muslim problems, and the alternative to contemporary Western secular democracy.

Granada was now home to all the defeated nobles of the north, deprived of their power and wealth. They lived in the past, bitter men who dreamed of regaining their lost emirates, but had no plan or ability to do so. It is said close to three million people lived in the tiny state, where increasingly the gap between the very rich and the poor was showing. The decay that had set in would set the scene for what in literary circles is known as the "last sigh of the Moor."

Among this nobility of the 14th century lived the intellectual politicians and academics who also played the roles of the judiciary and diplomacy. One name that stands out is that of Abd al-Rahman Abu Zaid Wali al-Din ibn Khaldun, better known as Ibn Khaldun. He was an African Berber, but claimed to have Yemeni ancestry. Ibn Khaldun created the science of the study of history and developed scientific methodology for calculating the rise and fall of civilizations. He conceived of a theory of social conflict and developed the dichotomy of "city" versus "desert," as well as the concept of a "generation" and the inevitable loss of power that occurs when desert warriors conquer a city. His teacher was a student of Averroes. Ibn Khaldun inherited the rationalism of the great Andalusian, but merged it with his concept of divine intervention, which he saw as the only reason why some civilizations survived the life cycle from birth to death that he had developed, while others did not. His theory of civilizations comes close to contemporary business models and the development of information technology. He wrote the *Muqaddimah* (*Introduction*), in which he developed a rational philosophy of history. He also wrote a history of Muslim North Africa, *Kitab al-'Ibar*.

In *Muqaddimah,* Ibn Khaldun came up with the concept of *asabiyah,* or the "group solidarity and tribalism" of the Arabs. He wrote that when a society becomes a great civilization and comes to dominate a region, this climax is always followed by a period of decay. He suggested that the group that conquers a decaying civilization is, by comparison, a group of barbarians. He may have been referring to the unfolding Christian conquest of Andalusia, but his theory applied equally to the demise of the Persian and Byzantine empires at the hands of the Arab Bedouin, whom Ibn Khaldun did not greatly respect. He felt that when unsophisticated groups topple a decaying civilization, they become a prisoner of their captives' refined tastes in arts, literature, and intellectual discourse.

The Islamic world during Ibn Khaldun's time was going through tremendous disruption. Palestine and Jerusalem had just come out of the trauma of the Crusades. In 1258 the Mongols had destroyed forever what was left of the Abbasid caliphate, burning Baghdad and slaughtering its citizens, and in his own Granada, the Spanish Christian Reconquista was becoming unstoppable.

Ibn Khaldun postulated that the expansion of Arab tribalism had resulted in a dynastic type of governance that was rooted in both nomadic and settled lifestyles. He felt that within this contradiction lay the seeds of its own destruction. He predicted the lifestyle of settled communities and the slothful luxurious lives of the ruling elite would compromise the people's ability to fight and survive—necessary skills especially for the nomads. Ibn Khaldun saw this decay unfolding among the Muslims of Spain, and had he been alive today, he would have said the same about the United States and its imperial vision of the world. Ibn Khaldun wrote that a people driven by desire to fulfill every want would face moral decline, resulting in the fall of dynasties from internal decay or conquest. His message may have been too late for the Nasrid sultanate of Granada, but may be applicable to Western civilization as we know it.

In Granada, the three sultans who played musical chairs in the last three decades of Muslim rule in Spain were the brothers Muley Abul Hassan and Muhammad al-Zaghal, along with the former's son Abu 'abd-Allah Muhammad, also known as Boabdil, the last king of Granada.

Abul Hassan, who became king caliph in 1461 after deposing his own father Saad and imprisoning him in the fortress of Salobrena, found out that his brother al-Zaghal had taken over the neighbouring city of Malaga. The enemy was breathing down their necks, but those in the elite of what remained as al-Andalus were fighting like hungry dogs at a butcher shop. Abul Hassan was the older son of the late Saad, but al-Zaghal had the support of the populace. Again, the absence of any succession rules would come to haunt the Muslims, even as they lay helpless in the corner of Spain.

Fortunately for the Muslims, al-Zaghal realized the peril facing the emirate, and in a display of humility rare in Islamic history, replicating the behaviour of Ali ibn Abu Talib, he approached his brother to make peace and to act in the larger interest of the community of Granada. A civil war was prevented and Abul Hassan began his twenty-year reign. His ambitious nature and his penchant for wine, women, and war ensured that the interests of the Ummah were the least of his priorities. While Berber invasions from the south chipped away at the limited military resources of the emirate, frustrated nobles and their legions of supporters who had lost their lands in the face of advancing Christian armies made for an explosive situation. Fearing a tribal uprising among some of the more established groups, the sultan invited the leaders of the Abencerrages to the great hall in Alhambra ostensibly to consult with them. When they arrived, he had them all slaughtered.

This may have provided Muley Hacen (as the Christians knew Abul Hassan) some temporary respite, but it generated deep hatred for the tottering monarch. Henceforth a tribe that had deposed Mohammad IX in 1429 would ally itself to anyone who was opposing the caliph. Abul Hassan's lust for bloodshed may have been sated, but this also gave him a false sense of power, which he now sought to exercise over his much more powerful Christian neighbours.

In 1453, Abul Hassan's grandfather Caliph Mohammed X had sought peace with the Castilian rulers by agreeing to pay an annual tribute. For ten years, this tribute had gone to Castile and had secured a semblance of peace on the western front.

However, in 1476 Abul Hassan refused to pay the tribute, leading to a strong protest from the newly formed Spanish kingdom that had emerged as a result of the marriage of Isabella and Ferdinand. When the Spanish monarchs sent an emissary, he is said to have remarked, "The mints of Granada coined no longer gold, but steel." Diplomacy had given way to open warfare and the first aggressive action was taken by Abul Hassan, setting the stage for serious internal strife and the inevitable fall of al-Andalus.

In 1481 Caliph Abul Hassan launched a surprise attack inside Christian territory and recaptured the fortress of Zahara, taking many prisoners. Some questioned the wisdom of initiating an attack on the new Kingdom of Spain, but with few advisers to temper the machismo of Abul Hassan, the attack went through. Despite the victory over the Christians and the recapture of Zahara, the mood in Granada was sullen. One Granadian *alfaki* (intellectual) is quoted as having remarked, "Woe is me! The ruins of Zahara will fall on our heads: the days of the Moslem empire are now numbered."

The significance of the fall of Zahara was not lost on this alfaki. It was Fernando's grandfather who had captured the fortress from the Muslims. This was a personal insult to the new Spanish king and he went about setting the stage for the final solution. He also recognized that despite its weakness, the military prowess of the Granadians should not be underestimated.

The Christian response was delayed, but when it came, it was swift and shocking. On a dark February night in 1492, the Lord of Cadiz, Ponce de León, launched a surprise attack on the town of Alhama, which lay on the road between Granada and Malaga. The fortress that had been deemed impregnable and had never been attacked in the past fell with little difficulty. The shock of this defeat was enormous. Repeated attempts by Abul Hassan to take back the city failed. In hand-to-hand fighting, the Muslims, despite breaching the fort, were driven back. A pall of gloom hung over all of what was left of al-Andalus. The enemy was now a mere forty kilometres from the capital. Stunned by the loss, the caliph ordered that any talk about the fall of Alhama would be punishable by death.

As the Christian noose tightened around Granada, Abul Hassan faced another rebellion—this time from his son, Boabdil, who with his younger brother had fled to the town of Guadix, where he declared himself the sultan, dividing the small emirate into two at a time it needed unity more than ever.

The motives of this sudden disruption are said to have come from the harem politics of the emirate. Abul Hassan's first wife was Ayesha, the mother of the runaway princes. However, Abul Hassan had been infatuated by another woman, Thuraiya, another wife or possibly a concubine. It is said that Ayesha was worried that the influence of Thuraiya would sway the decision of the caliph and that her son would be passed over. In trying to ensure that the son would have the rightful claim, it is said she engineered the secession. It was as if the *Titanic* was sinking, and the nobility was quibbling over who was getting served first.

In any case, in its dying days Granada was being ruled by two sultans, each trying to win over the loyalty of his subjects with outrageous military expeditions that would end in disaster but prove their prowess on the backs of dead soldiers and an impoverished citizenry. In trying to outdo his father, Boabdil launched an ill-fated raid into Christian territory, where he was captured and held prisoner for two years.

Boabdil was finally released by his Christian captors, but his sons were held as hostages. The Christians equipped Boabdil well and asked him to create strife inside Grenada while they prepared for its final subjugation.

In 1485, the ageing and ailing Abul Hassan decided to hand over power to his younger brother, Mohammad bin Saad al-Zaghal. Within a year of taking over, al-Zaghal had to face Boabdil, who had allied himself with the Christian kingdom. In 1487, while the sultan was in Velez Malaga, Boabdil again attacked the capital, resulting in much bloodshed. On April 29, 1487, the renegade prince took over the Alhambra itself and executed the warriors who had opposed him. He then sent a message to the Christian king in which he offered to hand over the city to them in exchange for a principality for him and one of his officials, his vizier.

Elsewhere, al-Zaghal valiantly fought to save the emirate, but it was a losing battle. Many leading Muslim notables sided with the Christians on the promise that they would be allowed to retain their holdings if they surrendered. One Muslim commander even converted to Christianity and abandoned his troops. First Baza fell, then Almeira, and finally when Guadix collapsed on December 30, 1489, al-Zaghal realized all was lost. Andalusia was lost not because Muslims capitulated, but because they were betrayed by their leadership. When al-Zaghal sent his cavalry to relieve Muslims in the city of Malaga, his troops were attacked by fellow Muslims and cut to pieces. William Prescott, in his 19th-century book *History of the Reign of Ferdinand and Isabella*, wrote:

The Moors were not unmindful of the importance of Malaga, or the gallantry with which it was defended. They made several attempts to relieve it, whose failure was less owing to the Christians than to the treachery and their own miserable feuds. A body of cavalry, which El Zagal (sic) despatched from Guadix to throw succours into the beleaguered city, was encountered and cut to pieces by a superior force by the young king Abdullah, who consummated his baseness by sending an embassy to the Christian camp, charged with a present of Arabian horses sumptuously caparisoned to Ferdinand.

Faced with such treachery, al-Zaghal surrendered in exchange for thirty thousand gold *castellanos*. After a brief stay in Spain, he sailed off to Oran in Morocco, where it is said he was looted by brigands and died in abject poverty. A sad and honourable man, al-Zaghal did in surrendering what so many defeated Muslim rulers have done since then and even before him. Blaming defeat on the will of Allah, he is reported to have told the emissary of Ferdinand, "What Allah wills, he brings to pass in his own way. Had he not decreed the fall of Granada, this sword might have saved it; but his will be done!"

Now Boabdil was the unquestioned king of Grenada, but with an ever-shrinking kingdom. He soon realized that the promises made by Ferdinand would not be kept. Despite the fact he had served the Spanish king and betrayed his own people, this treachery was not be sufficient to make the Reconquista desist at the borders of his beleaguered city. Throughout 1490 and 1491, the city was under siege. Famine now threatened mass unrest inside the city and, with no other option in sight, the halls of Alhambra were handed over to Ferdinand and Isabella.

On New Year's Day, 1492, Boabdil—Abu'abd-Allah Muhammad—handed over the keys of the city of Granada to the new rulers of Spain. Andalusia was lost forever that day. It is said that as the Muslim royalty moved south towards their exile, they reached a hilltop for a last look at the majesty of Granada, where Castilian flags were flying over the castle of Alhambra. Boabdil burst into tears. Seeing him cry, his mother, Ayesha, remarked sarcastically, "You do well to weep like a woman for what you could not defend like a man."

This hilltop from which Boabdil is said to have looked for the last time on Granada is now a tourist spot and is commemorated in the poetic name *el Ultimo suspiro del Moro*—"The last sigh of the Moor."

CHAPTER 10

Baghdad—Islam Embraces the Persians

IN THE YEAR 750 CE, the Syrian city of Damascus was in turmoil. The Umayyads—the descendants of Abu Sufyan, the great tormentor of the Prophet who had usurped the caliphate—were now on the run. The Abbasids—great-grandchildren of the Apostle's Uncle al-Abbas—were hunting them down, one by one. These two clans from the Meccan Arab tribe of the Quraysh were once more at each other's throats, except this time the family that had stolen Islam from under the very noses of the Prophet's family faced extinction.

The Umayyads had destroyed the mighty Persian Empire and brought the Byzantines to their knees, but now they were begging for mercy, with no place to hide in their huge domain, which stretched from Spain to the River Indus in India and the borders of China. Within a matter of months, the Umayyads would be literally exterminated from the face of the Earth and the Abbasids would assume power in Damascus.

In the complex, multi-tiered story that the Abbasid period proved to be, conflicting ideologies, social movements, theologies, and wars shaped the narrative of Muslims irrevocably. Almost every Muslim today belongs to one of the five schools of Islamic thought that were created during the first two centuries of the Abbasid era. The period is rife with contradictions. On one hand, for example, there was a broad acceptance of gays and erotic poetry, while on the other, laws were being developed to institute the death penalty for homosexuality. While music and dance, wine and women were staples of the caliph's courts, theologians were desperately trying to ensure that laxity of morals was adequately punished and prohibited.

In its cultural and intellectual makeup, the Abbasid period of Islamic history stands in sharp contrast to its predecessor, the Umayyad era. The Umayyads were essentially the regime of the Syrian soldiery and aristocracy, imitating Byzantine governance while invoking its Meccan Quraysh tribal ancestry to legitimize its hold on power; the Abbasids can be remembered as the dynasty that introduced Persia to Islam. The Damascus Umayyads invaded and occupied vast tracts of land and took booty; the Abbasids embraced the occupied people's knowledge and included them in the decision-making structure. The Umayyads were essentially an Arab state invoking Islam to justify their rule over non-Arabs; the Abbasids came to power as a result of a revolt of the Persians against Arab supremacy in Islam.

The British Islamic historian De Lacy O'Leary, in comparing the Umayyads with the Abbasids, wrote that the intellectual output of the Umayyads was made up totally of poetry, "largely of the old desert type." He continued: "Its poets praised their patrons, derided their rivals and enemies, pictured the perils of the desert life, or sang the echoes of the ancient tribal wars. The culture and science of the Greek world found no place in their compilations, apparently meant nothing to them."

Resentment over the institutionalization of Arab superiority over non-Arab Muslims was the catalyst that triggered the bloody collapse of the mighty Umayyad dynasty. Under Caliph Umar bin Abd al-Aziz (d. 720), some discriminatory practices against non-Arab Muslims had been suspended. However, even though granting non-Arab Muslims the same tax exemptions as Arab Muslims led to the pacification of the Egyptians, Berbers, Indians, and Iranians, the exemption adversely affected state coffers. This loss of tax revenue meant that members of the Umayyad elite were hit in their pockets. Competing nobles could not be bribed with lavish gifts, and this led to new strains on the stability of the caliphate. In addition, even though financial discrimination against non-Arabs ended, the deep-seated cultural stigmas could not be wiped out overnight. The friction between the Arabs and the Mawalis (as non-Arab Muslims were referred to, at times in a derogatory manner) led to revolts in Africa. In Persia, the resentment took a different turn.

The Persians were still smarting from their defeat at the hands of the Arab armies a hundred years earlier. Their second-class status, despite their conversion to Islam, added to their hurt pride. (Even today, Iranians have not forgotten the humiliation of the defeat at the hands of the Arabs. This is one reason why Persian nationalism is so different from Arab nationalism. Iranian nationalism is essentially anti-Arabian and tries to distance itself from Islam. On the other hand, Arabian nationalists, even the atheists and

Marxists among them, are at home in an overtly Islamic environment, quite oblivious to the Persian angst.

In the 8th century, the resentment among Persian Muslims against the Arab establishment of Damascus made them natural allies of the Arab Shias of Kufa and Basra. The descendants of Banu Hashim—the Prophet's clan that had so far been shut out of power—had new allies.

The Arab rebels were led by Abu al-Abbas Abd Allah, who traced his lineage to the Prophet's tribe via al-Abbas, an uncle of the Prophet. After Umayyad caliph Hisham had put down the 736 Shia revolt in Kufa, Abu al-Abbas moved farther east to Khurasan in eastern Persia. In 743, on hearing of the death of Hisham, Abu al-Abbas took advantage of the crisis in Damascus and supported a broad coalition of Shia, Kharijis, and Persian Muslims in Khurasan. From here, he led this army and advanced on the Umayyad capital, Damascus. In 750 this broad coalition, under a Persian general, Abu Muslim, captured Damascus, deposing and decapitating the last Umayyad caliph, Marwan II, thus ending the ninety-year rule of the Umayyads.

Contemporary Sunni Muslims and orthodox Arab Islamists take a rather dim view of the role of the Persians in this conflict. *The History of Islam,* a Saudi-published work, laments the fact that the Persian language survived and was not replaced by Arabic. The book describes the survival of the Persian language as a disaster, and blames the Abbasid revolt against the Umayyads as the reason Persian was not eradicated. Recounting the massacres that followed the uprising against the Damascus Umayyads, the book says:

> The Arab tribes which reached Khurasan in large numbers and were succeeding in turning the country's language and society into Arabic were all put to death, and the Arabic factor . . . suddenly lost its power and died. That was how the Iranian language, culture, society and morality, which were dying, got a new lease on life and Iran and Khurasan which could have been Arab countries like Egypt, turned into Persian countries again. Abu Muslim himself was a Khurasani and Iranian by race and for him there was no job more interesting and enjoyable than killing the Arabs.

The History of Islam paints the early Abbasids as puppets of the Persian Muslims, and depicts Abu Muslim with disdain, portraying him with the same contempt that is usually reserved for the Mawali, an attitude towards non-Arab Muslims that still permeates Saudi society.

The divisions in Umayyad society were not confined to Arab–Persian, Arab–Indian or Arab–Berber tensions. Within Arab society, the Banu Hashim versus Banu Umayya tussle became a Shia Uthman versus Shia Ali divide.

This political division was further complicated by the tribal origins of the Arabs who had now settled into Syria, Iraq, Egypt, Iran, and elsewhere. The tribal and clan division was made even more complex by the tension between the Yemenite and the Qays. The latter were Arabs from northern Arabian tribes while the former were from southern Arabia. The Qays dominated the Syrian cavalry and nobility in the Umayyad elites, and were dependent on a continuation of jihad for their economic prosperity; the Yemenites were settling in the villages and towns and were, in contrast, more involved in the commerce and development of trade. Just as the military–industrial complex in the United States thrives on conflict, the Qays-dominated Umayyads needed war.

These fissures were signs that the message of the Quran had long been forgotten and the teachings of the Prophet were no more than rhetoric falling on deaf ears. The tribalism that was given a fresh lease on life on the night the Prophet died would bleed Muslims for centuries, as we killed each other in the name of our Prophet and with the aim of establishing the Islamic State. The Umayyad Islamic State was dead, and the Abbasid Islamic State was born. Both gestated in the womb of carnage, and both would die in a torrent of bloodshed. I wonder which of the two would work better for latter-day Islamists who wish to emulate the political structures of the "Golden Age of Islam."

In Damascus, the new caliph was worried. Remnants of the Umayyad family were still alive and might strike back. To lure them into a trap, Caliph Abu al-Abbas declared amnesty for all surviving members of the deposed caliph's family. After the first round of massacres, the survivors had gone into hiding. The caliph sent out the message that all Umayyads were welcome to a grand reconciliation dinner party. Except for Abd al-Rahman I, grandson of the Caliph Hashim, they all fell for the ruse and were slaughtered as they sat down to eat dinner. It is reported that even as the dead and wounded lay bleeding on the floor of the caliph's court, Abu al-Abbas ordered that dinner be served and the revelries of the victorious continued amid the groans of the dying.

Abd al-Rahman I was lucky to have escaped the massacre. He fled to Andalusia in Spain, where he would resurrect the Umayyad caliphate. Because he missed his dinner date, the Umayyads would endure for three more centuries in Spain. Due to the brutality with which he eliminated the Umayyads, Caliph Abu al-Abbas has ever since been as *as-Saffah*—The Slaughterer.

Abu al-Abbas died four years later. His short reign was marked by his efforts to consolidate and rebuild the caliphate with a ruthless determination, and to move the capital from Damascus to a castle near Kufa, which he named Hashimiyah. The capital was later moved to Anbar, in Iraq. Caliph Abu al-Abbas is recognized as having introduced an era where Jews, Christians, and Persian Muslims were given prominent roles in government. He set the standard of pluralism that served as a model for future caliphs to follow.

Surprisingly, the Shia stood out as the one group not accorded a senior position. Soon after deposing the Umayyads, Abu al-Abbas reneged on his promises to the Shia community in claiming the caliphate for himself. Despite feeling betrayed and alienated, the Shia supporters of Abu al-Abbas did not make their feelings public. Shia forbearance and perseverance had by now become one of their cultural and religious characteristics. This resulted in less conflict during the Abbasid era than there had been during the Umayyad dynasty.

Caliph Abu al-Abbas as-Saffah died of smallpox on June 10, 754. He had appointed his brother Abu Jaffer Mansoor as his successor. For once, the transfer of power was without incident. Thus began an era in Islamic history in what is today Iraq and Iran that would parallel the dazzling dynasty in the Muslim-governed areas of the Iberian Peninsula known as al-Andalus, but like its counterpart thousands of miles away, the glory of Abbasids would continue to be tainted by bloodshed and civil strife. Both dynasties failed to create the institutions of political power and succession that would have been necessary for long-term governance. The caliphs struggled to maintain a monarchist dynasty, and they also wanted to show a semblance of legitimacy by invoking authority derived from being the family of the Prophet. Many fell in the process of trying to manage this high-wire act.

Caliph as-Saffah laid the foundation of the Abbasid dynasty, but it was his brother Mansoor who should be credited with ensuring its continuity and preservation. No fewer than thirty-five Abbasid caliphs descended from him. Though by all accounts a harsh and angry man, Caliph Mansoor was able to keep his rage under control and avoid bloodshed. He subdued a few uprisings, but then settled down, emerging as a king who cared for all his subjects and one who had a vision for the future. But Mansoor knew that to be an effective and respected ruler of the Muslim domains, he needed control over his military, which was largely in the hands of Abu Muslim, the Persian general who had stormed Damascus and defeated the Umayyads.

At first Mansoor offered Abu Muslim the governorship of Egypt, but the Persian declined, recognizing that far away from Persia, he would not be able to rely on his fearsome Khurasani troops. Abu Muslim recognized the authority of the caliph, but made no attempt to show any reverence to the young king. The tussle between Caliph Mansoor and General Abu Muslim was now public, and the new king realized that if he didn't act, he would remain a puppet in the hands of the general.

In February 755, Mansoor acted. He invited the Persian general to a sumptuous dinner, suggesting to Abu Muslim that he needed advice on a military mission. After luring the conqueror of Damascus to his court, it is reported that the caliph clapped his hands, and in an instant, the palace guard snatched the unsuspecting general and beheaded him. Thus ended the life of the kingmaker who had put the Abbasids in power. Death was swift. Power was consolidated in an instant. Henceforth Mansoor would face some rebellions, but no major challenge to his caliphate as he set forth to plan the most beautiful city on earth—Baghdad.

Before Baghdad could be built, the nagging problem of dealing with the progeny of the Prophet had to be resolved. Mansoor and his family had laid their claim to the caliphate on the basis that they were from the family of Muhammad, but they were aware this was only partly true. Despite their legitimacy as the descendants of the Banu Hashim clan of the Prophet, they knew they were not from his bloodline—they were not from the *Ahlul Bayt*, the family of the Prophet's only surviving child, Fatima, and her husband. These were the Shia, the offspring of the survivors of the massacre of Karbala. Some had escaped to India, others were in Medina and Basra, and they still had the sympathy of the masses, especially among the people of Iraq. This attachment is undiminished and visible even today. For Mansoor, the problem was to identify which one of the many great grandchildren of the Prophet would rise to challenge the authority of the new caliph. He would soon find out.

Mansoor was an astute politician, and started by offering the carrot before he would consider using the stick. He invited every member of the Prophet's family to be resident at his court, to avail themselves of handsome pensions, and to stay within sight of his spies, where they could be monitored for any subversive activities. Most of the family took the bait and made peace with Mansoor. Others had misgivings. The claim of Mansoor to be God's deputy on Earth was scoffed at. Soon the caliph was told that two younger members of the Prophet's family, the great-grandsons of Hassan ibn Ali, had disappeared.

In 756, Muhammad ibn Abdullah and his younger brother, Ibrahim— convinced they had been deceived by the Abbasid family—refused to give their oath of allegiance to Mansoor and withdrew to the City of the Prophet, Medina. Where better to raise the flag of rebellion than in the Mosque of the Prophet, they thought. In the spiritual sense, the brothers were right, but in the world of war and politics, Medina had lost all significance. The first city of Islam had become the backwater of the empire, far from the riches of Egypt, Syria, Iraq, and Persia. The city had long been abandoned by the ruling elite as the centre of Islam, and was a place primarily reserved for pilgrims and piety.

Muhammad ibn Abdullah, also known as *Nafs al-zakiay* (Pure Soul), soon had the support of the people of Medina and Mecca. Muhammad then sent Ibrahim to find support in Basra and Kufa, while he controlled the lands of Hejaz. He had not declared open rebellion, but his defiance, though a minor irritant at this stage, was angering the monarch. Muhammad mocked the new caliph, stating openly that while he had descended from the daughter of the Prophet, Caliph Mansoor's mother was a mere Berber concubine.

The rabble-rousing continued as Mansoor's troops tried in vain to hunt down the two brothers. Muhammad is said to have had many narrow escapes as he tried to evade his captors, even losing his newborn son temporarily as he ran to safety through deep craggy ravines.

In 761, the caliph himself went to Medina on his way to Mecca for hajj. He ordered the two brothers to present themselves in his court. Muhammad and Ibrahim refused, and hid out in the hills. Enraged by this defiance, Mansoor ordered the arrest of the entire family of the two brothers—including their ageing father, Abdullah ibn Hassan—who were put in iron shackles and made to walk all the way back to the caliph's court in Iraq. Many died on the march. The old man was brought before the caliph and flogged repeatedly. "Where are your sons? Where is that *al-muhammam* [charcoal face]," he was asked. Mansoor was referring to Muhammad, who was of dark complexion; such a derogatory reference to skin colour reflected the prejudice against Blacks that existed in the early Islamic empires and continues to this day. Of course, the old man could not say where his sons were and faced the whip again.

On September 23, 762, after being on the run for a year, Muhammad emerged in Medina and declared himself the caliph, urging his followers to take over the city and arrest the officials of the Abbasids, but to ensure that no one was killed or hurt. The city was soon in the hands of the rebels. Within days, Mecca was also under the new Caliph Muhammad ibn Abdullah. Hejaz had once again seceded from the Muslim empire. Memories of Abdullah ibn al-Zubayr's rebellion against the Umayyads were still fresh. A companion of the Prophet had set up his own independent caliphate.

But like Abdullah ibn al-Zubayr, the new renegade caliph would find his revolt was short-lived.

With two men now claiming to be the caliph, yet again Muslim was willing to kill Muslim in the name of Islam. Before the battle of Medina between the Mansoor's Abbasid army and Muhammad ibn Abdullah, great-great-grandson of the Prophet, letters were exchanged between the two claimants to the title of caliph. These provide an insight into the drifting attitudes towards women under Islam and the disdain towards non-Arabs. Whereas Muhammad proudly make reference to his lineage from Fatima, the daughter of the Prophet, Mansoor mocks Muhammad's manhood for relying on the bloodline of a woman in making his claim.

Caliph Muhammad ibn Abdullah wrote to Caliph Abu Jaffer Mansoor:

> You have laid claim to this office only through us. You made your uprising (against the Umayyads) to acquire it through our support and attained it only thanks to us. Our paternal ancestor, Ali, was the *wasi* and the *iman*, so how could you have inherited his *wilayah* when his own descendents are still alive.* Further, you well know that no one has laid claim to this office who has a lineage, nobility, and status like ours. By the nobility of our fathers, we are not the sons of the accursed, the outcast and the freedmen! . . . My paternity is purest among them, undiluted by non-Arab blood and no concubines dispute for me (in precedence).†

Caliph Mansoor must have been deeply incensed at this personal attack on his mother as a concubine and a non-Arab. In his reply, he dismissed Muhammad ibn Abdullah's claim to the caliphate based on hereditary lineage, but did not address the insult to his non-Arab bloodline. He wrote back:

> My, how you pride yourself on kinship through women, as to delude the uncouth and the rabble! But God did not make women equal to uncles and fathers or (even) paternal relations and guardians. . . . The best of your

---

* In classical Shia thought, the religio-political authority (*wilayah*) of the leader or guide (*iman*) of the community is secured through designation of one who stands in hereditary succession from the original agent (*wasi*).

† This is an allusion to Mansoor's mother, Sallamah, being a Berber concubine.

forefather's sons and the most excellent people among them are nothing but concubines' sons. After the death of God's Messenger there was no one born among you who was more excellent than Ali ibn Hussain,* yet he was the son of a concubine. He was certainly better than your grandfather Hasan ibn Hasan. After Ali there was no one among you to equal his son, Muhammad bin Ali,† yet his grandmother was a concubine. He was certainly better than your father. Further, there is no one the equal of his son, Jaffer,‡ yet his grandmother was a concubine. He is certainly better than you. Whereas you say that you are the descendent of God's Messenger, God in his book says, "Muhammad was not the father of anyone among your men." You are the descendents of his daughter, which is a close kinship. But it does not legitimate inheritance, not does it bequeath the *Wilayah*, neither does it confer the *Imamah* on her. So how could it be inherited from her? . . . We, not you, are the heirs to the seal of the Prophets.

The exchange of letters between the two claimants for the title of "Caliph of Islam" highlights some disturbing realities. The rights accorded to women during the time of Prophet Muhammad had already slipped precipitously, while Muhammad's exhortation to Muslims to renounce racial superiority had fallen on deaf Arab ears. The historian Tabari devotes an entire volume to this conflict, but he and later commentators seem to be quite oblivious to the blatant disdain the Arab elite had towards non-Arab Muslims.

Within three months, Medina was surrounded by Abbasid troops and their black flags, while the renegade caliph's supporters wore white, ironically the colour of the Umayyads. The resistance was futile, and within a few hours the Abbasids had entered Medina and beheaded Muhammad ibn Abdullah. His head was placed on a pike and carried to Mansoor in Kufa, presented on a silver platter as he met with notables in his court. Once more, for the sake of Islam, the blood of the Prophet's family had been spilled and the family humiliated in defeat. Muhammad's younger brother Ibrahim put up a more effective resistance to Mansoor's army in Basra, but he too was defeated and his head too was put on a platter and presented to the Abbasid caliph. Tabari reports that on seeing the head of the great-great-grandson of the Prophet, Caliph Mansoor wept openly. Here he was, the "Caliph of

---

* This is a reference to the only male member of a family who survived the massacre of Karbala.
† Grandson of Hussain bin Ali, acknowledged by Shia as their fifth imam.
‡ Jaffer al Sadiq.

Islam," having presided over the killing of two of the Prophet's great-great-grandsons, looking at the severed head of one of them. I am sure he must have wondered "Is this what Islam was about?"as he wiped his tears. In all of human history, no other religious community has presided over the annihilation of its own prophet's family, and no one has questioned how such a tragedy could unfold.

One aspect of the uprising by the Prophet's great-great-grandsons has been lost in many Muslim chronicles. While Muhammad ibn Abdullah was taking control of Medina, he sent his son Abdullah Ushtar to the province of Sind in India (now in Pakistan), where the governor Umar ibn Hafs was sympathetic to the Shia. The governor agreed to a date when he would renounce his allegiance to the Abbasids and support the new caliph in Medina. However, before this could happen, news came of the defeat of Muhammad ibn Abdullah. Caliph Mansoor found out about the Sind conspiracy and transferred the governor to Afriqiya (Tunisia today). The lone descendant of Prophet Muhammad now had no place to hide in the entire Muslim world. Once more, a direct descendant of the Prophet had to find refuge and protection with a Hindu prince of India. No school textbook in Pakistan recognizes this historic act of hospitality by a Hindu ruler in Sind who gave sanctuary to escaping descendants of the Prophet. When Mansoor found out that the young son of the defeated Muhammad had been given sanctuary in a Hindu kingdom, he sent an army detachment with specific instructions to capture and kill the young man and destroy the Hindu kingdom for giving refuge to a descendant of the Prophet. Abdullah Ushtar was hunted down and killed on the banks of the River Indus. His Sindhi wife, daughter of the Hindu king, was captured and taken away to Medina. She would never see her family again.

This branch of the Prophet's progeny would have been exterminated, but for the youngest of the three sons of Abdullah ibn Hassan. After his older brothers were defeated and beheaded, the youngest brother, a lad named Idris, escaped from the rule of the Abbasids in the year 786, taking refuge in what is now Morocco. He went on to establish the Idrisid dynasty in North Africa, outside the reach of the Abbasids. Idris founded the town of Moulay Idriss, and later on, the city of Fez, which his son Idris II turned into the capital of his kingdom. The birth of the Idrisid dynasty is considered the birth of Morocco.

BAGHDAD

After putting down the rebellions in Medina and Basra, Mansoor turned his attention to the task that would leave an indelible mark on Muslim history and heritage—the building of the city we know as Baghdad. In the spring of 762, Mansoor attended a ceremony to lay the foundation of the city he baptized as *Madinat al-salam*, the "City of Peace."

In selecting the site Mansoor was guided by his Persian adviser, Khalid ibn Barmak, and two astrologers, Nawbakht, a Zoroastrian, and Marw, a Jew. The caliph is said to have remarked: "This is a good place for an army camp. Here is the Tigris, with nothing between us and China, and on it arrives all that the sea can bring, as well as provisions from the Jazeera, Armenia, and surrounding areas. Further, there is the Euphrates on which can arrive everything from Syria and surrounding areas."

The site selected for Baghdad was a point where the Tigris and Euphrates rivers were thirty kilometres apart. The Isa canal connected the two rivers at this point, meaning goods from India and the Persian Gulf could be transported upstream to Syria and beyond. By involving the Persians, Jews, and Zoroastrians, Mansoor was laying the foundations of the Abbasid capital in a manner that demonstrated his emphasis on merit, not race or religion. He was starting a new chapter, distancing himself from the Umayyad notion of Quraysh superiority and the Shia notion of a theocracy. At the time suggested by the astrologers, with Sagittarius rising, the caliph initiated the digging of an immense circular shallow ditch, more than 2,740 metres in diameter. The ditch was filled with cotton and naphtha, which was then lit. Baghdad's birth was in a circle of fire, which could be seen for miles. Five hundred years later the city would burn again as the Mongols sacked it. Another 1,200 years later, in 2003, fire would rain from the skies over Baghdad as the United States invaded Iraq.

A hundred thousand workers laboured under the direct supervision of the caliph for four years. It is said the entire project cost nearly five million dirhams. The work involved demolishing of parts of the fortress city of Ctesiphon and bringing the bricks and columns to Baghdad. Immense blocks were transported from Mount Hamrin, about 130 kilometres from the city. When completed, the grand capital had a double surrounding wall of brick, a deep moat, and a third inner wall, 27 metres high, surrounding the royal palace of the caliph. The city had four main entrances, gates that were in the direction of Damascus, Kufa, Basra, and Khurasan. Although the city was on the banks of the Tigris, its water was piped in from the Euphrates.

Baghdad may been the crowning glory of Caliph Mansoor, but his true legacy lay in his effective and frugal management of the state's resources, his hard work and supervision of the affairs of his empire, and above all, the introduction of the world's first postal system. However, by moving the capital to Baghdad, the Abbasids also made a profound change in the direction of the Islamic empire. While Damascus looked westward towards the Mediterranean and Europe, Baghdad had its culture influenced by the East, primarily Persia. Had Damascus remained the capital of Islam, the Crusaders in 1099 might not have been able to inflict the humiliating defeat they did when Jerusalem fell to them as warring Muslim camps tried to undermine each other and facilitate the Crusaders. Constantinople too would not have waited until the 15th century before falling to a Muslim army.

Mansoor died a satisfied man in 775, having laid the foundation of a city and a dynasty that would be the envy of the world. However, if there was one failure that nagged him, it was the secession of Spain from the caliphate. The last surviving Umayyad, Abd al-Rahman I, had taken over al-Andalus. When Mansoor sent his emissaries to exert control, Abd al-Rahman sent their heads back, embalmed in salt and camphor, with their names tagged to their ears. The Islamic caliphate had already divided in two. Under later Abbasids, Egypt was lost, as well as the rest of North Africa. Yet, in the 21st century, Muslim youth in the West believe there always was a single caliphate that unravelled due to European Christian machinations of the 19th and 20th centuries. Oblivious to their own history, these young Islamists are satisfied with mythologies sung to them by Islamist clerics who are afraid of their diminishing power.

When Mansoor died, he was succeeded by his son Muhammad Mehdi. The young prince continued down the path of his father, but with a far more forgiving and compassionate nature. He is credited with introducing the world's first disability allowance, which ensured that lepers and other people who were unable to work for a living would not have to beg to survive.

Mehdi ruled for ten years, during which he made another attempt to conquer Constantinople in 782. The Muslim army was led by Haroon Rashid, the illustrious prince who would go on to become the most legendary of Abbasid caliphs. Haroon failed to conquer the Byzantine city, but was able to extract a humiliating peace treaty, signed near the Straits of Marmara. The deal forced Byzantine Queen Irene to pay a tribute of seventy thousand to ninety thousand dinars every year to the caliph's treasury.

Caliph Mehdi's ten-year reign was also marked by a shifting away from religious orthodoxy to a more secular environment where wine, music, and song made an appearance in the caliph's court. While both Abu al-Abbas and Mansoor were strictly against music and wine, the Persian influences started creeping in and were reflected in the relaxed attitude of Mehdi. In a poem written to celebrate the freeing of his favourite slave, Caliph Mehdi wrote:

My good fortune I pray that my God may prolong
Through Abu Hafs, the friend of my leisure.
For the joy of my life is in wine and song,
Perfumed slave girl and music and pleasure.

These were times of eloquent poetry patronized by the caliph himself. Some of the verses were highly erotic and wildly suggestive, oozing with sensuous sexuality, celebrating wine and women, tagged with titillating innuendos that might offend the middle-class intelligentsia of today's Arab elites.

Caliph Mehdi would die at the age of forty-three on a hunting trip when he fell off his horse and broke his spine. His son Haroon was at his side and could have claimed the throne for himself. However, in a display of maturity that was rare among Muslim princes, Haroon sent the Prophet's staff—the symbol of the caliphate—and his oath of allegiance to his brother Musa Hadi who was campaigning in Iran.

Caliph Musa Hadi was something of an interim ruler who, it is said, was murdered at the request of his own mother, so that the dynamic Haroon Rashid could take the throne. Caliph Hadi remained only a year in office and most of this was spent trying to manipulate the system to have his son Jaffer named as his successor. This despite the fact the late Caliph Mehdi had clearly designated the line of succession as being first Hadi and then Haroon. The power struggle became so intense that Hadi tried to poison his brother Haroon, who fled Baghdad.

The queen mother was alarmed at the ambitions of her caliph son; she is said to have had him smothered by two slaves. This paved the way for Haroon Rashid to return to Baghdad. He took up his role as caliph in September 786.

Even though his reign was short, Caliph Musa Hadi had managed to trigger a revolt among the descendants and followers of Ali ibn Abu Talib. The caliph cut off the pensions of the Prophet's family, and a fresh revolt broke out in Mecca, ending in yet another tragedy. One more descendant of the Prophet, another Hussain ibn Ali, was beheaded and his head presented to the caliph in his Baghdad palace, where it is said more tears were shed.

If there was one person who epitomized the Arab–Persian mix of the Abbasid caliphate and its resulting relaxed norms, it was the poet-genius Abu Nuwas (757–814). He was born in Basra to a Persian seamstress and an Arab father who died soon after the boy's birth. Although Abu Nuwas is the quintessential Arab poet, Persian culture had an impact on his life and left a stamp on his work. The poet wore his locks long, celebrated Nauroze,* and his vocabulary was sprinkled with Persian (his mother had never spoken Arabic, and the language of Abu Nuwas during his childhood had been Persian).

Abu Nuwas was openly gay, and his relationship with young men was widely known and accepted by the people of Basra. He was a poet to reckon with and not to be antagonized, for fear of a satirical reprisal that would become the source of amusement and mockery in the marketplace and wherever the nobility sipped fine wine or paid to watch damsels dance to the voices of minstrels. He was lucky to be living in the time of Caliph Mehdi, not his predecessor, Mansoor. He was lucky he wasn't living in today's Basra. Not even his Persian ancestry would have saved him from being stoned to death. Persians in the 21st century hang gays from cranes in soccer stadiums. But the Basra and Iran of Abu Nuwas' days was a city of tolerance and pluralism.

When Abu Nuwas took a fancy to a beautiful girl, Janan, it became the talk of the town. How could the lover of young boys fall for a woman? Abu Nuwas, who had little patience for piety, even went along to perform hajj when he found out Janan was going there. It is said that Abu Nuwas and Janan were finally able to get close to each other as they kissed the black stone of the Ka'aba, when they brushed against each other and allowed their cheeks to touch. Despite the melee of the hajj, Abu Nuwas was spotted and reprimanded for his disrespect for the House of Allah. No one harmed him due to his prestige—or perhaps because the Islam of the Abbasids was such that an openly gay poet courting a beautiful woman in the Ka'aba was not considered a catastrophe, as it would be in Mecca today.

The pair broke up when the young woman insisted that Abu Nuwas commit to monogamy and stay away from male sexual partners. The poet walked away, saying he could not abandon his homosexuality.

---

* Nauroze: The Persian and Zoroastrian New Year festival that is celebrated to mark spring.

In 786, in the year Haroon Rashid became the caliph, a broken-hearted Abu Nuwas also moved to Baghdad. The grandest of the Islamic caliphs and the most daring of the Arab poets in the same city at the same time—only a divine hand could have pulled off this miracle. Fortunately, there were no Syed Qutbs or Maudoodis in 9th-century Baghdad to sour the joy and revelry of classic Islamic civilization under a dynamic Arab caliph and a rebellious Arab poet.

Abu Nuwas was a Muslim, but had little respect for the clerics. He possessed a sharp sense of humour tinged with a naughty streak and a low threshold for tolerating dogma. Once, while attending prayers, when the imam recited the Quranic verse, "O ye unbelievers . . . ," Abu Nuwas interrupted him, saying, "Here I am [labbay-ka]" He was briefly detained on a charge of heresy when he questioned the hereafter, claiming that since no one had returned from there to confirm its existence, it could not exist.

Though he was best known for his genre of "wine poetry," Abu Nuwas' erotic poems about seduction and rape defy the image of the pompous piety that the Islamists would have us believe dominated the medieval Muslim world.

It wasn't just romantic erotic poetry and the taste of fine wines that exemplified the Abbasid caliphate. The arts and literature flourished hand in hand with philosophy, sciences, astronomy, and engineering. The Arabs were dazzling the world and the rest of it watched in envy. In fact, historian Philip Hitti makes the claim that what rendered this age most illustrious in world annals is the fact that it witnessed the most momentous intellectual awakening, not only in the history of Islam, but also "the most significant in the whole history of thought and culture."

The intellectual curiosity and hunger of the Arab Bedouin came face to face with the more advanced and cultured civilizations of the people they conquered. Indian, Persian, and Greek works of philosophy and science were translated into Arabic. In less than a century after the foundation of Baghdad, people in the city were reading neo-Platonic commentators, the works of Aristotle. Astronomy from India was introduced when Mansoor had the *Siddhanta** (*Sindhind* in Arabic) translated from Sanskrit into Arabic. Baghdad triggered a fusion of thought from the known centres of the world: Greece, India, Persia, and even China. "The famous al-Khwarizmi based his widely known astronomical tables (*zij*) on the Persian mathematician al-Fazari's work and syncretized the Indian and Greek systems of astronomy, at the same time adding his own contribution."

---

* *Siddhanta*: Sanskrit; roughly translates as the "Doctrine" or "Tradition." It denotes the established and accepted view of a particular school within Hindu philosophy.

The impact India had on medieval Abbasid Islam has gone largely unnoticed. Every page of every Quran anywhere in the world today bears witness to India's influence on how Muslims read the Quran. The pages of the Quran are numbered according to Indian numerals, not Arabic—the Arabic numerals having been seconded by the European languages long ago.

THE AGE OF IMAMS

Science, engineering, mathematics, music, dance, and poetry flourished even as caliphs conspired in palace corridors to retain power or to eliminate enemies. However, the impact of all of these endeavours of the Abbasid period pales when compared to the birth of the five Islamic schools of thought, whose Arabic name roughly translates as "religious jurisprudence."

Soon after the death of the Prophet, a number of such "schools" of Islamic jurisprudence emerged, many created by the companions of Muhammad. Some of the Damascus-based schools survived as the Maliki *madhhab*,* while other Iraqi schools developed or merged into the Hannafi madhhab. The Shafi and Hanbali schools emerged much later during the Abbasid era. Of course, Shia Islam had its own school of law, the Ja'fari school, founded by Imam Ja'far as-Sadiq (702–65), who chroniclers say was often imprisoned and ultimately poisoned to death by the early Abbasid administration. What is fascinating about Ja'far as-Sadiq is that both abu Hanifa and Malik ibn Anas, the founders of the Hannafi and Maliki Sunni schools, were his students, when he was the founder of the Shia school. The body of work these five imams created is today known as *sharia* law.

The reason I am telling the story of the five founders of major Islamic schools of thought is to demonstrate that even they—the most pious, who posed no threat to the Islamic political system—ended up as victims of the obsessive and suspicious nature of the Abbasid monarchs. Ja'far as-Sadiq was not the only one to suffer death or imprisonment as caliphs attempted to snuff out any possible challenge to their authority and authoritarianism.

Between 700 and 900 CE, the period when sharia law was created and the hadith—the sayings of Prophet Muhammad—were compiled, about forty-five Muslim versus Muslim wars, assassinations, revolts, and counter-revolts took place. That makes one incident of violent conflict every five years. These soon developed into a culture of violence within Muslim society,

---

* *Madhhab*: An Arabic term that refers to an Islamic school of thought.

one that is still the dominant method of political action among supporters of sharia-based political Islam.

Imam Abu Hanifah (699–767) was a student of Imam Ja'far as-Sadiq, but developed the most widely accepted Sunni school of thought. He was born in Basra to a family of traders from Kabul, and was the author of thousands of literary works.

In 763, Caliph Mansoor offered Abu Hanifa the position of chief judge of the state. When Abu Hanifa declined the offer, the caliph had him locked up in prison, where he was tortured. For having the audacity to reject a caliph's favour, Imam Abu Hanifah spent the rest of his days in a Baghdad jail, until death gave him liberty.

Imam Malik (715–96) was the founder of the Maliki school of thought, which today dominates North and West Africa. Born in Medina of a Yemeni family, Imam Malik was also an outspoken critic of authoritarianism in the politics of the time, and issued fatwas against the practice of being forced to pledge allegiance to Caliph Mansoor. He too was punished and flogged in public for his insolence. Other reports say the imam faced the public whipping because he issued a rule that a divorce obtained under coercion was invalid. The ruling had more serious political implications, because it validated critics of the caliph who claimed that Mansoor had no authority as he too had secured power by means of coercion.

Because of his vast knowledge, Muhammad ibn Idris ash-Shafi, also known as Imam al-Shafi (767–820) was given the honorific title "Father of Usul Al-Fiqh," the Foundation of Islamic Jurisprudence."

Born in Gaza, Palestine, Imam al-Shafi moved to Mecca and later to Medina, where he became a disciple of Imam Malik ibn Anas. Imam al-Shafi was the only one of these imams who went into the service of the caliph's government, an experience that did not go well for him. After Imam Malik's death in 796, Caliph Haroon Rashid appointed Imam al-Shafi as a judge in Yemen. Because he offended the governor, Imam al-Shafi was falsely accused of aiding a revolt against the caliph. From behind bars, Imam al-Shafi had to convince Haroon Rashid of his innocence, and was set free, but the experience ensured he never worked for the government again.

Al-Shafi's student Ahmad ibn Hanbal (780–855), who founded the Hanbali School, had to endure long sentences of imprisonment and public torture.

He was born in the city of Merv, Persia, but grew up in Baghdad. He lived during the great debates between the rationalist Mutazalites, who relied on

* Fiqh: Means understanding and refers to the study of the law in Islam.

reason and logic for their inspiration rather than dogma. The Mutazalites had a strong influence on Caliph Abdullah Mamoon (786–833). A clash between the traditionalists and the rationalists was inevitable, and the debate between the two camps is known as the trial of "the creation of the Quran."

Caliph Mamoon backed the Mutazalites, who espoused the belief that, even though they accepted that the Quran was the speech of Allah, they felt it was created by human endeavour.

Mamoon introduced a milder but reverse version of the Spanish Inquisitions, the institution of *Mihna*. This allowed the official jurists, who were mostly from the rationalist camp, to interrogate all scholars. Whoever opposed the Mutazalites was jailed. When Ahmad ibn Hanbal was put to the test on the order of Caliph Mamoon, he refused to acknowledge the possibility of the "creation of the Quran," other than it being the very word of God. Because of his refusal to follow the official line, Ahmed ibn Hanbal was imprisoned.

The persecution of traditional scholars was continued by Mustasim, the successor of Mamoon, who it is said was most brutal towards Sunni scholars in general, and Imam Ahmad in particular. The frustrated caliph finally ordered Ahmad to be flogged in public. After Caliph Mustasim's death, Wathiq took over the office, and had Imam ibn Hanbal banished from Baghdad.

It was only after Mutawakkil took over as caliph in 847 that this inquisition ended and all prisoners of faith were released. In a reversal of fortunes, the new caliph turned against the Mutazalites, purging them from the courts and issuing an order that all Mutazalite judges be cursed by name from mosque pulpits.

By 847, the tide had turned against the rationalists and Ibn Hanbal, who had hitherto maintained his silence, re-emerged in public as a scholar and imam. It is said that when he died in Baghdad on July 31, 855, more than 800,000 people attended his funeral.

A number of significant questions emerge from the study of the founders of the Islamic schools of thought. All five scholars were born in the same region and in the same time period, the 8th and 9th centuries; they were all linked to each other as students or teachers. However, as soon as the Abbasid empire started to stumble and splinter, no new school of thought emerged. It was as if Islamic thought itself came to a standstill, stuck in a quagmire of inertia. This begs the question: Is the development of Islamic thought restricted to the geographical areas of what we know as the Middle East? Could it be possible that not a single scholar arose in the Ganges delta of Bengal, the archipelago of Indonesia, the Atlas Mountains of Morocco, or the plains of Punjab? Or were they stamped out and eliminated like the Mutazalites of Baghdad?

In addition, we must ask how the development of Islamic thought could be restricted to a hundred-year period in the 8th and 9th centuries and hence arrested? Either we Muslims believe that human intellect reached its height in the 9th century and that men and women of subsequent centuries leading up to the present went into a decline, unable to match the philosophical, sociological, and scientific prowess of the men who became our imams forever, or we raise a ruckus and say these gentlemen may have been scholars of their time, but they did not speak in our name, nor were we asked by Allah or his Apostle to obey with blind conviction laws written by men we never knew and may never question.

Then there is this question: If in the 9th century Muslims could vigorously—though admittedly with risk to their lives—debate an issue as sensitive as the creation of the Quran, why cannot Muslims do it today?

And finally, if Islamists would have us believe that the models we have to implement for our future can only be derived from the era of the Abbasids, how do we explain why all five imams that Muslims have come to follow were tortured, jailed, or even killed in the name of Islam itself? And if the model being proposed involved the extermination of Islamdom's entire rationalist movement, the Mutazalites, what room would there be for those who challenge established mythologies? Would there be room for Adonis or Faiz Ahmed Faiz, let alone an Abu Nuwas?

HAROON RASHID

Caliph Haroon Rashid's reign over the Islamic empire lasted from September 786 to March 809, a mere twenty-three years, but in these two decades he shaped the future of his dynasty. Under his rule, Baghdad flourished into the most splendid city of its time. It is said that for thirty kilometres on both banks of the Tigris were wharves mooring hundreds of craft from as far away as China and India, intermingled with the *zouraq* gondolas that ferried Baghdadis from one shore to the other. The markets of the city carried goods from across the world, including places where slaves were bought and sold—not just Black Africans, but even White Russians. Despite the urgings of Prophet Muhammad, slavery flourished throughout Islamic history and across the Muslim world; from the times of the first caliph Abu-Bakr right up to the current Saudi dynasty in the 20th century. If there was one institution over which all the sects of Islam agreed, it was slavery, and Haroon Rashid's caliphate was no exception.

A superbly handsome man, Haroon was in his twenties when he took over as caliph. His mother, who was instrumental in ensuring her son was not bypassed, was a strong influence in the governance of the empire until her death in 789. Caliph Haroon Rashid was also assisted by his vizier, Yahya the Barmakid, a member of a prominent and wealthy family of Baghdad, Persians who had been in the service of the Abbasids from the days of caliphs Mansoor and Mehdi. The Barmakids controlled the financial administration of the government and had considerable freedom of action. Yahya had aided Haroon in securing the caliphate, and he and his sons were in high favour until 798, when the caliph, outraged that his sister Abbasa was having an affair with Yahya's son Ja'far, had him murdered by cutting him in two, then put his body on display on the bridge across the Tigris, and had the entire family arrested and its wealth and property confiscated.

Abbasa had a son as a result of her affair with Ja'far. To hide first her pregnancy and then the child, Abbasa was spirited away to Mecca on the pretext of wanting to perform hajj, where she gave birth. She left her son in the care of a woman in her service. Chroniclers say that years later, when the caliph was told about the young boy, he went to Mecca to meet him and had his nephew smothered to death. On his return to Baghdad, he had Abbasa killed in her own chamber.

It is said that a part of Haroon Rashid died with the death of his favourite sister Abbasa and her lover Ja'far, who was also the caliph's closest friend. Six years later the caliph died, in his early forties, never having recovered from presiding over the deaths of the two people closest to his heart. Robert Payne, in his book *A History of Islam*, writes:

> The most succinct account of the tragedy was given by a visitor to the Treasury who found in one of the ledgers the entry: "For a robe for Ja'far ibn-Yahya—400,000 dinars." A few days later, he noted another entry: "For naphtha and shavings for burning the boy of Ja'far ibn-Yahya—10 kirats." A kirat was one twenty-fourth of a dinar.

Haroon Rashid could tolerate a homosexual poet singing bards about beautiful sensuous women but, when it came to his family's honour, nothing less than the killing of his own favourite sister would suffice. Centuries later, another Muslim king, Moghul Emperor Aurangzeb, followed the example set by Caliph Haroon Rashid. He threw his own sister over the walls of Delhi's Red Fort for the crime of falling in love with a commoner.

Haroon Rashid brought immense wealth to the Muslim empire. The historian Tabari concludes his account of Haroon's reign with these words: "It has been said that when Harun Rashid died, there were nine hundred million odd [dirhams] in the state treasury."

Haroon had three sons. Abdullah Mamoon was born on the day of his accession; his second son, Muhammad Amin, was born some time later to another wife, Zubaida, a granddaughter of Caliph Mansoor. Since Mamoon's mother was a Persian slave, he was considered inferior to his younger brother. Even in the best of times, even under the wisest of the caliphs, race and bloodline mattered more than merit or faith. If Haroon Rashid could not, and did not, develop the political institutions that could have facilitated succession or the transfer of power, it is doubtful that any other Islamic leader could. This fact has been validated by history.

In 798 Caliph Haroon Rashid announced that the younger prince, Muhammad Amin, would succeed him, followed by the older brother. The problem was that there were more princes than there were positions. Soon, the caliph had to deal with the demands of another son, who was given the title of Mustasim. To settle the power-sharing arrangement among the brothers, the caliph took all three to Mecca in 802 and had them sign an elaborate contract, witnessed by leading judges, clerics, and generals. According to the contract, after Caliph Haroon Rashid passed away, Amin would succeed him as the caliph, but would not interfere in the affairs of his two other brothers, who were placed as governors: Mustasim of al-Jazeera and Mamoon of Persia. Amid oaths of loyalties and much fanfare, the Mecca document was signed in the shadows of the Ka'aba and then placed to hang from the walls of the House of God for added solemnity. But like many other Mecca declarations throughout history, including the Hamas–Fatah rival Palestinian factions deal of late 2007, Haroon Rashid's contract would not be worth the paper it was signed on. Effectively, the caliph had divided the empire into three parts. Neither God nor country mattered when family interests were concerned.

In 808, the great Haroon Rashid passed away, and with his death, the empire faced yet another civil war, this time from within the ruling family. As soon as news reached Baghdad that the caliph had died, Prince Amin took over as caliph, God's representative on Earth, and leader of the world's Muslims. Mamoon, who was at his father's side when Haroon Rashid died while watching the brutal murder of a rebel in the north, took the slight without much fuss, quite content that he would be the de facto ruler of the eastern part of the caliphate. Amin, on the other hand, had other ambitions. He first dismissed brother Mustasim as governor of Jazeera, and then tried to exert his control in areas that had been allotted to brother Mamoon.

For three years, a cold war existed between the two sides, but in 812, the bickering broke into a full-scale civil war in which Amin was badly defeated. The entire empire fell into the hands of Mamoon.

ABDULLAH MAMOON AND THE RATIONALISTS

Abdullah Mamoon (786–833) was the seventh caliph of the Abbasid dynasty, and his reign is best remembered for the rise of Islam's one and only rationalist movement, the Mutazalites. During his time the study of Greek thought absorbed the scholars and the balance of power shifted significantly from Arabs to the Persians and other non-Arabs.

Despite having defeated his brother Caliph Amin in a civil war, Mamoon did not move to the capital Baghdad, preferring to live in the Persian city of Merv in Khurasan. His army had won the civil war, but Baghdad had become a lawless area, that had yet to be brought under the authority of the caliph.

As rival interest groups elbowed for power, Mamoon tried to bring Sunnis and Shias together in 817 by designating Imam Ali Reza (Ali ar-Rida to the Arabs), a seventh-generation descendant of Prophet Muhammad, as his heir and successor. Instead, this step provoked a revolt in Baghdad. The caliph's uncle, Ibrahim bin Mehdi, incensed at the thought of a Shia heir to the caliphate, rebelled and proclaimed himself as the caliph. Mamoon had no choice but to stamp out the rebellion: he led his army into Baghdad in 819 and ended the revolt. However, Ali Reza died in Meshed of poisoning. Once more the absence of a political system within Islamic jurisprudence continued to bleed the Muslims in civil war and the assassination of political rivals. Added to this were the machinations of the harem, where the many competing wives and dozens of concubines conspired against each other in attempts to promote the fortunes of their sons. Polygamy, more than any other Islamic institution, caused immense grief to innumerable Islamic rulers, let alone to the women involved.

Having secured his caliphate, Mamoon also gave his blessings to the rising movement of Muslim rationalists who adhered to and promoted the Mutazalite philosophy. Mutazili theology had originated in the 8th century in Basra during the dying days of the Umayyad era when one Wasil ibn Ata (d. 748) fell out with his teachers on the question of whether a Muslim who commits grave sins (such as murder or rape) was to be regarded as non-Muslim or merely a Muslim who had sinned. The debate became known as the question of *al-Manzilah bayna al-manzilatayn* (the intermediate position between positions). Wasil and his followers argued that as long as a sinner or criminal accepted the unity of God (*tawheed*) and Muhammad as the Messenger of God, such a person cannot be cast aside as an infidel. Labelled as the Mutazili, they called themselves *Ahl al-tawhid wa al-'adl* (People of Divine Unity and Justice). However, it was not until Caliph Mamoon's reign in the early 800s that a theologian by the name of Abu al-Hudhayl al-Allaf (d. 849) in Basra systematized and formalized the Mutazili movement.

Though the Mutazalites based their philosophy on logic and aspects of Greek philosophy, their point of reference was Islam. Their opponents in rival schools of theology—traditional Sunnis as well as Shia—accused them of heresy, suggesting that their reliance on reason as the primary tool for understanding revelation was contrary to Islam.

From Islam's earliest days, Muslims had raised basic questions with their theologians: Was the Quran created or was it eternal? Was evil created by God? How was the free will of man to be reconciled with predestination set by Allah? If an ordinary leaf did not move without the permission of God, why would God not simply put an end to all evil? Muslims, especially during the Abbasid period, debated whether God's attributes in the Quran were to be interpreted allegorically or literally.

Mutazalites believed that human beings should use their intellectual power to determine whether God exists or not, instead of having blind faith. They urged Muslims to conduct an inner search and to become knowledgeable of God's attributes. They suggested that humans owe it to their intellect to ask why something exists rather than nothing. According to their theology, if one comes to believe that there is a God who created this universe, then one must be motivated to determine what this Creator wants from us humans. They believed that without this questioning, human beings only end up harming themselves by ignoring the whole mystery of existence and, consequently, the plan of the Creator.

Caliph Mamoon's backing of the Mutazalite philosophy proved to be a mixed blessing. Although this privileged position allowed the Mutazalites the freedom to propagate their views without the fear of being accused as heretics, their zeal took on an oppressive nature. In becoming the official creed of the caliphate, Mutazalism lost its original radical appeal and soon became seen as yet another institution of the state. The persecution campaign Mutazalites waged against the traditionalist imams cost them the sympathy of the ordinary Muslim masses, leading to a backlash.

The Mutazalites had overplayed their hand and, for most of the past millennium, no one has dared follow them for fear of being declared an apostate. It is only recently that there has been a revival of the Abbasid Mutazalite philosophy in some parts of the Muslim world, particularly in Indonesia, where the modernist scholar Harun Nasution* began writing about rationalism in Islam in the 1970s.

In 847, Caliph Mutawakkil withdrew official backing of the Mutazalites and soon they were on the defensive. By the end of the 9th century, the

---

* Harun Nasution: Part of a small but significant new trend within the Islamic debate to champion rationalist and humanist principles.

Mutazalites were subjected to attacks from not just the traditionalists, but also the growing number of atheist intellectuals.

Even though Mutazili theologians came under attack, their ideas were not instantly quashed. In fact, they thrived in the port city of Basra, where the prominent Abd al-Jabbar became the most celebrated proponent of Mutazalism in the late 10th and early 11th century. With the onset of the Abbasid decline and the coming of the Crusaders, there was a rise in Islamic fundamentalism. After the fall of Jerusalem to the Crusaders, Islam itself was thought to be in danger at the hands of Christendom. In a climate of fear and possible Armageddon, there was little appetite for rationalism as espoused by the Mutazalites. The slogan "Islam in Danger" has always resulted in setback to those who asked for critical inquiry and rational thought. The period from 1099 to 1258—from when Jerusalem fell to when the Mongols wiped out the Abbasid empire by burning Baghdad—was not conducive to the propagation of Mutazalite philosophy. With every defeat, with every division, with the onset of decay, orthodoxy and ultra-conservatism gained ground. The self-confidence that allowed for debate and critical analysis was waning. As in the 21st century, Muslims were paranoid and defensive, viewing the rest of the world as conspiring against their faith. By the time Baghdad fell, the rationalism of the Mutazalites in Islam had long been dead and buried.

Harun Nasution, the Canadian-educated Indonesian scholar who is a contemporary neo-Mutazalite, suggests the rise of the rationalists in the 9th century was a response to the decline of ethics in Islamic politics and theology. Richard Martin, Mark Woodward, and Dwi Atmaja, in their book, *Defenders of Reason in Islam,* write:

> Harun Nasution begins his treatise with an equally important Mutazalite claim that Islamic politics and Kalam (theology) arose out of a single troubling event in nascent Islam, the assassination of the third caliph of the Muslim community, Uthman ibn Affan (d. 656). That the civil war which soon followed had enormous implications for subsequent Islamic political and social history is not in dispute . . . Nasution's text reminds us that the *fitnas** first occurred as political and social conflicts that generated theological discourses.

The main challenge to Mutazalite thought came from the Ashari theology, founded by Abu al-Hasan al-Ashari (d. 936). The Ashrites were instrumental in drastically turning Islamic theology away from Mutazalism.

---

* *Fitnas*: Conflicts.

The Asharite view was that comprehension of the characteristics of God was beyond human capability. They believed that while human beings had free will, they had no power to create anything. It was a view that assumed human reason could discern morality. This was in sharp contrast to the Mutazalite school of Greek-inspired theologians.

The founder of their movement, himself a former Mutazalite, wrote that the divine had a physical shape, something that was foreign to the Quran, yet as blind faith spread, his ideas received acceptance. He wrote: "We confess that God is firmly seated on his Throne . . . We confess that God has two hands, without asking how . . . We confess that God has two eyes, without asking how . . . We confess that God has a face . . . We affirm hearing and sight."

The philosopher Ghazali (d. 1111) was the most prominent of this school's adherents. He is best known for his influential work *The Incoherence of the Philosophers*, a thorough and comprehensive attack on rationalist Hellenic thought and its influence on Islam. He is considered to have laid the foundation stone of the movement to shut the door of Ijtehad* and in the words of Syed Hossein Nasr, "saved orthodoxy by depressing science." While Ghazali may have not intended such an outcome, interpretation of his work led the Islamic societies to do just that. Works of his critics, including the Andalusian rationalist Averroes (Ibn-Rushd), were forbidden for centuries. Ghazali denounced Muslim Aristotelian philosophers, accusing them of being outside the fold of Islam. He declared: "We must therefore reckon as unbelievers both these philosophers themselves and their followers among the Islamic philosophers, such as Ibn-Sina (Avicenna), Farabi, and others, in transmitting the philosophy of Aristotle."

According to the Asharites and Ghazali, the movement of the world is not based on physical sciences, but rather on God's will. He believed that when cotton catches fire, it is not because of the heat of the flame, but because of God's will. According to Ghazali: "This we deny, saying: the agent of the burning is God, through His creating the back in the cotton and the disconnection of its parts, and it is God who made the cotton burn and made it to ashes either through the intermediations of the angels or without intermediation. For fire is dead body which has no action, and what is the proof that it is the agent. Indeed, the philosophers have no other proof than the observation of the occurrence of the burning, when there is contact with

---

* *Ijtehad:* The process through which Islamic scholars could generate new rules for Muslims. It was one of the recognized sources of Islamic knowledge by early Islamic scholars.

fire, but observation proves only simultaneity, not causation, and, in reality there is no cause but God."

Today's Islamists want to return to the era when it was acceptable to propagate a view that it is God, not heat, that is the cause of fires. It was the Asharites, the followers of Imam Hanbal and other ultra-conservatives, who killed rationalism in Islam, halted the development of sciences and philosophy, and rendered the Islamic empire impotent in the face of the rise of sciences and the Renaissance in Europe. Today, Islamists celebrate Ghazali's anti-science as inspiration for their own work. The president of the pro-sharia Canadian Islamic Congress, a scientist himself, says: "My teacher and spiritual guide, while we have never met in this life, has been Imam Abu Hamid Muhammad al-Ghazali (1058–1111 AD). I admire his writings for he is the best Muslim scholar to introduce Islam to Westerners."

The Muslim dynasties of medieval times are littered with decapitated bodies of religious scholars who refused to sanction the rule of the sultans and caliphs. In India, it was not uncommon for Muslim rulers to kill their prisoners by having them tossed around by trained elephants that had sharpened double-edged swords tied to their tusks. Golden age? Not even close, by the standard of any age.

The Quran did not provide a basic framework for statehood. The Prophet did not rule on the issue of political leadership and succession. Perhaps this is because God never wanted state authority to have a role in the growth of Islam. All three of Islam's founding dynasties and the era of the first four caliphs succeeded in many areas, but failed dramatically in the area of political stability. The Abbasids succeeded in creating an environment and a society where philosophy, literature, art, music, and dance thrived, and where the rights of ordinary citizens emerged as a concept, where even the lepers were awarded lifelong pensions. However, time after time, this progress was interrupted by bloodshed and political upheaval. The rise of conservative theologies as a response to rationalism also contributed to the caliphate's long journey on the road to decay.

THE DECLINE

The decline of the Abbasid caliphate was not simply a result of an intellectual relapse: it had political, financial, and economic causes. Two events stand out among the factors that led to the breakup of the Islamic State in the 9th century, and the creation of smaller successor states. First, Turks were introduced into the Abbasid armies. They were brave, courageous, and swift on horseback, but soon came to dominate the entire military structure, making the later caliphs mere puppets. Second, Black African slaves rose in revolt in what is known as the rebellion of the *Zanj*.* These factors, together with unending violence between religious sects, did permanent damage to the Abbasid caliphate.

The Turkish military units were first created during the reign of Mustasim (833–42). In the beginning the Turkish soldiers, who had been brought in as slaves, provided the caliph with a loyal force capable of dealing with domestic challenges, but the general public resented their presence in Baghdad. To avoid the rising friction between the citizenry and the non-Arabic-speaking troops, Mustasim made the blunder of trying to start afresh and moved his government to the city of Samarra, north of Baghdad on the shores of the Tigris. This move turned out to be the first step towards the eventual dissolution of the Islamic State.

Eventually the Turkish troops created their own independent community, which led to clashes and rebellions against Baghdad. Upon the caliph's death in 842, the power the Turks wielded became evident. It was they who managed the succession and put Caliph Mutawwakil on the seat of power. Samarra remained the Abbasid capital for fifty-six years (836–892), during the reign of eight successive caliphs.

Caliph Mutawwakil knew the weakness of his position. When he tried to diversify his army by recruiting soldiers from North Africa and Armenia, he was murdered. From this time on, Baghdad and Samarra were constantly at war with each other, which had a huge impact on the economy of the region. The decline in agricultural production, the loss in revenue from taxation, and the general lawlessness of Baghdad compounded the problems.

With the near absence of central authority, regional warlords rose in rebellion in Egypt, Armenia, and Arabia. The Turkish army had been recruited to save the caliphate. Ironically, it was their presence as "foreigners" that led to the collapse of the state. While other non-Arabs, primarily the Persians, had assimilated into the Arab culture of the state, and were content with the indirect influence they exerted while retaining their own distinct identities, the Turks had other ideas. They were the military might of the empire and felt they didn't have to play second fiddle to the caliphs.

In 869, when the Turks had already killed two caliphs, they installed Mutamid as caliph. He had barely taken charge of his nominal role when a rebellion broke out in Basra, the slave capital of the caliphate. Over the

---

* *Zanj*: Literally, land of the Blacks.

years, tens of thousands of Black slaves captured in East Africa had been bought and sold in the Basra region. The working conditions of these men were appalling, even by the standards of medieval times. They were from Ethiopia, Somalia, and Zanzibar, kidnapped by slave traders and sold to Arab and Persian nobles, and they had to toil in the marshes and the saltpetre mines of the lower Euphrates. They were all Muslims, but they were Black. They were part of the Ummah, but they were African. Centuries later, even the great Ibn Khaldun would describe them as near animals. They had been slaves for more than a hundred years, yet had not seen or experienced the so-called Golden Age of Islam under the Abbasids.

In one of the most dramatic uprisings by slaves anywhere in human history, the African slaves of Basra organized themselves into an army and laid siege to their former masters. Ordinary men, kidnapped from their homes in Africa, converted to Islam and then were made to live in a hell on Earth, right under the shadows of immense wealth and pomp. They rebelled. They invoked the Quranic verse in which God told them that they had the right to the wealth of the rich. They told their Arab and Persian masters to remember the words of Prophet Muhammad that their masters had taught them: "Do not suffer nor inflict inequity."

Their leader, Ali ibn Muhammad, was not a slave. He was known as *Sahib al-Zanj* (Gentleman of the Black Lands), and claimed to be a descendant of the Prophet's family from his daughter Fatima, and hence a Shia. Ali ibn Muhammad's grandmother was an Indian woman from the province of Sind. He came to the slaves after some of them had already rebelled and moved out of their camps on the shore of the Euphrates. Seizing the moment, he joined them and promised to live and die with them in their struggle. His passionate oratory lifted their morale as he urged them to take up arms and rise against their masters. Freedom was what he promised, and freedom is what he delivered.

While the caliph in Samarra and his Turkish generals were playing cat-and-mouse games to test the boundaries of their power, band after band of African slaves were joining Ali ibn Muhammad's ragtag army. In ferocious clashes, the Zanj army advanced from one city to the other, defeating the caliph's forces and killing their former masters. The historian Tabari has dedicated an entire volume of his thirty-volume history of medieval Islam to the Zanj rebellion. His account is unique because he was living in Baghdad as the mutiny unfolded.

For fourteen years the rebellion enjoyed success and expanded the territory under its rule. The Zanj republic was proving to be more dangerous to the Abbasids than they had imagined. Neither the salaried Turkish troops nor the recently recruited North Africans proved to be any match for the newly liberated slaves of the empire. After capturing Basra, the Zanj army built its own capital and a fort in al-Muhtara. At its height, the Zanj rebellion spread to Iran and advanced to within 112 kilometres of Baghdad itself.

It wasn't until 883 that the caliph's army attacked the fortress. In the fighting, Ali ibn Muhammad was killed. The revolt of the slaves was put down, but the fourteen-year rebellion destroyed the economic heartland, the caliphate. Historian Philip Hitti estimates that half a million people died in the rebellion and its aftermath. He writes that the rivers were clogged with skeletons of the dead that could not be buried.

The rebellion came at a time when Iraq was already in decline. After it was crushed, the region's economy, which depended on the slave trade, collapsed. Basra never recovered. The slave trade continued at a low level from Africa to the Arab heartland, and even the coastal areas of India, for many more centuries. The curse of slavery would not end in some of the Islamic countries until the 20th century.

During the Zanj revolt, Egypt would break away from the Abbasid empire under the rule of Ahmed ibn Tulun (835–84). He had been sent by the caliph as governor, but instead broke away and founded the Tulunid dynasty, which would rule Egypt from 868 until 905, when the Abbasids reconquered Egypt.

While the African slaves were fighting the Turkish–Arab–Persian armies, another event was unfolding in Shia Iraq. In 874, the eleventh imam of the Shia, Hasan al-Askari, died while under house arrest in Iraq. Upon his death, the Shia believed that his infant son, Muhammad al-Mehdi, who was five at that time, went into hiding. They believed then (as they do even now) that this divine child, whom they consider the "twelfth imam," would one day return as the Messiah. And until he did, they could not give allegiance to any of the Abbasid caliphs.

To this day the Shia, including President Ahmadinejad of Iran and Syed Hassan Nasrallah of Hezbollah, believe that this being will emerge from hiding after more than a thousand years. Sunni Muslims scoff at the idea, much to the chagrin of their Shia cousins.

Up until the time of the doctrine of the hidden imam, the differences between Shia and Sunni Muslims were solely of a historical and political nature. However, after the death of Imam Al-Askari, the divide became unbridgeable because of the theological disputes. The events of the 9th century not only caused the decline of the Abbasid caliphate, but also set the scene for a seemingly permanent division in Islam.

THE CRUSADES

When the Crusaders arrived in 1099, the Abbasid caliphate was a mere shell of its original self. Most of the Muslim world had broken off from the centre, while the Baghdad caliphs were puppets in the hands of the Turkish military commanders. There were three competing caliphates in the Islamic empire, with numerous petty sultanates in the hinterland. Iraq was ruled by the Abbasids, Egypt and Palestine by the Fatimids, and Spain by the Umayyads.

The Sunni Abbasids had lost Jerusalem to the Shia Fatimids without much fanfare. They engaged in a Sunni–Shia war of words and swords, which has continued ever since. Of all the Islamic cities, Jerusalem had until recently been the most multi-religious, considering its Jewish and Christian roots. However, in the year 1009, the Fatimid caliph, al-Hakim bi-Amr Allah, ordered the Church of the Holy Sepulchre destroyed. Even though his successor in 1039 permitted the Byzantine Empire to rebuild the historic church, its destruction sent shock waves throughout Christian Europe and provided the papacy with the justification to call for the military attack to free the Holy Land from the Muslims. The Fatimid provocation could not have come at a worse time. In Spain, the Muslims were being pushed back, while the Sunni–Shia conflict between the Fatimids and Abbasids ensured a complete lack of cooperation in the face of the threat from Europe.

On Friday, July 15, 1099, the city of Jerusalem fell after a forty-day siege by the Crusaders. For two days the Europeans slaughtered citizens, until no Muslim was left alive. The Jews were surrounded in their quarter, which was set alight, to die en masse in an inferno. The question has always been asked, but rarely answered: How did this happen? How could God allow his holiest city to burn like hell? And how did the caliphs, who claimed to be God's shadow on Earth, fail to protect the city they called their third holiest place on Earth?

Amin Maalouf's *The Crusades through Arab Eyes* reveals a disturbing picture about the reaction of the Abbasid caliphate to the fall of Jerusalem. It is an eye-opener. Maalouf writes about the arrival of Abu Saad al-Harawi—the *qadi** of Damascus—in Baghdad along with his companions to alert the people of the capital city of Islam about the calamity that had hit Jerusalem.

Maalouf's account begins with a Friday during the month of Ramadan, when everyone was supposedly fasting. Al-Harawi and his companions entered the great mosque of Baghdad, spread out a prayer mat, and started eating a

---

* *Qadi*: Civil judge.

meal. The congregation was horrified. Eating in the middle of the day, during Ramadan, and on a Friday, was blasphemous. Soon an angry crowd surrounded al-Harawi and his companions, who refused to stop their meal. When soldiers came to arrest him, he stood up calmly and asked them how it was that they were indignant at his violation of their fast whereas the massacres of thousands of Muslims and the destruction of the holy places of Islam were met with complete indifference. Having made his point, which still carries merit today, al-Harawi stepped out and took his protest to the palace.

The Afghan-born cleric burst into the court chambers of Caliph Mustazhir Billah, with a throng of companions trailing behind him. He had come to apprise the caliph of the catastrophe that had unfolded in the Holy Land. Brushing aside the courtiers with disdain, al-Harawi proceeded to lecture the caliph and his court: "How dare you slumber in the shade of complacent safety leading lives as frivolous as garden flowers, while your brothers in Syria have no dwelling place save the saddles of camels and the bellies of vultures? Blood has been spilled! Beautiful young girls have been shamed, and must now hide their sweet faces in their hands! Shall the valorous Arabs resign themselves to insult, and the valiant Persians accept dishonour?"

The entire audience broke into wails and lamentations, but al-Harawi had not come to elicit sobs. "Man's meanest weapon," he shouted, "is to shed tears when rapiers stir the coals of war." Al-Harawi and his companions had walked all the way across the Syrian desert to come to Baghdad and ask the caliph for help for the victims of the Jerusalem massacre, but he had not counted on the apathy of his hosts. After listening to the qadi's speech and his description of the horrors inflicted on the city and people of Jerusalem, twenty-two-year-old Caliph Mustazhir expressed his sympathy and set up a seven-member committee of wise men to investigate the issue. The seven wise men have yet to report back to the caliph in Baghdad.

What most Muslims do not know, and perhaps do not wish to know, is the amount of complicity various Muslim rulers had in the fall of Jerusalem. When the Franks surrounded the city, General Iftikhar al-Dawah, the Fatimid commander of Jerusalem, abandoned the city instead of putting up a fight. He left the civilians to the mercy of the Crusaders. Little is said of the delegation and gifts the Fatimids sent to the advancing Crusaders when they took the Turkish city of Antioch. In fact, the Fatimids were so obsessed with their hate for the Sunni Turks, the Seljuks, that they proposed an alliance with the Europeans to keep the southward advance of the Turks from reaching Egypt. The Crusaders spurned the Fatimid offer, instead entertaining the Egyptian delegation with a display of three hundred heads of Turkish soldiers they had massacred in the capture of Antioch. The Fatimid prime minister,

Vizier el-Fadl, is said to have congratulated the Franks on their success, and then returned to Cairo.

Such was the sorry state of affairs of the Islamic world when the Crusaders arrived in the Levant. The Shia Fatimids, the descendants of the Prophet and Ali ibn Abu Talib, after centuries of being oppressed and marginalized had achieved their desire to rule in the name of the Prophet. However, perhaps unknowingly, they were now working to facilitate the sacking of Jerusalem. The Shia leadership would fall into the same kind of trap in the Baghdad of 1258 that, some say, it would fall into again in 2003. The fear of the Sunni domination would force the Shias into many historic errors. But that is another story.

Amin Maalouf in the epilogue of his classic book writes: "At the time of the crusades, the Arab world, from Spain to Iraq, was still the intellectual and material repository of the planet's most advanced civilization. Afterwards, the centre of world history shifted decisively to the West. Is there a cause-and-effect relationship here? Can we go so far as to claim that the crusaders marked the beginning of the rise of Western Europe—which would gradually come to dominate the world—and sounded the death knell of Arab civilization?"

Maalouf answers his question with a qualified yes. He writes that the Arabs were already suffering from certain weaknesses, which the Crusaders "exposed and perhaps aggravated, but by no means created."

Even a brilliant Arab writer like Maalouf succumbs to the notion of Arab superiority over non-Arab Muslims. He bemoans the fact that non-Arab Muslims were at the head of the Muslim world and suggests this was one of the reasons for its collapse. In a startling remark, he writes: "The people of the Prophet had lost control of their own destiny. Their leaders were all foreigners."

Wait a minute. Foreigners? Does Maalouf consider only Arabs to be the "people of the Prophet"? Perhaps a slip from a brilliant author, but a slip that is indicative of the deeply rooted, centuries-old view about the Arab and the Mawali non-Arab, the master and the client, that even today affects the relationships among Muslims.

Notwithstanding Maalouf's view of Persians, Kurds, and Turks as "foreigners," and not "people of the Prophet," his book delivers a breathtakingly accurate depiction of the Muslim world after its clash with the Crusaders. He writes: "Although the epoch of the Crusades ignited a genuine economic and cultural revolution in Western Europe, in the Orient these holy wars led to long centuries of decadence and obscurantism. Assaulted from all quarters, the Muslim world turned in on itself. It became over-sensitive, defensive, intolerant, sterile—attitudes that grew steadily worse as world-wide evolution continued. Henceforth progress was the embodiment of 'the other.' Modernism became alien."

If the Crusades were not sufficient enough a jolt to the Muslim psyche, there was more to come. Muslims under the Kurdish general Saladin had barely recaptured Jerusalem and defeated the Crusaders in 1187 when the Mongols came calling. In 1258, in an orgy of bloodshed, the hordes from the East inflicted on Baghdad a punishment that rivalled what the Crusaders had done to Jerusalem in 1099. The fall of Baghdad also heralded the end of the 500-year-old Abbasid caliphate.

The caliph who presided over the fall of Baghdad was Mustasim, thirty-seventh in the Abbasid line. He was placed in power in 1242, and like his predecessors, ruled with the confidence that his house would reign until the Day of Judgment. In late 1257, he was told of the approaching Mongol army, but instead of preparing for the defence of the capital, he scoffed at the threat. After all, he reassured his court, Baghdad had been attacked by the Mongols once before during the reign of his father, the late caliph Mustansir, and had been beaten back. The Mongols were no match for the army of the mighty Abbasid caliphate, he argued.

But the Mongols had learned from their past failure. This time they were led by Hulagu Khan (1216–65), a grandson of Genghis Khan.

Hulagu set out in 1253 from Mongolia, marching westward at the head of perhaps the largest Mongol army ever assembled, along a well-prepared path. After an eighteen-month march during which he defeated a number of Ismaili Shia forces, Hulagu's army reached the mountains of Persia. Here they surrounded the fortress of Alamut, hitherto considered the impregnable home of the *Hashshashin* (the Assassins),* a dreaded extreme Shia sect that terrorized neighbouring rulers by sending young men on suicide missions to kill them. It is said that the sight of the mammoth Mongol army and the massive artillery barrage it let loose on the fort so frightened these extreme Shia that they surrendered unconditionally. Yet they could not avoid a massacre in which, as Philip Hitti writes, "even the babes were ruthlessly slaughtered."

By the summer of 1257, Hulagu had reached the vicinity of Baghdad and he sent an invitation to Caliph Mustasim to come to him and surrender the city. The caliph, who considered himself God's shadow on Earth, did not take kindly to the invitation and sent a message to the invading Mongol to go back to where he came from, reminding him that all of Islam was ready to defend Baghdad.

---

* *Hashshashin*: Young men who were drugged with hashish (source of the Arabic word for "assassins") and told that when they died they would immediately go to Paradise, where women and other pleasures awaited them. This tradition is kept alive even today by the suicide bombers of Al-Qaeda and Hamas.

In November 1257, the City of Peace—which had been built by Mansoor five hundred years before and shone like a glittering diamond on the bosom of a beautiful woman, the envy of the world—witnessed on the horizon the darkened mass of a horde approaching from all sides. Nearly a million Mongol troops, strengthened by a Christian army from Georgia, had Baghdad surrounded. Mustasim sent a force to stop the encirclement from the west, but the Mongols trapped his army by breaking dikes on the Tigris and flooding the area. Most of the Muslim troops either drowned or were slaughtered trying to escape the deluge.

Hulagu wasn't just relying on military advantage. He was also exploiting the deep divisions that permeated Iraqi society, pitting the Shia population against the Sunni caliph. In 2003, another invader of Iraq would rely on the same dynamics of Iraqi society. The US invasion to topple Saddam Hussein would have the blessings of the country's Shia population.

Caliph Mustasim, a drunkard who preferred the company of musicians and clowns to poets and philosophers, had made no secret of his contempt of the Shia, mocking their beliefs and insulting their leaders publicly. Some Shia, now finding the hated Sunni caliphate under attack, facilitated the Mongol advance by volunteering to help the Mongols in capturing cities along their route to the capital. It is widely believed that Caliph Mustasim's chief minister, the vizier al-Alkamzi, who was a Shia, betrayed the caliph. To solidify support of the Shia population, Hulagu promised to not destroy the Shia shrines in Najaf and Karbala.

The attack on Baghdad began on the morning of January 29, 1258. As Hulagu's Chinese units breached the outer eastern wall of the city, the caliph offered to negotiate. He came out of the city in person, along with his army and the citizenry. Hulagu refused the surrender offer, had the caliph arrested and ordered his troops to kill everyone. For a period of seven days, the Mongols sacked the city, killing almost a million people. The river turned red with Muslim blood. The Mongol hordes had no way of differentiating between Shia and Sunni: all perished in the City of Peace.

The Persian historian Abdullah Wassaf, a contemporary of Marco Polo, described the apocalyptic end of Baghdad:

> They swept through the city like hungry falcons, attacking a flight of doves, or like raging wolves attacking sheep, with loose reins and shameless faces, murdering and spreading terror . . . beds and cushions made of gold and encrusted with jewels were cut to pieces with knives and torn to shreds. Those hiding behind the veils of the great Harem were dragged . . . through the streets and alleys, each of them becoming a plaything in the hands of a Tartar [Mongol] master.

Ian Frazier, in a 2005 article for *The New Yorker*, "Destroying Baghdad," wrote that Hulagu, whose wife was a Christian, ordered all Christians of Baghdad to take refuge in the churches, which he had ordered off limits to his troops. Frazier said that the Mongols' Georgian Christian allies particularly distinguished themselves in slaughter:

> Plunderers threw away their swords and filled their scabbards with gold. Silver and jewels and gold piled up in great heaps around Hulagu's tent. Fire consumed the caliph's palace, and the smoke from its beams of aloe wood, sandalwood, and ebony filled the air with fragrance for a distance of a hundred *li*. (A *li* equalled five hundred bow lengths—a hundred *li* was maybe thirty miles.) So many books from Baghdad's libraries were flung into the Tigris that a horse could walk across on them. The river ran black with scholars' ink and red with the blood of martyrs.

The last caliph of the Abbasids was now a prisoner of Hulagu and it is said that the Mongol took immense pleasure in mocking the leader of the Muslim world. One story has it that as Baghdad burned and its people were being butchered, Hulagu amused himself by dining with the caliph, pretending to be his guest. Another account describes how Hulagu offered the caliph gold and jewels for dinner. When Mustasim protested that he could not eat gold, Hulagu asked him why he hadn't used his treasures to strengthen his army and defend himself against the Mongols. The caliph said, "That was the will of God." Hulagu replied, "What will happen to you is the will of God, also."

With Baghdad destroyed, Hulagu had two problems to resolve. First, the stench of the dying and the rotting corpses was overwhelming. To escape the stench, Hulagu moved his camp upwind to the north. The next challenge was what to do with his prisoner. Rumours and superstition had it that if the blood of the caliph of Islam was spilled on earth, God would let loose a catastrophe. Astrologers predicted an earthquake. However, chroniclers report that the learned Shia imams who were now advising Hulagu argued that the Mongol had nothing to fear from God. After all, they argued, no catastrophes had followed the bloody deaths of John the Baptist, Jesus Christ, or even the grandson of the Prophet, Imam Hussein. They urged Hulagu to kill the caliph. To be on the safe side and to ensure that the caliph died in such a way that no blood would spill on the earth, Hulagu had the caliph wrapped in a carpet and then trodden to death by horses. Thus ended the 500-year rule of the descendants of Abbas, the uncle of Prophet Muhammad..

Thus far in this book, I have travelled a long journey of many centuries looking for an era in the Islamic history of its caliphates that could provide the model Islamists offer as a political salvation for contemporary Muslims. I have sincerely attempted to find the so-called Golden Age of Islam that was free of bloodshed, civil strife, palace intrigues, outright racism, slavery, and pillage. I have failed. From the Ridda (Apostasy) Wars of Caliph Abu-Bakr to the humiliating defeat of Caliph Mustasim, I have not found a single period that I could in all honesty say I would trade for my 21st-century existence as a Muslim living in a secular democratic society. Why Islamists would crave the bloody past is beyond rational explanation, but rationality was a victim of the caliphs.

Of course, Muslims conquered not just land, but the sciences and philosophy too. However, they proved completely inept in creating political institutions that would withstand the scrutiny of today.

It is true that no other empire, from the Indian to the Chinese, the Roman, the Byzantine, the Persian or the Mongol, was free of the tyranny, war and looting, and mass killing that were witnessed during the Islamic caliphates. The difference is that there are no demonstrations in India with people chanting slogans to bring back the rule of Shivaji or masses of people in Tiananmen Square sloganeering for a return to the Ming dynasty. The reason I have critiqued the notion of the Islamic State and shown its inadequacies is because of the Islamists' clamour for the return to a mythical golden period. Of course, there were golden moments in Islamic history, but they did not occur because of the development of progressive political institutions of an Islamic State. They happened in spite of the attempts to create an Islamic State.

Professor Pervez Hoodbhoy, the Pakistani peace activist who teaches nuclear physics at the Massachusetts Institute of Technology and Islamabad's Quaid-e-Azam University, makes a compelling case for Muslims to take a critical look at how we treated the best brains among the Ummah. He writes: "The great scholars of Islam were often endangered not by Mongol hordes or infidel Christians, but instead, by home-grown religious orthodoxy."

Hoodbhoy devotes a chapter of his book *Islam and Science* to the individuals he refers to as the "Five Great Heretics." They are: mathematician Al Kindi (801–73); physician Ar Razi (865–925); Aristotelian jurist Ibn-Rushd, or Averroes (1126–98); physician Ibn Sina, or Avicenna (980–1037); and the father of the study of history, Ibn Khaldun (1332–1406).

Islamists cite these men as evidence of the greatness of an Islamic political system. What they fail to mention is that the great ones were all accused of heresy and blasphemy.

So why is it that Islamists dream of the so-called Golden Age that never occurred? Is it because when today's young men and women look around, they see so little of themselves in the progress the world has made in the past two hundred years? They have no stake in the success of human society and would rather not be part of this world. In the failure of their ancestors, they reject this world for either a fictitious past or the promissory notes of paradise in the hereafter.

If I could make a heartfelt case to my sisters and brothers who wear Islam on their sleeves, I would say this: "You are in a trap. Make no mistake about it. The way out is to identify all of humanity as the Ummah, as God's children, and not think of ourselves as apart from all others. The accomplishments and success of all human beings belong to us Muslims as well. Embrace equality, just as the Arabs embraced Aristotle. I know this is more easily said than done, but you and I do not have a choice. This is it. This *is* the heaven we were promised. Let us not turn it into hell."

PART THREE

The Consequences

CHAPTER 11

Sharia—God's Law or Man's Flaw?

HASAN MAHMUD WAS EMPHATIC. Sharia is not a benign legal system, he said. "It is the foundation for building a global theocratic Islamic State. Further, sharia is not entirely compatible with the spirit of Islam." In what way, I interjected. "Because most of sharia law comes from outside the Quran," he responded. "No law that perpetuates injustice against our mothers and daughters can be considered Islamic. Sharia forces Muslims to turn away from Islam's spirit of moral guidance, and instead makes ordinary Muslims pawns in a man-made political power struggle."

It was the summer of 2003. A few of us at a Muslim Canadian Congress (MCC) strategy meeting had been discussing how to thwart a move to introduce sharia law into Ontario's family law regime. Canadian Islamists had for years been lobbying the government to put its stamp of approval on sharia law.

"Isn't your description of sharia a rather bleak indictment of what the imams say are laws based on the Quran?" I suggested to Mahmud. "Not at all," he responded. "An overwhelming number of laws contained in the books of sharia were written by men. How can such laws then be defined or categorized as divine or Quranic? Here, take a look at them," Mahmud said, pushing a sheaf of photocopies towards me. "Read them," he said angrily. "Do these laws appear to be Islamic?" The paper contained a long list of interpretations of the sayings of the Prophet, and a selection of sharia laws extracted from Islamic law books. Two of them caught my attention:

- The Head of an Islamic State cannot be punished under Islam's Hudood laws that govern acts of murder, rape, and thievery.
- If the husband's body is covered with pus and blood, and if the wife licks and drinks it, her obligations to her husband will still not be fulfilled.

"You can't be serious," I exclaimed. "Are these part of sharia law?" "Yes," replied Mahmud. "The Head of an Islamic State is protected from all criminal prosecution under Law #914 C in volume three of the Codified Islamic Law, while the quote about a wife's obligation to her husband comes from none other than Imam Ghazali's classic, *Ihya ulum al-din*. Can such an opinion about women be considered Islamic? Yet it is right there in black and white."

No analysis of the Islamist agenda in North America can be complete without a post-mortem of this attempt to impose sharia in Canada's most populous province, Ontario. The Islamists almost pulled it off. In the words of another anti-sharia Muslim activist at the 2003 strategy meeting, "The Islamists are banking on guilt-ridden bleeding-heart liberals and leftists, who can easily be fooled into believing that sharia law in Canada fits our multiculturalism policy. What the mullahs have not taken into account is the fact that in Canada, unlike Europe, the opposition to sharia will come from within the Muslim community."

Leading up to the campaign to introduce sharia, its proponents carefully concealed the fact that one of the men behind the move to bring sharia law to Canada was the late Syed Wasi Mazhar Nadvi, the former religious affairs minister in Pakistan. Nadvi, a member of the Jamaat-e-Islami Islamist group, had recently moved to Canada. He came with impeccable Islamist credentials. It was he who, under Islamist dictator General Zia-ul-Haq, had introduced sharia in Pakistan. His work in Pakistan to this day has convulsed the nation and has led to discrimination against religious minorities and women, resulting in the deaths of many on charges of apostasy.

Syed Nadvi was one of the key people who set up the *Darul qada*, the thirty-member, all-male "Muslim House of Judges" that was to implement sharia, if and when it was permitted by the Ontario government. Defending the introduction of sharia law in Canada, Nadvi wrote in an ultra-conservative Islamist magazine: "Muslims can only be permitted to resolve their personal conflicts and disputes according to God's laws and instructions [not laws created by parliamentarians]. In this connection, the Holy Quran is explicit where God says to Muslims, those of you (Muslims) who do not settle their affairs based on the laws revealed by Allah, they are the infidels, they are the cruel, and they are the *Fasik*."*

The public face of Ontario's pro-sharia forces was the retired barrister Mumtaz Ali, who had created the self-styled "Muslim Court of Arbitration" alongside his Islamic Institute of Civil Justice. Mumtaz Ali went a step further than Syed Nadvi in stating that Muslims who opposed the introduction of sharia or who refused to accept its legitimacy were apostates. In an interview published on his website, Syed Mumtaz Ali says: "As a consequence, on religious grounds, a Muslim who would choose to opt out at this stage, for reasons of convenience would be guilty of a far greater crime than a mere breach of contract—and this could be tantamount to blasphemy—apostasy."

The interview, first published in 1995, was widely distributed in 2003 during the heated and often angry debates on sharia that took place in Toronto. This was an alarming declaration, a warning that had serious consequences for Muslims opposed to sharia, because the traditional punishment for blasphemy—apostasy is death.

The objective of the likes of Syed Mumtaz Ali, Syed Wasi Nadvi and the wider Islamist network was twofold: first, they wanted an Islamist toehold in North America in order to establish an Islamist agenda for the Muslim community, with the patronage and blessing of various levels of government and all political parties. With Canada as a model of multiculturalism and pluralism, the Islamists would have forced this option on European countries such as Britain and the Scandinavian nations, where there is still a well-meaning naivety in dealing with Islamists (unlike among the German and French).

The second and more immediate goal was to keep an iron grip on the Muslim communities of North America, especially the large South Asian Muslim population that increasingly finds itself caught in an identity crisis in which its members distance themselves from their parents' Indo-Pakistani background and act as if they were of Arab ancestry. They make up one of the few Muslim groups who have been convinced that their own culture—Indian—is un-Islamic and therefore needs to be discarded.

The plan was that once the Islamic arbitration courts applying sharia law were established, the mullahs and imams would narrow the definition as to who could be considered a Muslim. Whereas Arab and Iranian Muslims, when excluded from this club, can always fall back on their ethnic and cultural customs, the South Asian Muslim gets trapped in the Islamists' clutches.

---

* *Fasik*: Can mean godless, sinful, licentious, fornicator, or adulterer.

Leading up to the decision by the Ontario government to ban the use of any religion-based legal system, the debate between opposing Muslim groups was vigorous. The liberal and secular Muslim Canadian Congress (MCC, which I helped found) led the charge against the proposal to introduce sharia in Canada, arguing that the proposed use of religious laws to settle family disputes had deeply divided the Muslim community and caused serious concern among women's groups, children's advocates, and supporters of the separation of religion and state. The MCC said:

> It [the proposal to introduce sharia] ghettoizes the Muslim community . . . into one second-class compartment in the determination of human and family law rights, which are of public importance and domain. This insidious and discriminatory ghettoization and marginalization, into "out of sight" only plays into: i) The hands of the extremist political and ideological agenda of a certain sector of Muslim-Canadian proponents of "Muslim Law" that is antithetical to the Canadian Constitution and values; and ii) Equally into the hands of the reactionary, intolerant and otherwise racist segments of Canadian non-Muslim society who want nothing better than to exclude Muslims from the mainstream; all of this, behind the dishonest guise of religious tolerance and accommodation.

Critics of the proposal to introduce sharia law in Canada urged the premier of Ontario, Dalton McGuinty, to reflect on the consequences of increasing the power of religious clerics, especially in view of events where religion has been used to inflict terror instead of building peace and harmony. The opposition to sharia was not to downplay the important role of religion in our lives, but to highlight the dangers of bringing religion into public policy, thus risking further divisiveness in our society which is already threatened with religious conflict.

The government appointed a former attorney general of Ontario, Marion Boyd, to study the issue and give recommendations. Boyd, who came to power with the left-wing New Democratic Party (NDP), shocked the country when she recommended in a report that "Muslim principles" be permitted in arbitration as a substitute for the Family Law Act. She carefully skirted around the word "sharia," trying to mellow its impact by using the questionable term "Muslim principles."

Boyd was not the only one from the left who supported the introduction of sharia in Canada. The ultra-left Trotskyites even advanced the idea that since Lenin had permitted the continuation of sharia courts in the Soviet

Union's Asian republics after the Bolshevik Revolution, support for the Islamists was in line with socialist principles.

The flamboyant and controversial left-wing British politician George Galloway joined the Islamist cause while visiting Canada. In a spirited support of sharia, he defended the rights of Muslims to be governed by their own laws. In a speech at the University of Toronto, he taunted the Ontario NDP leader Howard Hampton to rise up and defend the interests of Canadian Muslims and support the introduction of sharia in Canada. Hampton and his party had just come out in opposition to what they said would amount to the privatization of the judicial system. Galloway's endorsement of sharia was another reflection of the close working relationship between the ultra-left and the Islamists. Of course, neither Galloway nor Toronto's ultra-left would refer to Lenin's warnings about "the need to combat Pan-Islamism and similar trends," which, he wrote, strove "to combine the liberation movement against European and American imperialism with an attempt to strengthen the positions of the khans, landowners, mullahs, etc."

The Muslim Canadian Congress was quick to denounce the Boyd report, saying what Boyd was recommending under the cover of "Muslim principles" was, in fact, "sharia by stealth"—man-made laws that had been erroneously given divine authority and that cannot be debated or amended by any Canadian jurisdiction. Other Muslims voiced opposition to the introduction of sharia into the Canadian judicial system. Professor Omid Safi, the Iranian-American professor of Islamic studies at Colgate University in New York State, said: "The use of religious law as a substitute for laws created by Parliament, and the establishment of a multi-tier legal system—one for average Canadians and one for Muslim Canadians—is not only unjust, but also detrimental to the well-being of all Canadian citizens." Furthermore, progressive Muslims argued, introducing sharia into the judicial system will ghettoize the Muslim community, making their already difficult task of integrating into Canadian society even more onerous.

And from Europe, Professor Tariq Ramadan—who was then teaching at the University of Fribourg in Switzerland—told an Egyptian magazine there was no need for Canadian Muslims to set up their own sharia courts, because they were not necessary. He said demanding such courts "is another example of lack of creativity" among Muslims. Of course, Tariq Ramadan's statement could easily be read as tactical advice to Muslims, to bide their time and only make this demand for sharia when the soil was fertile for such ideas. His "lack of creativity" remark was another reason why so many people feel he still adheres to his family tradition of the Muslim Brotherhood, but employs very sophisticated tactics to make his politics palatable to secular audiences.

If Tariq Ramadan's critique of sharia was wrapped in double-talk, Nobel Peace Prize-winner Shirin Ebadi's position was an example of clarity. She took a firm stand against the introduction of Islamic tribunals in Canada, warning that they would open the door to potential human rights abuses.

While the supporters of sharia had the entire mosque establishment backing them, the opponents could reach the Muslim community only through the columns of the mainstream press, which allowed both sides to express their views. Not a single mosque in Canada permitted the Muslim opponents of sharia to make their case. In August 2005, I wrote in Kitchener-Waterloo's *The Record*: "I believe that mosques, churches, temples and synagogues have an important role to play in the community, but their role should be restricted to mediation and reconciliation, not interfering with the Canadian justice system and running a parallel private-sector judiciary with self-styled religious judges for hire."

In what was essentially an open letter to the premier of the province, I stressed the international implications of the outcome, and that McGuinty's decision would have a profound long-term impact on Canadian society as well as across the Muslim world, "where progressive and liberal men and women are fighting to keep sharia out of the political system." I wrote: "My position is not against religion. On the contrary, I stand for the constitutional guarantee of freedom of religion. However, freedom of religion does not mean that we dilute laws and strengthen the power of imams, rabbis and priests over their communities—especially the most vulnerable."

Professor Omid Safi, who at the time headed the Progressive Muslim Union of North America, wrote:

> We are alarmed at the prospect of repressive Muslim governments around the world pointing to Canada, and the implementation of sharia within Canada, as a justification for their oppressive legal systems. This is not a comment on Islamic jurisprudence as a whole, but rather on the repressive interpretations of sharia found in those countries. It is unrealistic to think that the ayatollahs of Iran or the proponents of Wahhabism in Saudi Arabia will not use this to promote the viability of their oppressive visions.

From France, the grand mufti, or Muslim legal expert, of Marseilles added his voice to those who were opposing the application of sharia laws in family matters. Mufti Soheib Bencheikh, who is also the highest official of religious law for Marseilles, told a Montreal conference that sharia was developed exclusively by men centuries ago and is subject to interpretation. He said these interpretations may not apply to contemporary Canadian society. "Is it possible to apply the sharia in societies that are governed by constitutions that stand for gender equality?" asked Mufti Bencheikh. "It's illogical to apply today the precepts conceived [in tribal, patriarchal societies] to safeguard the interests of yesterday."

Taj Hashmi, then a professor at Vancouver's Simon Fraser University, wrote an article for the online magazine *MuslimWakeUp.Com* that bore the headline "Sharia Is Neither Islamic, Nor Canadian." Hashmi suggested that the Islamists and their left-wing supporters were relying on the naivety of the ordinary Canadian. He wrote:

> To the uninformed, Marion Boyd sounds quite "reasonable" in the way she has argued her case. In her view the "Muslim principles" should be considered an acceptable method of religious arbitration as long as they do not violate Canadian law. . . . Surprisingly, she tells us: "We're being very clear, this is not Sharia law." What is even more surprising is that Syed Mumtaz Ali, the main advocate of Sharia arbitrations in Ontario, is "delighted" with the Boyd Report, given that many of the 46 recommendations of the Report came from him. Ali glorifies the proposed Board as "a model for the world to see how Sharia law can be used in a Western society." The ambivalence in Boyd's and Ali's statements on the true colour of the Report smacks of duplicity. It seems, Boyd is playing a hide and seek game with us, trying to introduce Sharia with a different name.

Hashmi, who now teaches at Honolulu's East-West University, warned that "Canada's adopting of Sharia law may legitimize the excesses of sharia committed elsewhere in the Muslim World."

Female legislators in Ontario from all parties stood against the Islamist proposal. The Quebec National Assembly, thanks to an initiative by Muslim MNA Fatima Houda-Pepin, voted unanimously to reject the introduction of sharia law in Quebec and requested the Ontario government to follow suit. This added to the general outrage among Canadians, who were shocked to find out that Islamists were slipping in their agenda through the back door. Separately, but significantly, women's groups led by the Canadian Council of Muslim Women (CCMW) and their president Alia Hogben carried out an effective and impressive lobbying effort to stop the Islamists in their tracks. The effort by the CCMW and their work with Ontario's female MPPs tipped the scale.

Lined up against the Muslim opponents of sharia were powerful Muslim organizations and virtually the entire mosque establishment of the country. The Canadian Islamic Congress and the US-based Council for American-Islamic Relations (CAIR) were joined by two more US-based Islamic organizations—the Islamic Society of North America (ISNA) and the Islamic Circle of North America (ICNA). These campaigned vigorously, suggesting that denying sharia in Canada would amount to discrimination against Muslims.

The Islamists who demanded to implement sharia in the Ontario Family Law Court system even received the blessings of *The Globe and Mail*, as well as a senior editor at *The Toronto Star*. In his twice-weekly column, Haroon Siddiqui of the *Star* mocked Muslim opponents of the law, describing one of them, a Quebec Muslim legislator, Fatima Houda-Pepin, as "not a practising Muslim" and suggesting she was "reviled" by many Muslims. This was not the first time he had defended sharia. In January 2001, during the infamous case of the Nigerian teenager who was sentenced by a Nigerian sharia court to one hundred lashes, he trivialized the outcry against the punishment. Defending sharia as a "good law," Siddiqui wrote, "The sharia, however, is popular. It has restored order to a corrupt, lawless society."

The president of the Canadian Islamic Congress was quoted in *The Toronto Star* as saying Muslims who opposed sharia were "non-religious Muslims who had no right to tell religious people what to do," in essence asking 99 percent of the Canadian population to stay out of the debate while their country's legal system was being tampered with. The rationale that laws applying to orthodox Islamists should only be debated by them was contrary to the aspirations of the country's 750,000 Muslims.

On September 11, 2005, Premier McGuinty announced that his government had rejected the proposal by former attorney general Marion Boyd to introduce sharia law in Ontario. After a year of debate, when the Ontario government outlawed all religious courts and effectively put an end to the attempt to introduce sharia in Canada, Islamist groups responded by staging a series of protests, for which they enlisted groups with links to the Egyptian Muslim Brotherhood, Pakistan's radical pro-Taliban Jamaat-e-Islami, and the ruling Iranian ayatollahs.

At a news conference, supporters of sharia threatened to mount a constitutional challenge to force the government to reverse the decision; they raised the spectre of discrimination and hinted that the outlawing of sharia courts was an act of racism. At the head table sat representatives of the Muslim Association of Canada (MAC). This was a significant development as MAC makes no attempt to hide its links to the banned and secretive

Muslim Brotherhood organization. Its website says: "MAC adopts and strives to implement Islam . . . as understood in its contemporary context by the late Imam, Hassan Albanna, the founder of the Muslim Brotherhood." The Muslim Association of Canada subscribes to the philosophy of the Muslim Brotherhood, which aims to restore Islamic laws and values in the face of growing Western influence.

Although the Muslim Brotherhood has influenced a generation of violent, radical groups, MAC spokesman Yaser Haddara told the news conference, without blinking an eye, that the group's core values are consistent with Canadian values. MAC states on its website that "we do have a firm belief that our philosophy and vision are superior to others and we strive to ensure that they are actualized." How MAC will "actualize" the Muslim Brotherhood "philosophy" in Canada is not elaborated.

At the same news conference, ISNA spokesperson Kathy Bullock conceded that she did not agree with Canadian laws that treat men and women as equals. She told the reporters: "The main understanding of women's equality in the West is the liberal feminist version, which is that if men and women are not treated equally and in an identical manner then women are being oppressed . . . There are other understandings of what women's equality means, and one that is best expressed from the Quranic point of view is that women are different but equal."

Citing an example of the "different but equal" application of gender equality, Bullock said that although sons inherit more than daughters under sharia, men are also supposed to "maintain" women, so the imbalance is justifiable. According to its website, ISNA wants to build an "Islamic way of life" in North America and is guided by "correct faith and correct understanding and practice of sharia" and advocates "Islamic solutions to societal problems" and to effecting "righteous change in North America."

The defeat suffered by Islamist groups at the hands of the secular MCC, the CCMW, and the International No-Sharia campaign (headed by Iranian exile Homa Arjoumand), has continued to rile the mosque establishment in Canada. The Islamists have made a concerted effort to repackage themselves and appear mainstream and palatable to the political establishment. Flush with funds and possessing unchallenged access to the pulpit, many imams have taken advantage of the inherent decency as well as naivety of Canadian society to pursue their goals. They demonize any Muslim who dares challenge their authority. The Islamist attempt to hoodwink the mainstream establishment, combined with the unfortunate need of politicians to dip into the "ethnic vote bank," has ensured that radicalism and calls for segregation from Western society continue unabated across the Western world.

In 2007, another group of Islamists, this time in Britain, started a campaign to introduce sharia. The sharia package in Britain was marketed as being helpful in reducing the high level of crime within Muslim youth. The fact that the British government would even consider such a Trojan horse speaks volumes about its naivety and lack of understanding of the objectives of the world Islamist movement.

Syed Aziz Pasha, secretary-general of the Union of Muslim Organisations of the United Kingdom and Ireland, in demanding the introduction of sharia law in Britain, told the British press: "If you give us religious rights we will be in a better position to convince young people that they are being treated equally along with other citizens." He had just met with Britain's deputy prime minister John Prescott, along with ninety so-called Muslim leaders, and was responding to the discovery of a terror threat by British Muslims who wanted to blow up planes over the Atlantic. Sharia as a panacea to counter Islamist-inspired terrorism? It was a mind-boggling suggestion.

Responding to the demand for sharia as an instrument to counter Islamic extremism among British Muslim youth, Shahid Malik, who currently sits as Britain's first-ever Muslim cabinet minister in Prime Minister Gordon Brown's government, and who was then a Labour MP, told reporters: "If you want sharia law, you should go and live in Saudi Arabia."

British Islamists were outraged. Lord Nazir Ahmed, a Muslim member of the House of Lords who has close links with Canadian Islamists, was quick to attack Shahid Malik, accusing him of doing the work of the racist British National Party (BNP). Malik had first come to prominence when he was beaten by police as he tried to stop a racial flare-up between BNP thugs and Muslim youth. He responded to Ahmed's allegation by asking him not to play with the truth. He wrote: "When Lord Ahmed, the Muslim Labour peer, heard my comments—I said essentially that if Muslims wanted sharia they should go and live somewhere where they have it—he accused me of doing the BNP's work. He is entitled to his opinion. However, a little honesty, like mine, in this whole debate might just restore trust in politicians and ease the population's anxieties."

While Islamists in Canada were defeated in their attempt to introduce sharia, they are still in the country and will use every possible opportunity to revive the issue. The reason is that even the victims of sharia law have been brainwashed into believing that their suffering is a stepping stone towards pleasing God.

The author Hasan Mahmud describes this phenomenon as something akin to the Stockholm Syndrome, in which the hostage starts to admire the captors.

WHAT IS SHARIA?

Despite the claim of Islamists that sharia is the universally accepted law of Islam, the word is controversial and, as the debate in Canada demonstrated, its opponents are mostly Muslims. Islam is essentially a religion based on the Quran—the revelations received by Prophet Muhammad from Allah through the agency of the Angel Gabriel. The word "sharia" appears in the Quran only three times: once as a noun in chapter 45, and twice as a verb in chapters 5 and 48. The term sharia means "way" or "path to the water source," and in Islamic religious vocabulary it stands for the body of Islamic law.

Sharia is the legal framework within which the most private aspects of life are regulated for those living in a Muslim society. These laws are often in conflict with the laws of the country. Medieval in nature and its origin, sharia tries to deal with all aspects of modern day-to-day life, including politics, economics, banking, business law, contract law, family, sexuality, hygiene, and social issues. However, most of these laws are the work of ordinary mortals and have never been debated in any parliament, nor would they ever be put to such scrutiny. Legal scholar L. Ali Khan writes that there is "a muddled assumption that scholarly interpretations are as sacred and beyond revision as are the Quran and the Sunnah." He continues: "The Quran and the Sunnah constitute the immutable Basic Code, which should be kept separate from ever-evolving interpretive law (*fiqh*). This analytical separation between the Basic Code and *fiqh* is necessary to dissipate confusion around the term sharia."

In actuality, sharia is derived from at least ten sources. They are:

The Quran	Local Customs
Sunna, or the Prophet's examples	Independent opinion
Consensus	Public interest
Reasoning	Equity consensus
Old laws of culture and scriptures	Presumption of continuity

Except for the Quran, sources of sharia are human. How then can sharia—an overwhelming percentage of which is man-made—be called Allah's Law and imposed on Muslims? Added to this is the fact that many celebrated Muslim scholars never agreed to the use of Quranic verses to frame historic sharia laws. They showed alternate meanings and interpretations of those verses. Examples are polygamy, wife-beating, men's right to have concubines, and slavery. Even a cursory study of the development of sharia from medieval times would demonstrate that far from being Quranic, these laws were man-made, at times backdated, with the objective to Islamicize harsh tribal and misogynist laws and to keep the masses from questioning the rule of the monarchs.

A better understanding of sharia is possible if we look at a timeline:

I. 610–32: The Quran, God's revelations to Muhammad, is completed. God says in the final verse: "Today I have completed your religion for you."

II. 700–850: Sharia, the codified laws, are formulated by the five imams:

Imam Abu Hanifa (699–767)

Imam Jaffer Sadiq (702–65)

Imam Shafi'i (767–820)

Imam Malik (712–95)

Imam Hanbal (778–855).

III. 800–900: Compilations of the sayings of Prophet Muhammad are recorded, more than two hundred years after the death of the Apostle. They include:

Sahih Bukhari, compiled by Imam Bukhari (d. 870)

Sahih Muslim, compiled by Imam Muslim (d. 874)

Sahih Tarmidhi, compiled by Imam Tarmidhi (d. 870)

Sahih Abu Dawood, compiled by Imam Abu Dawood (d. 888)

Sahih Malik Muatta, compiled by Imam Malik (d. 795)

Sahih Ibn Majah, compiled by Imam ibn Majah (d. 886).

Considering the fact that Islam does not permit the dynastic rule of kings, the above timeline clearly indicates that the Muslim kings (caliphs) first created sharia laws (700–850) to give Islamic legitimacy to their un-Islamic rule. Then, for the next hundred years, from 800 to 900, the books on the hadith, the Prophet's examples, were written to legitimize sharia as Islamic law. It almost seems the entire exercise is rife with backdated, re-written minutes of meetings that were part of a massive cover-up to hide the fact that Muhammad's religion of Islam had been taken over by those monarchs.

The Holy Quran lays down fundamental laws, and the working details are left out to be determined by the people according to their specific circumstances. Staying within the framework of these fundamental laws, these details could be changed if circumstances so warranted. If these details are called sharia, then the fundamentals would remain unchangeable whereas the sharia would continue changing, like the flowing fresh water coming from a spring. If this water were to become static, resulting in stagnation, it would, instead of giving nourishment to life, become harmful. Islamic law as represented by modern-day sharia has been stagnant for centuries. No wonder, wherever it is applied, sharia triggers "convulsions" and has proven to be extremely harmful to the human spirit. What is being touted as sharia should be known as *kara'un*—the word for stagnant rainwater.

Hashim Kamali, one of the world's leading Islamic jurists, suggests the application of sharia is affected by the arbitrary nature of Muslim rulers of the time. He writes: "A Quranic injunction may simultaneously possess a definitive and a speculative meaning . . . At times seven or eight different juristic conclusions have been arrived at, on one and the same issue . . . When the ruler authorizes a particular interpretation of the Quran and enacts it into law, it becomes obligatory for everyone to follow only the authorized version."

Disciples of four Islamic jurists codified the Islamic dictums in the names of their four respective masters: imams Abu Hanifa, Shafi'i, Malik, and Hanbal. The four versions are strikingly similar in major laws. Even today Sunni Muslims consider themselves followers of one or other of these four imams. The Shia version was developed much later. It is significant that these four jurists kept their distance from the power centre, despite repeated invitations from the caliphs. For defying political authority, they were severely dealt with: Imam Abu Hanifa was imprisoned and poisoned, Imam Malik's hands were publicly torn apart, Imam Shafi'i was imprisoned, and Imam Hanbal was killed. The laws we are told were written by these four imams were, in fact, written by their disciples who codified the sharia in the name of their masters. We have no way to determine exactly which laws were defined by the imams and which were inserted by their disciples.

The very existence of not one but five shariahs, with contradictions and variations among them, prove that these are not God's law but human endeavours. In addition, sharia laws include the seven *hudood** laws, such as stoning to death and cutting off a thief's hands. Islamists have declared that these laws are beyond human capacity for any change, amendment, updating, addition, or subtraction.

As Abul Ala Maudoodi, the father of modern Political Islam, says: "Where an explicit command of God or His Prophet already exists, no Muslim leader or legislature, or any religious scholar can form an independent judgement, not even all the Muslims of the world put together have any right to make least alteration to it."

Such absolute declarations allow sharia to become a very effective political tool against which few Muslims can argue without fearing for their lives. Sharia has become the governing tool of Political Islam. Its followers believe that God's divine command is to establish a global Islamic State to apply sharia. In that sense, sharia is the informal constitution of the institution of Political Islam, which is defined by its founding father Abul Ala Maudoodi in these frank words: "Islam wishes to destroy all States and Governments anywhere in the face of the earth which are opposed to the ideology and program of Islam. . . . If the Muslim Party commands adequate resources, it will eliminate un-Islamic governments and establish the power of Islamic governments in their stead."

This is the type of arrogant and supremacist ideology that today encourages Muslim youth towards violence and terrorism as a path towards the creation of an Islamic State.[†]

Some of the sharia laws are not only an embarrassment to Islam, but also a serious liability on Muslims. Calls to annul them or reject them outright have been met with fatwas of apostasy. Yet the outrageous nature of these laws makes it incumbent upon Muslims to stand up and say, "Not in our name."

Hashim Kamali says in his *Principles of Islamic Jurisprudence*: "I have consequently commented on the nature of the challenge that Muslim scholars and jurists must take up if the methodology of *Usul-al-Fiqh*[‡] and *Ijtehad* are to be revitalized and integrated into the process of law and government in modern times."

---

* *Hudood* laws in Islam: Considered immutable and cover criminal and family laws.

† It is worth noting that not a single woman has authored any of the sharia laws, yet Islamist women are today its most vigorous promoters.

‡ *Usul-al-fiqh*: Literally, "roots of the law"; refers to the study of the origins, sources, and practice of Islamic jurisprudence.

It is not surprising that adherents to Political Islam have not taken up the task of revising these archaic and medieval texts. The reason seems threefold:

- Sharia is simply irreparable. Its methodology disregards the contextual and normative aspects of the Quran. Kamali rightly says: "Owing to a variety of factors, *Usul-al-Fiqh* is no longer capable of serving the goals for which it was originally designed and developed. *Usul-al-Fiqh* has often been described as a theoretical discipline that has lost touch with the realities of social change."
- The sort of intellect, intelligence, knowledge, wisdom, and poetic faculty—including a sense of humour—that is required to reform a society is conspicuously absent from the traditional conservative leadership of the Islamists. When the clergy get insulted by even the most innocuous observations, they show their insecurity. They are the least likely of all people to bring about a renaissance among their congregations or within religion.
- Current international law opens another challenge to sharia: the concept of universal human rights. Abdullahi an-Na'im, a Sudanese-American professor of law at Emory University, in his book *Toward an Islamic Reformation*, writes: "Current international law, including the human rights standards established thereunder, cannot co-exist with corresponding principles of sharia."

Hashim Kamali says the tool of creating sharia did not differentiate between contextual and normative aspects of Islam. This created a fatal vacuum in sharia's elemental structure. He says: "The legal theory of *Usul* falls short of integrating the time-space factor into the fabric of its methodology." Another formidable Islamic scholar, Abdul-Aziz Sachedina, writes in his book *Islamic Roots of Democratic Pluralism*, "The problem arises when these historical necessities are used to justify contemporary political policies."

Article 1 of the United Nations Universal Declaration of Human Rights states: "All human beings are born free and equal in dignity and rights." Article 2 continues: "Everyone is entitled to all the rights and freedoms set forth in this Declaration, without distinction of any kind, such as race, colour, sex, language, religion, political or other opinion, national or social origin, property, birth or other status." Article 7 adds: "All are equal before the law and are entitled without any discrimination to equal protection of the law. All are entitled to equal protection against any discrimination in violation of this Declaration and against any incitement to such discrimination." And Article 16.1 states: "Men and women of full age, without any limitation due to race, nationality or religion, have the right to marry and to found a family. They are entitled to equal rights as to marriage, during marriage and at its dissolution." Article 18 goes so far as to state: "Everyone has the right to freedom of thought, conscience and religion; this right includes freedom to change his religion or belief, and freedom, either alone or in community with others and in public or private, to manifest his religion or belief in teaching, practice, worship and observance."

Sharia law contravenes all of these articles. When sharia supporters say, for example, that sharia respects women's rights, they don't mean that women are given the same rights as men. They mean that sharia respects the rights that sharia gives to women. Sharia also prescribes penalties against those who deviate or depart from the "true faith." Sharia therefore violates Articles 1, 2, 7, 16, and 18 of the UN declaration. No wonder so many human rights advocates around the world have been fighting against sharia. Women's groups in particular have led the fight to remove sharia from the world's legal systems.

The authoritarian and autocratic nature of sharia violates the Quran, which clearly declares that the responsibility of prophets was not to govern, but only to deliver God's message. In the Quran, God reminds Muhammad and the Muslims many times: "We have not sent thee to be their keeper"; "Say: I am not placed in charge of you"; "We have not appointed you a keeper over them, and you are not placed in charge of them"; "I am not a custodian over you"; "We have not sent thee [O Muhammad] as a warden over them"; "whoever errs, he errs only to its detriment; and you are not a custodian over them"; "Thy duty is but to convey [the Message]"; "Therefore do remind, for you are only a reminder. You are not a watcher over them."

Islam's five pillars—the declaration of faith in the oneness of God; prayers; fasting; paying the charitable tax of zakat; and the hajj pilgrimage— are non-political. Had the governing of people by sharia-based laws in an Islamic State been so important to God and the Prophet, we would have expected Muhammad to have said so, at least once in his lifetime. He did not. Nowhere among the forty thousand reported hadith—the Prophet's examples—does Muhammad suggest the structure for an Islamic State or the rules of governance and succession. Even in his last sermon, Muhammad gave no instructions about governance and sharia.

Despite evidence that aspects of sharia violate the Quran, sharia is still treated by many as "Allah's Law." There is little doubt that 1,400 years ago, Islam initiated some revolutionary steps in terms of women's rights. The question is, why did the Quran not finalize the process of establishing full human rights? Why didn't it explicitly abolish slavery? Is it possible that God did not feel it was the right time to correct the inhumanity of human beings? Perhaps Allah in his wisdom knows that socio-cultural progress is better achieved by evolution than by revolution. If the society is not ready, forced implementation of any system, however good it is, is bound to throw people into utter confusion, leading to chaos and devastation. Perhaps we have to keep in mind the psyche of a desert society of the distant past.

A thorough study of Islam and Muslims shows that in spite of many initial conflicts, Islam's Prophet slowly and steadily prepared his followers for equity and equality by taking tiny but significant steps a few at a time. After his death, instead of continuing his journey towards complete equity between race and gender, Muslims fell back on the familiar turf of their pagan forefathers. Today, by invoking hadith, Islamists present the beginning of the journey as its natural end. The saying that power corrupts and absolute power corrupts absolutely applies very well to Muslims. Once a system falls into the trap of power politics it is difficult to maintain ethics. Political kings ruled Muslims in the name of Islam and Islamic law for 1,300 years, quite long enough to ingrain anything they wanted as part of Islam.

The word "sharia" first appeared in the Quran, so it is perhaps worthwhile to try to understand the history of this book, which changed the course of human history. The 6,326 Quranic verses were revealed to Muhammad over a period of twenty-three years. These verses were never compiled in any order during his lifetime. Ideally they should have been compiled sequentially as they were revealed, but they were not. The first known compilations took place under Caliph Uthman, who, instead of compiling the revelations according to a chronological order, sorted them by the size of the verses. However, there is at least one record of another compilation of the same Quran. *Hadis al Kafi,* the major Shia collection of the sayings of the Prophet, records:

There is no dispute between scholars, whether they be Sunni or Shia, concerning the fact that the *Amirul Mumeneen* [Ali ibn Abu Talib, the Prophet's cousin and son-in-law] possessed a special transcript of the text of Quran, which he had collected himself. This transcription had the following particularities and special points. It was collected together according to the order in which the revelations had been sent down.* This copy of the Quran contained commentary and hermeneutic interpretation from the Holy Prophet, some of which had been sent down as revelation but not as part of the text. This transcript also contained references to the persons, places etc., about which the verses were revealed. After he had collected this transcript together, *Amirul Mumeneen* [Ali ibn Abu Talib] took it and presented it to the rulers† who followed the Holy Prophet, but they did not accept it. Thereupon *Amirul Mumeneen* took the transcript and concealed it, and after him it passed to the [Shia] Imams who also kept it concealed. It remains concealed with the Imams to this day.

Notwithstanding the claim by the Shia theologians that Ali possessed a different compilation of the Quran, the difference between the two versions was only the order of the verses and the accompanying commentary. However, the fact remains that many sharia laws were at variance with the Quran. Hasan Mahmud's book *Islam and Sharia* has a detailed list of sharia laws that violate corresponding Quranic verses, as well as the mechanism employed in such violation. Here are a few of the sharia laws he lists:

- The sharia law of stoning to death of adulterers violates chapter 24, verses 2 and 3; chapter 4, verses 15, 16, and 25. The Quran does not prescribe death sentence for adulterers, but accepts repentance for such an act.
- The sharia law requiring a raped woman to produce four adult male Muslim eyewitnesses to prove her case makes a mockery of the Quranic injunction that requires the state to produce four eyewitnesses to prove adultery: an almost impossibility. There are seldom four witnesses to a rape. Proof of rape under sharia is almost impossible.
- The sharia law rejecting women's eyewitness in *hudood* or criminal cases violates chapter 24, verses 4 and 11–20. The verses require not the accused (as stipulated by sharia), but the accuser to produce

---

* In other words, Ali had compiled a copy of the Quran arranged in the chronological order of the revelations received by Muhammad.
† The ruler mentioned in this Shia hadith is the third caliph, Uthman.

four adult male eyewitnesses to prove adultery or fornication. The verses were revealed to stop men from unjustly accusing women of adultery.

- The sharia law permitting unrestricted polygamy violates chapter 4, verses 3, 4, and 127. Polygamy is admissible only in case of vulnerable orphans in specific circumstances and restricted by behaviour codes.
- The sharia law permitting the killing of apostates violates chapter 4, verse 94; chapter 2, verse 256; chapter 3, verse 88–89; chapter 16, verse 106. During the life of the Prophet, three persons are recorded as having left Islam. Not one of them faced the death penalty.
- The sharia law allowing a Muslim husband to issue an "instant" divorce to his wife violates chapter 2, verses 228 and 229, and chapter 65, verses 1 and 2.
- If a divorced Muslim woman wishes to re-marry her former husband, a sharia law makes it mandatory on her part to first marry a complete stranger, have sexual intercourse with him, and then obtain a voluntary divorce from this stranger. Only after she obtains this divorce is she permitted to remarry her former husband.

SHARIA BANKING

Family law is not the only place where the introduction of sharia law is being sought in Canada. While Islamists may have suffered a setback in their attempt to introduce sharia law in this country, they have not accepted defeat. In fact, their plan is to introduce "sharia" in any form, wherever it would gain acceptance as a legitimate part of the Western lexicon. The recent attempt to obtain government validation and funding of sharia-based private Islamic schools in the province of Ontario almost sneaked in, but for a public outcry. Sharia-compliant music, sharia-sanctioned soccer, sharia-based health practice (in which physicians refuse to treat patients of the opposite gender)—you name it and the Islamists are trying to push some aspect of sharia into our lives. However, the one area where their efforts are making the most ground is in sharia banking, where they have the help of some extremely powerful allies.

On one hand Islamists have made common cause with such figures of the left as London Mayor Ken Livingstone and maverick British MP George Galloway, denouncing capitalism as the source of all ill. However, a closer examination suggests Islamists are also lining up with such icons of global capitalism as Citibank NA, HSBC Holdings PLC, and Barclays PLC, which have all endorsed sharia banking and started offering Islamic financing products to a vulnerable Muslim population.

While sharia-style family law was essentially promoted by imams and the mosque establishment, sharia-based banking is being promoted by well-heeled Muslim bankers and investment lawyers, who are driven not by teachings of the Prophet but the lure of profits.

The Globe and Mail reported in May 2007: "Several Canadian financial institutions are preparing sharia-compliant mortgages, insurance, taxi licensing and investment funds to help serve the country's fastest-growing part of the population." Promoting it of course is a prominent Muslim corporate lawyer with close ties to Canada's Conservative Party, Walied Soliman. A lawyer at Ogilvy Renault LLP, Soliman told *The Globe*, "I expect it [sharia banking] to grow exponentially in Canada in the next couple of years." He confessed that the promotion of sharia banking has become a priority practice area for his firm.

This push from Muslim banking executives working inside the corporate world has had some success. Most big Canadian institutions are treading carefully, and not all are jumping on board. *The Globe* reported that while the Royal Bank of Canada quietly tested a sharia finance product a few years ago and didn't find enough market interest, other Canadian banks, smelling easy pickings, are lining up to wear the Islamic mantle. Scotiabank and Toronto-Dominion Bank have been quietly considering whether to start offering sharia-compliant products as part of the big banks' strategy to reach out to a growing "immigrant population." I doubt very much if Hindu, Sikh, and Chinese "immigrant" Canadians are excited at the prospect of halal banks.

The promoters of sharia banking are Islamists, and their target is to control the Muslim population and segregate them from the rest of the world, one bank account at a time. With every mortgage signed, the family has to take ownership of sharia and disown the rest of society as the impure moneylenders.

While Scotiabank and TD officials were rubbing shoulders with two hundred delegates at a Toronto Islamic Finance World conference in Toronto in summer 2007, Canada's Office of the Superintendent of Financial Institutions (OSFI), which regulates financial institutions, said their staff was being pushed to brush up on the fine points of sharia law to cope with the anticipated expansion of Islamic financial services in Canada. Normand Bergevin, managing director at OSFI's approvals and precedents division, told *The Globe* that several people on his staff were learning about business plans, legal structures, accounting methods, types of governance and other issues related to Islamic finance. He told the newspaper: "It's fairly new to us. There's not a whole lot of experience here in terms of supervising or even understanding the different types of products. They all have little twists on them that make them very unlike anything we've ever seen before."

Guess who is going to fill the knowledge gap and find jobs in high places of Canada's financial watchdog?

While Canada's banks salivate at this supposed untapped niche market, one Muslim-owned financial institution with strong marketing and social links to most Islamist events in Canada has been doing a brisk business. Omar Kalair, the chief executive officer of UM Financial, has said demand for his group's sharia-compliant products has been so great that UM has stopped all marketing and has a five-thousand-person waiting list of people who want to switch over from conventional mortgages to ones that are sharia-compliant. Kalair however admitted that from among the 200,000 Muslim households in Canada, his target is the capture of 2.5 percent of this market, and that too with the help of one of the big five banks.

ORIGINS OF ISLAMIC BANKING

Islamic banking traces its roots to the 1920s, but did not start until the late 1970s, and owes much of its foundation to the Islamist doctrine of two people: Abul Ala Maudoodi of the Jamaat-e-Islami in Pakistan and Hassan al-Banna of the Muslim Brotherhood in Egypt. While these two pillars of the Pan-Islamist movement propagated jihad and war against the West, they also recognized the role international financial institutions could play in carrying out their political objectives. Since 1928, when it was created, the Muslim Brotherhood has placed a high emphasis on the creation of a so-called Islamic economic system. Banna and his successor Syed Qutb even laid down principles of Islamic finance. Millard Burr and Robert Collins in their book *Alms for Jihad* claim that the Muslim Brotherhood watched, waited, and learned the management of money that was essential to finance a worldwide organization devoted to spreading their Islamist ideology. But the theory was only put into practice once the US-backed Pakistani military dictator General Zia-ul-Haq overthrew the government of Z.A. Bhutto and established sharia law in Pakistan, forcing the country's public-sector banks to run their operations based on Islamic principles and without the role of interest.

The proponents of Sharia banking rest their case on many verses of the Holy Quran, which in their interpretation outlaw any business or personal financial transaction involving interest. There is no unanimity among the Muslims who, in voting with their feet and chequebooks, have overwhelmingly rejected banks that operate in a supposedly interest-free environment. Most Muslims can see through the fog of deception, but we are a billion strong worldwide, and even if a small minority falls prey to the Islamist propaganda, there is lots of money to be made.

Quranic verses that address the question of the role and the question of loans and debts include:

- Al Baqarah (2:275): "God hath permitted trade and forbidden usury. Those who after receiving direction from their Lord, desist, shall be pardoned for the past; their case is for God [to judge]; but those who repeat [the offence] are companions of the Fire: They will abide therein [forever]."
- Al Baqarah (2:276): "Allah does not bless usury, and He causes charitable deeds to prosper, and Allah does not love any ungrateful sinner."
- Al Baqarah (2:278): "O you who believe! Be careful of (your duty to) Allah and relinquish what remains [due] from usury, if you are believers."
- Al Baqarah (2:280): "If the debtor is in a difficulty, grant him time Till it is easy for him to repay. But if ye remit it by way of charity, that is best for you if ye only knew."
- Al Nisa (4:161): "And their taking usury though indeed they were forbidden it and their devouring the property of people falsely, and We have prepared for the unbelievers from among them a painful chastisement."
- Ar Rum (30–39): "And whatever you lay out as usury, so that it may increase in the property of men, it shall not increase with Allah; and whatever you give in charity, desiring Allah's pleasure—it is these [persons] that shall get manifold."

From these Quranic verses it is abundantly clear that the Quran is addressing the rich money lenders to show compassion towards the borrower and give him or her more time to pay back the loan. In fact the Quran suggests to the lender that it would be far better if the money lender forgave the loan altogether. To suggest that the onus of complying with sharia rests on the weaker borrower is obscene and against the spirit of equity in Islam. I say this because what the imams and self-styled scholars of sharia banking are proposing makes it easy for the wealthy to be pious simply by not having to do anything, while the poor who need to borrow are told to stay away from banks that lend.

Once more we see an example of Islam attempting to bring justice to the poor while Islamists make it difficult for the poor to access funds they don't have. Today, owners of Islamic banks are billionaires—the practitioners of sharia banking are among the richest men in the world,* while the vast majority of Muslims still struggle to eke out a living beyond one dollar a day. Sharia banking fattens the bottom lines of the imams, the bank owners, and the lawyers who pull out their best to Islamicize anything that sustains their handsome hourly rate.

Every translation of the Quran into the English language has rendered the Arabic word *riba* as "usury," not "interest," yet Islamists have deliberately portrayed bank interest, the cost of borrowing money, as usury. For Islamists, there should be a cost to renting a car and renting a DVD, but when renting money for a period of time, there should be no cost of this capital. Instead, Islamists have created exotic products with names that are foreign to much of the world's Muslim population This is where interest can be masked under the *niqaab* of *Mudraba, Musharaka, Murabaha,* and *Ijara.*†

Whereas interest is the charge for the privilege of borrowing money, typically expressed as an annual percentage rate, usury is the practice of lending money and charging the borrower interest, especially at an exorbitant or illegally high rate.

Two senior Muslim banking experts-turned-authors have written scathing critiques of sharia banking: Muhammad Saleem has labelled the practice as nothing more than deception, while Timur Kuran has suggested that the entire exercise was "a convenient pretext for advancing broad Islamic objectives and for lining the pockets of religious officials." Why Canadian banks would contribute to this masquerade is a question for ordinary Canadians to ask.

Muhammad Saleem is former president and CEO of Park Avenue Bank in New York. Before that he was a senior banker with Bankers Trust, where among other responsibilities he headed the Middle East division and served as adviser to a prominent Islamic bank based in Bahrain. In his book *Islamic Banking: A $300 Billion Deception,* Saleem not only dismisses the founding premise of Sharia and Islamic Banking, but says: "Islamic banks do not practise what they preach: they all charge interest, but disguised in Islamic garb. Thus they engage in deceptive and dishonest banking practices." He writes: "Proponents of Islamic banking say that Islam bans all interest. But an understanding of pre-Islamic and Islamic history and keeping in mind the context would lead one to conclude that what the Quran bans is usury,

---

* "The reason [why they are so wealthy] was a two-page report on the wealth of 15 ruling dynasties, seven of which are Arab," Refaat Jaafar, managing editor of Dubai-based *Forbes Arabia,* told Reuters. In October 2007, *Forbes Magazine* reported on the wealth of 15 ruling dynasties, seven of which are Muslim. Saudi Arabia banned the issue after it ranked Saudi King Abdullah third, behind the rulers of Brunei and the United Arab Emirates.
† Arabic names given to various banking products.

not interest. Usury can be defined as interest above the legal or socially acceptable rate. Phrased differently, usury is the exploitative, exorbitant interest rate."

While Saleem goes to great lengths in exposing the intellectual dishonesty surrounding the marketing of sharia-compliant banking, Professor Timur Kuran, who taught Islamic Thought at the University of Southern California, mocks the very idea. In his brilliant book *Islam and Mammon: The Economic Predicaments of Islamism,* Kuran writes: "There is no distinctly Islamic way to build a ship, or defend a territory, or cure an epidemic, or forecast the weather." He says the effort to introduce sharia banking "has promoted the spread of anti-modern currents of thought all across the Islamic world. It has also fostered an environment conducive to Islamist militancy."

Islam's essence is its quest for equality and social justice. Muhammad Saleem says that any banking or economic system that purports to be "Islamic"—including the current crop of Islamic banks—should answer two questions: By supposedly staying away from interest and sharing risks with their clients, were they able to help make the economic system more just, fair and equitable, and honest? Secondly, were these banks able to promote economic development in the Muslim world? In the words of Saleem: "Sadly, the answer is a resounding no. There is absolutely no evidence that the Islamic banks have made any contribution in either of these two areas."

The fact is that China and India, two countries that have had some measure of success in alleviating poverty and enhancing development, have outpaced all the Muslim countries put together despite their enormous natural resources and strategic locations. Sharia banking may not have alleviated poverty or generated economic development, but it has been a boon to the mullah class on one hand and, on the other, to the yuppie Muslim bankers and investment lawyers who have created a niche for themselves at the expense of the larger Muslim masses.

Saleem, who saw the functioning of Islamic banking from the inside, writes: "In promoting the establishment of Islamic banking, the Sharia scholars have played a critical role. Lacking any knowledge of banking, economics and for many even Islamic history, in interpreting *riba*, they have confused interest with usury.... Secondly, as Sharia advisers to Islamic banks, they have blessed many transactions as Islamic—meaning non-interest bearing—when in fact they are clearly charging interest, but interest payments are masked."

Dozens of Islamic scholars and imams now serve on sharia boards of the banking industry. If Canada's TD Bank, BMO, and RBC join the league, it will be interesting to see how the ultra-left Trotskyite allies of the Islamists view their partners hobnobbing with the bankers atop Toronto's TD Tower.

Moreover, a new industry of Islamic banking conferences and forums has emerged, permitting hundreds of sharia scholars to mix and mingle with bankers and economists at financial centres around the globe. In the words of Saleem, who attended many such meetings, they gather "to hear each other praise each other for all the innovations they are making." The Toronto conference promoting sharia banking and Islamic investments was part of this worldwide touring circuit that allows banks to keep the sharia scholars pampered and well looked after. There are at least five international conferences every year and these have been going on annually for the past twenty-five years. Saleem estimates that the cost of each conference exceeds $2 million and so far more than $200 million has been spent just keeping the sharia banking circuit alive.

He cites one example of how sharia scholars only care for the money they get from banks, and are willing to rubber-stamp any deal where interest is masked. Saleem describes one such incident as "comical":

I have first hand seen comical cases where the sharia scholar of an Islamic bank only spoke Arabic, but a lending officer only spoke English and Urdu. A particular financing transaction was structured in English with such terms as x% over LIBOR.* So we had an interpreter who would translate from English to Arabic, explaining this convoluted transaction to the Sharia advisor. It was at times painful and other times comical to watch the proposal being presented to this religious scholar for his blessings to ensure that it was consistent with the principles of sharia. The "sharia scholar," elderly and partly deaf, had little experience in modern banking and finance. However, mindful of the fact that the bank was paying him a generous retainer, he gave his blessing to the deal, after being fully made aware that the bank wanted to do this deal, even though from the look on his face it was obvious that he could not tell the difference between a trade deal and a leveraged buyout transaction.

In the name of Islam, what amounts to deception and dishonesty are being practised while ordinary Muslims are being made to feel that their interaction with mainstream banks is un-Islamic and sinful. As the Muslim banker asked: "Through various devices—mostly cosmetic—[Islamic] banks end up with virtually no risk. If Islamic banks label their hamburger, a Mecca

---

* LIBOR is the London Interbank Offered Rate, much like the US Federal Bank rate or the Bank of Canada rate.

Burger, as long as it still has the same ingredients as a McDonald's burger, is it really any different in substance?"

Muhammad Saleem laments the fact that few people are exposing the deception of this exercise in the name of Islam. "We should be able to point out the failures and shortcomings of Islamic banking and economics without being accused of being anti-Islamic," he says. Perhaps Scotiabank, the RBC, BMO, and the Office of the Superintendent of Financial Institutions will pay heed to this former banker's words of caution.

The sharia-banking charade is a sad indictment of the Muslim community. Islamic banking is not some resurrection from a golden period—it is a 20th-century creation that flies in the face of reason, logic, and the spirit of Islam, yet is being thrust on us for no fault of ours.

As Muslims approach the first 1,500 years of their faith (2008 corresponds to year 1429 of the Muslim calendar), we need to take a serious look at how we can move forward without having to carry the baggage of the past that has no relevance to the five pillars of Muslim faith. Some medieval feudal and tribal laws have clung to Islam like parasites, devouring our spirit and our freedom from the clergy, which Muhammad offered, and the equality of men and women that we all deserve. These man-made laws must be discarded despite the threats of the zealots. When God revealed in the last verse of the Quran that "Today, I have completed your faith for you," we need to trust him to be right. Progressive and liberal Muslims need to step up, take responsibility, and defend the gains of democracy and human rights that all of humanity has accomplished since the days of the American and French revolutions. All laws that have come from outside the realm of democratically elected parliaments cannot be called laws.

Muslims living in Muslim countries may not have the courage or capability to fight the introduction of sharia, but those of us who live in North America and Europe carry the responsibility to stand up to the thugs who relish authoritarianism. We need to realize that segments of the non-Muslim community in the West, especially the guilt-ridden Left that comes out in support of sharia, are practising racism of lower expectations, where, under the garb of diversity, Muslims are being encouraged to ghettoize and withdraw from the mainstream.

In pleading to my Muslim sisters and brothers for an abandonment of man-made sharia laws, I would like to quote a great Iranian philosopher and revolutionary who has experienced the ire of both the Marxist Left of the country and the ruling ayatollahs—Ali Shariati (1933–77). He argued that there were two types of Islam that have faced each other throughout Islamic history: on one hand, "the degenerate and narcotizing religion," and on the other, "the progressive and awakening religion."

Shariati pleaded for the destruction of all the degenerating factors which, in the name of Islam, have stymied the process of thinking and the fate of the society. Shariati called for eliminating the spirit of imitation and obedience that is the hallmark of the popular religion, and replacing it with a critical revolutionary, aggressive spirit of independent reasoning (Ijtehad).

American author and psychologist Laleh Bakhtiar, in her book *Shariati on Shariati*, quotes the Iranian philosopher as saying:

> The Islam of tomorrow will not be the Islam of the pseudo-religious scholars. The Islam of Qum and Mashhad will also change. The young theological students have shown that they will no longer accept things which are dictated to them without first questioning them . . . Tomorrow's Islam will not be the Islam of the book of prayers. It will be the Islam of the Quran . . . Tomorrow's religion will no longer be the religion of ignorance, tyranny, prejudice, and ancient superstitions, habit, repetition, tears, weakness and abasement.

Can we, Muslims living in democratic societies, heed the call of Dr. Shariati?

CHAPTER 12

Jihad—Permanent War or Continuous Struggle?

THOMAS JEFFERSON and John Adams sat at a table in the London Chambers of Abd al-Rahman al-Ajar, the representative of the Ottoman pasha of Tripoli (now in Libya). What transpired between the two American founding fathers and the nobleman from Tripoli in 1785 would be the United States' first exposure to the sense of entitlement with which most Muslim rulers governed—and still do. These caliphs and sultans considered their rule to be a God-given trusteeship, with an obligation to conduct first *dawah*[*] and then jihad.[†]

In the late 18th century, the United States had no navy, while the North African Muslim states of Morocco, Algeria, and the Ottoman vassal of Tripoli had a combined naval strength that rivalled their European neighbours and

---

[*] *Dawah*: Literally, "invite." Islam considers it an obligation on Muslims to invite others to Islam, but Islamic rulers have invoked *dawah* as an institution of the state to "invite" a non-Muslim country to accept Islam or pay a poll tax. If both offers are rejected, Islamic scholars have ruled that a Muslim ruler may wage war or jihad against the non-Muslim state.

[†] *Jihad*: Although in Arabic it means to strive or exert oneself, Islamic scholars have distinguished between the "greater jihad" (a spiritual struggle against one's ego) and a "lesser jihad"(war in the cause of Islam). The connotation and common usage of "jihad" in the Muslim narrative has been this lesser jihad, meaning military action for either the defence of Islam or its spread through *dawah*. This chapter expands how latter-day Islamists have mocked the notion of the greater jihad and have laid the foundations for jihad to have only one meaning: a war against the infidel until it accepts Islam or prepares to pay a tribute. (Jihad is also a common male name, spelled various ways in English.)

facilitated the largely undocumented European slave trade—White men enslaved to work in Africa.

In the 1780s American merchant ships in the Mediterranean, having lost the protection of the British Navy, were subject to attack by pirates and slave traders from Morocco, Tripoli, Tunis, and Algiers. Jefferson and Adams, recognizing the limits of US naval power, were meeting with the Ottoman representative Abd al-Rahman al-Ajar to offer him a tribute of $25,000 in exchange for his protection. The French were already paying. Jefferson told al-Ajar that although the United States was "eager to avert bloodshed" and therefore willing "to offer a treaty of lasting friendship with Tripoli," he was intrigued and wanted to know under what moral authority the Muslim nobleman was demanding the bribe.

The answer Jefferson got was the United States' first exposure to the sort of protection racket Muslim rulers had been running in the name of Islam. The Muslim ambassador gave the two Americans a crash course in dawah and jihad. The doctrine, as laid into law by medieval Muslim theologians, did not consider such a tribute as a bribe, but rather an interim arrangement until the non-Muslim party accepted the invitation to Islam or was conquered by force of arms. Ambassador al-Ajar told the two Americans: "It was . . . written in the Koran, that all Nations who should not have acknowledged their [Muslims'] authority were sinners, that it was their [Muslims'] right and duty to make war upon whoever they could find and make Slaves of all they could take as prisoners, and that every Mussulman who should be slain in battle would surely go to paradise."

Jefferson and Adams were taken aback. They had just glimpsed the mindset that drew inspiration from the medieval application of jihad. Most Muslim rulers from the earliest caliphates to the Ottomans of the 18th century self-righteously saw themselves as saviours of the human race, "Shadows of God on Earth," and thus entitled to rule. From the perspective of the Ottoman official, the United States was a non-Muslim Christian entity. It was perfectly justifiable for him to ask for the tribute, since the United States had not accepted the Muslim caliphate's invitation to Islam. The Americans denied that they were a "Christian" country. The Treaty of Tripoli became one of the early documents recording the US separation of church and state.

Other countries in Europe had their own system of exacting tribute from weaker nations, so the practice was not the exclusive preserve of the Muslim rulers. Muslims, however, like the Popes during the Crusades, were invoking religion to justify what might be regarded as an ocean toll tax.

The link between "inviting the infidels" to the fold of Islam and demanding a tribute if they turned the invitation down was sanctioned by most medieval Islamic scholars in the 9th and 10th centuries. Imam Muslim (d. 875)—in his collection of the sayings of Prophet Muhammad, *Sahih Muslim*—indicates that a dawah is the first of three "courses of action" to be undertaken prior to war with non-Muslim enemies. In 1368, Ahmad ibn Naqib al-Misri wrote the classic work of Shafi Islamic law, *Umdat as-salik* (*Reliance of the Traveller*). In his book, al-Masri is quite frank about the link between dawah and jihad:

> The caliph makes war upon Jews, Christians, and Zoroastrians (provided he has first invited them to enter Islam in faith and practice, and if they will not, then invited them to enter the social order of Islam by paying the non-Muslim poll tax *jaziyah*—which is significance of their paying it, not the money itself—while remaining in their ancestral religions) and the war continues until they become Muslim or else pay the non-Muslim poll tax in accordance with the word of Allah Most High.

Americans would soon discover that the Muslims they encountered in North Africa were quite sure of their place in the world—right at the top and with a dogged sense of entitlement. The United States' first war would be with the Islamic states of North Africa and it would be over the "tribute." Americans had already encountered Muslims, but the circumstances were very different. Long before Jefferson and Adams dealt with the Ottoman pasha in the 1780s, thousands of Black Muslims were kidnapped from West Africa and sold as slaves in Britain's American colonies. There, they were forced to renounce their faith and adopt the religion of their new masters—Christianity.

While some non-Muslim critics of Islam used the word "jihad" as a lightning rod with which to berate the faith of the Muslims, the response of the Islamists has merely facilitated the work of these hate mongers. The Internet is awash with sites dedicated to the critique of jihad and the portrayal of Muslims as essentially a violent people. One would have hoped that the Islamist response would be to admit to the fact that, yes, the doctrine of jihad does permit acts of war, and yes, Muslims have invoked religion to fight wars, but just like the institution of slavery, which Muslims now distance themselves from, the doctrine of jihad as an instrument of war and violence is no longer applicable. However, that appears to be too much to ask for.

Instead, Muslim leaders, especially in the United States and Canada, have stuck to the now familiar script: "*Jihad* does not mean holy war. *Jihad* is the Arabic word meaning 'to strive or struggle.'" Of course they are right, in that the meaning of the word "jihad" is to strive, but the actual use of the word is not so innocent. Who are we fooling? Not only is this carefully crafted spin disingenuous, it is an exercise in intellectual dishonesty that cannot withstand the slightest scrutiny.

The Saudis have funded North American Muslim organizations and also sent their textbooks, Qurans, and their versions of *Sahih al-Bukhari* for many years. These books include commentaries that promote jihad as war. Take a look at this reproduction of a Quranic verse in the Saudi publication *Summarized Sahih al-Bukhari:* "Jihad (Islamic holy fighting) is ordained for you (Muslims) though you dislike it, and it may be that you dislike a thing which is good for you and that you like a thing which is bad for you."

The Saudis repeatedly say that the word "jihad" does not mean holy war, yet they go out of their way to ensure their Muslim target audience in North America is told exactly what jihad means, that is, "Islamic holy fighting." These are the words they have sneaked into the translation by including them in parentheses in the previous paragraph.

At every occasion they get, Muslim leaders take to the pulpit and state with disarming smiles and polite language that jihad is a peaceful exertion of spiritual warfare waged against oneself—against one's ego and against one's evil intentions, a sort of a cleansing of the soul. Again, this is all true, because the Prophet after returning from a battle told his colleagues: "You are returning from a lesser *jihad* to a greater *jihad*," and when asked to clarify, he said the greater jihad "is the jihad against your passionate souls."

But make no mistake: the jihad that Osama bin Laden has launched against all of us is, unfortunately, the lesser jihad. Had Bin Laden taken the route of the "greater jihad," the world would not be sitting on a powder keg (although US President Bush would certainly have discovered other reasons to invade Iraq). Bin Laden and the Muslims who admire him for launching his jihad against the West make no mistake about the meaning as well as the connotation of the word "jihad." They cite the sharia, the legal medieval texts, the Quran, the hadith, and the Islamic books preceding the hadith to justify their jihad against not just the West, but fellow Muslims who stand in their way. Bin Laden not only has the ancient texts to back him; he relies on validation provided by such 20th-century scholars as Hassan al-Banna, Syed Qutb, and Abul Ala Maudoodi. It is these three men who are the intellectual gurus of all Islamist organizations in the West, yet when these leaders appear before cameras or politicians—even the ones they hate, like Bush and former British prime minister Tony Blair—they parrot their denunciations of Islamic terrorism while refusing to distance themselves from the doctrine of jihad as military action. Curiously, no one ever asks them to do so!

The verse in the Quran that jihadis use to legitimize their terrorism says:

But when the forbidden months are past, then fight and slay The Pagans, wherever ye find them. And seize them, beleaguer them, and lie in wait for them in every stratagem (of war). But if they repent and establish regular prayer and practise regular charity, then open the way for them; For God is Oft-forgiving, Most Merciful.

Jihadis use this verse to justify their actions, not realizing that the verse was revealed for a specific narrow application for a particular skirmish with pagan Arabs. Early classical commentators stated very clearly that this was not an all-encompassing direction for the future. Sadly, other theologians with a radical streak have used this verse as their clarion call for jihad against the infidel. This is insane. Imagine using Winston Churchill's wartime speeches as a call to wage war on Germany today.

More than the Quran, it is the hadith literature that incites radicals to fight in the name of Allah as the highest form of worship. In the 8th century, the first of the books on jihad was published by a central Asian Muslim, Abdullah bin al-Mubarik (d. 797). In his book *Kitab al-jihad*, al-Mubarik goes to great lengths to document the various stages of jihad, the different levels of martyrdom, and the now well-known doctrine that says when a sinner dies fighting in a jihad, God forgives all his sins.

Later in the 9th century, al-Bukhari's canonical collections of the sayings of the Prophet appeared. In his commentary on jihad, al-Bukhari invokes the Quranic verse 9:111 to explain jihad, which he believes is incumbent on all Muslims and is a contractual obligation to Allah, a bargain whereby Muslims, in obtaining his pleasure, promise to give up everything in return. Bukhari writes: "God hath purchased of the Believers (Muslims) their persons and their goods; For theirs (in return) is the garden of Paradise; They fight in His cause, And slay and are slain; A promise binding on Him in truth through the law. The Gospel and the Quran; and who is more faithful to His covenant than God? They rejoice in the bargain Which ye have concluded: That is the achievement supreme."

Others presented apocalyptical imagery and suggested that the end of the world was in sight and that Muslims owed it to Allah to spread his message to all corners of the Earth. In fact, Abu Daud in his *sunan* hadith collection says that jihad is and will be in force until the Day of Resurrection. He also predicts that one particular group among the Muslims will be continuously victorious till the end of time and the return of the hidden imam, the Mehdi.

But consider this: If the so-called lesser jihad is an act of defensive war, how do we Muslims explain the Muslim invasion of Egypt and Persia by the early caliphs? Neither Persia nor Egypt was posing any military threat to the nascent Muslim community in Arabia. In fact, Persia and the Byzantines were so exhausted by their unending conflict that invading the deserts of Arabia could not have been on their mind. One explanation is that the earliest invasions were not to acquire territory, but an expression of the zeal with which Muslims were ready to do dawah, to spread the word of the Quran and the message of Muhammad to all of humanity and to invite the infidels to the one true religion—Islam. There was the atmosphere of apocalyptic fears and need to spread God's word before it was too late. The intention was not to conquer, but to do dawah.

However, spreading the invitation to Islam was fraught with danger and was impossible unless the proselytizers had the protection of an army behind them. The zeal with which these early desert Arabs took the message of Islam to the fertile lands of Syria, Egypt, Persia, and India was matched by the impact of these advanced societies on the Bedouin. Soon the zeal to spread Islam was complicated by the desire of these Arabs to live in comfort of the new societies and not have to return to the deserts. It is not a coincidence that both Mecca and Medina, where Islam was born, were abandoned soon after the death of Muhammad and the centre of Islam moved to Damascus, Baghdad, Cairo, Cordoba, and Delhi. No dynasty ever returned to Medina. However, to remain in these new lands where Muslims were a tiny minority (they didn't become a majority in Egypt until three hundred years after the coming of the Muslim armies) was not possible without the protection of military might. Thus what started as an earnest attempt to "invite" the non-Muslims soon turned into "defensive war." It was under these circumstances that military actions were sanctified as religious with the label "jihad."

Which begs the question: If the purpose of this lesser jihad, as in military jihad, was merely to provide protection to those involved in the pursuit of dawah, hasn't the so-called lesser jihad outlived its purpose? After all, in this day of the Internet and the mass media, dawah can be done without leaving home. Why then are today's Islamists reluctant to state emphatically and without qualification: "There is no need for jihad in the 21st century because dawah can be done without waging war." Period. No "ifs," "ands," or "buts." Sadly, wisdom and intellectual integrity are two gifts of the Creator that seem to be in serious short supply among Islamists.

I believe the agenda of the Islamists is not to spread the message of peace and justice on Earth with people submitting to the Creator. For these people who treat Islam as a brand name, not a religion, it seems their motivation is one of revenge, or an outburst on seeing themselves as unable to compete in or contribute to a globalized world. For others it is a continuation of a response to the Crusades. It appears the defeat of Richard the Lion-Hearted was not enough. They would like to see both Muslim and non-Muslim collectively submit to their fascist ideology of hate and supremacy where instead of life, death is to be celebrated.

The doctrine of armed jihad against the non-Muslim "enemy" would take on a more robust and political form in the early 20th-century interpretations among such Islamist scholars as the trio mentioned earlier in this chapter: Hassan al Banna, Abul Ala Maudoodi, and Syed Qutb. These men have laid the foundation of a new form of jihad, patterned on the tradition of the underground communist parties of Europe and at times resembling the anarchists of the 19th century. Today, it has evolved into a form of a death cult, where the highest level of Islamic worship is to die and leave this world to its "satanic existence." This blending of the death cult and jihad has translated into the martyrdom sought by so many brainwashed young Muslim men and women.

While many Islamists in the West are careful about what they say to the media, Islamists from the Muslim world are not so guarded. Justice Muhammad Taqi Usmani is a sharia judge in Pakistan's Supreme Court and one of the world's most respected Islamic scholars from the Deobandi Sunni school. This is the sect of Islam that dominates the Taliban and has a presence in most Indo-Pakistani mosques in Britain and Canada. Though not directly linked to the Saudi Wahhabi strain of Islam, the Deobandi school has historical links with the Saudis. The learned judge, who advises many multinational companies on halal investments, has some eye-opening thoughts on jihad. Usmani is a regular visitor to Britain, where in 2007 he declared in a London *Times* interview that Muslims should wage military jihad "to establish the supremacy of Islam" worldwide.

He told the newspaper that Muslims should live peacefully in countries such as Britain, where they have the freedom to practise Islam, but only until they gain enough power to engage in battle. He told the prestigious *Times*: "The question is whether aggressive battle is by itself commendable or not. If it is, why should the Muslims stop simply because territorial expansion in these days is regarded as bad? And if it is not commendable, but deplorable, why did Islam not stop it in the past?"

He then proceeded to answer his own question: "Even in those days . . . aggressive jihads were waged . . . because it was truly commendable for establishing the grandeur of the religion of Allah."

The United States did not hesitate to tap into this vast reservoir of brainwashed jihadis. In fact, the United States would finance the jihadis, using them to fight its global war on communism. For decades the United

States had clandestinely helped jihadi groups quash pro-communist and nationalist Muslims inside the Muslim world. By the end of the 1970s, this covert practice was more visible, and the United States had become a covert supporter of international jihad.

Perhaps the clearest example of US endorsement of jihad came in the January 1980 photo-op showing President Carter's national security adviser, Zbigniew Brzezinski, standing at the historic Khyber Pass that marks the border between Pakistan and Afghanistan. Pointing a rifle at Kabul, Brzezinski declared: "We know of their deep belief in God and we are confident that their struggle will succeed. Your fight will prevail because your cause is right and God is on your side."

Standing alongside Brzezinski were Pakistani military officials, CIA operatives, and the much-loved *mujahideen* (Muslim guerrilla fighters) of the time. Brzezinski urged the warriors to go forth and commit jihad. As the turbaned men who would later metamorphose into the now-hated Taliban cheered, Brzezinski, resplendent in a traditional Afghan woollen cap, basked in their adoration. The Americans had finally found the dupes who were willing to die serving US imperial interests.

Thus began the ten-year CIA-sponsored jihad against the Soviets, which one CIA officer said was "a war that was fought with our gold, but with their blood." It was a US-sponsored jihad; even the textbooks for the jihadi madrassahs came from the United States. In these books, the alphabet consisted of *jeem* for "jihad," *kaaf* for "Kalashnikov," and *tay* for "tope" (cannon). It's this sponsorship of jihadi doctrine that has come back to haunt the United States. The same jihadi doctrine of the Muslim Brotherhood that made the Taliban and Al-Qaeda allies of the United States during the Cold War has now become the genie that cannot be put back into the bottle.

Few non-Muslims can understand the psychology of the person who wishes death more than life. Jihadis have not been the first to die for their cause, but their passion for death far exceeds that of the kamikaze pilots or the Tamil Tiger suicide bombers.

An example of this death cult was reported in *The Sunday Times*' coverage of the Pakistani military action that ended the Islamabad Red Mosque siege in the summer of 2007. On July 15, a few days after the fighting had died down, the newspaper interviewed a fifteen-year-old girl who had witnessed the fighting. Asma Hayat said that she was handing out water to children affected by tear gas near the main gate of the mosque when her friend Nasmeen, seventeen, was shot in the side. When she went to help her, Nasmeen pushed her away, saying: "It feels good, it's martyrdom."

It makes one wonder what would make a seventeen-year-old girl, wounded in battle, deny help simply because "it feels good to be martyred." This bizarre behaviour has no precedent in the Quran or the Prophet's teaching. It is the result of the unchallenged death cult being taught to young Muslim girls and boys in private Islamic schools throughout the world—teachings which, in the words of Hassan al-Banna, claim that "jihad is obligatory on every Muslim." And that martyrdom in the name of Allah is better than life on Earth.

Islamists are no longer restricting their activities to the mosques or Islamic centres. In October 2007 they even set up a stand at Toronto's annual "Word on the Street" book festival, which was staged on the leafy lawns of Queen's Park, home of Ontario's legislative building. At this event, another US-based Islamist organization, the Islamic Circle of North America (ICNA), distributed a free booklet titled *Towards Understanding Islam,* written by Abul Ala Maudoodi, the founder of the radical Jamaat-e-Islami, and the intellectual guru of Islamists and jihadis around the world.

In the booklet, Maudoodi exhorts ordinary Muslims to launch jihad, as in armed struggle, against non-Muslims. "Jihad is part of this overall defence of Islam," he writes. In case the reader is left with any doubt about the meaning of the word "jihad," Maudoodi clarifies: "In the language of the Divine Law, this word [jihad] is used specifically for the war that is waged solely in the name of God against those who perpetrate oppression as enemies of Islam. This supreme sacrifice is the responsibility of all Muslims."

Maudoodi goes on to label Muslims who refuse the call to armed jihad as apostates: "*Jihad* is as much a primary duty as are daily prayers or fasting. One who avoids it is a sinner. His every claim to being a Muslim is doubtful. He is plainly a hypocrite who fails in the test of sincerity and all his acts of worship are a sham, a worthless, hollow show of deception."

Two thoughts troubled me as I read the above passage. First, why was a Canadian Muslim organization distributing this call to arms against Canada at a book festival? Second, I wondered, if such hateful and inflammatory literature was being distributed openly in downtown Toronto, what was being said in the confines of private gatherings and the new mini-mosques that have sprouted across all major metropolises in the West? It is clear that jihadi extremists are taking advantage of Canada's liberal democracy to spread their fascist ideology, while the liberal-left custodians of fair play and equity are being taken to the cleaners. Taunting peaceful Muslims to commit jihad against Canada should certainly deserve a challenge, but few are willing to speak up.

The problem is compounded when many of the Western writers and academics with a sound knowledge of Islamic politics treat the subject matter with kid gloves, instead of stating the facts about the dangers of spreading the doctrine of jihad among Muslim youth followers of Qutb and Maudoodi. Take the example of John Esposito, a professor of religion and international affairs at Georgetown University. In discussing jihad, it seems he goes out of his way to not offend the Islamists, appearing to gloss over the threats they pose, if not apologizing for them. In mid-2007, in a piece for *The Washington Post* titled "Want to Understand Islam? Start Here," he wrote:

> Muslims also argue over what some refer to as Islam's sixth pillar, *jihad*. In the Koran, Islam's sacred text, *jihad* means "to strive or struggle" to realize God's will, to lead a virtuous life, to create a just society and to defend Islam and the Muslim community. But historically, Muslim rulers, backed by religious scholars, used the term to legitimize holy wars to expand their empires. Contemporary extremists—most notably Osama bin Laden— also appeal to Islam to bless their attacks. My book *Unholy War: Terror in the Name of Islam* tackles this theme.

John Esposito knows very well that the problem is not simply Osama bin Laden, but that it lies in the doctrine of jihad as espoused by such 20th-century Islamists as Hassan al-Banna and Abul Ala Maudoodi, who have a large following among American Muslim organizations and their leaders. He could have asked Muslims to distance themselves from these two purveyors of Islamic extremism, but instead chose to gloss over the subject, trivializing the real danger this ideology poses to secular civic society. Instead of promoting his book, Esposito could have used the space to explicitly denounce the application of jihad as a political tool. He did not.

Not only did the late Hassan al-Banna make it seem obligatory for all Muslims to conduct jihad, but he was quite clear that "jihad" meant armed conflict. He mocked the concept of the lesser and greater jihad, suggesting that this theory is a conspiracy so that "Muslims should become negligent." Syed Qutb, another Egyptian stalwart of the Islamist movement and the Muslim Brotherhood, wrote in his classic book *Milestones*:

> Can anyone say that [if] Abu Bakr, Umar or Othman had been satisfied that the Roman and Persian powers were not going to attack the Arabian peninsula, they would not have strived to spread the message of Islam throughout the world? . . . It would be naïve to assume that a call is raised to free the whole of humankind throughout earth, and it is confined to preaching and exposition.

Qutb is blunt about his expectations of Muslims living in the West. He writes:

A Muslim has no country except that part of the earth where Shariah of God is established and human relationships are based on the foundation of relationship with God; a Muslim has no nationality except his belief, which makes him a member of the Muslim community in Dar-ul-Islam; a Muslim has no relatives except those who share the belief in God. . . . A Muslim has no relationship with his mother, father, brother, wife and other family members except through their relationship with the Creator, and then they are also joined through blood.

He goes on to urge Muslims living in non-Muslim countries to work towards domination of their religion: "Indeed, there is no Islam in a land where Islam is not dominant."

From India to Indonesia and Morocco to Malaysia, the Muslim Brotherhood ideology of jihad and Islamic supremacy is being challenged by fellow Muslims. However, in Canada, the United States, and the West, it seems the Muslim Brotherhood and its Pakistani wing, the Jamaat-e-Islami of Abul Ala Maudoodi, dominate the Muslim narrative. The few voices that do stand up to the open exhibition of jihadi ideology in Canada and the United States face serious obstacles. For example, two Muslim experts who were hired by the US TV network PBS to advise it on a series on Islam ensured that Canadian filmmaker Martyn Burke's documentary *Islam vs. Islamists* was excluded. It was later widely reported that the two knew the very Islamist groups that were the subject of the documentary investigation. It took months of lobbying by the producer, including a viewing for members of the US Congress, to compel PBS to lift what amounted to a covert ban.

One needs to read what is being distributed by Islamists around the world to recognize the threat this propaganda poses. The booklet *Call to Jihad* by the founder of Jamaat-e-Islami is sold in most Islamic bookstores in North America and is distributed by Muslim youth organizations on campuses. Maudoodi urges young Muslims to consider themselves under attack if any Muslim country is threatened. He writes that it is "the categorical injunction of the Islamic shariah that whenever an enemy attacks any part of *darul Islam* [the Muslim world], Jihad for its defence becomes obligatory (*fard*) on every Muslim." Little wonder that so many young Muslims give up on the country that nourished them through birth, schooling, and youth, and transfer their loyalties to some Islamist cause overseas.

Maudoodi makes another significant clarification. He writes that even though jihad is separate from *qetal* (warfare), they are complementary. He says warfare may end, but jihad does not. He writes: "In terms of Shariah or Islamic Law, *Jihad* and *Qetal* are two separate things. *Qetal* is actual warfare and clash of arms of the fighting forces against the armies of the enemy. The *Jihad* on the other hand means the struggle as a whole—the entire war effort which the nation collectively puts forth in order to achieve the objective for which war takes place. In the course of *Jihad*, *Qetal* is, at times, put off or temporarily suspended, but *Jihad* goes on and continues until the object for which it was undertaken is realized."

Muslim youth in the West are being made to feel guilty if they do not commit to jihad. They are being told they are sinners if they don't take up arms and join the jihad. One wonders if there are any books that urge young Muslim Canadians to be true to their soil, their neighbours, their community, and their country. Is anyone asking them to dedicate themselves to becoming ambassadors of Islam serving Canada rather than undermine the very values that have made Canada the best country on Earth in which to live?

Again from his book *Milestones*, Syed Qutb writes: "Any place where Islamic shariah is not enforced and where Islam is not dominant becomes the Home of Hostility (Dar-ul-Harb) . . . A Muslim will remain prepared to fight against it, whether it be his birth place or a place where his relatives reside or where his property or any other material interests are located."

Qutb describes jihad in this manner: "Since the objective of the message of Islam is a decisive declaration of man's freedom, not merely on the philosophical plane but also in the actual conditions of life, it must employ *Jihad*."

Are the distributors of Maudoodi's and Qutb's books in Canada urging Muslim youth to consider Canada as a "Home of Hostility"? In the same book, Qutb writes: "In this world, there is only one party of God; all others are parties of Satan and rebellion." Syed Qutb reduces the message of Islam to the rejection of all laws made by parliaments: "The basis of the message [Islam] is that one should accept the Shariah without any question and reject all other laws in any shape or form. This is Islam."

Following every terrorist act, the aftermath is predictable: there are public denunciations from the very people who support jihad. How is that possible? Just look at the incident involving the Glasgow airport attack in July 2007. No sooner had the sight of a burning suv stuck at the entrance of Glasgow airport's passenger terminal gone on live tv than ordinary Muslims around the world were begging God for reprieve. "Please let it not be a Muslim," they prayed. But the odds were stacked against us. Deep down all of us knew that such acts of callous cowardice have become the hallmark of our co-religionists. Yet we crossed our fingers and hoped for a miracle.

In the offices of the hundreds of Islamist groups that dot the British political landscape, activists were churning out denunciations of the terror attack. As usual, Islamic groups lined up to utter cliché-ridden denunciations without attacking the ideology of jihad that provides the fertile soil for Islamic extremism. The condemnations were just enough to put some distance between themselves and the jihadis, and to absolve themselves of any responsibility. At the time I wrote in the *Ottawa Citizen*:

> The current state of affairs in Britain is not just the fault of the Islamists and their apologists. It is also the fault of politicians such as Tony Blair, who, after foolishly entrenching Islamists at every level in British society . . . set up state-funded Islamic schools and knighted a known Islamist, a person who had defended the death sentence on Salman Rushdie. Mr. Blair appointed another Islamist, an admirer of Ayatollah Khomeini, to the House of Lords. To make matters worse, Mr. Blair endorsed and funded the so-called "Radical Middle Way" for British Muslim clerics. This "middle way" has become a front for all those who provide convoluted academic analysis, explaining the root causes of Islamic terrorism and falsely promising the British taxpayer that they will counter the ideology of hate against secular societies. But its media savvy scholars promote a very narrow view of Islam, carefully avoiding any rejection of the doctrine of jihad, choosing instead to suggest that Britain's foreign policy is at the root of terrorism.

The reaction was swift. Fuad Nahdi, a respected Muslim journalist in London and a director of the "Radical Middle Way,"* sent me a terse e-mail referring to my piece as "rehashed neo-con shit." Others from that movement were a bit more generous. Abdul-Rehman Malik, one of Canada's

---

* The Radical Middle Way is a British organization funded by the UK government, ostensibly committed "to the emergence of a distinct British Muslim identity that encourages the active involvement of British Muslims in social, public, and economic life of Britain." However, it is as male-dominated as any other Islamist organization in the UK, boasting 20 scholars of which just one is a woman. Its roster is restricted to ultra-conservative clerics with not a single liberal or secular British Muslim author, artist, singer, or politician.

brightest young Muslims and now a British resident who is also intimately involved in the Blair project, protested that I had lumped his group with other Islamists. He challenged my suggestion that the Radical Middle Way distance itself from the doctrine of jihad. He wrote:

> Define doctrine of jihad, Tarek? Jihad is a term—a word—that exists with divergent meanings, interpretations, applications and contexts. This kind of totalising of terminologies puts you into the same intellectual frame as totalising jihadists. The issue of jihad has been addressed, was addressed and [is] continuing to be addressed. Jihad, its notion of struggle, is certainly open to much interpretation and application. Our scholars have been clear: suicide bombing is not jihad, killing innocents is not jihad. Don't confuse us with some Islamists who have different moral values for Israeli civilians. The message has been categorical and, in some segments of the Muslim community, unpopular.

He was right, but had ducked my question. The jihad doctrine that needs to be rejected is the one that is espoused by the Islamists. I would hope that intelligent young Muslims would gather the courage to say, "Jihad, as promoted in Britain and North America by Hassan al-Banna, Abul Ala Maudoodi, and Syed Qutb has no relevance in the 21st century. Like slavery, the time of jihad has gone." While the jihadis continue to take inspiration from this trio of Islamist intellectuals—the Marx, Engels, and Lenin of Islamic extremists—their opponents within conservative and classical Islam oppose them, but are unwilling to go that necessary extra step to distance themselves from the so-called lesser jihad that holds the rest of the world hostage.

The time has come for this to change. The time has come for ordinary Britons, Americans, and Canadians to say that if our politicians do not have the spine to stand up to the Islamists, we will. We have to say to those apologizing for Islamists, "Enough is enough," and stand up to the jihadis and jihadi-Lites. We must not hesitate to say to those who do not embrace the principles of secular democracies, "Shape up or ship out."

My passport is not for rent. My country is not a parking lot and neither is it a port of convenience. It is my adopted home and I am not willing to let it decay at the hands of parasites.

The victimhood mentality forced on young Muslim men, mixed with the exultation of martyrdom and the doctrine of jihad, has been at the root of Islamic terrorism in Britain, Continental Europe, Pakistan, Indonesia, Morocco, and Bangladesh. When modern-day Muslims get involved in three-pronged car-bomb attempts in London's West End and the Glasgow airport,* the groups who instilled this frenzy in them are equally guilty of the crime, if not more guilty. Those who incite young Muslim men in Britain and Canada to believe that Western society is satanic and that the West is waging a war against Islam have a moral obligation to take responsibility when these same men become suicide bombers and terrorists.

Muslim organizations in Europe and North America must do more than simply pay lip service to cliché-ridden patriotism while preaching against the values and foundations of this great country. They must state clearly that the only laws that matter in Canada are the laws of this country, not medieval sharia laws from the 9th century. If they do not reject the doctrine of jihad as an option for Muslims, they should be considered part of the problem, not the solution. These organizations have no vision of the future for their community or for humanity. Their goal is to seek paradise, not in life, but in death.

Tariq Ali, one of the few left-wing activists who still openly criticizes the Islamo-anarchists (as he prefers to call them), has repeatedly exposed the bankruptcy of their jihadi agenda. Speaking at a conference in Karachi, Pakistan, in September 2007, Ali said: "The jihadis have no social vision. They speak about getting the US out. I asked them, fine, you're right, but what next? And they said, 'Allah will take care of the rest.'"

Unless this trend is reversed, the fatalism associated with the jihadi doctrine of the Islamists will succeed. It will instill a sense of vitcimhood in the minds of young Muslim professionals, a rejection of Western values and institutions. When we start wondering if a neurologist[†] has been brainwashed, who next—a nuclear physicist?

---

[*] On June 29 and 30, 2007, there were two thwarted car bombings in London and a failed car-bomb attack at Glasgow International Airport, all immediately linked to Muslims.

[†] Suspects in the failed car-bomb attack on Glasgow airport included a neurologist.

CHAPTER 13

Hijab—Islamic Piety or Political Islam?

IN KHALED HOSSEINI'S soul-piercing novel *A Thousand Splendid Suns,* the character Nana, a poor unwed mother, tells her five-year-old daughter, Mariam: "Learn this now and learn it well, my daughter: Like a compass needle that points north, a man's accusing finger always finds a woman. Always. You remember that, Mariam."

Hosseini's novel is about life in Afghanistan, but in the thirty words above he sums up the way men govern the lives of women across most of the Muslim world. Like Mariam, millions of Muslim girls are told very early in life by their mothers that their place in society is one of submission; submission, not to God, but to Man. No other institution confers this status of submission and possession more than the *hijab*—the two-metre-long cloth that today stands as the universal defining symbol of Islam. Failure of Muslim women to submit to wearing the hijab can lead to serious consequences, especially if they are under statutory requirements to do so in an Islamic State.

An example of this came in a chilling letter from the Palestinian Islamist group Swords of Islamic Righteousness, to TV newscasters in the Middle East. "You are without shame or morals," the letter said. The jihadis were addressing their "sisters" who work for Palestinian Television in Gaza. Demanding that the women start wearing the hijab, the group threatened that if they did not see heads covered, the Swords of Islamic Righteousness would "cut throats, from vein to vein, if needed to protect the spirit and morals of this nation."

The threat was sent as a text message to Lana Shaheen, a prominent TV host. Even though the incident rattled her, Shaheen remained defiant. "I am taking the threats very seriously, but I will not start wearing the hijab," she told reporters. However, that was June 2007. Within a month, Gaza fell to the gunmen of the fundamentalist Hamas movement, and the agenda of Swords of Islamic Righteousness came into effect. As this book goes to press, few women appear publicly in Gaza without a hijab.

What is it about this piece of cloth that triggers so much self-righteous angst among Islamists? What is it about a women's hair, the most inanimate part of her body, that arouses so much passion among some Muslim men? Moreover, why would so many Muslim women, educated and supposedly enlightened, submit to the dictates of the men in their lives—their husbands, brothers, sons, and of course, the clerics and male scholars who have laid down the law for these females for centuries? How could the covering of a woman's head—a requirement that does not merit explicit mention in the Quran—end up as the most defining symbol of Islam? And what is the rationale behind this Islamist obsession? Will God really be offended if a woman shows a bit of her bangs?

In Muslim-majority countries, where Islamists have a free hand—if not in the political arena, definitely in the theological—jihadis do not mince their words or actions. However, in the West, the Islamist tactics are deceptively employed to generate support from liberal-left segments of society—even from feminists—without appearing to be coercive. In North America and Europe the mantra is an easily marketable word—"choice." It's a matter of choice, they say. A woman may choose whether or not to wear a hijab. Who can argue against a woman's right of choice, a word that has a ring of liberation associated with the early days of the feminist struggle.

Though carefully concealed, the true agenda of Islamists is to promote fear among young Muslim girls about not wearing the hijab. This was very evident during the infamous tae kwon do controversy in Quebec in the spring of 2007. At the start of the tournament, a team of young Muslim girls sponsored by the Muslim Community Centre of Montreal mosque refused to participate unless they were allowed to wear the hijab under their helmets. The organizers insisted that the rules of the event did not permit anything other than the prescribed helmets, and since the helmets covered the girls' hair more than the hijab, there was no need for the hijab. In addition, officials said the decision was taken for security reasons. They pointed out that tae kwon do is a martial art that involves mainly kicking and throwing, and expressed fear that part of the hijab could come loose during a bout.

The parents of the young girls, as well their coach from the mosque, refused to allow the girls to participate. The team, made up of girls between the ages of eight and twelve, went home following the decision. One team member, Bissan Mansour, told reporters, "I feel very sad because we practised so hard. We pulled out for a useless reason."

The next day the news was on the front pages of all Canadian newspapers. Islamist groups sounded exhilarated. The incident had given them one more opportunity to drive home the propaganda among vulnerable Muslim youth that Canada is essentially an anti-Muslim country and that Muslim youth are the targets.

What went unreported by all the newspapers was the fact that even under the harshest interpretation of the sharia, Muslim girls below the age of puberty are not required to cover their heads. Here was an eight-year-old girl being forced to wear a hijab, and not a single reporter or columnist dared to challenge the parents or the mosque. The Muslim Canadian Congress (MCC) took up the case and issued a statement expressing "concern and disappointment that the hijab is once again being used as a political tool by Islamists to further their agenda in Canada." The statement said:

> The helmets were sufficient substitutes for the hijab. However, the parents of these very young girls—who are not required to wear the hijab even according to the strictest interpretations of Quranic injunctions—decided to turn this into a political statement of Muslim identity.

There was another twist to the story that also went unreported. The fact the mosque in question was a hotbed of pro-Hezbollah activity in Montreal was not relevant to the hijab story. What went unreported was the warning from the mosque to the young girls that if they discarded the hijab, they risked getting raped. In a message posted on its website, the mosque declared that if the young girls took off their hijab, they could end up having "illegitimate children." One can only imagine the trauma of a ten-year-old girl being warned of possible rape. Is this how Islamists offer choice?

The mosque website listed the "Advantages of Observing Hijab," which included "guarding oneself from the lustful looks of men." The mosque also listed "The Disadvantages of *Discarding* the Hijab." These included:

- divorce, adultery, rape, and illegitimate children
- stresses, insecurity and suspicion in the minds of husbands, ultimately disturbing the familial harmony
- instigating young people to deviate towards the path of lust and immorality.

If the threat of rape and the fear of illegitimate children were not enough, these pre-teen girls were told that if they took off their hijab, they would cease to be Muslims. The website said: "By removing your hijab, you have destroyed your faith. Islam means submission to Allah in all our actions. Those who refuse submission cannot be called Muslims." Little wonder then, that the girls walked away from the tae kwon do tournament rather than remove their hijab.

And if the threats of eternal damnation were not enough, the mosque then told the girls that the consequence of removing their hijab would be that all of society would suffer. It said young men might resort to criminal activity, including armed robbery and murder, and that on the Day of Judgement they, the girls, would have to bear the full responsibility of these young men's crimes. Here is part of the message to young Muslim women, as posted on the mosque's website:

> Then Allah commanded our sisters to observe Hijab, it was because of the universal damages that would be caused by refusing to observe It. It is not a matter of individual behavior, as many people may think. A woman going out exposing her charms attracts men, which sets off a chain of undesirable events, causing lot of harm to several people. Discarding Hijab will harm not only one's own self but also millions of others. Exposure of physical charm of our women may destroy many homes and cause innumerable rapes and murders for which we all are responsible. It is pertinent to relate one of the several heart-breaking stories caused by discarding Hijab: A young innocent man, who saw the photograph of an attractive woman, was immediately infatuated by her physical charm. Unfortunately, he had neither wealth nor position to get closer to her. To fulfill his desire, he thought of getting money quickly by any means and resorted to stealing. Finally, he ended up in prison for robbing a few people and killing one. Who is to be blamed for all the consequences but the person who caused them? Had that woman observed Hijab and refrained from displaying her attractions, these crimes would not have taken place.

The belief that women are to blame for bringing sexual assault and rape on themselves has unfortunately gained wide acceptance among Islamists as well as the leadership of conservative Muslim women's groups. These women have been duped into believing that sexual offences committed by men are their own fault, rather than an outcome of the rapists' pathological tendencies. Sadly, feminist groups in Canada, the United States, and Europe have abandoned their duty to confront the growing acceptance of misogyny in Islamist circles. It seems that as long as US troops occupy Iraq and the likes of George W. Bush occupy the White House, feminist groups will unwittingly give free rein to mosque leaders like the one in Montreal in the name of multiculturalism, a philosophy which has of late come to be adopted with absolutist zeal.

MUSLIM WOMEN AS THE GUARDIANS OF MUSLIM HONOUR

It was shortly after midnight on Saturday, September 1, 2007. A twenty-four-year-old Muslim woman was working all alone in the chemistry laboratory at Carleton University in Ottawa. She had been alone for a few hours. Suddenly she heard the sound of the door opening. As she turned, she saw a broad-shouldered, bald white male, about five-feet eight-inches tall, carrying a white plastic bag, enter the lab. As the two exchanged a few words, she realized he had been drinking. The clean-shaven twenty-something, who spoke English without an accent, did not have chemistry on his mind that Labour Day weekend. Before the woman could grasp the danger he posed, the young man in the blue hoodie sweatshirt was all over her.

The two grappled, but she was no match for the predator. With a swift blow, he broke the victim's jaw, dislocated her shoulder, and knocked her unconscious before removing her clothes and sexually assaulting her. Newspapers report that when the student was brought to the hospital, she was in a state of shock and not fully conscious.

The young Muslim woman went through a horrifying trauma with physical injuries and emotional scars that she may never be able to get rid of. However, what happened in the days following this incident tells the true story of the terrible burden that Muslim men and Islamic society have placed on the backs of Muslim women.

Four days after the sexual assault, the student told Christine Baker, a sexual assault nurse examiner at the Ottawa Hospital, that although she had been sexually assaulted, she had not been raped. The student reportedly expressed concern that if the rape was not denied, the "incorrect information would destroy her future." This young woman, who did not wish to be identified, said she was making the clarification in an effort to save herself grief as an unmarried Muslim woman. She said that in Islamic countries, victims of rape are considered unclean by potential future husbands. The sexual assault examiner would later tell the media: "As part of her culture, being a virgin is very important and, if, all of a sudden, everybody looks at her and says she's not a virgin, she's a lot less desirable as a wife." In an unprecedented statement, Baker then added: "There was no penetration of her body, and for her, that's a huge distinction that has to be made."

By any standards this was an outrageous development. The victim of sexual assault had to explain herself as if she was guilty of the crime, not the assailant. The fact is that it is not just in "Islamic countries" that victims of rape are considered guilty. The feeling seems to exist inside the community in Canada. Why else would the woman go to such lengths "to clear her name"? The reaction of Muslim leaders in Ottawa made it obvious that this viewpoint is widely held by conservative and fundamentalist circles. Read the words of the president of the Ottawa Muslim Association. He said he supported "the woman's decision to clear her name." *Clear her name!* She didn't do anything wrong; she shouldn't have to clear her name. Another sentence uttered by Mumtaz Akhtar, president of the Ottawa Muslim Association, gave away the prevalent mindset in the community. He said, "Who are we to judge somebody else, especially if a person is innocent?" Which begs the question: Had she been raped, she wouldn't have been innocent?

While Western society has a long way to go before it can claim to have truly introduced gender equality, one cannot deny that in the last hundred years we have made huge progress and women are no longer considered the chattels of men or the source of sin. Unfortunately, the followers of a religion that gave women the right to property and divorce have failed to keep up. Only a few brave souls have dared to criticize the Islamic institutions of concubinage and polygamy that lie at the heart of gender apartheid and its various manifestations, including the *niqab*,* the hijab, and the refusal to acknowledge the right of women to stand in the front rows of a mosque.

When the young Canadian woman was sexually assaulted, she was a victim of two attacks. For the first—the crime of sexual assault—the assailant will get caught and face justice. However, the second crime committed against her—making her feel guilty for no fault of hers—will go unpunished. The people responsible for creating the climate where victims of rape fear reporting it are doing more damage to the Muslim community than the sick men who rape helpless young women. These are the imams and sheikhs who have perpetuated the myth that a woman is essentially the source of all sin.

In October 2006, an Australian imam of Lebanese descent, the country's most senior Muslim cleric, triggered outrage when he described women

---

* *Niqab:* Face-covering veil that can be part of a body outfit (a.k.a. burka).

who dress immodestly (in his view) as "uncovered meat" who invite sexual attacks. Sheikh Taj Aldin al-Hilali, the so-called Mufti of Australia, condemned women who he said "sway suggestively," wear makeup, and do not wear the hijab. The idea that women are to blame for rape is preposterous, but that is what the sheikh suggested while delivering a sermon during the month of Ramadan. Not a single member of the congregation protested or challenged the imam. Later, the imam apologized for his comments, but his apology reflected the deep-seated attitudes among many clerics of Islam about women. He told reporters, "I had only intended to protect women's honour." During the sermon, al-Hilali had said:

> If you take out uncovered meat and place it outside on the street, or in the garden, or in the park, or in the backyard without cover, and the cats come to eat it . . . whose fault is it—the cats' or the uncovered meat? The uncovered meat is the problem. If she was in her room, in her home, in her hijab, no problem would have occurred.

Women, al-Hilali said, were "weapons" used by "Satan" to control men.

If Sheikh al-Hilali of Australia believes that women are Satan's weapons against men, he is relying on the long history of interpreting the Quran in a particularly misogynistic manner. These interpretations that place women as sexual objects are not just the work of medieval scholars, but the leaders of the contemporary 20th-century Islamist movement. Such leaders include the late Abul Ala Maudoodi, who worked closely with the Egyptian Muslim Brotherhood. Maudoodi's writings are widely read and believed as absolute truths in Islamic schools and mosques in North America and Europe. Maudoodi gives a nod to the rape of non-Muslim women who are captured in war, and yet few Muslim women have stood up to condemn an ideology that gives religious sanction to rape. Little wonder that Pakistani troops in the Bangladesh war had no hesitation raping Bengali women after clerics had declared these Muslim women as non-Muslim enemies of Islam. The same theology today gives religious license to the Janjaweed Arab militia in Sudan to rape Darfuri women—their very own Muslim sisters.

Maudoodi's commentary on one verse of the Quran demonstrates the kind of liberties that Islamists have taken with the Muslim holy book to serve their sexual perversion and legalize sex slaves for Muslim soldiers. In his commentary, he uses convoluted language to permit the rape of captured non-Muslim female prisoners of war; their slavery; and the right of Muslims to buy and sell non-Muslim women. Here is how verse 24 of chapter 4 of the Quran actually reads:

Also (prohibited are) women already married, except those whom your right hands possess: Thus hath Allah ordained (Prohibitions) against you: Except for these, all others are lawful, provided ye seek (them in marriage) with gifts from your property, desiring chastity, not lust, seeing that ye derive benefit from them, give them their dowers (at least) as prescribed; but if, after a dower is prescribed, agree Mutually (to vary it), there is no blame on you, and Allah is All-knowing, All-wise.

The way Maudoodi sees it, this verse gives him the liberty to institutionalize sex slavery and the treatment of women as commodities that can be bought and sold. The following commentary by Abul Ala Maudoodi on the above verse comes from his six-volume translation and interpretation of the Quran, *Tafhim ul Quran*:

Those women who become prisoners of war, while their *kaafir* [non-Muslim] husbands have been left behind in *dar ul harb* [the non-Muslim country with which Muslims are fighting, or the "home of war"], are not prohibited to you [for sexual intercourse]. The reason is that as soon as these women crossed over from *dar ul harb* to the *dar ul Islam* [the Muslim country], their marriage contract with their husbands became null and void. You can either marry such women or, if your right hand possesses these women, you can also have sexual relations with them. However, there is a difference of opinion among the scholars in case both husband and wife are captured together. Imam Abu Hanifa says that the marriage of the [non-Muslim] husband and wife will remain intact, while Imam Maalik and Imam Shafi'i say their marriage contract is void. As there are many misunderstandings exist in the minds of people concerning taking advantage* of [having sexual intercourse] with slave-girls captured as prisoners of war, the following principles must be carefully understood:

I. It is not lawful for a soldier to have sex with a captured woman as soon as she falls into his hands. According to Islamic law such women should be first handed over to the government, which then has the right to set them free; ransom them; or exchange them for Muslim prisoners of war in enemy hands. Or, if the government so wishes, it can distribute these

---

* In the original Urdu-language version of Maudoodi's book, he uses the word *tamatto*, the literal meaning of which is "to complete delight." The word has been deleted from the English translation of his work.

  non-Muslim women among the Muslim troops to serve as their sex-
  slaves. However, a soldier can have sex with only that woman who has
  been formally given to him by the government.
2. After taking possession of this woman, a soldier should not have sex
  with her until after she has had her monthly periods and it is clear that
  the woman is not pregnant. To have sex with the captured woman prior
  to her periods is *haraam* [prohibited].
3. It does not matter whether the female prisoner of war belongs to
  "people of the book" [Christian or Jew] or not. No matter what her
  religion, the soldier has the right to have sex with her if he has been
  given possession of her.

Elsewhere in the same commentary, Maudoodi writes: "The proprietary rights over a slave, male or female, as given to a person by the government, are transferable, like all other proprietary rights."

Unfortunately, until 2007 only men had translated the Quran and interpreted it. The very idea of a woman translating the holy book offends Islamists. Take for example the reaction to the first-ever translation by a woman—Laleh Bakhtiar's *The Sublime Quran*.

Mohammad Ashraf, secretary general of ISNA-Canada, a branch of the Indianapolis-based Islamic Society of North America, told *The Toronto Star* that he would not permit *The Sublime Quran* to be sold in the ISNA bookstore. "Our bookstore would not allow this kind of translation," he said. "I will consider banning it." He claimed his objection was not because Laleh Bakhtiar is a woman, but because "she was not trained at an academic institution accredited in the Muslim world." He cited the University of Medina in Saudi Arabia as one such a place, but apparently failed to disclose to *The Toronto Star* reporter that this Saudi university, which is the world centre of Wahhabi ideology, refuses to admit female students, let alone accredit them! Instead, he went on to claim: "This woman-friendly translation will be out of line and will not fly too far."

What had Laleh Bakhtiar done to deserve the punishment of having her translation of the Quran banned from ISNA's Islamic bookstores? Her fault in the eyes of Islamists is that she believes the Quran does not condone spousal abuse, as claimed by Islamists. It took Bakhtiar seven years to write her English translation of the Quran, a version that she says was written from a woman's point of view. She says of the ninety thousand words she translated, there is just *one*—in chapter 4, verse 34—that led to sharp criticism and controversy. It's from the section on women and describes how to deal with a wife who is disobedient. All translations of the Quran by men claim the Quran sanctions the beating of a wife. Laleh Bakhtiar, however, discovered what it seems no male Islamic scholar wanted Muslims to know: that this is not what the Quran says.

"When I got to chapter four I had to really look at this carefully," Bakhtiar told *The Toronto Star.* She concluded that the Arabic word *idrib*, which literalists and Islamists say means "to beat," could have twenty-six different meanings. She feels the Quran asks husbands "to go away" or "to leave," not "to beat." For suggesting an end to religiously sanctioned wife-beating and for standing up to centuries of misogyny, it appears that Laleh Bakhtiar paid the penalty: ISNA—the organization that champions the introduction of sharia law in Canada, runs a large Islamic school, and has received funds from Saudi-based sources—banned her Quran from their Islamic bookstore.

WHAT IS THE HIJAB?

It is not just non-Muslims who ask what the hijab is. Most non-Arab Muslims had not been exposed to the word or its application until they arrived in North America or Europe, or went to work in the Middle East. Even in the most conservative parts of India, Pakistan, and Bangladesh, the obsession of tucking every little piece of hair under an elastic sort of a wrap was unheard of before the 1970s oil boom. The *dupatta* or the *sari-pallu** would loosely be thrown over the head at times of prayer or in the presence of elders. In Somalia and much of sub-Saharan Muslim Africa, the term "hijab" did not exist and the head cover was colourful attire, more a fashion statement than a symbol of piety. Today, the resurgence of the hijab seems both a rise of Islamic fundamentalism and a visible way for Muslim women to show that they do not wish to identify with the West. In imitating the custom of the Middle Eastern hijab rather than wearing the South Asian dupatta, the women indicate that the issue is not one of hiding hair, but one of reaffirming their identity as "authentic" Muslims (as opposed to ones tainted by their Indianness).

So what exactly is the hijab? There is no denying that covering the head is a cherished part of Muslim social custom, tradition, and heritage for women. A Muslim woman should have the right to wear a hijab. But Islamists take it a step further, a giant step further, and state that the hijab is compulsory attire and that women who do not wear it are not Muslims at all. The hijab has become more of a political statement than an act of piety.

---

* The *dupatta* and the *sari* have been the head cover and dress of choice among Indian, Pakistani, and Bangladeshi Muslim women for centuries.

What Islamists do not admit is that the custom of the veiling of women in early Islam was not part of the dress code until Muslims conquered Persia and the Byzantine territories in the 7th century. It was only after this assimilation of the conquered cultures that head covering and veiling were viewed as appropriate expressions of Islamic practice. Since the veil was impractical attire for working women, a veiled woman was a sign that she belonged to the upper class and that her husband was rich enough to keep her idle.

Ibrahim B. Syed, a professor at the University of Louisville, Kentucky, and president of the Islamic Research Foundation, writes that hijab literally means a "curtain," "partition," or a "separation." According to Syed, when pre-Islamic Arabs went to battle, Arab women on seeing the men off to war would bare their breasts to encourage them to fight, or they would do so at the battle itself. This changed with Islam, when the Prophet received a Quranic revelation asking women to cover their breasts with the garment the Quran refers to as the *khimar*, worn by Arab women as a head covering.

The respected Polish Islamic scholar Muhammad Asad, commenting on this verse of the Quran (24:31), writes:

The noun *khimar* (of which khumur is plural) denotes the head-covering customarily used by Arabian women before and after the advent of Islam. According to most of the classical commentators, it was worn in pre-Islamic times more or less as an ornament, and let down loosely over the wearer's back. In accordance with the fashion prevalent at the time, the upper part of a woman's tunic had a wide opening in the front, and her breasts were left bare. Hence, the injunction to cover the bosom by means of a khimar does not necessarily relate to the use of a khimar as such. Rather, it is meant to make it clear that a woman's breasts are not included within "what may decently be apparent" of her body, and should not, therefore, be displayed.

The Quran itself does not state explicitly either that women should be veiled, or that they should be kept apart from the world of men. On the contrary, the Quran is insistent on the full participation of women in society, and in the religious practices prescribed for men. The Lebanese scholar Nazira Zain Ad-Din argues that self-control is far better a moral standard than the practice of draping women from head to toe.

In her book *As-sufur wa'l-hijab*, Zain Ad-Din proves it is not an Islamic duty of Muslim women to wear the hijab. She adds that in enforcing the hijab, society becomes a prisoner of its own customs and traditions. Zain

Ad-Din argues that imposing the veil on women is the ultimate proof that men are suspicious of their mothers, daughters, wives, and sisters. This means that men suspect "the women closest and dearest to them."

It is difficult to say exactly when the head cover and the face mask became part of Islamic law. What we do know is that the laws that emerged as sharia were first developed during the 8th and 9th centuries, when the Abbasid caliphs of Baghdad were ruling Islamdom. The "lawyer-theologians of Islam," as Professor Ibrahim Syed refers to these clerics, operated in a religious environment with a self-imposed duty of formulating Islamic law and code of morality. It was these theologians who interpreted the Quranic rules on women's dress in increasingly absolute and categorical terms, reflecting the practices and cultural assumptions of their place and age.

Fatima Mernissi, the Moroccan sociologist and feminist, in her book *The Veil and the Male Elite: A Feminist Interpretation of Women's Rights in Islam*, writes that the sayings of Prophet Muhammad and the Quranic teachings have been manipulated by a male elite whose power could only be legitimized by religion. She says the Prophet's sayings were fabricated to protect the privileges of men, while denying women full participation in Islamic societies. Mernissi attacks the age-old conservative focus on segregation of women. She argues that this is achieved by way of manipulation of the sacred texts, "a structural characteristic of the practice of power in Muslim societies."

In Canada, feminist Farzana Hassan, author of *Islam, Women and the Challenges of Today*, has been a vocal critic of the Islamists who prescribe the hijab head cover as a mandatory dress code for Muslim women. For speaking her mind, she has received death threats and accusations that she is an enemy of Islam, an apostate deserving of death. Addressing the meaning of the word "hijab," she says: "The Quran speaks mostly of modesty when it enjoins 'hijab.' . . . Besides, hijab is more a state of mind. The modesty recommended in the Quran has more to do with modesty in conduct and demeanour."

Elsewhere she writes, "the Quran remained silent as to the specific apparel to be worn [by women] . . . except for the occasion where it specifically suggested covering the bosom with a *khimar* . . . this was specifically designed to discourage the practise of earlier times when women dressed scantily with their bosoms remaining exposed."

If Allah wanted women to cover their heads or their hair, why was he not explicit about it in the Quran? After all, nothing would have prevented him from sending a Quranic revelation, saying to Muslim women, "cover your heads," but he did not. The Arabic word for "chest" is *gayb*, which is in the verse 24:31, but the Arabic words for head (*raas*) or hair (*shaar*) are not part of the verse. The commandment in the verse is clear: Cover your chest or bosom. But, because of the fabrication of medieval scholars and the cowardice of contemporary translators who do not wish to appear as transgressing these scholars, Muslims are being told that the Quran prescribes the covering of one's head or hair.

Asma Barlas, professor of politics at Ithaca College, is also of the view that the head-covering hijab is not a mandatory dress code for Muslim women. She believes that "Conservatives read these Ayat [verses] as giving Muslim males the right to force women to don everything from the *hijab* ... to the *burka* ... They justify such forms of veiling on the grounds that women's bodies are pudendal, hence sexually corrupting to those who see them; it is thus necessary to shield Muslim men from viewing women's bodies by concealing them." Barlas writes that while none of these ideas about the female body derives from the Quran, conservative Muslims continue to cling to them.

Fatima Mernissi points to another meaning of the word *hijab* in the Quran, where it depicts a veil that "hides God from men," describing the inability of certain individuals to perceive God. In yet another occurrence in the Quran, she points out that the word hijab is "something that diminishes human intelligence." Mernissi believes that sometimes the meaning of the word hijab takes on "an eminently negative significance."

In one Toronto bookstore, the title of a gaudy glossy paperback screamed at passersby: *Women Who Deserve to Go to Hell*. The book, which is also widely available in British libraries and mosques, lists the type of women who will face eternal damnation. Among them are:

- The Grumbler . . . the woman who complains against her husband every now and then is one of Hell.
- The Woman Who Adorns Herself.
- The Woman Who Apes Men, Tattoos, Cuts Hair Short and Alters Nature.

The book is not an isolated attempt by a zealot, but part of a growing trend. Mernissi writes that new editions of medieval books on women, Islam, and the veil are being mass-produced by religious authorities who she sarcastically says are "concerned for the future of Islam"; these books state in their introductions that their aim is to "save Muslim society from the danger represented by change." She writes that at a time when the Arab publishing industry is in the doldrums, it is indeed surprising to find new editions of old texts in luxurious gilded bindings at astonishingly low prices. In particular, she points to the latest edition of the medieval classic by 13th-century scholar Ibn al-Jawzi (d. 1257), *Kitab ahkam al-nisa* (Stautory Provisions Concerning Women) published in Egypt.

Women such as academic Asma Barlas, author Amina Wadud, sociologist Fatima Mernissi, and activists Farzana Hassan and Raheel Raza (who led the first women-led Muslim prayer service in Canada) are vocal and courageous, but they have the powerful Islamist elite lined up against them. Two other women, authors Irshad Manji *(The Trouble with Islam Today)* and Asra Nomani *(Standing Alone in Mecca)*, have thrown a more robust challenge to the Islamic establishment, but instead of being debated on the merits of their case, the two were unfairly dismissed as attention-seeking apologists for the West. Other Muslim writers treat the subject very cautiously so as not to be seen to be offending the women who wear the hijab. They ask the tough questions that may lead to some soul-searching, but avoid answering the questions. An example of this is in Syed Osman Sher's book *Religion, God and Islam*. Sher, a retired senior civil servant of Pakistan, now settled in Canada, writes:

> Can the women now be protected from molestation simply by wearing an outer garment, or by being recognized as Muslims? . . . Are the Muslims living in the dark streets of Makkah and Medina of those days that they need protection through such contrivances? If a veil is prescribed for the streets, is it applicable also when a woman is inside a building among the family members, close relatives and friends? Does it become obligatory for a woman to cover herself from head to foot, sometimes only to bare the eyes?

The most troubling aspect of the hijab controversy is that it is not only men but also ultra-conservative Muslim women who have taken the lead in promoting the head cover or the face mask as a mandatory obligation of Islam. The defence of the hijab has become the defence of Islam, as if Islam and the hijab are one and the same. However, the defenders cannot explain why the only legitimate covering of the head has to be one that originates from among the Muslim Brotherhood followers in Egypt and Palestine, and not the head covers worn in Bangladesh or Somalia. Perhaps these young women know that what they wear on their heads is a political symbol, not religious, one that says, "I am hereby rejecting what the West stands for, and in doing so, I will also reject my own heritage, my mother's, and my grandmother's and mimic an adopted identity of an Islamist activist working for the Muslim Brotherhood."

WHY ARE WOMEN WEARING THE HIJAB?

Notwithstanding the fact that there is ample evidence—both historical and theological—that the head covering is not mandatory attire for Muslim women, the reality is that a rising tide of hijab mania has been sweeping the Muslim middle class. The question is, why are Muslim women falling for this fad when the Quran does not require them to do so?

In 2003 the Canadian Council of Muslim Women invited scholars in the fields of anthropology, history, Islamic studies, and sociology to carry out a systemic study of the issues surrounding the resurgence of the hijab in Canada.

Reem Meshal, then a PhD student at the University of Toronto, was one of the scholars who studied the reasons why women adopted or rejected the hijab. The results may provide some idea why so many women are wearing the hijab despite evidence that it is not an obligation. Meshal writes that when asked "what sources most influenced their position on *hijab*," an overwhelming number of hijabi women said the Quran or the hadith. However, when asked to identify the text that mandates the wearing of the hijab, they were not able to provide these references. Commenting on her findings, Meshal writes:

> Despite protestations to the contrary, the women in our survey had only a vague grasp of the Quranic verses that have been interpreted as prescribing *hijab*. Here are a few sample remarks made by them [*hijabi* women] concerning Islamic scriptural references to *hijab*:
> - I know it's in the Quran, but I don't know where
> - In the verses everyone talks about
> - Ask an *alim* [a Muslim scholar]

Meshal concludes that the respondents had little familiarity with Islamic texts, thus reinforcing the idea that religious knowledge for these women was primarily coming from oral transmission and the filtration of religious dogma through family and the mosque.

Meshal's report found that Canadian mosques promote the hijab as the ideal for a Muslim woman. From the mosques, the message is that Muslim women who do not wear the hijab are shameful or weak in faith. Unfortunately, women then internalize this dogma and carry it with them to educational institutions and national Muslim organizations. Meshal writes:

> The message that our informants claim is being propagated by mosques has also found its mark in national and campus organizations, which are also largely pro-*hijab* . . . One Edmonton woman reported the following incident during "Islam Awareness Week" at her campus: "[T]he women in our [Muslim campus] association were informed by the male students that any woman not wearing the *hijab* was not welcome to sit at the [information] table."

Another respondent noted the pressure she had from her family to don the hijab. "My father refused to come to my graduation ceremony if I did not wear it," the young woman told Meshal.

At times one is left scratching one's head, wondering how so many Muslims could treat the hijab as a central pillar of Islam. What would make a father boycott his daughter's graduation ceremony simply because her head was not covered? And what about the woman convicted of welfare fraud, who filed a lawsuit for damages because the police asked her to take off her hijab while she was in their custody?

Meet Souhair Khatib of Santa Ana, California. Khatib and her husband, Amro, were convicted of welfare fraud in 2006 and sentenced to three years' probation and thirty days of community service. Not at all embarrassed at her conviction for welfare fraud, Souhair Khatib told the *Los Angeles Times* that when jail officials forced her to remove her head scarf for eight hours, it caused her "extreme mental and emotional distress." She told the newspaper that wearing the hijab "is an obligation," and being without it is embarrassing because a woman's head and neck are exposed to strange men in the courtroom and to male deputies in jail. Apparently, she felt no such urge to adhere to Islam's teachings when she was committing welfare fraud. She also disclosed that while living in Lebanon, she had never covered her head, but after coming to the United States, she had ended her "sin."

The above incident also gives a rare insight into the minds of the Islamists. What went unsaid in the above story is the belief among many Islamists that laws created by mere mortals—congress and parliaments—are not applicable to Muslims. As such, it is no big deal to violate California laws against welfare fraud. But when it comes to the hijab, well that is another story, since many women mistakenly believe and are told by men that it was God who wrote the law on head coverings.

HIJAB AS A MATTER OF CHOICE?

Then there is the argument that the hijab is a matter of choice. Of course, no one can deny the right of a woman to wear a hijab, but the argument of choice espoused by non-Muslim feminist defenders of the hijab falls flat. The same Muslim women who demand the right to choose hijab refuse to accord the same right of choice to their sisters who refuse to wear it.

This double standard was evident when in 1999 I interviewed Merve Kavakci for the *Muslim Chronicle* TV show. Kavakci is the Turkish–American Islamist who was elected to the Turkish parliament, but claims she was not allowed to take her seat because she refused to take off her hijab. The Turkish government for their part said Kavakci was barred because she was an American citizen and thus was not permitted to sit in the Turkish parliament. During the interview, I empathized with her situation, but asked her: "If you demand that the Turkish parliament should not bar women MPs who wear the hijab, are you also willing to demand that the Iranian parliament not bar women who *do not* wear the hijab?" Her response startled me. She defended the Iranian parliament for making the wearing of the hijab compulsory. She said Iranian women MPs who do not wear the hijab must respect Iranian laws, which she said were Islamic. The irony of her statement was lost on her. For a second I was at a loss for words. When I pointed to her double standards, she was mildly offended, but unshaken in her belief that wearing the hijab should be enforced in Iran.

Merve Kavakci is not alone. This double standard is widespread among Islamist women. On a freezing Canadian winter morning—Saturday, January 17, 2004—I joined about a hundred young women protesting the French ban on the hijab. Even though I am opposed to the headdress as an Islamic dress requirement, I fully support the right of a woman to wear it. Some see this as a contradiction, but I don't. Exposing and opposing a religious myth does not mean I would agree to legislation banning the hijab. Myths cannot be outlawed.

The young hijabi women and their "brothers" stood shivering outside the French consulate, waving placards and raising slogans. However, as I marched in solidarity with my fellow Muslims, I couldn't help but realize that our reaction to the French initiative was not based on universal principles. The French law may have been foolish, if not outright racist, but our outrage left the door open for others to accuse Muslims of double standards.

If Muslim Canadians feel governments have no business dictating what their citizens should or should not wear, we need to apply this principle to all governments, not just the French. If Muslims considered the French law against the hijab offensive, then the Saudi and Iranian laws enforcing compulsory wearing of the hijab should also be condemned because they take away a woman's right to choose. While the French law has banned the wearing of the hijab in school, Saudi and Iranian laws bar women from appearing in public without the hijab.

In the most atrocious application of the Saudi law, fifteen schoolgirls perished in March 2002 when they were not permitted to flee their burning school in Mecca because they were not wearing so-called proper Islamic dress. Why then were these hijabi Muslim women protesting outside the French consulate, not challenging the hijab laws of Saudi Arabia and Iran? Why were they not protesting outside the Saudi and Iranian consulates? Why is it that Musim anger is directed against the French alone? Is it because Saudi Arabia and Iran are Muslim countries that claim to be true representations of the fabled Islamic State?

I asked a number of people that freezing Saturday outside the French consulate whether they were willing to stage a similar protest against Saudi Arabia and Iran. While some agreed with my rationale, many more answered my questions with empty stares or a flat refusal to have such a discussion. The fact is that the situation of Muslim women in Saudi Arabia and Iran is far more serious than the problems their sisters face in France. Yet most of the young female Muslim protesters were quite comfortable turning a blind eye to oppression in Muslim countries. It was deeply disappointing to see them oblivious to the double standard they were practising.

In an animated exchange with one articulate hijabi student from Toronto, I showed her an article by a French Muslim writer, Mouna Naim, who had written a month earlier in *Le Monde* about a thirteen-year-old Saudi girl who asked, "Why was I born a girl? This is a country of men, and I wish I was one." The *Le Monde* correspondent wrote that while many Saudi women voluntarily wear the head cover, many others "find the wearing of the garment intolerable because they see it as embodying the raft of restrictions they have to endure, which include the requirement that the slightest patch of flesh must remain covered, reducing women to formless, uniform shadows."

I asked the Toronto hijabi what she had to say to her Saudi sister. The response I got was the same lazy rhetoric I find spouted by so many Islamists. "This is nothing more than French propaganda. I think *Le Monde* is a Zionist newspaper," she said as she shrugged her shoulders and walked away to join the orchestrated chant.

In the days leading up to the Toronto demonstration outside the French consulate, there was considerable debate on the Internet about whether the French and Saudi laws were flip sides of the same argument, that is, state enforcement of citizens' dress codes. Judy Rebick, former head of Canada's National Action Committee on the Status of Women, and currently a professor at Ryerson University in Toronto, supported the protest outside the French consulate, but said demonstrating only against France without at the same time criticizing Saudi Arabia would send the wrong message. She wrote:

> I have heard similar concerns expressed by women's groups from the Middle East. If we lived in France it would be a different story, but since we are protesting the action of a foreign government, I think we should protest both sides of the problem. I think if we are going to protest against a state forcing woman not to wear the *hijab*, we should also protest forcing women to wear the *hijab*.

Rebick went on to say: "In France, it is racism and Islamophobia. In Saudi Arabia, it is fundamentalism and sexism. I think it is a good time to make the point that we are for freedom from oppression everywhere."

Muslim women advocates of the hijab would be well served if they took Rebick's suggestion to heart. Failure to apply the principle of universality, and the refusal to double-critique our positions, has seriously hurt Muslim credibility.

When we Muslims demand that others respect our rights, we need to be courageous and honest enough to recognize the oppression within our own community and speak out against it. However, for Islamists, human rights are not universal principles based on reason, rational argument, and equality of all humans. When they invoke human rights, they do so to protect the medieval misogyny they have packaged falsely as divine revelations. One does not have to imagine how these attitudes would play out in a state run by Islamists. One has to only look at the state of women inside Iran and Saudi Arabia, two alternative models of the Islamic State, one Shia, the other Sunni, at loggerheads with each other, yet unified in their conviction that women are divinely ordained to be subservient to men.

Music Ban

The Islamist obsession with head coverings is matched only by their contempt for music. This was quite evident in the summer of 2004, when SoundVision, a Chicago-based Islamist bookstore and publisher that sells Maudoodi's works and has close ties to Saudi Arabia, announced plans for what it called a "MuslimFest" in Toronto. Supposedly this was to be a festival of culture and art where Muslim youth could participate and show off their talent. However, no sooner had the "Call for Talent" notice gone out than it was clear that far from festivities, this was one more attempt by Islamists to spread their message under the cover of culture.

Three clauses buried in the "Submission Guidelines" gave away the true agenda and the misogynist nature of the event. Instead of stating unambiguously "No Women Singers Allowed," the guidelines carried a convoluted instruction that read: "Songs performance can be male voices only," leaving one wondering if recent transvestites with male voices would be permitted.

And if the message about the Islamist nature of the event was not clear enough, the guideline carried the explicit warning: "All submitted artwork must be compliant to the boundaries set by *Shariah*." The organizers of the event also made it clear that no musical instruments would be permitted at the MuslimFest except for the Saudi camel-skin drum known as the *daff*—and even that, only "if needed." To clarify what they meant by sharia-compliant art, the organizers said in a footnote: "No hand drawn faces. Silhouettes may be acceptable in some cases . . . Photographs of people will be allowed *if they* conform to the contents allowed by *shariah*."

Few people noticed the sharia clause or the no-women-allowed-to-perform instructions buried in fine print. Later, many Muslim artists would discover that their entries were rejected without explanation. Asma Arshad, a Toronto artist whose multimedia installations have been on display at the Royal Ontario Museum, wanted to enter her work, but she told *The Globe and Mail* that she didn't do so because she was uncomfortable with the "narrow interpretation of Islamic culture that excludes the depiction of faces in artwork, sitar and guitar music, and even clapping." Bewildered by the restrictions, the mother of two said, "What is un-Islamic material exactly . . . Why do they call it MuslimFest when their interpretation of Islam is so narrow?"

What was particularly disturbing about the exclusion of women at the MuslimFest was the fact that it was young women who were given the task of implementing the "no women" and "no musical instruments" policies and were made to believe that in enforcing their own second-class status, they were empowering themselves.

MuslimFest is now a regular feature in the Toronto-area Islamist calendar. However, this exclusion of women, enforced by women, did not go unchallenged. In the 2005 MuslimFest, Zuriani (Ani) Zonneveld, a Grammy Award-winning Muslim singer from Los Angeles who would like to have been part of the festival, received a cold shoulder from the organizers. She told *The Globe and Mail*, "I feel discriminated against." Zonneveld accused the

MuslimFest organizers of "misrepresenting what Islam is about." Referring to the ban on female performers, the singer asked, "Where does it say this in the Koran?"

Zonneveld disclosed to the *Globe* reporter that festival organizers SoundVision of Chicago had declined to sell her CD through their website. She wrote them a letter, complaining that they were perpetuating what she called a "male chauvinist" version of Islam.

There is a relentless and continuous attack by Islamists on all aspects of spontaneous happiness and merriment. Whether it is the destruction and burning of video rental stores in Islamabad or the ban on the sitar and guitar at Toronto's MuslimFest, the ascending forces of puritanism are depicting any expression of joy as a satanic act. Today it is not uncommon to witness a complete ban on the clapping of hands at exclusive Muslim events. Invariably, a young man will stand up at the first hint of spontaneous applause and start yelling, "*Takbeer... Takbeer*" to drown out the sound of clapping, followed by a quick reprimand from the Red Guards of the new Islamic Cultural Revolution who will descend on you like hawks to say, "Brother, it is forbidden to clap ... Allah is not pleased with the sound of clapping."

The Islamist contempt for singing and musical instruments is perplexing, considering the fact that there is not a single word of censure against music in the Quran. In fact music was, and still is, an indispensible part of Arab social life.

Islamists who despise music and singing should pay heed to Ibn Khaldun, the great Muslim philosopher and sociologist of the 14th century. In listing the hierarchy of professions, he categorized music and writing as the highest ranking crafts in a society. In his 1377 classic, *The Muqaddimah,* Ibn Khaldun said the disappearance of music from a community is one of the signs of its decline. He wrote, "The craft of singing is the last of the crafts attained to in civilization ... It is also the first to disappear from a given civilization when it disintegrates and retrogresses."

A PLEA TO MY SISTERS

Originally a reflection of modesty, the hijab has now become a political tool. All women have, at some time in their lives, chosen to wear a head cover, whether in a snowstorm or freezing rain. At times, the covering of the head, irrespective of what religion one practises, is crucial to one's survival. In the deserts of Arabia, whether one is a Muslim or a pagan, the covering of one's head and face is an absolute necessity—not just when facing a blistering sandstorm, but any time one steps out of the home into the searing sunshine.

But what is essentially attire for a particular climate and weather has been turned into a modern symbol of defiance and, at best, a show of false piety by Islamists and orthodox Muslims.

As discussed in this chapter, there is not a single reference in the Quran that obliges Muslim women to cover their hair or their face, or to lower the voice. The only verse that comes close to such a dress code (Sura 24, "The Light," verse 31) directs believing women to cover their bosoms. Yet, in the past few decades, Islamists and orthodox Muslims have made the covering of a woman's head the cornerstone of Muslim identity.

It is true that through history some Muslim women have chosen to wear the hijab for reasons of modesty. Today, however, some wear it for the opposite reason. "Young women put on a hijab and go dancing, wearing high heels and lipstick. They wear tight jeans that show their bellies," seventy-five-year-old Nawal Al-Saadawi, Egypt's leading feminist, noted recently, adding that "The *hijab* has nothing to do with moral values."

Beyond fashion, however, this supposed symbol of modesty has assumed a decidedly political and religious tenor, dominating the debate on civil liberties and religious freedoms in the West. Any opposition to the hijab is viewed as a manifestation of Islamophobia.

It should be noted that the khimar, the head scarf that pre-dated the hijab, was worn by Arab women before the Quran's stipulations on modesty of dress and demeanour. Verse 24:31 did not introduce the garment, but modified its use when it said that Muslim women should "wear their Khimar over their bosoms"—previously, breasts were left bare, although bedecked with jewellery and ornaments.

Therefore, to turn the hijab or khimar into a religious and political issue belies its original intent. Muslim women who so vociferously defend its use should consider its history before deciding whether they must wear it. Islamists have turned the hijab into the central pillar of Islam. The odd thing is that one could try as much as one wants to, but it is virtually impossible to see a single Muslim women in hijab also wearing the khimar! If these women are invoking the Quran to cover their heads, why are they not wearing the khimar as explicitly mentioned in the Quran?

Islamists consider Muslim women who do not cover their heads—the majority—as sinners or lesser Muslims. They ban the books of women who stand up to spousal abuse and depict Muslim feminists as women of questionable character. As despicable as this blackmailing is, it pales in comparison to the fact that these men in robes are using young Muslim girls as shields behind which they pursue a political agenda. Can God be fooled?

CHAPTER 14

The Islamist Agenda in the West

IT WAS A COLD January morning in 2003 as I walked through ankle-deep icy snow into the Toronto Convention Centre. I was attending a conference of Muslims arranged by groups allied to the Saudi-based World Assembly of Muslim Youth—WAMY. The freezing temperature and the frosty welcome I received at the hands of the young Islamists had not prepared me for the chilling lecture I was about to hear. The speaker, a Kuwaiti politician, said: "Western civilization is rotten from within and nearing collapse . . . it [the West] will continue to grow until an outside force hits it and you will be surprised at how quickly it falls."

The crowd burst into applause. Just sixteen months beforehand, an "outside force" had hit the New York Twin Towers on 9/11, and here was Tareq Al Suwaidan, a member of the Muslim Brotherhood from Kuwait, rubbing salt into the wounds of the West. The audience of more than two thousand young Canadian Muslims, many of them associated with the Muslim Students Association (MSA), carefully segregated into male and female sections, listened in awe. Suwaidan used elaborate charts to draw projections about the impending collapse of the West. His words were worrisome, but the response to his speech by the young Muslim Canadians was deeply troubling. They lustily cheered the Kuwaiti Islamist as he predicted the doom of the very civilization these young men and women were living in.

Why were these Muslim youth, born and educated in Canada, cheering the fall of the West? Did they not consider themselves to be part of the West?

If they did, why would they be cheering its imminent collapse and who were they expecting to carry out the "outside force" attack? How could they, as citizens of a democratic Western country, allow a Kuwaiti politician to write the obituary of the West, but also cheer him on as he did so?

Two newspaper stories that appeared soon after 9/11, one in *The Toronto Star* and the other in *The Globe and Mail*, give us an insight into the thinking of Islamist youth organizations that operate in the schools and universities of Canada and the United States.

On October 21, 2001, Richard Gwyn of *The Star* wrote in his regular column about a Friday sermon inside the York University mosque. A graduate student, acting as the imam, targeted Jews and Christians in his sermon, exhorting his congregation to segregate from non-Muslim Canadians. The student imam was quoted as saying: "We Muslims should not be friends with Jews and Christians . . . they'll never accept us . . . only Muslims will go to heaven and Jews and Christians to hell."

The York University Muslim student leader was preaching the ideology of the Egyptian Muslim Brotherhood. What was remarkable is that this ideology has found fertile soil among the radical Islamists in Canadian campuses. These true believers have succeeded in wrapping themselves in the cloak of respectability accorded to a victimized and marginalized minority. This portrait of the victim draws credence from the guilt-ridden liberal-left establishment functionaries in charge of Canada's educational institutions. Gwyn identified this Islamist ideology correctly in the student leader's tirade. He wrote:

> There is an inherent isolationist strain in Islam. It divides the entire world into Dar al Islam, the House of Submission (to God) and Dar al Harb, the House of War. Osama bin Laden repeated this concept when he declared in his highly effective video speech that this was a war between believers and those without faith.

The ink on the *Star* column had barely dried when, on October 29, 2001, Jan Wong of *The Globe and Mail* brought to light support for the militant Taliban movement by a leader of the Muslim Students Association. In a conversation over lunch with four Muslim students after a class on Islamic history at the University of Toronto, Wong asked Muhammad Basil Ahmad, then twenty-two, how he felt about the Taliban's mistreatment of women. Ahmad, vice-president of the University of Toronto's MSA, and another female student, Nora Hindy, told Wong that they *understood* why the Taliban refused to educate girls.*Justifying the Taliban's ban on women's education, the MSA leader said, "Have you seen the infrastructure? What schools are they going to go to?" His wife, a biology student at York University, sat silently beside him.

However, after defending the Taliban and citing logistic and economic reasons to justify the virtual banishment of women from Afghan society, the MSA leader in an unguarded moment revealed his true feelings. He asked his female Muslim colleagues a couple of questions that must have stunned Jan Wong: "Do you agree that women are more emotional than men? In a court of law, would you be overcome by emotion?" Instead of protesting this outrageous assumption, Hindy, who was wearing a hijab, looked at him and nodded in agreement! As if to ensure his point had not been misunderstood, Ahmad went on to say, "The Taliban bring 'law and order' to Afghanistan."

Who are these people that reject the values at the very foundation of liberal democratic society? How could one participate in student life at a leading Canadian university while holding the view that the brutality of the Taliban represents "law and order"?

After the terrorist attacks of 9/11, all of us in the West—Muslim and non-Muslim—could have used the opportunity to take a closer look at the behaviour of radical Muslim organizations that have been functioning and flourishing in the Western world. We might have used this time to begin rectifying the trend that was, and is, contributing to a reactionary and militant vision of Muslim identity in the West. Unfortunately, an incompetent President George W. Bush, himself prone to view the conflict from a religious perspective, has provided comfort to the very people who have contributed to a dysfunctional Muslim identity. At the time it went unnoticed, but when Bush aligned himself with leadership of the conservative American Islamists, instead of the mainstream Muslim community, he gave legitimacy to these conservative groups as the *de facto* voice of Islam. Within days of the attacks, Bush made a statement at the Washington National Cathedral in which he

---

* The Taliban, who were forcibly removed from power in Afghanistan, are notorious for, among other things, refusing to educate girls past the age of eight, and up to that age allowing them only to study the Quran.

condemned the terrorists, but he did this while standing beside some of the most pro-Saudi Islamists in the United States.

These men included Muzammil Siddiqui of the Islamic Society of North America (ISNA), and Nihad Awad of the Council on American-Islamic Relations (CAIR). According to Suleyman Stephen Schwartz, executive director of the Center for Islamic Pluralism, "both organizations began with financing from terror apologists—ISNA from the official, ultrafundamentalist Wahhabi sect in Saudi Arabia and CAIR from Hamas."

By June 2007, US federal prosecutors had named CAIR, ISNA, and the North American Islamic Trust (NAIT), as participants in an alleged criminal conspiracy to support a terrorist group. Each of the three groups was labelled as an "unindicted co-conspirator" in connection with a trial in Texas for five officials of a defunct charity, the Holy Land Foundation for Relief and Development. However, in October 2007 after the jury could not agree on a verdict, the judge declared a mistrial.

A court filing by the government that listed the three Islamic groups as co-conspirators gave scant details, but prosecutors described CAIR as a present or past member of "the U.S. Muslim Brotherhood's Palestine Committee and/or its organizations." The government listed ISNA and the NAIT as "entities who are and/or were members of the U.S. Muslim Brotherhood."

How could Bush and his advisers have made such a critical error in judgment? They failed to realize how much authority and influence they were bestowing on these men and these two organizations by having them present at such a pivotal point in history. And it sent a strong message to mainstream Muslims: as far as the White House is concerned, a Muslim American is considered Muslim only if he or she fits the Islamist stereotype.

Weeks after this photo op captured a grinning Bush and his uneasy, sheepish Islamist guests, *The New York Times* ran a story headlined "Stereotyping Rankles Silent, Secular Majority of American Muslims." It reported on the silent majority of American Muslims, those who have nothing to do with the self-styled Islamist leaders who purport to speak in the community's name and are able to play both sides of any issue with ease. These "liberal" or "cultural Muslims" told the *Times* that they "have been overlooked in the portrayal of Muslims after the Sept. 11 attacks, with devout Muslims regarded as the norm, even in the United States. Cameras have homed in on women in head scarfs and bearded men on their knees facing Mecca."

But the ordinary 9-to-5 Muslim has little chance of competing with the large Islamist networks in Canada and the United States who have not just the ideological but also financial support of Saudi Arabia and other Islamic countries and institutions. Saudi money has helped many Muslim causes worldwide, but support for North American Islamic organizations such as CAIR and ISNA has ensured that the Muslim narrative is dominated by the various shades of Wahhabism.

CAIR's links with Saudi Arabia rarely make news in the Western media, but occasionally they do come to light elsewhere. On July 12, 2002, the Saudi newspaper *Ain al yaqeen* carried this story in its "Briefs" section:

> The Secretary General of the Muslim World League (MWL), Dr. Abdullah Ibn Abdul Mohsin Al Turki, has stressed the necessity of promoting effective coordination among Islamic organisations in the United States of America. During a visit to the Headquarters of the Council of American-Islamic Relations (CAIR), Dr. Al Turki said: "This coordination will achieve the best results for the future of Muslims in the U.S., strengthen relations between them, and highlight the comprehensive principles of Islam." Dr. Al Turki expressed the League's readiness to offer assistance in the promotion and coordination of Islamic works, and noted that it will establish a Commission for this purpose.

The Saudi-based Muslim World League's readiness to "offer assistance" to CAIR may or may not have resulted in funding of the organization, but another Saudi individual, Prince Al-Walid Bin Talal, came up with a $500,000 donation soon after 9/11 "in order to defend Islam in the American society."

This story too would have remained unreported had it not appeared in the Saudi magazine *ArabicNews.Com,* which reported on November 19, 2001:

> The office of the Saudi prince al-Walid Bin Talal announced in a statement it issued yesterday that it offer[ed] a donation of USD half a million to finance a campaign organized by the Council of the Arab-Islamic Relations CAIR in the USA in order to defend Islam in the American society.

CAIR did not disclose this Saudi donation until the story was broken by the *Los Angeles Times,* which reported that the Saudi donation to CAIR had sparked a "blunt debate" among US Muslims, many of whom expressed fears that Saudi Arabia was trying to "co-opt" Muslim organizations.

CAIR dismissed the concerns of fellow Muslims who feared that too many mosques and organizations were becoming dependent on Saudi money, thus inhibiting them from criticizing the racist and medieval practices carried out by Riyadh under the cover of Islam. Responding to the criticism, CAIR told the *LA Times* that critics of Saudi funding were aiding "a campaign by fundamentalist Christian and conservative Jewish groups to demonise the Saudis."

If the Saudi donation to CAIR, which has branches in Canada and a number of US cities, was a matter of concern, it was small change compared to what was coming down the pipeline. On May 21, 2006, the official website of the government of the United Arab Emirates disclosed a massive investment in CAIR by the UAE minister of finance, who is also the deputy ruler of Dubai. The announcement revealed that the "Deputy Ruler of Dubai and UAE Minister of Finance and Industry has endorsed a proposal to build a property in the United States to serve as an endowment for the Council on American-Islamic Relations (CAIR)." It continued:

> The endowment will serve as a source of income and will further allow us to reinvigorate our media campaign projecting Islam and its principles of tolerance, which is based on promotion of peace, co-existence and dialogue among various religions and cultures," said Nihad Awad, Executive Director of CAIR, following a meeting here on Saturday between Sheikh Hamdan and representatives of the North American organisation.

The exact amount CAIR will receive from the endowment is not certain. Suffice it to say that CAIR won't have to worry about its core funding for some time to come. The Al-Maktoum Foundation of Dubai put up more than $978,000 for the property that is now the head office of CAIR at 453 New Jersey Avenue S.E. in Washington. While the foundation holds the rights to sell it, CAIR is said to manage the property and collect rents from other tenants in the multi-storey red-brick building.

At about the time CAIR and the Dubai deputy ruler were negotiating the funding of CAIR's operations in North America, the former president of CAIR's Canada operations was praising Dubai in an op-ed piece for *The Globe and Mail*. In the article, titled "Don't Be Fearful of Dubai," Sheema Khan gave a sanitized view of the Gulf monarchy. Presenting it as a model to the world, she wrote:

> Dubai is a mixture of the old, and definitely, the new. It combines the business acumen of Hong Kong, the discipline of Singapore, and the best of Arab hospitality. This city-state is open to the world, and the world has come flocking.

Dubai a symbol of Arab hospitality? Perhaps Jenin in Palestine or Cairo's Rawd al-Faraj district, but referring to Dubai as a symbol of Arab hospitality is insulting to Arabs. Dubai is a city built by its Indo-Pakistani workers living in near slave-like conditions, and it is teeming with prostitutes from Central Asia in brothels run by the Russian mafia. But all of this is swept into the shadows of the tall skyscrapers. The city-state may excite visitors from the West like Sheema Khan, but its Muslim slave-labourers may not share her views. Dubai is the place where little Muslim boys from Bangladesh and Pakistan are used as camel jockeys, risking death and injury, while sheikhs in flowing robes charm their Western guests with so-called Arab hospitality. Praising Dubai's policies on immigrants, CAIR's former president had the audacity to mock Canada and offer Dubai as the alternative. Khan wrote: "Canadians fearful of immigrants with 'strange' attire and values should look at Dubai, where immigrants form 85 per cent of the population. New arrivals need not wear indigenous attire (*abayas* or *chadors*), nor are they screened for their values." What Khan failed to disclose in her favourable travelogue on Dubai was the fact that this "85 per cent of the population" of immigrants and new arrivals were treated as third-class people with absolutely no citizenship rights.

In contrast to *The Globe and Mail* piece, the *Asia Times* of Hong Kong carried a more realistic and honest article on Dubai. Pepe Escobar, the author of the piece, went to the heart of the Dubai economy, which is being touted as a model for all Arab countries by corporate America, but which Escobar refers to as a model that "spells out an apolitical, consumer-mad, citizenship-free society," built on "post-modern slavery." He wrote that the Dubai social pyramid is "unforgiving," and that:

> At the base is the average construction worker, inevitably South Asian, either Pakistani or Indian. He's invisible. But he and his fellow workers now comprise an astonishing 80% of the UAE's population. Human Rights Watch has repeatedly complained that this archetypal construction worker is never treated like a human being. But the UAE power structure couldn't care less. He works a minimum of 12 hours a day in [temperatures of] up to 50 degrees, with a half-hour break, six days a week, and earns no more than $150 a month. He lives in a camp, four and sometimes as many as 12 to a 15-square-meter room lost in the dreary al-Quoz industrial suburb. . . . He has no rights. Trade unions are banned. If he speaks up, he's instantly deported.

Escobar went on to write, "Racism in Dubai—as in the US south—is pervasive, but off-limits to discussion." He describes the country as "the new medievalism," where "unelected male elders of a single ruling family may control it with no opposition . . . but the Emirates' medieval feudalism somehow has managed to impress global perceptions as the most 'progressive' state in the Middle East."

CAIR is not the only Islamic organization that has been receiving monies from Saudi Arabian sources. Another recipient of this largesse is ISNA—the

Indianapolis-based Islamic Society of North America that has a large chapter in Canada. News of Saudi funding for Canadian Islamic organizations was first broken by Robert Fife in the *Ottawa Citizen* in July 2004.

In a news story titled "Saudis Fund Radicals in Canada," Fife reported:

> A task force report on terrorist financing by the Council on Foreign Relations, which included former White House counter-terrorist chief Richard Clarke and David Cohen, the CIA's former director of operations, says U.S. strategic interests are threatened by Saudi efforts to extend its brand of extremist Islam to North America and elsewhere. . . .
>
> The task force said Saudi Arabia has spent hundreds of millions of dollars to fund 210 Islamic centres and 1,359 mosques around the world, including in Canada.
>
> It cites an official Saudi report in 2002 that stated "King Fahd donated $5-million US for the cost of an Islamic centre in Toronto, Canada, in addition to $1.5-million US annually to run the facility."
>
> The Saudi government's official Web site also states that King Fahd provided funds to the Calgary mosque, the Ottawa mosque, and the Islamic centre in Quebec.
>
> Toronto has numerous Islamic centres, and the Saudi embassy in Ottawa refused to say which received millions of dollars from King Fahd.

The *Ottawa Citizen* said it had made "numerous telephone calls to Islamic organizations in Toronto," but had still not been able to find out which was the Saudi-financed centre. Further, Gamal Solaiman, imam of the Ottawa mosque, could not tell the paper how much money the Saudis had given his mosque, and the Calgary mosque's Hussein Paiman, whose imam was a professor at Saudi Arabia's King Saud University, told the *Citizen* he did not know how much the Saudis had contributed.

Sheikh Syed Bukhari, who runs the Islamic Centre in Quebec (located in Liberal leader Stephane Dion's riding) and is a graduate of Medina University in Saudi Arabia,* also could not discuss the Saudi funding with the *Citizen*.

The mystery of the Toronto-area mosque that had received $5 million in Saudi funding remained unsolved for more than a year.

The fact is that the monies were received by the Canada branch of ISNA. Islamic ethics would have dictated that ISNA reveal its Saudi funding to the

---

* The Medina Islamic University is the pre-eminent centre of learning for strictly orthodox Wahhabism. Its graduates today dominate the world Islamist movement and influence events and thought in Islamic academic institutions and organizations as far apart as McGill University in Montreal and the Islamic University in Kuala Lumpur.

media, but it didn't until two reporters from *The Globe and Mail* broke the story after a lengthy investigation. In November 2005, Omar Al Akkad and Marina Jimenez finally identified ISNA as being the mystery mosque that had received the funds. The two reporters wrote:

> ISNA is also one of a few facilities in Canada that is funded by the Islamic Development Bank [IDB], which is based in Saudi Arabia.
>
> In 2002, the Saudi Ministry of Culture and Information announced that King Fahd gave $5-million (U.S.) and an annual grant of $1.5-million to the Islamic Centre in Toronto. (The Islamic Centre of Canada is also housed at ISNA.) This year, the IDB announced a $275,000 grant to ISNA's high school, as well as a scholarship program.
>
> The IDB funding—touted on ISNA's website, although officially denied by a society spokeswoman—is of concern to some Canadian Muslims who advocate for a secular government. They worry about the potential ideological parity between the society and its funder.

The spokesperson for ISNA Canada, Kathy Bullock, acknowledged that ISNA had received money from the Saudi-based Islamic Development Bank (IDB). She said there was no pressure to follow Wahhabism as a result of the IDB money. "It is like a grant," she said. ISNA later claimed that since the money came from the IDB, it could not be called Saudi funding. It is interesting to note that the IDB, which has its headquarters in Jeddah, says its mandate is to "to foster the economic development and social progress of member countries and Muslim communities in non-Muslim countries in accordance with the principles of Shari'ah (Islamic Law)."

ISNA is not alone in trying to mask its Saudi funding. In October 2006, *Toronto Star* reporter Heba Aly wrote about another mosque that initially denied it was the recipient of Saudi funding, but when presented with the evidence, acknowledged such monies.

When the *Star* approached the Scarborough Muslim Association about foreign funding, management committee member Saleh Hafejee first said there had been none since about 1998, when the Scarborough Muslim Association mosque accepted $100,000 from a wealthy Saudi individual. But the mosque's president, Yakub Hatia, later confirmed what the *Star* had found on an IDB website—that the mosque had accepted a $270,000 grant in 2006 to build an Islamic school.

Many Muslims across the West are deeply angered that their mosque leadership employs such deception to hide overseas funding. The lack of transparency has always been a hallmark of the Islamist culture. An authoritarian streak is the defining characteristic of the Islamist culture, but the lengths that Islamists have gone to deceive their critics and confuse governments is one of their singular achievements. Counting on the sincere efforts by many governments in the West to embrace diversity, Islamists have draped themselves in the garb of multiculturalism and diversity to position their agenda as mainstream. This is nothing more than hypocrisy masquerading as diversity.

Despite the evidence that the Saudis are funding Islamists in Europe and North America, the West's embrace of the Islamists does not stop. Time and time again political leaders in the United States, Canada, and Britain have aligned themselves with the ultra-orthodox in the Muslim community. Instead of working with the vast majority of Muslims in the West, whose lifestyle is totally in step with that of Westerners in general, Bush and former prime ministers Tony Blair and Paul Martin kept catering to and accommodating the militants and the mullahs.

Just after the 7/7 bombings in London in 2005, Canadian prime minister Paul Martin decided to reach out to Canada's Muslim community and a meeting was hurriedly arranged. Guess who came to dinner? Nineteen men—heads of mosques and imams—most in full mosque regalia, with not a single woman present. Did this mean the prime minister did not consider women as Muslim? Or was he advised that the only good Muslim is a bearded Muslim? When reporters asked him about the absence of women as well as secular and liberal Muslims in his list of invitees, Martin was tongue-tied. It seemed he realized his mistake, but could not get around to admitting that the word "Muslim" had conjured up the image of a bearded, turbaned cleric, so that is whom he decided to invite.

Political correctness and liberal guilt over historic colonial abuse in the Muslim world can easily blind Western leadership and society to the anti-social agenda of radical Islam. The unspoken policy is to keep blinders on and mouths shut in the name of cultural relativism. This is a mistake. To redress the wrongs of colonialism and imperialism, the West can take a myriad constructive steps, including withdrawing support for the despots and kings it props up and opening Western markets to goods and services from the developing world. But capitulating to Islamists camouflaged as moderates and validating them up as genuine representatives of the West's Muslims is simply repeating the mistake of propping up the Saudis as the legitimate spokesmen of Muslims worldwide.

Since 9/11, the modus operandi for those Islamist individuals and organizations who want to manipulate Western pluralism has been to pass themselves off as moderates. They use the language of left-wing activists; they sprinkle their language with references to the World Bank, social justice, debt relief, poverty, and that key word "equity" to get well-meaning leftist liberals on side. And it has worked. What you see now is an unholy alliance between conservative Muslim organizations and the progressive liberal movement—two sets of ideologies that are diametrically opposed on every social issue. But they are now, since 9/11, bedfellows.

Organizations like the MSA, which acts as a farm team, cultivating future members for ISNA and CAIR, are far more sophisticated than naive Westerners are ready to acknowledge. These aren't just makeshift student organizations or community groups holding bake sales and cute cultural festivals. These are well-oiled, foreign-inspired, politically driven machines that have their hooks in every corner of Western society. It is not a coincidence that so many Muslims who were just average American teenagers in high school get recruited by radicals and end up emerging from universities with a deep-rooted hatred for the country that has been their home all their lives.

There are more then two hundred MSA chapters on college and university campuses throughout the United States and Canada. Their public online mandate suggests that they are a non-political organization devoted to the development of Islam for students in North America. They claim no links to foreign governments. However, MSA and its partner ISNA have been closely associated with Saudi Arabia from as far back as the 1960s, when both groups were first established. In an essay on Wahhabism, Hamid Algar of the University of California–Berkeley writes:

> Some Muslim student organizations have functioned at times as Saudi-supported channels for the propagation of Wahhabism abroad, especially in the United States . . . Particularly in the 1960s and 1970s; no criticism of Saudi Arabia would be tolerated at the annual conventions of the MSA. The organization has, in fact, consistently advocated theological and political positions derived from radical Islamist organizations, including the Muslim Brotherhood and Jamaati Islam.

Algar goes on to write that the MSA has played a major role in spreading Wahhabism. At every Friday prayer sermon, he says, the many local chapters of the MSA would have large stacks of publications from the Mecca-based World Muslim League at hand—in both English and Arabic. "Although the

MSA progressively diversified its connections with Arab states, official approval of Wahhabism remained strong."

In the United States, the MSA has been linked to charities such as the Holy Land Foundation, Global Relief, and the Benevolence Foundation—all three have been investigated by the FBI for links to terrorism, and all three have been shut down. The MSA's international links to Islamist figures and the Muslim Brotherhood have been widely reported. In 1995, Youssef Qaradawi, the Qatar-based imam who is widely seen as a spokesman for the Muslim Brotherhood movement, attended an Islamic conference in Ohio. In a speech in which he said, "We will conquer Europe, we will conquer America, not through the sword but through dawah,"* the imam credited the MSA as being one of the groups created by the exiled Muslim Brotherhood leaders from Egypt who came to the United States to "fight the seculars and the Westernized."

The Washington Post reported on the third anniversary of 9/11 that "the MSA—using $21 million raised in part from Qaradawi, banker Nada and the emir of Qatar—opened a headquarters complex built on former farmland in suburban Indianapolis. With over 150 chapters, the MSA is one of the nation's largest college groups."

Stephen Schwartz of the Center for Islamic Pluralism goes further. In his June 2003 testimony to the US Senate's Subcommittee on Terrorism and Homeland Security, he said:

> Shia and other non-Wahhabi Muslim community leaders estimate that 80 percent of American mosques out of a total ranging between an official estimate of 1,200 and an unofficial figure of 4,000 to 6,000 are under Wahhabi control. . . . Wahhabi control over mosques means control of property, buildings, appointment of imams, training of imams, content of preaching including faxing of Friday sermons from Riyadh, Saudi Arabia, and of literature distributed in mosques and mosque bookstores, notices on bulletin boards, and organizational and charitable solicitation. . . . The main organizations that have carried out this campaign are the Islamic Society of North America (ISNA), which originated in the Muslim Students' Association of the U.S. and Canada (MSA), and the Council on American–Islamic Relations (CAIR).

---

* *Dawah:* As noted earlier, this is the Arabic word for "invitation." It has a political connotation that means aggressively converting the non-Muslim world to Islam. In fact, dawah is a necessary prerequisite to the declaration of jihad.

Both in Canada and the United States, CAIR has pretended to be a civil rights organization and has had some success in linking up with Amnesty International, the American Civil Liberties Union, and other human rights organizations in its effort to position itself. However, CAIR's concept of human rights does not appear to be based on the acceptance of universal human rights and seems to be restricted to the human rights of Islamists alone or Muslims whom CAIR considers "authentic." Thus, while CAIR was on the frontlines of the fight to get justice for Maher Arar, who was wrongfully deported to Syria where he was tortured, CAIR refused to seek the freedom of another Muslim Canadian, Muhammad Essam Ghoneim el-Attar, who was being tortured in Egypt.

El-Attar was just like Maher Arar. Arar was Arab, and so was el-Attar; Arar was a Muslim, and so was el-Attar; Arar was arrested by a dictatorial Arab government, and so was el-Attar. Arar said he was tortured, and so was el-Attar. So what was the difference? While Arar was straight, el-Attar was gay. Because of that, not a single Muslim organization other than the Muslim Canadian Congress spoke about el-Attar. It was no surprise for me that Muslim organizations would refuse to advocate for a gay man, but the silence of the left and mainstream human rights groups was disturbing.

On February 14, 2007, an event was held in Ottawa to honour Maher Arar and his wife, Monia Mazigh. Few events in Ottawa have attracted such a phalanx of human-rights activists rubbing shoulders with Muslim glitterati. Imam Aly Hindi chatted with Stephane Dion, the leader of the Liberal Party. NDP leader Jack Layton mingled with the mosque establishment. Speaker after speaker spoke about the courage of Mazigh and the injustice inflicted on Arar. They also denounced the continued detention of Egyptian nationals Mahmoud Jabalah and Hasan Mrie in Canada under Canada's security certificates.

But while these politicians apologized to one Arab Canadian who had suffered torture, they were careful not to mention the name of another Arab Canadian who was enduring a similar experience in Egypt. As our politicians denounced the confessions forced out of Arar under duress, another Canadian Arab was going through a similar ordeal. But not one speaker that night made mention of this Canadian languishing in an Egyptian prison. It wasn't as if they didn't know about this new victim of torture: newspapers had carried the story on the front page for some time.

Thirty-one-year-old Muhammad Essam Ghoneim el-Attar had been arrested as he flew into Cairo from Canada on January 1, 2007. Authorities in Egypt claimed he had confessed that he was an Israeli spy working for Mossad in Toronto. El-Attar may or may not be an Israeli spy, but the fact remains that he is an Arab Canadian, just like Maher Arar, who had "confessed" to a crime, just like Maher Arar, likely after being tortured, just like Maher Arar.

I wrote to CAIR asking them why they had not raised the case of Muhammad el-Attar. They had no answer. It seems for CAIR only the human rights of Islamists matter. If a gay Muslim ended up in jail, I guess some would argue this must be God's way of punishing the man for being homosexual. Why would Islamists intercede on behalf of a man deemed to be a sinner? He could rot in jail for all they care.

The Islamist agenda works because too many decent, well-meaning, otherwise thoughtful and genuinely welcoming politicians who wear the liberal or left stripe of politics are gullible and naive when subject to the aggressive tactics of the Islamists. This fear of the aggressive Islamist agenda and the submissive response to it by the mainstream, motivated eleven Canadian academics and activists with roots in Iran, Iraq, Palestine, Pakistan, and Bangladesh to write a joint opinion piece in *The Toronto Star*:

> A curtain of fear has descended on the intelligentsia of the West, including Canada. The fear of being misunderstood as Islamophobic has sealed their lips, dried their pens and locked their keyboards. . . . Canada's writers, politicians and media have imposed a frightening censorship on themselves, refusing to speak their minds, thus ensuring that the only voices being heard are that of the Muslim extremists and the racist right.

The signatories included Jehad Aliweiwi, former executive director of the Canadian Arab Federation; El-Farouk Khaki, then secretary general of the Muslim Canadian Congress; Munir Pervaiz, a PEN Canada director; Professors Amir Hassanpour and Shahrzad Mojab (University of Toronto), Tareq Ismael (U of Calgary), Haideh Moghissi and Saeed Rahnema (York U); and myself. We were responding to the aftermath of the Danish cartoons controversy,* which was used by Islamists around the world to fan fanaticism to extraordinary levels, leading to many deaths and countless death threats.

---

* On September 30, 2005, the Danish newspaper *Jyllands-Posten* published twelve editorial cartoons, mocking Prophet Muhammad. While Danish Islamist organizations objected to the depiction, by holding public protests, the protests fizzled out until many months later when two Danish imams went on a tour of the Middle East and whipped up a frenzy. That resulted in world-wide protests by Islamists, and led to hundreds of deaths.

In the article we described how, "emboldened by the free rein" they had come to enjoy, Muslim extremists and their supporters had turned out at Queen's Park in Toronto to hear speakers promise such violence as drowning Danes "in their own blood," while in Pakistan a Muslim woman was shown carrying a sign reading GOD BLESS HITLER. We noted that a Muslim cleric had offered a $1-million reward for the cartoonist's murder, and we made mention of the burning of embassies, the desecration of churches, and the hundreds of deaths that had taken place in Muslim countries since the controversy had erupted.

The authors of the article pointed out:

> For too long the media have created an image that portrays communities from the Muslim world as a monolith entity, best represented by extremists. . . . It is time for Canadians to stand up for the hard-won democratic values that the Muslim extremists oppose. By rejecting the agenda of the extremists, Canada's intelligentsia would be standing shoulder to shoulder with the Muslims and secular individuals from the region who reject both Islamophobia and Islamism. Islamism is not the new revolutionary movement against global forces of oppression, as a section of the left in this country erroneously perceives.

The authors brought to attention the agenda of "the religious right and autocracies in the so-called Islamic world [that] are united in their call for passing legislation to make any discussion on religion a criminal offence. This, at a time when many writers in Jordan, Iran, Yemen, Pakistan and Afghanistan are rotting in jails, facing charges of apostasy and blasphemy."

We urged Canada's politicians and intellectuals to "stand up for freedom of expression. Our democratic values, including free speech, should not be compromised under the garb of fighting hate. To fight Islamophobia and racism, we do not need to sacrifice free speech and debate."

Whether Canada's political leaders respond to such a call has yet to be seen, but Islamists have certainly not been backing down from aggressively occupying the Muslim podium and trying to deceive these politicians.

One aspect of the Islamist agenda in Canada and Britain, but less so in the United States, is to keep pushing the mainstream community with outlandish demands in the hope of provoking a racist backlash. This has succeeded. In Ottawa, the lobbying by Islamist groups is relentless, putting politicians of all stripes on the defensive as they fear they might be labelled racist or Islamophobic if they criticize Islamists. The summer of 2007 in Quebec will long be remembered for its debate about "reasonable accommodation" to discuss issues of immigrants and religious minorities. While most Québécois were asking for immigrants to adopt and adapt to their new homelands and respect the separation of religion and state, rednecks and racists came out of the woods in a bizarre display of xenophobia and hate. Instead of focusing on the Islamist agenda of segregation and sharia, the debate shifted to cover the bigotry of the racists. The Islamists had won.

The Islamists have also made impressive allies with a section of the left. One of the most detailed analyses of this new-found love affair between the left and the Islamists has been penned by Fred Halliday, an authoritative scholar on Middle Eastern affairs and a professor of international relations at the London School of Economics. In an article for *Open Democracy* titled "The Left and the Jihad," Halliday asks: "The left was once the principal enemy of radical Islamism. So how did old enemies become new friends?"

Halliday acknowledges that the intervention in Afghanistan and the invasion of Iraq by the United States generated considerable sympathy for Islamist groups from far beyond the Muslim world. However, he notes that "there are signs of a far more developed and politically articulated accommodation in many parts of the world between Islamism as a political force and many groups of the left." He writes:

> The latter show every indication of appearing to see some combination of al-Qaida, the Muslim Brotherhood, Hezbollah, Hamas, and (not least) Iranian president Mahmoud Ahmadinejad as exemplifying a new form of international anti-imperialism that matches—even completes—their own historic project. This putative combined movement may be in the eyes of such leftist groups and intellectual trends hampered by "false consciousness," but this does not compromise the impulse to "objectively" support or at least indulge them.

Halliday concedes that Islamists themselves are a diverse political movement and that the movement in its current form is indeed opposed to the United States, but he says to remain there omits a deeper, crucial point: that, "long before the Muslim Brotherhood, the jihadis and other Islamic militants were attacking 'imperialism'—they were attacking and killing the left and acting across Asia and Africa as the accomplices of the west."

In July 2002, Professor Khaled Abou El-Fadl of the University of California at Los Angeles (UCLA) wrote in *The New York Times*: "Moderate Muslim intellectuals have been combating continued and well-funded efforts of Saudi Arabia to regain ground for its Puritan Islam–Wahhabism." That statement accurately reflects the situation today in both North America and Europe.

CAUGHT BETWEEN THE US HAMMER AND THE ISLAMIST ANVIL

Back at the Toronto Convention Centre on that cold January morning, I was deeply troubled by the hostility towards the West and the thunderous applause of the young audience. With friends like these, did Muslims need enemies, I wondered. All I could do was muster the courage and stage a polite walkout.

As I made my lonely walk through the convention hall, I reflected on this growing chasm between Western civilization and its young Muslim citizens. I realized it was having two dangerous effects. First, it highlighted the failure of the West to provide a safe space for Muslim youth. Second, it revealed the success that Islamist Muslims have had both in positioning the West as essentially evil and in the incessant incitement that goes on at mosques and supposed conferences.

In the words of British author Tariq Ali, today's Muslims are caught between the "hammer" of American military adventurism and the "anvil" of Islamist extremism. Many Muslims find themselves hostages of an Islamist leadership that feeds on their genuine grievances, but offers them little hope of success or any chance of escape, except in the hereafter.

The US–Islamist alliance is best detailed by Robert Dreyfuss in his book *Devil's Game: How the United States Helped Unleash Fundamentalist Islam*. Dreyfuss, who is an investigative journalist and whose work appears in *The Nation* and *Rolling Stone*, exposes the links between right-wing and hard-line elements in the US government and fundamentalist groups in the Middle East. He discloses how Citibank helped create the Islamic banking system that would become the financial foundation of violent anti-Western Islamism. He quotes top US military and intelligence officials to give the reader an alarming insight into the shadowy origins of a US foreign policy strategy of strengthening Islamists as way of combating communism.

Zbigniew Brzezinski, President Carter's national security adviser, is quoted as saying, when asked in 1996 if he regretted supporting the Islamic fundamentalists: "What is more important to the history of the world? The Taliban or the collapse of the Soviet empire? Some stirred-up Muslims or the liberation of Central Europe and the end of the Cold War?" This was the same Brzezinski who had stood at the Khyber Pass in Pakistan in 1980 and exhorted the Islamists to go forth and commit jihad.

In one chapter on the war in Afghanistan, Dreyfuss describes how the United States deliberately channelled money to the "nastier, more fanatic types of mujahideen" in Afghanistan in order to do the most damage to Soviet troops. This included Gulbuddin Hekmatyar, Pakistan's and the CIA's favourite mujahid who is known to have skinned his prisoners alive and who approved the practice of throwing acid in the faces of women who did not wear the burka. Today, Hekmatyar and his forces are back in reckoning, fighting side by side with the Pakistan-based Taliban against Canadian and British troops serving the International Security Assistance Force's (ISAF's) NATO troops.

MASQUERADING AS ANTI-IMPERIALISTS

When US jets bombed Yugoslavia in the 1990s, the same Islamists who now march to denounce the United States were out celebrating in the streets of Europe and the United States. For the Islamists, US military intervention in a foreign land was not a problem. Their objections to US imperial ambitions came into play only when those ambitions affected Muslim lands. Thus, throughout the war in Vietnam, the large Muslim organizations that dot the US urban landscape were completely absent from the anti-war marches. Ordinary American and European Muslims participated wholeheartedly in the anti-Vietnam War movement, but nary an imam or sheikh was visible during the 1960s. The Islamist leadership that today sprinkles its terminology with anti-imperialist speak has no answer when asked: "Where were you during the Vietnam War? Where were you during the civil rights movement? Where were you when Reagan invaded Grenada?" In 1985, when the Sudanese government hanged renowned Islamic scholar Muhammad Mahmud Taha as Muslim Brotherhood vigilantes cheered, not even a single letter to the editor from a Muslim leader appeared in any Toronto newspaper. I doubt if any other Western newspaper carried op-ed pieces by Muslims protesting the outrage.

Today, Islamists in North America and Europe are playing multiple roles; some having falsely appropriated the "moderate" label, while others have stuck to spreading their contempt for anything that has any semblance of a modern secular democratic institution. The prime target of both variations of these Islamists is the ordinary Muslim, who refuses to be bound by the mosque establishment or by the sectarianism and medieval obscurantism that governs the day-to-day life of the mullahs and imams. Any society that ensures a semblance of equality of all citizens and justice, and which is based on laws created by mere mortals, is an affront to the religious beliefs of most

Islamists. For them, no laws made by parliamentarians are acceptable unless they are scrutinized and vetted by self-anointed Islamic scholars. In fact, what the Islamists look up to is the Iranian model of the ayatollahs where laws and even election candidates can be vetoed by the *velayat-e faqih*—the Supreme Leader, answerable only to God.

Islamists and the clerical establishment they represent are deeply fearful of secular democratic societies, where their grip on individual Muslims and the mosque congregations would come undone. In societies such as Iran and Saudi Arabia, social, cultural, and feudal pressures force even the most secular Muslim to pay deference, if not homage to the imam, sheikh or ayatollah; Muslims in countries such as India, South Africa, the Caribbean, and in North America and Europe, are less likely to toe the party line of the medieval theocrats. This is why an attempt was made to introduce sharia law in Canada, the defeat of which has left the Islamist establishment deeply embittered against the small group of Muslims who exposed the truth behind what was being deceitfully presented as a docile family law arbitration issue.

THE TORONTO TERROR SUSPECTS

The June 2006 arrests in Canada and the alleged role of young Muslim men in a terror cell may not have been inspired by the fiery rhetoric of a visiting Kuwaiti scholar. But if the RCMP allegations are true, the actions of this terror group definitely have roots in the cult of hate and death that is glorified by a tiny segment of Muslim clerics. While the overwhelming majority of Canada's Muslims were stunned by the discovery of alleged terrorists in their own backyard, few can honestly deny that they had not seen this coming. Fewer still were willing to confront and expose the cancer destroying our future as Muslim citizens of a Western country.

Frustrated at the rumours circulating in the community that the busting of the alleged terror cell was a conspiracy against Islam, I wrote in the *Toronto Star*:

> Enough is enough. Muslims cannot go on behaving as if everything is normal. We cannot sit still while a fascist cult of Islamic supremacy takes over our mosques. We cannot afford it any more because we risk losing a generation to the temptation of simple answers to life's challenges; a solution that states that life on Earth is meaningless because it is temporary and therefore not worthy of sustaining, not worthy of enjoying. Muslims need to recognize that a mosque is not the places for politics; it is a place

of worship. . . . Let us tell our imams to keep their politics to themselves and not to stain our religion by using the divine texts to score political points and promote terror.

But other Canadian Muslims disagreed. In a live debate on Canada's TVO station, Toronto imam Ali Hindy clearly insinuated that the entire RCMP operation that led to the June 2006 arrests was being conducted to justify the continuing war in Iraq and Afghanistan. He referred to the arrests as "show business" and stated sarcastically, the "show must go on." During the discussion, Imam Hindy claimed he knew eight of the accused. According to his analysis, the suspects may have been involved in military training to fight a jihad overseas. He went on to say that when young Muslim men come to him asking to go overseas to fight, he discourages them and tells them to fight their jihad "here."

Flabbergasted, TV host Paula Todd asked him, "Why? What do you mean?" Cornered, he took refuge—as so many Muslim clerics who encourage jihad do when trapped—in philosophy: "By jihad, I mean the inner jihad . . . "

This discussion on TVO and other TV networks in Europe and North America are also significant because it is only in non-Muslim institutions that Muslims can debate from adversarial positions. There is hardly a mosque in Canada, Britain, or the United States where Muslims with opposing views can debate anything political, social, or theological. The doors of debate are shut by the cement of orthodoxy. Only doublespeak and hypocrisy are allowed to flourish. It seems that as long as Muslims can find someone else to blame for our ills, the problem is seen as resolved.

While the rest of the world gallops into the future, harnessing new technologies, debating globalization, fighting poverty, working towards the emancipation of women, confronting diseases, and developing novel ideas to foster learning, the one billion Muslims are lagging in all respects. Socio-economic, political, cultural, scientific, and historical growth is often minimal and in some countries regressing. Muslims have been led to believe by their leaders that the panacea to their pain is not a historical correction in their view of the world and their role in the emergence of multi-ethnic, multi-religious nation-states, but in turning to the past as their path to the future.

The Muslim leadership today can best be compared to someone driving in a car rally with their eyes fixed on the rear-view mirror. As they crash into one obstacle after another, instead of changing their driving habits and focusing on what lies ahead, they believe the obstacles they crash into have been deliberately placed in their path by the "enemies of Islam"—the West, the Jews, the communists, the atheists, the Hindus, the banking world, the entertainment industry, and the rest of what is perceived as the hedonistic "Islam hating" infidel universe.

Instead of trying to understand and analyze the challenges of poverty, underdevelopment, illiteracy, racism, and disease that Muslims face alongside other peoples of the developing world, Muslim leaders have craftily framed their problem as essentially a Muslim versus Non-Muslim conflict. Inside the Muslim majority countries, promotion of this false dichotomy has helped the mosque establishment tighten their grip on the prevailing Muslim narrative and project themselves as the guardians of the faith and true patriots of Islam. The so-called US War on Terror has permitted them to raise a frenzy of fear that has stifled any attempt to challenge their version of Islam and the crimes that are being perpetrated in the name of Allah.

Faint voices of protest, whether from writers like the Syrian poet Ali Ahmad Said Asbar, better known as Adonis; Egyptian feminist Nawwal El Saadawi; or academics like Pervez Hoodbhoy of Pakistan and Farish Noor of Malaysia, are drowned out in a chorus of denunciations, where such dissent is depicted as reflective of links to neo-conservatives in the United States. The same strategy has been applied in North America and Europe, where any Muslim speaking out against Islamic extremism and the worldwide jihadi movement has been threatened and denounced with the much-misused labels of neo-con or neo-liberal.

The eloquent left-wing thinker and activist Tariq Ali has taken a more cautious approach in condemning the Islamists. Despite his contempt for what Islamists stand for, he blames the United States for creating the conditions in which he says these "Islamo-anarchists" have found strength. In his now famous "Letter to a Young Muslim," written in the aftermath of the 9/11 tragedy, Tariq Ali goes to great lengths to explain why, despite being an atheist, he marches in solidarity with the Muslim community, while rejecting the ideology of the Islamists. For example, in a stinging rebuke of the wearing of the burka or the niqab, he talks about a "shrouded corpse."

Tariq Ali has been a thorn in the side of US foreign policy since the Vietnam War, but he too dismissed the notion that the attack on the Twin Towers was a justified response to US actions in the Muslim world. He wrote:

But none of this justifies what took place. What lies behind the vicarious pleasure is not a feeling of strength, but a terrible weakness. The people of Indo-China suffered more than any Muslim country at the hands of the US government. They were bombed for 15 whole years and lost millions of their people. Did they even think of bombing America? Nor did the Cubans or the Chileans or the Brazilians. The last two fought against the US-imposed military regimes at home and finally triumphed.

Responding to a young British Muslim who challenged his atheism during an anti-war march, Tariq Ali challenged his young British Islamist critic in the letter, which he included in *The Clash of Fundamentalisms:*

> What do the Islamists offer? A route to a past, which, mercifully for the people of the seventh century, never existed. If the "Emirate of Afghanistan" is the model for what they want to impose on the world, then the bulk of Muslims would rise up in arms against them. Don't imagine that either Osama or Mullah Omar represent the future of Islam. It would be a major disaster for the culture we both share if that turned out to be the case. Would you want to live under those conditions? Would you tolerate your sister, your mother or the woman you love being hidden from public view and only allowed out shrouded like a corpse?

After the 7/7 bombing in London, Tariq Ali referred to the suicide bombers as "Islamo-anarchists," whom he said were small in number, "but whose reach is deadly." In justifying the use of this new terminology to describe Britain's jihadi fringe, Ali wrote, "I coined Islamo-anarchism to counter the 'Islamo-fascism' of American and Brit neo-cons." Ali's effort to create a new terminology is just one indication of the tough task facing many leftists who abhor the Islamic religious right, but in their criticism do not wish to be seen as serving the interests of the White House. Other leftists, such as George Galloway and Ken Livingstone, have thrown caution to the wind and have swung so far to the Islamist cause that, unlike Tariq Ali, they seem to have become the literal mouthpieces of Sheikh Qaradawi and the Muslim Brotherhood.

In academic circles, no one has been more consistently critical of the Islamist agenda than the UCLA's Kuwaiti-born Professor Khaled Abou El-Fadl. The author of numerous books, and a scholar of Islam with a brilliant mind and a sharp wit, he has single-handedly been demolishing the Islamist agenda from an Islamic perspective. In 2005, El-Fadl wrote in his book *The Great Theft: Wrestling Islam from the Extremists,* "To win this very real war that has done inestimable damage to so many Muslims and to the truth of the Islamic faith, it is absolutely imperative that moderates declare a counter-jihad against puritan heresy."

In one of his rare visits outside California, El-Fadl addressed a conference of Muslim women in Toronto in 2002 in which he lambasted the Muslim community and its leadership. I was one of the few men in the room and was struck by his frank discourse. El-Fadl visibly stunned the women when he said:

Our Muslim scholars must be the most dull and the most boring products that humanity has known, because each of them can say, "What I am going to do with my life is I'm going to write exactly the same things that were said for the past 600 years."

The question to my fellow Muslims is this: If we consider these two Kuwaiti-born academics, why does a speech by Tareq Suwaidan, who talks about the destruction of Western civilization, attract two thousand screaming and chanting young Canadian Muslims, but one given by Khaled Abou El-Fadl, who advocates "counter-jihad against puritan heresy," attract only two hundred? Have moderate Muslims conceded defeat at the hands of their more vociferous and fanatic Islamist opponents and their bullying tactics?

DESPAIR AND MARGINALIZATION

Muslim communities around the world today are perhaps the most marginalized, but misled, group of people on Earth. After the damage done by centuries of European occupation, instead of re-emerging in the image of their illustrious ancestors such as the Umayyads of Spain, the Abbasids of Baghdad, and the Mughals of India, Muslims today have sunk into a collective sense of despair and a loss of confidence that belies their own rich heritage. Nations such as India and China, with few natural resources other than their burgeoning populations, and with the challenge of widespread poverty, have nonetheless carved out the future and emerged as the next superpowers. Muslim countries, despite enormous natural mineral resources, have generally wasted their wealth, failed to capitalize on their strategic geopolitical locations, and failed their populations, miserably.

Now at the mercy of US imperial interests and witnessing the collapse of societies in Palestine, Iraq, and Somalia, Muslims have a sense of alienation from the rest of the world that is growing and being encouraged by the mullahs around the globe who have an unchallenged stranglehold on our collective narrative. Instead of a people who once represented modernity and progress, scientific endeavour, and critical thinking, we have descended into the path of segregation, fear, and suspicion that is making our societies worse off than they should be, given the circumstances. The paranoia of the non-Muslim world, which is unjustified yet understandable, created an uphill and unenviable struggle for moderate Muslims who are liberal and have a secular and progressive perspective on life.

In Muslim-dominated societies, as much as the vast number of ordinary Muslims may wish to reject oppressive theocracies (like those in Iran and

Saudi Arabia) and enjoy democracy and dignity for themselves, they are getting little help. Their brothers and sisters in the diaspora, with all the advantages of living in democratic societies, have managed to reduce the Muslim faith and identity into little more than a trivial quest for the exhibition of specific attire, an endless role as lard busters reading food labels to detect the faintest presence of prohibited ingredients. An obsessive aversion to anything that contributes to joy and happiness, such as music and dance. No more are Muslims known for their uninhibited quest for the unknown and the undiscovered; no more are others looking at the dynamism of our poetry, dance, philosophy, and architecture, or our ability to challenge the norms of existing religiosity and, yes, sexuality. No, today's Islamic leadership has rendered us collectively impotent, brainwashed our youth into a pervasive thirst for victimhood, derailed all attempts to rejuvenate and re-interpret the faith, and as the Muslim masses stumble along and trip at every challenge, the Islamists lay the blame at the feet of their former masters—the United States.

Undoubtedly, Muslims today face discrimination, oppression, and massive obstacles as they try to overcome centuries of stunted development and come to terms with the rest of the world that is outpacing them in every sense of the word "progress." However, this hostility and obstruction is not necessarily only coming from non-Muslims. The worst perpetrators of crimes against Muslims are fellow Muslims. Consider this little list:

- It is four Muslim countries—Turkey, Iraq, Iran, and Syria—that have been occupying Kurdistan for the past eighty years, denying the sons and daughters of Saladin a country they could call home.
- It is Muslim Morocco that has occupied Western Sahara now for thirty-five years.
- The territory of Aceh (the first place Islam is said to have been established in Southeast Asia) is seeking freedom, not from the Dutch but from Muslim Indonesia.
- Darfur is raped not by some infidels, but by fellow Muslims.
- It was Syria that tortured Maher Arar.
- It is Pakistan that refuses to give dignity and self-rule to the Baluch, Pukhtoons, and Kashmiris, not India.
- It is Saudis and Gulf Arabs who treat Indo-Pakistani Muslims like dirt in slave-like conditions.
- It is Arab Muslims who refer to fellow Muslims from Sub-Saharan Africa as "Ya Abdi" (oh Black slave).

We Muslims must not forget that it is not the infidel who forces Muslim women to the back of the mosques or relegates them to basements or hidden balconies—it is the Muslim men who do it; it is not non-Muslims who have planned the destruction of Prophet Muhammad's home in Mecca—it is the Saudi.

The list of Muslim oppression of Muslims is long. It is not the heretics who massacred 100,000 Iranians after the Islamic Revolution—it was the ayatollahs. And who was it who carried out the genocide of a million Indonesian leftist Muslims in 1965? Was it not the Indonesian Muslim fanatics backed by the CIA who carried out the worst massacres in the world's largest Muslim nation? And why did the Islamists sit in silence as Islamic vigilantes, inspired by the words of Abul Ala Maudoodi and Syed Qutb in former East Pakistan, collaborated with the West Pakistan army to carry out genocide of fellow Muslims that killed close to a million? The infamous Al-Shams and Al-Badr brigades associated with the Jamaat-e-Islami and the Islamic Chatro Sangho decimated the ranks of Bengali Muslim intellectuals and activists, killed poets and writers, hanged communists and nationalists, as the Muslim world slumbered. These were, after all, dark-skinned Bengali Muslims dying at the hands of fairer-skinned Punjabi Muslims. There were no Muslim George Harrisons orchestrating a concert to raise money for Bangladeshis, the victims of the genocide. That job was left to the former Beatle himself as the leadership of the Muslim world abandoned the children of Nazrul Islam.

To understand the mindset of contemporary Islamists, and their contempt for all things Western and joyful, one needs to read what the Islamist magazine *Crescent International* had to say about the assassination of John Lennon. As the world wept, the magazine's editorial read, "Lennon Killed by his Own Image"—blaming Lennon for his own death. The *Crescent International* opined:

Did John Lennon commit suicide? Perhaps the gun was in Chapman's hand and it was Chapman who fired the fatal shots. But did Chapman and his gun represent the values that produced Lennon himself, the "pop" rock, drugs and promiscuous culture that Lennon promoted and symbolized, and the frustration and the psychological disorder that is the inevitable result? . . . If he created bent and twisted minds with such lines as "happiness is a warm gun" and "thank you girl," then it is right that he should be one of the victims of his own creation. Lennon's life was also a reflection of western civilization. This civilization too will die at the hands of the evil it has let loose on God's earth.

Revealing words, written at a time of tremendous sadness, but they give us all an insight into what we are up against. The Islamists were warning us. It was a finger waving "I told you so," a reprimand to all of us in the West. More than twenty-five years after Lennon was killed and got blamed for his death by the Islamist magazine, another Islamist, Tarek Suwaidan from Kuwait, would come to Toronto to utter the same celebratory prognosis—the end of Western civilization.

I believe the fight for civil liberties and human rights is incomplete if one does not oppose fundamentalism. For it is fundamentalism, whether it is American or that of bin Laden, that poses a threat to Western civilization—a civilization built by all of humanity including the Prophet Muhammad and his followers.

Today, if not living under foreign occupation, the largest numbers of Muslims are citizens of countries ruled by military dictators, self-appointed monarchs, and oppressive theocracies, all invoking religion, race, dynasty, or class to justify a relationship that is better suited to the 12th century than the 21st. In the diaspora, the Muslim communities are under the thumb of well-funded and -organized conservative Islamist groups who control most of the mosque establishment—almost all of the imams who conduct weddings and death ceremonies and thus have managed to control the community, which is marginalized and thus vulnerable to clerical control.

We have succumbed to the lure of falsehoods that parade as facts. We Muslims have murdered our own history, distorting facts, deceiving our own selves, and then wondering why no one believes us. Professor K.K. Aziz of Pakistan, in his book *The Murder of History*, produced hard evidence of how Muslim youth were being deliberately fed lies in their textbooks to render them impotent as far as their intellectual development was concerned. Seeing Muslim youth cheering hate, or being attracted to lectures by hate-spouting imams, demonstrates that Aziz was right.

Islamist Muslim youth, nurtured in the climate created by Saudi and Iranian-influenced youth organizations, seem to excel in the "Don't Ask, Don't Think" school of thought. K.K. Aziz's Pakistan is not alone. Iran and Saudi Arabia lead the way in falsifying history and encouraging hatred of Baha'is, Jews, and Hindus very early in school life.

Imagine your child in Grade 9 being taught:

- The clash between this [Muslim] community (umma) and the Jews and Christians has endured, and it will continue as long as God wills.
- It is part of God's wisdom that the struggle between the Muslim and the Jews should continue until the hour [of judgment].

Imagine your child in Grade 8 being taught: "As cited in Ibn Abbas: The apes are Jews, the people of the Sabbath; while the swine are the Christians, the infidels of the communion of Jesus."

The brainwashing starts early. Imagine your child in Grade 1 being asked to fill in the blanks of this sentence: "Every religion other than _____ is false. Whoever dies outside of Islam enters _____."

The above quotes are all from Saudi textbooks that were part of the Saudi school curriculum as recently as 2005. But the teaching of hate is not restricted to schools in Saudi Arabia. Within the United States, private Saudi-funded schools carry on this jihad too.

Five months after 9/11, *The Washington Post* reported on a Saudi Islamic school in the District of Columbia area where Grade 11 students were being taught that on the "Day of Judgment Muslims will fight and kill Jews, who will hide behind trees that will say: 'Oh Muslim, Oh servant of God, here is a Jew hiding behind me. Come here and kill him.'"

The Islamists would have many of us believe that their struggle is against the West, but that is not true and does not withstand the test of scrutiny. For the past few centuries (and, some may argue, from the earliest days of Islam following the death of Prophet Muhammad), the primary target of Islamists, those who invoke Islam to retain political power, has been fellow Muslims. It is ordinary Muslims who will suffer most if the Islamist agenda succeeds.

The Islamists would have us believe that as Muslim Canadians, Muslim Americans, or Muslim Britons, our loyalty must be to the so-called Ummah— the worldwide Muslim body—not to the neighbourhoods and countries we live in. What they are asking us to do is submit to the will and machinations of the ayatollahs of Iran or the imams of Saudi Arabia.

One of the few Islamic scholars in the West who has denounced this notion of loyalty to foreign governments is Sheikh Hamza Yusuf of California. I do not entirely share his vision of the Muslim community, but Hamza Yusuf makes it very clear that Muslims who hate the West should find abode elsewhere. Barely a month after 9/11, he told the British newspaper *The Guardian*: "I would say to them [Muslims in the West] that if they are going to rant and rave about the West, they should emigrate to a Muslim country."

The mythological oneness of the Muslim family stands shattered among the corpses that litter Darfur. Muslims are exhorted by the Islamists to live by the rules of the divine texts, not the laws made by mere mortals; to disavow any links to the notion of "life, liberty and the pursuit of happiness," or "peace, order and good government." Instead, the Islamists want us to subject ourselves to sharia and give allegiance to the mullah-led Ummah. The caveat, though, is that they and only they—the Islamists—would have the authority to determine the leadership of the Ummah. The Islamist path for the Muslims has been determined as one that will achieve the mythical "Islamic State," but the fact is most Muslims merely wish to live in a "state of Islam"—two concepts that could complement each other, but in reality and in history have been diametrically opposed and on a collision course. This obsession with the Islamic State has created turmoil, bloodshed, and conflict ever since the day the Prophet Muhammad died in Medina.

From that day on, Muslims have made their choices—one path leading towards the mirage of the Islamic State, the Xanadu-like entity that we are still chasing all these years later. The other path is a state of Islam that is within our grasp, right now as we speak. Millions of Muslims have died in the pursuit of the former. After more than 1,400 years, this mythical Islamic State has been like a shimmering mirage in the desert, deceptively visible to the eye, seemingly within grasp, but never actualized.

"Morality is doing what is right, regardless what we are told;
Religious dogma is doing what we are told, no matter what is right."
—Elka Ruth Enola

Conclusion

ISLAM AND THE UNITED STATES may be intertwined forever historically. But seventy years from now, two anniversaries could bring them firmly together in contemporary life, or set them well apart. The paths of these two civilizations will cross as each commemorates its roots: in 2076, the Muslim world will celebrate the 1,500th anniversary of Islam,* while the United States celebrates its 300th birthday year—the tricentennial. Most of us will not be around for these events, but what we Muslims do today will determine whether our great-grandchildren will proudly celebrate their state of Islam arm in arm with Americans celebrating their tricentennial, or whether these children will be sulking in anger at the Americans, and putting on fake smiles while still chasing the elusive mirage of an Islamic State.

What we do today will determine the outcome. It all depends on whether we Muslims are able to separate our religion from politics or whether we continue to wallow in the nostalgia of a lost golden age. Will an Averroes have been born by then to inspire new philosophies and thought, urging us to reason, or will we be remembered for the insufferably sullen faces of men like Osama bin Laden and Ayatollah Khomeini? That choice is ours, not one of fate. No messiah is going to appear and save us from the hellish hole we have dug ourselves into. It's time to stop the digging. It is time to start climbing out.

---

* The Muslim year, based on the *hijera* lunar calendar, is ten days shorter than the Gregorian calendar year of 365 days. The year 2008 CE corresponds to the Islamic year 1429.

Only if we Muslims start building institutions on the basis of reason will Muslim children of 2076 remember us with fondness. Otherwise, they will continue to speak of Islam's past glory, taking their pick from 9th-century Iraq, 10th-century Spain, 16th-century Turkey, or 17th-century India. But no one will have time for our rhetoric anymore, and the world will join the United States in the revelry of its tricentennial year, leaving us sulking on the sidelines.

Al Gore in his stimulating book *The Assault on Reason* writes: "Fear is the most powerful enemy of reason." He warns Americans to restore the rule of reason if they wish to safeguard their future. Gore warns: "Both fear and reason are essential to human survival, but the relationship between them is unbalanced. Reason may sometimes dissipate fear, but fear frequently shuts down reason."

Gore's reference to the "politics of fear"* concerns the driving force propelling the American neo-conservative agenda. But he could very well be speaking about the "theology of fear" that has been the theme of Islamist neo-conservatives. If the Bush White House has successfully made the American public sphere inhospitable to reason, then Islamists have been even more successful in using fear to drive away reason from the Muslim realm.

In the case of the Muslim world, the Islamist-induced "fear of God" has blinded the community from seeing reason and thinking rationally. Clerics don't invoke the "Love of God." Instead, there is an incessant downpour of threats about punishments in the hereafter, numbing the Muslim ability to engage in any objective critical thinking. In the words of Edmund Burke, "No passion so effectually robs the mind of all its powers of acting and reasoning as fear."

Today we are paying the price for opportunities wasted in the past. Let us learn from these mistakes and start building for the future.

Abdullah Hakim Quick, a respected academic and American scholar, has presented evidence that Muslims were part of the Americas before the arrival of Columbus. In his book *Deeper Roots*, Quick documents the presence of Muslims in the western hemisphere, including a map of the Americas by the 10th-century historian and geographer al-Masudi. There is no doubt that the centuries of slavery eliminated Islam as a native religion in North America, but even in modern times, Muslims have been in the United States and Canada since the 19th century. The first recorded Muslim names in

---

*The subtitle to his book is: *How the Politics of Fear, Secrecy, and Blind Faith Subvert Wise Decision-Making, Degrade Our Democracy, and Put Our Country and Our World in Peril.*

Canada appear as early as 1897, when Major Kadir Khan led a contingent of the British Indian Army across Canada on its way to England for Queen Victoria's diamond jubilee celebrations. In the United States, there was a Muslim presence in Detroit, Chicago, and New York. There were Muslims among the African Americans, and among Arab and Indian immigrants. Muslims had found their way into Iowa in the Cedar Rapids area as early as 1885, a year before the golden-domed Iowa Capitol State Building was completed in Des Moines. In 1914, a Canadian-American Muslim of Indian ancestry named Hussain Rahim was the editor of a community newspaper in Vancouver; he would later lead the protests in the infamous *Komagata Maru* affair.*

The excuse therefore that Muslims have failed to leave an impact on the United States because we are "new to America" is not true. The fact is that in the 1960s, American and Canadian campuses had large numbers of Muslim students, but few were involved in any human rights causes. Individual Muslims such as the revolutionary Pakistani American Eqbal Ahmad (1933–99) were outstanding in their involvement with the civil rights movement as well as the anti-Vietnam War campaign, but they were few and far between. By and large as a community, Muslims shied away from human rights causes. While other equality-seeking groups in the United States marched shoulder to shoulder with Black Americans, both the Islamic Society of North America (ISNA) and the Muslim Students Association (MSA)—who speak endlessly about human rights—were conspicuously absent from these rallies. More so, one would be hard-pressed to find someone at the head of any of today's Islamic organizations (barring Black Muslims) who was involved at any time in the struggle for the rights of African Americans, or defending affirmative action, or protesting US intervention in Grenada or Vietnam.

While other racial and religious minority groups participated in the civil rights movement for Black Americans, many Muslim immigrants and their second-generation children were listing themselves as "White" in the US Census. Today, when they march for human rights, is it only because their own human rights are under threat?

No incident better reflects the ineptitude and selfishness of the conservative Islamic organizations than their reaction to the police killing

---

* *Komagata Maru* was a Japanese freighter that brought 376 Sikh, Muslim, and Hindu Indians to Canada in 1914, but was forced to leave port by the Canadian cruiser HMCS *Rainbow* on orders from the Canadian government.

of African immigrant Amadou Diallo on the night of February 4, 1999, in New York. The Liberian-born bicycle messenger and street merchant was returning to his apartment that night when an unmarked car pulled up and four plainclothes policemen got out. They attempted to question Diallo and, in the ensuing argument, the four officers began firing their weapons. In all, forty-one shots were discharged. Nineteen of those bullets hit Diallo and he died instantly. The shooting set off a firestorm of protest in New York City. Black leaders staged a three-week protest outside City Hall. Many were arrested, including Rev. Al Sharpton; Rev. Jesse Jackson; Kweisi Mfume, president of the National Association for the Advancement of Colored People (NAACP); former New York mayor David Dinkins; and actress Susan Sarandon. Hillary Clinton called the shooting a murder.

Missing in action were City of New York and national Muslim leaders. That is, until it turned out that Amadou Diallo's full name was Ahmed Ahmedou Diallo and that he had been a Muslim—it was only then that the Muslim leaders came out of the woodwork to join the protests. As long as the dead man was "Amadou," these groups couldn't care less, but when Amadou turned out to be Ahmed, he became a victim of police oppression. This attitude reflects the lack of understanding of universal human rights that is so pervasive among the Islamists who govern the community. When it became know that Diallo was a practising Muslim who prayed five times a day, Islamic organizations even joined the lawsuit against the New York City Police Department. And in 2004, when a $3-million settlement was reached, the Council on American-Islamic Relations (CAIR) sent out a news release asking its members to congratulate just one of the co-counsels who was a Muslim. There was no mention of the non-Muslims who were instrumental in the Diallo case. In fact, since 9/11 Diallo has been turned into a Muslim martyr. His name is disingenuously invoked as a symbol of Islamophobia in the United States, whereas it is likely Diallo died because he was Black, not because he was Muslim.

The movement by Muslims for their human rights is valid, but unfortunately does not carry moral weight. Had those who speak on behalf of Muslims a track record for standing up for the "other," the situation would be far different. The men who speak for us today are not men of courage like anti-war activist Eqbal Ahmad. In fact, they considered Eqbal Ahmad to be outside the fold of Islam.

However, there may still be some hope for redemption. We can learn from our errors and start afresh today. To begin this process, the mosque establishment should embrace liberal and secular Muslims as part of the Ummah. If this is not possible, we need to build a space and a voice for Muslims who do not feel represented by existing organizations that are either sectarian or ethnocentric, are largely authoritarian, and are influenced by a fear of modernity and an aversion to joy. We should never be seen as opportunists who one day back Bush for the presidency, and the next label him as the arch-enemy. The Islamists in the United States did just that.

We are from all parts of the world, with diverse ethnic and racial backgrounds. We are proud of our heritage and the contribution of Islam to human civilization, but we need to move beyond that pride. We need to focus our strategies and build for the future, without having to compromise on the spirit of Islam as represented by its five pillars. We need to look to the future and not to the past for the best days of the Muslim community—a community that needs to integrate and participate with other people on Earth to be a beacon of hope, peace, prosperity, and joy for the rest of the world.

We need to include as Muslim any person who identifies himself or herself as Muslim. No longer should a person die in the name of God. As Muslims, we need to believe in a progressive, liberal, pluralistic, democratic, and secular society where everyone has freedom of religion as well as freedom from religion. Our communities should be equal and active contributors in the development of a just, democratic, and equitable society on Earth. We need to fight oppression—not just against ourselves, but also the injustices committed in our name by other Muslims.

Unless we start believing in the separation of religion and state in all matters of public policy, we will continue to do a tremendous disservice to Islam and our great-grandchildren. We need to understand that a separation of religion and state is a prerequisite to building democratic societies where all religious, ethnic, and racial minorities are accepted as equal citizens enjoying the full dignity and human rights enunciated in the 1948 United Nations Universal Declaration of Human Rights. Only by the unqualified embracing of human rights, not just our own, but those of our adversaries, will we be respected as the "best among the peoples."

Religion, including Islam, can be the moral compass that guides us towards good deeds and restrains us from arrogance and self-righteousness. Islam should help us curb our anger, not ignite it. The challenge posed by fanaticism and extremism within the Muslim community needs to be confronted by Muslims, not left to the rest of a world that views us with deep suspicion. We Muslims must oppose the extremists and present the more humane and tolerant face of our community.

And unless the gender apartheid that is practised in large parts of our community is stamped out in letter and spirit, we will make no progress even if the wealth of a hundred Saudi Arabias is left at our feet. A community that treats its mothers as second-class citizens cannot and should not expect its daughters to be treated with respect and dignity by others. Making women walk behind men or pray behind men is contrary to the equality among men and women enshrined in Islam. Muslim men and women should work together, shoulder to shoulder, in their effort to rejuvenate our community and shed the burden of medieval misery.

In writing this book, I talked to many Muslims, asking them what they felt was the way out of the "Muslim predicament." I talked to men and women, gay and straight, Arab and Iranian, Turk and Kurd, Black and White, as well as atheists and believers. Here is some of what they said.

- **Roshan Jamal**, a chartered accountant of South African ancestry who became the first woman to head an Islamic centre in North America and turned the mosque into a cultural hub of Toronto's Muslim community:

The Muslim predicament arises partly because not every Muslim interprets and applies the faith consistently since our faith has no higher human connection to God (like a priest in Christianity for example). Secondly, the current predicament arises due to marginalization felt by the communities. . . . All that can be done about the predicament is that each Muslim should embrace the challenge of living a just life and shift his /her worldview from fear to wonder.

- **Mahfooz Kanwar**, a Pakistani-Canadian professor of sociology at Mount Royal College in Calgary:

As a progressive Muslim I feel that the Muslim predicament can only be resolved through the creation and nurturing of a Muslim reformation movement and the advent of a renaissance of sorts that would embrace all of humanity, espouse secular values, establish man-made laws as supreme, treat all citizens as equal under the law, and reconnect with the world at large and contribute to the arts, technology, design and sciences. . . . Even utopian ideas gain traction given human will, courage, and inner strength.

- **Aysal Ozkan**, a Turkish-Canadian realtor and board member of the Muslim Canadian Congress:

There are a lot of misunderstandings about Islam, and the situation we Muslims are in. Partly it is our mistake, because we could not enlighten Christians and members of other religions and explain our point of view. We also should learn openly to criticize ourselves and not just others.

This however requires a higher level of maturity. Islam, throughout history, unfortunately was in the hands of the wrong people. The interpretation of Islam which was mostly in the hands of uneducated people with their own agendas, was not done rightly. Unfortunately the problem still exists. Educated mullahs, clerics who are not power hungry or corrupt are needed. Separation of religion and government affairs is a must.

- **Farzana Hassan**, Toronto author of *Islam, Women and the Challenges of Today*:

Muslims often speak nostalgically of their past glory but fail to recognize that Islamic civilization was at its peak only when Muslims chose a path of tolerance, humanity, honesty and open-mindedness rather than being overly preoccupied with dogma, as they are today. Rigid adherence to dogma causes nothing but division and friction in societies and is a barrier towards overall civilizational advancement. A paradigm shift is therefore needed in the collective psyche of Muslims so as to enable them to develop political, social, and educational institutions that embrace universal human values. These must of necessity be based on democratic principles and social equality regardless of race, creed, class or gender.

- **Jane Khan**, a Ukrainian-Canadian convert to Islam:

I was raised a Catholic up to 1968, when I met my Pakistani husband (God bless his soul). All that I had heard or read about Muslims was derogatory and negative. Over the years, I have met some extraordinary outgoing, loving, capable Muslims and also have had to contend with some negative, niggardly, legalistic, arrogant, ignorant Muslims. . . . We need to counteract the mullahs and impress upon those we meet by our acts of kindness, courtesy, neighbourly behaviour, and good citizenship. Perhaps a single non-denominational school system is the answer. It is up to all moderate, educated, and progressive Muslims to continue to light that candle to illuminate the darkness of ignorance and prejudice.

- **Muhammad Ali Bukhari**, a Bangladeshi-Canadian journalist living in Toronto:

The greatest obstacle for Muslims has been the absence of democracy and their resultant backwardness in the realm of economic development. In the contemporary world, both geo-politics and interdependence control everything, and the most powerful force in this process, the United States, has always been a supporter of anti-democratic status quo around the world through its agenda of New World Order. Look at Iraq and Afghanistan—they are as much reminders of failure to implement democracy, as the Islamic republics in Iran, Pakistan, and Sudan are arguments against the establishment of Islamic rule anywhere else.

- **Summiaya Ahmad**, a Canadian-born Muslim school teacher in Markham, Ontario:

I have just come back from my first ever visit to a Muslim-majority country—Pakistan. What I saw over there was a very happy blend of modernism and tradition. This was contrary to what the Islamists in the West will have us believe. Over the past few years, Muslims in Canada have been exposed to a very strict and totalitarian version of Wahhabi Islam, whereas during my trip to Pakistan I witnessed people embracing a far more liberal Islam and relishing their freedom of choice. . . . Whereas the rest of the Muslim world is progressing in a rapid and contemporary manner, we Muslims in the West for some odd reason have become ultra-conservative, believing that the only true Islam is the Islam of the 7th century. Muslims should enjoy life as a gift from Allah, not as a perpetual punishment.

- **Edward Horne**, a convert to Islam living in Mexico:

The first time I worshipped at a mosque was sunset prayer on September 10, 2001. The next day, Muslim terrorists attacked New York City. I had an irrational terror that I had caused the disaster. I stayed away from mosques until I realized that the best way to oppose this evil was from within Islam, not from the outside. The medieval bloodlust of our Islamist enemies cannot survive the onslaught of modern life, the Internet, opportunity, prosperity, education. . . . Today we are forced to guard that religious lunatics do not obtain nuclear or biological weapons which certainly could destroy our world. But I foresee a day when the terrorists will be forgotten, along with the absurd notion of Islamic government, and mosques will be closing for lack of worshipers, just as Christian churches are today. That will be a day when the Quran and the teachings of Muhammad are recognized for their beauty and wisdom, not as an excuse for stupidity and mayhem.

- **Ali Abbas Inayatullah,** a businessman in Karachi, Pakistan:

As Muslims we are facing an existential crisis like never before. We are torn between different and competing political and socio-economic views of the way we need to live our lives. A false opposition has been created between secularism and being a Muslim. . . . My Muslim identity was greatly inspired by Imam Ali ibn Abu Talib. He encapsulated the qualities of compassion, justice, mercy, knowledge, chivalry, patience, humility like none before him. His spirit of fairness and egalitarianism are inspiring to all humanity but find no currency in the Muslim world. It is rather countries that are secular and care for their citizens where such qualities are evoked. It is only within such societies that humans can attain a degree of equality like never before and reach for the stars whilst simultaneously uplifting those who have slipped below. In the pantheon of the arts, sciences, and culture, we are nowhere to be found. In the gallery of whiners and underachievers, our numbers are ever increasing as we drift further into the jaws of Political Islam. As long as we cannot awaken our conscience, take responsibility for our actions, and reach out to the world, we are doomed.

It is not with a wish list that I conclude my book, but with a plea to my fellow Muslims: If there is one thing that we could do to help ourselves, it is to end the addiction to victimhood that has blinded our senses, rendering us incapable of moving forward. Almost everything that goes wrong in the Muslim world today, we are told, is the fault of the United States and those Jews.

Yet there was no Israel when Ibn Saud and his Wahhabi warriors invaded Iraq in the early 19th century, destroyed the city of Karbala, and massacred fellow Muslims. There was no United States when Damascus was ransacked by the Abbasids in the 8th century while rivers of Muslim blood flowed in the streets. The United States and Israel—no angels among nations—are not without blame, but please, a bit of honesty would go a long way. The Muslim malaise is not a result of a Zionist-US conspiracy. It is the inability of the Muslim leadership to realize that the days of emirs and caliphs belongs to the past. It is a failure of our scholars and clerics to reconcile Islam with modernity, individual freedom, and liberty. As long as we continue to blame others for our own shortcomings, we will continue to stagnate. Waiting for a Mehdi to emerge from a well, or dreaming of the kind of Islamic State that has eluded us for fourteen centuries, are not the answers to our dilemma.

My fellow Muslims, we have got to grow up. Let us stop chasing a mirage.

Afterword by
Husain Haqqani

FOR FOURTEEN CENTURIES Islam has been the faith of hundreds of millions. Its followers have included emperors and mystics, traders and farmers, soldiers and philosophers. Like all religions, Islam aspires to provide ethical and spiritual guidance to its followers. This guidance applies to all spheres of life, but cannot be described as a political or economic ideology in the contemporary sense. Throughout history, Muslims have had the sense of belonging to a community of believers, but they have hardly ever been organized into a single state.

Beginning with the 20th century, however, several interlinked movements seeking an Islamic revival have claimed that Islam lays the foundations for a specific political system, and that the principal objective of Islam is the creation of an Islamic State. The desire to revive something that historically did not exist has led to a partial erosion of Islam's ethical and spiritual heritage, and its replacement with totalitarian and semi-totalitarian versions of a political ideology that seeks legitimacy in Islam's name.

The Islamic political theory known today as Political Islam has developed largely in response to the breakdown of traditional order under the pressures of modernity. Several political models prevailed in the pre-modern Muslim world. Prophet Muhammad's immediate successor (the first of the "Rightly Guided Caliphs") was elected when the notables of the time gathered in a mosque. The first caliph designated his own successor, while the third was chosen by an appointed committee and then endorsed by the community. The Shia split with the majority Sunnis over the concept of the caliphate, and asserted that religious authority rested with those known as imams, all directly descended from the Prophet's daughter and son-in-law. Temporal power in Shia-majority Iran was exercised by kings ("shahs"), and the Fatimid offshoot of the Shia in Egypt preferred to call themselves caliphs, like their Sunni Umayyad and Abbasid predecessors.

The larger Muslim states were ruled by sultans, hereditary autocrats who derived their legitimacy from the implementation of sharia laws. Early Muslims did not accept the divine right of kings and considered the sharia as a means of tempering their rulers' authority. The Ottoman Empire in Europe and the Middle East, and the Moghul Empire in India, accommodated large non-Muslim populations within the sultanates. Sultans aided by the Ulema (religious scholars) also ruled parts of contemporary Malaysia and Indonesia. Smaller principalities, such as Yemen and the present-day Gulf States, were run by imams, emirs, or sheikhs, all of whom paid tribute to the major sultan in the region, especially the caliph in Constantinople after the 15th century.

Having lived on its own terms, and with few setbacks (such as the Mongol conquest of Baghdad in 1258), the Muslim world's ascendancy turned into a gradual decline that coincided with the rise of Europe. The Muslim world faced modern transformation over a relatively short time and mainly under pressure from the European powers. Unlike Europe and North America, Muslim territories did not get the opportunity to evolve into modern states over time. The British and the French in the Arabic-speaking lands, the Russians in Central Asia, the Dutch in Indonesia, and the British in India and Malaya penetrated and occupied Muslim lands. Once their authority was firmly established, the Europeans governed with an iron fist, with the help of elites trained by the colonial masters.

The earliest Western idea borrowed by Muslim modernizers, especially in the 19th century, was enlightened absolutism. Administrative and military reform within the decaying Ottoman Empire, for example, depended largely on the model of the enlightened despot. Numerous "partial modernizers" emerged in other parts of the Islamic world: primarily rulers who wanted to introduce selected Western social and economic ideas and technology without altering the basis of political power. Some Sultans even followed Europe's enlightened despots in introducing constitutions and assemblies of nobles, but these efforts did not go far enough for some and went too far for others within powerful elite groups.

Muslims responded to the challenge of the technologically and militarily superior West in one of two ways. One segment of the population accepted Western education and adopted the Western way of life, excluding religion from their discourse almost entirely. Others started defining politics in religious idiom, insisting that Islam offered a complete way of life distinct from that offered by the colonial powers and their modern ideas.

The beginning of the modern era thus marked the beginning of ideological conflicts within the Muslim world about politics and governance. Until then, traditional Islamic scholarship had focused on the divine message through critical evaluation of the Quran and extrapolation from the hadith, as well as through philosophy, reasoning—and some jurisprudence. With notable exceptions, Muslims paid little attention to political and economic theory. This absence of a consistent Islamic political theory has led scholars such as Bernard Lewis to argue that in Islam, "In principle, at least, there is no state, but only a ruler; no court, but only a judge." The alternative explanation is that Muslim politics is plural and changing, which renders redundant any monolithic interpretations of fourteen centuries of history by historians or by religious ideologues.

Muslims have a tremendous sense of history and of civilizational rise and fall. Having lost the status of world leaders to the West beginning in the 16th century, Muslims have developed a collective feeling of weakness and helplessness. Starting in the 19th century, Muslim scholars have spent a lot of time explaining the Muslim decline and proposing remedies for it. Of all the remedies proposed, the one with the most disastrous consequences has been the notion of Islam as political theory, resulting in what Tarek Fatah describes as "the illusion of an Islamic State."

The advocates of an Islamic State back their ideology with conspiracy theories about threats to Islam that have been popular among Muslims since the twilight years of the Ottoman Empire. Non-Muslim conspiracies are used to explain the powerlessness of a community that was at one time the world's economic, scientific, political, and military leader. The overarching Islamic State that would unite all Muslims and topple the ascendant powers from their perch is offered as the remedy to the Muslims' current weak situation. One can find evidence of fear of schemes by "freemasons" and "Zionists" being voiced since the late 18th century. The 19th and early 20th centuries saw wider discussion of how Muslims and Islam were being contrived against.

The erosion of the leadership position of Muslims coincided with the West's gradual technological ascendancy. Soon after the Ottomans took over Constantinople, Johannes Gutenberg printed a Bible using metal plates. Printing was introduced into the Ottoman Empire during the reign of Sultan Bayazid II (1481–1512), only to be virtually banned for use by Muslims in 1485.

In Europe, a full-grown book industry evolved, facilitating wide dissemination of ideas and knowledge. By 1501, more than a thousand printing presses had produced approximately 35,000 titles with ten million copies. But in the Ottoman Empire, only Christians and Jews used printing technology.

Muslim use of the printing press did not start until 1727, causing the Muslims to lose more than 270 years in the world's greatest explosion of knowledge. The Persian, Moghul, and Ottoman empires controlled vast lands and resources, but many important scientific discoveries and inventions that had occurred since the 15th century came about in Europe and not in the Muslim lands.

Ignorance is an attitude, and the world's Muslims have to analyze, debate, and face it before they can deal with it. The predisposition to rumour and conspiracy theories—and the presumption that an Islamic State is all that is needed to revive the Ummah's fortunes—prevents that frank discussion. The fifty-seven member countries of the Organization of the Islamic Conference (OIC) account for one-fifth of the world's population, but their combined GDP is less than the GDP of France. The twenty-two Arab countries, including the oil-exporting Gulf States, account for a combined GDP less than that of Spain alone. Almost half of the world's Muslim population is illiterate. Muslims are noticeably absent from the list of recent inventors and innovators in science and technology.

The OIC countries have around five hundred universities; by comparison, there are more than five thousand universities in the United States and more than eight thousand in India. In 2004, Shanghai Jiao Tong University compiled an "Academic Ranking of World Universities," and none of the universities from Muslim-majority states made it into the Top 500.

There is only one university for every three million Muslims, and the Muslim-majority countries have 230 scientists per one million Muslims. The United States has 4,000 scientists per million and Japan has 5,000 per million. The Muslim world spends 0.2 percent of its GDP on research and development, while the Western nations spend around 5 percent of GDP on producing knowledge.

Tarek Fatah rightly explains that the decline of the world's Muslims does not come from the absence of a puritanical Islamic state. It is the result of the state in which the Muslims currently find themselves. He also calls for making a distinction between pietistic Muslims and those pursuing power in Islam's name. Some of his views, especially in relation to US policies and the war against terrorism, are bound to generate controversy, and not everyone agreeing with his diagnosis will necessarily agree with his prescription. But Fatah joins the expanding list of Muslim authors who are challenging Islamism and demanding that Muslims revert to seeing Islam as an essentially spiritual and ethical belief system instead of stretching history to present Islam as a political ideology.

Contemporary Muslims need to understand the material causes of their material decline, recognize the sacred essentials of the Islamic faith, and acknowledge Islam's historic diversity and pluralism. Islamist demands for an Islamic State, accompanied by calls to arms and terror, are likely to only push Muslims further down the road of weakness and humiliation.

Husain Haqqani is director of Boston University's Center for International Relations, and co-chair of the Islam and Democracy Project at Hudson Institute, Washington, DC.

Acknowledgements

I FIRST MET NARGIS TAPAL at a noisy election rally on the campus of Karachi University in the winter of 1970. She was a Beatles fan, sporting a Ringo Starr mop of hair, while I was the rabble-rousing student leader of the Left. Since the day we met our paths have been the same, traversing three countries and three decades in a roller-coaster ride that has culminated in this book. For over a year, Nargis has endured my obsession with this book, from 5:00 every morning to midnight, with the patience of a rock. Without her support, the repeated requests to read my rants, and her ability to say, "this sucks," or "get your facts right," *Chasing a Mirage* would have been just another chase. Thank you, Nargis, for your support. Two other women helped with this project: my daughters, Natasha and Nazia. I placed an enormous burden on their time and space, and they did not complain. Thank you, kids.

This book owes its existence to two Catholic institutions, one in Pakistan and the other in Canada. First, I owe my quest for history and understanding of Islam to my alma mater, St. Lawrence's Boys School in Karachi, Pakistan. To Father Joshua, Father Trinidad, and Father Mascarenhas, I say thank you for the education you gave to me and for allowing Muslim students in a Catholic school to study Islam. Second, my current employer, St. Michael's Hospital—built by the Sisters of St. Joseph—permitted me time off to write this book. They were under no obligation to cater to my "extra-curricular" activities, but they did. Thank you, St. Mike's. My gratitude also goes to my co-workers Tasha Michael and Catherine Cameron, who in their own way ensured that I didn't fall behind schedule, and on my days of despair would give me pep talks to overcome the proverbial writer's block.

An anchor for me throughout this exercise were my friends Salim Ahmad and Intizar Zaidi. A successful real estate agent, Salim is an intellectual with an abundance of common sense and reason. His moral support to this project ensured I had a place to escape to when the writing got scary. Intizar Zaidi and I go back to the 1960s when we shared jail cells as political prisoners in Pakistan. His insight into the working of Islamists in Canada, especially Quebec, were invaluable.

The suggestion that I write this book came from two fellow Muslims: controversial Canadian author Irshad Manji (with whom I have had a public falling-out, but she is a courageous woman with a sharp wit and we still agree profoundly on many things) and Husain Haqqani, professor at Boston University and an aide to former prime minister Benazir Bhutto (I had never met him until he called me for a chat and suggested, two minutes into a doughnut at Tim Horton's, that I focus my critique into a book form). I would like to thank both Irshad and Husain for planting the seed.

Enter Don Loney, who came from nowhere the day after I resigned as communications director of the Muslim Canadian Congress in July 2006. My resignation followed a death threat which had left my family shaken. Don read about my ordeal in *The Globe and Mail* and that I planned to write a book about the challenges facing the Muslim community. The next day he called, saying Wiley would be interested in discussing the possibility of publishing my book, a possibility which became a reality.

I would also like to acknowledge others at Wiley for their professional efforts: Pamela Vokey, Liz McCurdy, Erin Kelly, and Robin Dutta-Roy. In addition, I would like to thank Cheryl Cohen for her copyediting expertise and Christine Dudgeon for creating such a comprehensive index.

Many of my friends went through the manuscript and helped me focus my thoughts: Edward Horne, former school teacher and a convert to Islam; Farzana Hassan, who was in the middle of her own second book; Terry Walker for helping me stay focused; Harminder Dhillon, who helped me gain access to precious material on Sikh history; and Jehad Aliweiwi, who painstakingly pored over part of the book. Thanks also to Keyvan Soltany; Ali Abbas; Raheel and Sohail Raza; Col. Anwar Ahmed, who opened his vast library to me; York University student Toomaj Haghshenas, who took time from his soccer matches to assist me in creating the bibliography, while engaging me in delightful debate about the Middle East and South Asia; and Salma Siddiqui in Ottawa and Tahir Aslam Gora in Burlington, who endured lengthy phone calls as I bounced ideas off them and who told me bluntly when those ideas sucked.

I would like to say a special "thank you" to Hasan Mahmud, whose book in Bengali, *Islam and Sharia,* has created a stir; his expertise on sharia law dwarfs that of many imams in Canada.

I wish my parents were alive to see this book. My father, because history was one of his passions. From Asoka to Napoleon, the Balfour Declaration to the Trieste Treaty, by the time I was ten, I had heard it all. My mother, who sacrificed a lot to ensure my schooling. She managed to put food on the table and books in our schoolbag, making sure adversity did not stand in the way of accomplishment. Thank you both.

Manufacturer's Warranty

ALL EXPRESS AND IMPLIED WARRANTIES made by the manufacturer will be considered void if any unauthorized third-party add-ons are installed on top of the basic operating system of Islam. Such add-ons are causing a worldwide system failure. The manufacturer is warning the general public to be wary of unscrupulous vendors who are marketing bootlegged versions of the product to unsuspecting customers. Users are hereby warned that the manufacturer does not guarantee the proper functioning of Islam if these add-ons are installed over the basic operating system. The manufacturer also cautions all users that there has been no new version of Islam since the last upgrade in 632 CE. Speculation that the manufacturer plans to release a new Service Pack are without foundation.

Access to manufacturers' on-line Help Desk and Call Centre is limited only to users of the original product, not the bootlegged versions. Unless callers can demonstrate that they have uninstalled all add-ons sold by third-party vendors, their calls will not be returned.

Users are warned not to install any upgrades to Islam being marketed by the following unauthorized vendors: Ibn Taymiyah Inc., Al-Wahhab Ltd., The Syed Qutb Corporation, Hassan Al-Banna Enterprises, Khomeini & Khamenei PLC, and Maudoodi Associates. The manufacturer reserves the right to prosecute all third-party vendors who tamper with the original product under chapter 5.0, verse 003 of the Quran, which states explicitly the perfection of the product and the guarantee of no further upgrades of add-ons: "This day have I perfected your religion for you, completed My favour upon you, and have chosen for you Islam as your religion."

— ☺ —

Notes

THE TRANSLITERATED spelling of authors' names below is based on the spelling used by their individual publishers, which may differ from the spelling in the chapters of this book.

PREFACE

xi   **a scathing report:** Arab Human Development Report 2002, *Creating Opportunities for Future Generations,* www.rbas.undp.org/ahdr2002.shtml (accessed October 12, 2006).

xii   **UNDP report:** "Tough report says Arab world stuck in Dark Ages," *The Toronto Star,* July 7, 2002.

xii   **freedom of the press in Egypt:** Mohamed Elmasry, "UN report ignores social progress made by Arab states," July 11, 2002.

xv   **Canadians to embrace Islam:** *The Michael Coren Show,* CTS-TV, September 26, 2007.

xv   **"educate non-Muslims":** "Islamic leader to Muslims: Educate others about Islam," *Detroit Free Press,* March 2, 2007.

xv   **falsehood of their ancestry:** K.K. Aziz, *The Murder of History,* 98–99.

xvi   **local converts:** Ibid, 98.

xviii   **Make mercy your Mosque:** W.H. McLeod, *Textual Sources for the Study of Sikhism,* 43.

CHAPTER 1: POLITICS AND THEOLOGY OF ISLAMIC STATES

3   **"Come to gloat":** Tariq Ali, *The Leopard and the Fox,* 163. *The Leopard and the Fox* is a play written by Tariq Ali on the trial and execution of Zulfi qar Ali Bhutto, which was commissioned by the BBC but subsequently dropped after pressure from the British government.

3   **signed confession:** Ibid.

4   **"Until we meet again.":** Benazir Bhutto, *Daughter of Destiny,* 22.

5   *fatwa* **issued:** Abdullah bin Baz was the head of the Council of Ulema (Islamic scholars) in Saudi Arabia. His fatwas were based on a literalist reading of the Quran and exemplified the Wahhabi stream of Islam, urging Muslims to return to Islam's origins for knowledge, rather than look to contemporary interpretations. As chief mufti, authorized to rule on religious issues, bin Baz wielded much power in Saudi Arabia. He made pronouncements on many social aspects of daily life–banning women from driving cars, for example, and granting Saudi men permission to use Viagra. But he is best known for his ruling in 1976 that the Earth was flat and that it was a great blasphemy to suggest otherwise.

6   **Taha's execution:** Samir Amin, "Political Islam," *CovertAction Weekly* 71 (Winter 2001): 3–6, Washington, DC.

8   **existence of Darul Islam:** S. Abul Ala Maududi, Call to Jihad, 4.

8   **"What are the fundamental objects":** Syed Abul Ala Maudoodi, *Islamic Law and Constitution,* 127–28.

8   **"enjoin good and forbid evil.":** Ibid.

9   **"eradicate and crush with full force":** Ibid.

9   **"conceived of as the 'Islamic State.'":** Muhammad Asad, *The Principles of State and Government in Islam,* v.

9   **Muslim history can offer us no guidance in our desire:** Ibid.

12   **The notion of a single Caliph:** Bernard Lewis, *The Emergence of Modern Turkey,* 257–58.

12   **I find the Turkish view is perfectly sound.":** Allama Muhamad Iqbal, *The Reconstruction of Religious Thought in Islam,* 124–25.

13   **"Such is the attitude of the modern Turk,":** Ibid, 125–26.

14   **Quran should be translated and read in the Berber language:** Ibid, 127–28.

14   **"non-Arab is really a complete Muslim.":** Wilfred Cantwell Smith, *Islam in Modern History,* 94.

15   **Turkey alone has shaken off its dogmatic slumber:** Charles Kurzman, ed., *Liberal Islam: A Sourcebook,* 262.

16   **successive Islamic declarations on human rights:** The Cairo Declaration on Human Rights in Islam adopted in 1997.

16   **According to the Foreword:** www.alhewar.com/ISLAMDECL.html.

17   **a "western construct,":** Faisal Kutty, *A Western Construct? The Legacy of the Universal Declaration of Human Rights,* www.counterpunch.org/kutty12092006.html.

18   **the pernicious seed that was sown:** S. Abul Ala Maududi, *The Sick Nations of the Modern Age,* 3.

20   **the Prophet's "heaven-appointed work":** Ali Abd al-Razik, *Islam and the Fundamentals of Authority,* 480.

22   **"constitutional problems with the sharia model":** Abdullahi Ahmed An-Na'im, *Toward an Islamic Reformation,* 77.

CHAPTER 2: PAKISTAN—FAILURE OF AN ISLAMIC STATE

27   **Hindus would cease to be Hindus and Muslims would cease to be Muslims:** Muhammad Ali Jinnah, inauguration speech to the first sitting of the Pakistan Constituent Assembly, August 11, 1947.

27   **Within months he would change course:** Zulqurnain Zaidi, The Emergence of Ulema in the Politics of India and Pakistan, 95.

28   **the gaudy ceremonials of the top offi ce:** Allen McGrath, *The Destruction of Pakistan's Democracy,* 39.

28   **"the Prime Minister will do what I tell him.":** Ibid, 38.

31   **Today, I beckon you Waris Shah:** English translation by the author.

33   **Jamaat-e-Islami:** The Jamaat-e-Islami, founded in India by Abul Ala Maudoodi, shifted its activities to Pakistan after August 1947. There, it led the campaign to introduce sharia law and turn the country from a constitutional democracy into a theocratic caliphate. The Jamaat-e-Islami has made significant gains in Bangladesh and Pakistan since the US intervention in Afghanistan and Iraq. Internationally, it has historic links with the Egyptian Muslim Brotherhood and has an active cadre running American, Canadian, and British Muslim organizations.

33   **"[secularism] is the creature of the devil.":** Justice Muhammad Munir, Commission Report to Enquire into the Punjab Disturbances of 1953 (constituted under Punjab Act 2 of 1954), 203.

34   **Khalifa of Pakistan:** Ibid, 213.

34   **whether a person is or is not a Muslim will be of fundamental importance:** Ibid, 214–15.

35   **Muslims according to the view of that *alim*, but *kafirs* according to the definition of everyone else.:** Ibid, 218.

36   **if Divine commands cannot make or keep a man a Musalman:** Ibid, 236.

37   **U-2 spy planes:** Gary Powers, the US pilot shot down over the Soviet Union on May 1, 1960, had flown out from Peshawar.

37   **martial law had been declared:** Mohammad Asghar Khan, *Generals in Politics: Pakistan 1958–1982*, 6.

41   **only recognizes religious minorities:** Asian Centre for Human Rights. *Pakistan: The Land of Religious Apartheid and Jackboot Justice.* www.achrweb.org/Review/2007/179-07.htm

41   **had to take his oath of office with a Quranic prayer:** *Times of India*, "Pak's Hindu CJ Took Oath with a Quranic Prayer," March 26, 2007, www.timesofindia.indiatimes. com//articleshow/1824483.

CHAPTER 3: SAUDI ARABIA—SPONSOR OF ISLAMIC STATES

44   **"I see earthquakes and dissension over there":** Muhammad Muhsin Khan, *The Translation of the Meanings of Sahih al-Bukhari, Kitab al-Fitan*, volume 9, 142.

44   **modern countries named after a person:** The Philippines was named after King Philip of Spain.

46   **assistance was possible "only if Hussein gave his word":** Haifa Alangari, *The Struggle for Power in Arabia*, 172.

48   **a horrible example of the Wahhabis' cruel fanaticism . . .:** Alexei Vassiliev, *The History of Saudi Arabia*, 97.

49   **His political ambition was to restore Muslim power in India:** William Cantwell Smith, *Islam in Modern History*, 44–45.

50   **"All control of power is with the Hindus":** R. Upadhyay, Shah Wali Ullah's Political Thought, South Asia Analysis Group. www.saag.org/papers7/paper629.html.

52   **"The house where the Prophet received the word of God is gone":** Daniel Howden, "The destruction of Mecca: Saudi hardliners are wiping out their own heritage," *The Independent*, August 6, 2005. www.news.independent.co.uk/world/middle_east/article304029.ece.

53   **The countries where they're located are simply trustees:** Tarek Fatah, "Saudi Royals destroying home of Muhammad," *The Toronto Star*, August 17, 2005.

53 **"It is hardly something we are going to allow to be destroyed.":** Prince Turki al-Faisal, Saudi Ambassador to the UK. "What Rubbish," letter published in *The Independent*, on August 12, 2005, in response to the article, "The destruction of Mecca: Saudi hardliners are wiping out their own heritage."

53 **"demolition of key archaeological sites":** Daniel Howden, "Shame of the House of Saud: Shadows over Mecca," *The Independent*, April 19, 2006, www.news.independent.co.uk/world/middle_east/article358577.ece.

54 **"we see no concern from Muslims.":** Irfan al-Alawi, Bulldozing Islam; Historic destruction, Wahhabi style, *The Weekly Standard*. www.weeklystandard.com/check.asp?idArticle=12759&r=cvwpc.

CHAPTER 4: IRAN—THE ISLAMIC STATE

56 **equate him to Simon Bolivar.:** The event was a lecture by Tariq Ali, titled "Imperial Blues: Afghanistan, Lebanon, Iraq and Palestine," on October 15, 2006, at the University of Toronto.

57 **"there is an absence of hierarchy in the clergy":** Quoted in Janet Afary and Kevin B. Anderson, "The Seductions of Islamism: Revisiting Foucault and the Iranian Revolution," *New Politics* 10, no. 1, 2004. www.wpunj.edu/~newpol/issue37/Afary37.htm.

57 **nobody in Iran means a political regime:** Ibid.

57 **"Between men and women there will not be inequality with respect to rights, but difference,":** Ibid.

58 **"participation in secular democracies or military juntas are two pitfalls":** Iqbal Asaria, "No Third World for us—we are Muslim," *The Crescent International*, Toronto. August 15–31, 1980.

58 **The establishment of Muslim rule:** Islamic Viewpoint, Grade 11 (2004) pp. 8–9, as reproduced in *The Attitude to 'The Other' and to Peace in Iranian School Books and Teacher's Guides*, The Center for Monitoring the Impact of Peace, October 2006, 22.

59 **Even if we are cut to pieces a thousand times:** Ibid, 29.

59 **The left had been warned of just such an event:** Bijan Jazani was assassinated in 1975, along with six of his fellow *Fidayeen* members and two from the *Mujahideen Khalq* in the hills overlooking Evin prison. SAVAK, the Shah's intelligence arm, claimed that the men were killed while trying to escape from prison, but it is widely believed the nine were executed.

64 **forklift trucks were used to make it easier for prisoners to be hanged from cranes:** "Khomeini Fatwa 'Led to Killing of 30,000 in Iran,'" Christina Lamb, *The Telegraph*, June 19, 2001.

64 **"The execution of several thousand prisoners in a few days will not have positive repercussions":** Ibid.

64 **"False comparisons are frequently made":** Samir Amin, "Political Islam," *CovertAction Quarterly* 71 (Winter 2001): 3–6, Washington, DC.

64 **"The club of the pen and the club of the tongue is the worst of clubs":** Shaul Bakhash, *The Reign of the Ayatollahs* (1984), p. 146.

67 **the office of the President is purely for Iran.:** "Bani-Sadr saga shows up the loopholes," *The Crescent International*, Toronto, July 16–31, 1981.

CHAPTER 5: PALESTINE—FUTURE ISLAMIC STATE?

73 **"homosexuals and lesbians, [are] a minority of perverts":** Zahar was interviewed by cnn's Wolf Blitzer on January 29, 2006. www.edition.cnn.com/TRANSCRIPTS/0601/29/le.01.html.

75 **Those secularists who support dictators and colonizers are mainly interested in living the good life:** Joseph Massad as quoted by Hussein Ibish in "Sense, Nonsense and Strategy in the New Palestinian Political Landscape," American Task Force on Palestine. www.americantaskforce.org/policy_and_analysis.

75 **"The position of Mahmud Darwish on Oslo":** As'ad AbuKhalil, The Angry Arab News Service, Monday, June 18, 2007. www.angryarab.blogspot.com/2007_06_01_archive.html.

75 **"I want Nobel. Please give me Nobel.":** Ibid. Saturday, July 21, 2007. www.angryarab.blogspot.com/2007_07_01_archive.html.

75 **"These hyperbolic, hyper-personalized and low-blow attacks":** Hussein Ibish, "Sense, Nonsense and Strategy in the New Palestinian Political Landscape," American Task Force on Palestine, September 7, 2007. www.americantaskforce.org/policy_and_analysis.

76 **opposed establishing any state on the basis of religion, "even if it's done by Hamas.":** Adonis was interviewed on Dubai TV on March 11, 2006.

77 **"And if the Mossad could arrange for Hamas . . . to take over the Palestinian streets from the PLO,":** Victor Ostrovsky, *The Other Side of Deception,* 196.

77 **"The Muslim Brotherhood leadership urged Fatah to purge its ranks":** Ziad Abu-Amr, Islamic Fundamentalism in the West Bank and Gaza, 49.

77 **the Israel secret service gave covert support to Hamas:** Robert Dreyfuss, *Devil's Game,* 208.

77 **acting "with the direct support of reactionary Arab re-gimes . . .":** *Corriere Della Sera,* December 11, 2001, as quoted in Robert Dreyfuss, *Devil's Game,* 209.

78 **"Can you blame Palestinians for now asking for a one-state solution?":** Jehad Aliweiwi in conversation with the author.

78 **"wrapping such organisations in the flag of Islam":** Samir Amin, "Political Islam," *CovertAction Weekly* 71 (Winter 2001): 3–6, Washington, DC.

82 **"Certainly Palestinian-Americans and their allies have to recognize that their traditional approaches have failed.":** Hussein Ibish, "Sense, Nonsense and Strategy in the New Palestinian Political Landscape."

82 **"Those liberals and leftists presently inclined to be sympathetic to Hamas need to step back":** Ibid.

82 **This scarred, marred brightness:** Faiz Ahmad Faiz, "The Dawn of Freedom," a poem written in August 1947 (translated by the author).

83 **Record!/ I am an Arab:** Mahmoud Darwish, "Identity Card," a poem written in 1964.

CHAPTER 6: THE PROPHET IS DEAD

88 **"out of their love for him, took an oath of allegiance.":** Abul Ala Maudoodi, *Khilafat o malooqiat,* 83.

89 **both accounts could be true, according to some sources:** Ali's claim came in a speech at the battle of Siffin ("Nasr Muzahim al-Minqari, Waqat Siffi ," ed. Abd al-Salam Muhammad Harun, Cairo 1962). For more on Aisha's claim, see Ibn Ishaq, *The Life of Muhammad.* Most historians and scholars of Islam side with Aisha's version of the

death of Muhammad, but some suggest that both accounts could be true (e.g., Barnaby Rogerson, *The Heirs of Muhammad*, 31).

90   **immediately after his death his companions started feuding over power:** Wilfred Madelung, *The Succession to Muhammad*, 43.

91   **ambition for the leadership replaced zeal for the religion:** Ali Dashti, *Twenty-Three Years: A Study of the Prophetic Career of Mohammad*, 167.

92   **the tendency to treat the religion as a means, rather than as an end in itself:** Ibid.

92   **"I know not if ever I shall meet you in this place after this year.":** Martin Lings, *Muhammad*, 334.

92   **"An Arab is superior to a non-Arab in nothing, but devotion.":** Maxime Rodinson, *Muhammad*, 286, from *Jahiz, kitab al-bayan wa-t-tabyin*, ed. Harun, Cairo.

93   **"We created you from a single (pair) of a male and a female,":** A. Yusuf Ali, trans. and commentator, *The Holy Quran*, verse 49.011, 1406.

93   **"I perfected your religion for you, completed.":** Ibid, chapter 5, verse 3, 240.

95   **"Dissensions have come like waves of darkness":** Hadith, or saying of the Prophet, as translated by Sir John Glubb, *The Life and Times of Muhammad*, 360.

95   **"Subversive attacks are falling one after another like waves of darkness":** Muhammad Husayn Haykal, *The Life of Muhammad*, 495.

95   **"Go, therefore and ask him if this affair [that is the caliphate] shall be ours":** Mahmoud M. Ayoub, *The Crisis of Muslim History*, 8, quoting Bin Qutaybah.

95   **"Stretch out your hand that I may pledge allegiance (ba'yah) to you":** Ibid.

96   **only Ali, his trusted lieutenant and son-in-law:** Martin Lings, *Muhammad*, 339.

96   **"Carry out the expedition to the Syrian border," he ordered.:** Ibn Ishaq, *The Life of Muhammad*, 173.

97   **"close them all save those which lead to the house of Abu-Bakr":** Ibid.

97   **"And this Ali is the guardian of all those for whom I am a guardian.":** Masnad Ahmad ibn-e-Hambal, vol. 4, 372, Ibn Kathir, *Al Bidaya wa nnihayah*, 209.

98   **"I have allowed only what the Quran allows":** Ibn Ishaq, *The Life of Muhammad*, 173.

98   **"a major contemporary Occidental work on the Prophet":** Edward Said, review of *Muhammad* by Maxime Rodinson, back cover.

98   **Those present were at first astonished, and then began arguing amongst themselves:** Ali Dashti, *Twenty-Three Years*, 174.

98   **Those present were much perplexed at this, wondering whether they ought to trust the abstractedness of a sick man.:** Maxime Rodinson, *Muhammad*, 288.

99   **However, Umar "held firmly to his judgment":** Muhammad Husayn Haykal, *The Life of Muhammad*, 500.

100   **"Oh men, if anyone worships Muhammad, Muhammad is dead.":** Ibn Ishaq, *The Life of Muhammad*, 651.

100   **Muhammad is only a messenger:** Ahmed Ali, trans. *Al-Quran*, 64.

101   **"everyone had forgotten the body still lying in Aisha's little hut.":** Maxime Rodinson, *Muhammad*, 291.

102   **"Strengthen your hold on this affair":** Mahmoud M. Ayoub, *The Crisis of Muslim History*, 9. Ayoub quotes from an early account of the Saqifah debate attributed to Abd Allah b. Muslim bin Qutaybah al Dinwari.

103   **"Nonetheless, a group of you have gone to the extreme of seeking to deprive us of our natural leadership":** Muhammad Husayn Haykal, *The Life of Muhammad*, 509.

103   he was "ready to put an end to this situation once and for all by the sword.": Ibid, 509.

103   "We are therefore the chiefs (Umara) and you (the people of Medina) are the subordinates (Wuzura).": Mahmoud M. Ayoub, *The Crisis of Muslim History*, 11. Ayoub quotes from Bin Qutaybah again.

103   "The Arabs do not and will not recognize any sovereignty": Muhammad Husayn Haykal, *The Life of Muhammad*, 509.

103   they should recognize the Meccan Arabs as the "leaders" and consider themselves as no more than the "helpers.": Tabari, *The History of al-Tabari*, vol. 10, 4–5.

104   "delegate the management of their affairs to those among whom prophethood appears": Ibid.

104   "If the men of Khazraj were to show their ambitions concerning this affair": Mahmoud M. Ayoub, *The Crisis of Muslim History*, 11–12. Ayoub is quoting from Uthman bin Bahr al-Jahiz.

105   "O Abu-Bakr, stretch forth your hand": Muhammad Husayn Haykal, 510.

105   Umar cursing the old man, "Kill Sa'ad, may God kill Sa'ad.": Mahmoud M. Ayoub, *The Crisis of Muslim History*, 15.

105   "By God, if you remove a single hair from it": Tabari, *The History of al-Tabari*, vol. 10, 8–9.

105   "Pre-Islamic mode of authority surfaced immediately after Muhammad's death": Liyakat N. Takim, *The Heirs of the Prophet*, 6.

106   "Islam came to be identified with the Arabs.": Ibid, 7.

106   At his public ceremony in the Prophet's Mosque in Medina, Abu-Bakr gave a stirring speech,: To this day, Abu-Bakr's speech is considered the standard that Muslim heads of government claim to aspire to. Few, if any, have met that threshold.

106   "I am appointed to govern you, although I'm not the best of you.": Ibn Ishaq, *The Life of Muhammad*, 175.

106   Ibn Khaldun (1332–1406) was a Tunisian Berber. As a historian, sociologist, and philosopher, his reputation rests on *The Book of Exemplaries and the Collection of Origins and Information Respecting the History of the Arabs, Foreigners and Berbers and Others Who Possess Great Power*. Just the introduction to this seven-volume work is considered a masterpiece. Titled "Muqaddima," it is a systematic analysis of the development of history and society, and one of the earliest rational philosophies of history.

107   Islamic scholars have discussed the qualities required in a caliph: Abd-al Aziz Abd-al-Qadir Kamil, *Islam and the Race Question*, 40.

108   only the ailing Saad bin Ubadah refusing to acknowledge Abu-Bakr's caliphate.: Saad bin Ubadah later left Medina and migrated to Syria, where he died in mysterious circumstances many years later, some say, at the instigation of Umar.

108   "Abu-Bakr, leading the funeral procession would appear as the Prophet's appointed successor.": Maxime Rodinson, *Muhammad*, 292.

108   only when she heard Ali and his Uncle Abbas digging the grave in the middle of the night.: Ibn Ishaq, *The Life of Muhammad*, 177.

108   approached the tribal leaders of Medina, seeking their support in his dispute with Abu-Bakr.: Mahmoud M. Ayoub, *The Crisis of Muslim History*, 19, from Bin Qutaybah, v. 1, 29–30.

108   "Should I have left the Messenger of God in his house unburied and gone to quarrel with men over his authority?": Ibid, 19.

109   "You would then have killed the brother of the Messenger of God.": Ibid, 20.

109   "That you are the servant of God, yes we agree": Ibid.

109   *Peshawar Nights* is a book written by one Sultanu'l-Wa'izin Shirazi. It claims to be an account of a public debate between Shias and Sunnis on January 27, 1927, in the city of Peshawar. The dialogue was held in Farsi and the transcript, made by four reporters and published in the newspapers, was published in book form in Tehran in 1971, the year Sultanu'l-Wa'izin died at the age of seventy-five.

109   "We prophets do not give any inheritance.": Mahmoud M. Ayoub, *The Crisis of Muslim History*, 21.

110   "You have defrauded us of our right and did not heed it.": Quoted in Mahmoud M. Ayoub, *The Crisis of Muslim History*, 23.

110   "I wish I had not searched the house of Fatima": Quoted in Mahmoud M. Ayoub, *The Crisis of Muslim History*, 29.

111   "The conquest . . . intoxicated the Arabs with pride.": Ali Dashti, *Twenty-Three Years*, 179.

CHAPTER 7: MEDINA—THE POLITICS OF THE RIGHTLY GUIDED CALIPHS

112   "The period of the 'Right-going' Caliphate": Abul Ala Maudoodi, "Political Thought in Early Islam," in M.M. Sharif, ed., *A History of Muslim Philosophy*, 665.

113   "the complete and perfect model of an Islamic political system does not exist today.": Jamal Badawi, "The Nature of the Islamic Political System," *IslamOnline.Net*, October 10, 2004, published online at www.islamonline.net/English/introducingislam/politics/Politics/article05.shtml.

115   "the Negro nations are, as a rule, submissive to slavery": Ibn Khaldun, *The Muqaddimah*, 117.

115   writes in glowing terms about the time of the first four Muslim caliphs: Abul Ala Maudoodi, in M.M. Sharif, ed., *A History of Muslim Philosophy*, p. 665.

115   "slave with a mutilated ear.": Tabari, *The History of al-Tabari*, vol. 14, 43.

116   "I am not the caliph of God": Ibn Khaldun, *The Muqaddimah*, 389.

116   "O People, I have been given authority over you; yet, I am not the best of you.": Barnaby Rogerson, *The Heirs of Muhammad*, 129.

117   the apostate is threatened with punishment in the next world only.: Verses 3:72, 3:90–91, 16:106, 4:137, and 5:54 of the Quran deal with apostasy directly and do not prescribe death or any earthly punishment.

118   "There is no compulsion and coercion": Abul Ala Maududi, trans., *The Holy Quran*, verse 2:256, 63.

118   Malik's head was struck off: Ali Abd al-Razik, *Islam and the Fundamentals of Authority*, 520.

119   There is no god, but God: Ibid, 522.

119   "Cover not Truth with falsehood": A. Yusuf Ali, trans., *The Holy Quran*, verse 2:42.

120   Abu-Bakr's injunction that the Quraysh Arabs of Mecca were divinely ordained to rule: Mahmoud M. Ayoub, *The Crisis of Muslim History*, 11, citing Bin Qutaybah.

120   obedience to the Imams is . . . obedience to God: Ali Abd al-Razik, *Islam and the Fundamentals of Authority*, 526–27.

122   **dirhams:** The silver dirham was the currency of early Islam, adopted from the name the Greek coin, the Drachm. The silver dirham and the Islamic gold dinar continued to be the dominant international currencies until the 13th century.

122   **Abu Bakr's allowance:** Reuben Levy, *The Social Structure of Islam*, 412.

123   **O guide of the way, it is either the light of dawn or evil!:** Tabari, *The History of al-Tabari*, vol. 11, 148.

125   *Mawali* is an Arabic word used to address non-Arab Muslims. In the early years of Islam, after the Prophet's death, the Mawali were considered second class in Arabian society, even beneath freed Arab slaves. After Umar set the rules of *sabiqa*, the term gained wide usage and was widely applied to many non-Arabs such as Persians, Egyptians, Indians, and Turks who had converted to Islam after Arab armies conquered these territories. Whereas the Quran and Muhammad spoke of the equality of all, irrespective of race, these new Muslim converts were treated as second-class citizens by the ruling Arab elite of the Umayyad dynasty.

125   **"Messenger of God was frugal":** Tabari, *The History of al-Tabari*, vol. 12, 206.

126   **"I will follow the example of the Messenger of God and Abu-Bakr.":** Al-Yaqubi. *The History of Al-Yaqubi*. vol. 2, 152–54.

127   **"Stoning is a duty laid down in Allah's Book":** Sahih Muslim, *Book 17*: 4194.

127   **"a goat ate the piece of paper while we were mourning.":** Sunan Ibn Maja, vol. 2, 39.

128   **"The messenger of God permitted it at a time of necessity.":** Tabari, *The History of al-Tabari*, vol. 14, 140.

128   **triggered the assassination:** Tabari, *The History of al-Tabari*, vol. 14, 90.

129   **had Ali ibn Abu Talib in mind as one of his targets:** Wilfred Madelung, *The Succession to Muhammad*, 69.

129   **"I commend to the caliph after my death the Arabs":** Tabari, *The History of al-Tabari*, vol. 14, 92.

130   **"The Bedouins, who are the original Arabs":** Ibid, 142.

130   **Speaking ill of the Companions of the Prophet:** Shaikh Faraz Rabbani, *SunniPath. com*, as seen on May 14, 2007.

131   **Abu-Bakr and Umar—carried on with his mission successfully.:** Abul Ala Maudoodi, *A Short History of the Revivalist Movement in Islam*, 26–27.

131   **weakened the Caliphate.:** Ibid.

132   **"What prevents you from appointing him":** Al-Baladhuri, *The Origins of the Islamic State*, vol. 2, 501.

132   **"When I am dead, hold your consultations for three days.":** Tabari, *The History of al-Tabari*, vol. 14, 146.

132   **"How eager you both are to get hold of the caliphate.":** Ibid, 93.

132   **"I do not like dissension in the family.":** Ibid, 145.

133   **"Umar had prepared the gesture for me.":** Mahmoud M. Ayoub, *The Crisis of Muslim History*, 51.

133   **"Today evil was born.":** Ibid.

134   **God has commanded the Imans to be shepherds.:** Tabari, *The History of al-Tabari*, vol. 15, 7.

134   **"I have decided to be generous towards my next of kin.":** Al-Baladhuri, vol. 2, 512.

134   **"O you who believe, obey God and the Prophet and those in authority among you,"** Ahmed Ali, trans., *Al-Quran*, chapter 4, verse 59.

136   **his exhortations against the wealthy elites:** Tabari, *The History of al-Tabari*, vol. 15, 65.

138   **blames the unrest:** Tabari, *The History of Islam*, vol. 2, 22.

141   **Ya'la bin Umayyah, stepped forward with a donation:** Tabari, *The History of al-Tabari*, vol. 14, 41–42.

142   **"I will seek revenge for his blood.":** Tabari, *The History of al-Tabari*, vol. 16, 52.

147   **"Authority belongs to God":** Tabari, *The History of al-Tabari*, vol. 17, 218.

CHAPTER 8: DAMASCUS—ISLAM'S ARAB EMPIRE

149   **Ali should not have become the fourth caliph of Islam:** Akbar Shah Najeebabadi, *The History of Islam*, vol. 2, 24. This book was originally written in the Urdu language in 1922.

150   **"cannot co-exist in our family.":** Ibid.

153   **When this ruse failed:** Wilfred Madelung, *The Succession to Muhammad*, 320.

154   **"He decreed that that there would be differences between Ali and Amir Muawiyah and the opportunities that followed.":** Akbar S. Najeebabadi, *The History of Islam*, vol. 2, 53.

154   **"tyrant kingdom,":** Abul Ala Maudoodi, *A Short History of the Revivalist Movement in Islam*, 26–27.

154   **"Whoever enters the house of Abu Sufyan shall be secure":** Husayn Haykal, *The Life of Muhammad*, 403.

155   **Arab sense of pride of Arab identity reasserted itself:** Liyakat N. Takim, *Heirs of the Prophet*, 7.

155   **the Umayyad government took on the colours of an Arab government:** Abul Ala Maudoodi, *Khilafat o malookiyat* (Caliphate and Monarchy), 169–70. Under the Umayyads, non-Arab non-Muslims would first be invited to enter Islam. Then the non-Muslim tax would be imposed on them because they were not Arabs. And if they wanted to revert back to their original faith, they faced the death penalty, which, contrary to the Quran, was instituted as the punishment for Muslims leaving Islam.

156   **the Berber African Muslims staged a rebellion:** Maribel Fierro, *Abd al-Rahman III*, 8–9.

156   **executed the Sindhi Muslim ruler:** Khalid Yahya Blankinship, *The End of the Jihad State*, 132.

156   **when Sind was invaded by Muhammad bin Qassim:** Andre Wink, *Al-Hindi: The Making of the Indo-Islamic World*, 172.

157   **Chroniclers write that Qassim brought back "120,000,000 dirhams.":** Ibid, 174.

157   **"120,000,000 dirhams.":** To this day, Muslims in Sind and the rest of Pakistan are taught to respect and eulogize the invading Umayyad army and to understand the plunder of their own land as a tribute to Islam. Textbooks in Pakistan don't mention that Sind already had a Muslim population and that many Muslims served as advisers to Rajah Dahir against Muhammad bin Qassim. It is little wonder that Umayyad rule in India did not last long and left little impact on the culture, cuisine, and language of the Sindhi Muslims. In fact, the Islam that gripped Sind, Baluchistan, and Punjab was deeply influenced by Persian and Turkish Sufis, and this is true even today.

158   **"you will give birth to a king":** Akbar S. Najeebabadi, *The History of Islam*, vol. 2, 27.

158 **"Jibril came to me and said, 'O Muhammad',":** Aisha Bewly, *Muawiyah*, 5.

158 **"Consult Muawiyah in your affairs":** Ibid, 5.

159 **"Do not refrain from abusing Ali and criticizing him":** Tabari, *The History of al-Tabari*, vol. 18, 123.

159 **"the instruction that in sermons from the pulpit, Ali should be reviled and insulted.":** Abul Ala Maudoodi, *Khilafat o malookiyat*, 174.

162 **He wrote a secret letter to the governor of Medina:** Tabari, *The History of al-Tabari*, vol. 19, 2–3.

163 **"Do not attack Mecca.":** Ibid, 12.

164 **"let us attack him in the heart of the Ka'aba":** Ibid, 12.

164 **asking him to come to Kufa to lead the challenge to Yazid.:** Ibid, 24–25.

164 **"The janab has grown green":** Ibid, 26.

165 **urging him to make the move to Kufa, where an army waited for him to lead:** Ibid, 57.

166 **Both Muslim and Hani were beheaded:** Tabari, *The History of al-Tabari*, vol. 19, 74–75, 89.

166 **"By God! We will not go back until we have taken our vengeance":** Ibid, 94.

167 **"A ballista with which we bombard the pillars of the mosque":** Ibid, 224.

169 **The caravans should not be set out except for three mosques:** Ahmad b. Abu Ya'qub, Ibn Wadih al-Ya'qubi, *Tarikh al-Yakubi*, vol. 2, 271, Darul Sadr, Beirut. Translation from http://www.islamic-awareness.org/History/Islam/Dome_Of_The_Rock/hajjdome.html, as seen on July 12, 2007.

170 **The reason for its construction:** Chase F. Robinson, *Makers of the Muslim World: Abd al-Malik*, 6.

170 **end of institutional discrimination against non-Arabs:** During the earlier caliphates, while non-Muslim Arabs were permitted to convert to Islam, non-Arabs were discouraged and even when they did convert, they could only do so through the sponsorship of an Arab *mawla*, hence the term *Mawalis*.

171 **Islam "as the property of the conquering aristocracy.":** G.R. Hawting, *The First Dynasty of Islam*, 4.

172 **Another nephew of his had a hand and foot chopped off:** Reinhart Dozy, *Spanish Islam*, 161.

CHAPTER 9: CORDOBA—ISLAM'S EUROPEAN VENTURE

173 **The rich synthesis of learning and culture nurtured in Muslim Spain:** Erna Paris, *The End of Days*, 46–47.

174 **"the very idea of pluralism was perceived as a threat:** Ibid, 47.

174 **"The arrival of the Almohads":** Ibid, 49.

176 **Attempts to move south towards the fabled Wangara:** Marq de Villiers and Sheila Hirtle, *Timbuktu*, 10.

176 **"Ye Muslims whither can you flee?":** Syed Azizur Rahman, *The Story of Islamic Spain*, 22.

178 **there was no religious stipulation:** Linda Zagzebski, *Philosophy of Religion: An Historical Introduction*, 217.

178 **clerics publicly burned many of Averroes' books:** Centuries later, the works of Averroes would again be tossed into mountains of burning books by conquering Christian armies who set fire to all Jewish or Muslim texts as they captured Grenada in 1492.

178 **"If one has the means to provide either the [Sabbath] lamp":** Moses Maimonides (Ibn-Maimon), *Misneh Torah.*

180 **"What is the point of life without our books of learning?" he cried through scorching lungs.:** Tariq Ali, *Shadows of the Pomegranate Tree,* 4–5.

181 **"not a tax-collector.":** Reinhart Dozy, *Spanish Islam,* 123.

181 **"God sent Mohammad to call men to the true Faith":** Ibid, 130.

182 **"its van will be upon them before the rear has left Damascus.":** Ibid, 133.

182 **"behead all that fell into his hands":** Ibid, 133.

185 **The Umayyad emirs** of al-Andalus were: Abd al-Rahman I (756–88), Hisham I (788–96), al-Hakam I (796–822), Abd al-Rahman II (822–52), Muhammad I of Cordoba (852–86), Al-Mundhir (886–88), and Abdallah ibn Muhammad (888–912).

185 **"The Golden Age of the Umayyad Caliphate,":** Hugh Kennedy, *Muslim Spain and Portugal,* 82.

186 **Hisham III** was the last of the Umayyad caliphs, who included: Al-Hakam II (961–76), Hisham II (976–1008), Mohammed II (1008–9), Suleiman (1009–10), Hisham II again (1010–12), Suleiman again (1012–17), Abd al-Rahman IV (1021–22), Abd al-Rahman V (1022–23), Muhammad III (1023–24), and Hisham III (1027–31).

188 **The Spanish term** *Taifa* in the history of Iberia refers to an independent Muslim-ruled principality, an emirate or petty kingdom, of which a number were formed in Andalusia after the final collapse of the Umayyad Caliphate of Cordoba in 1031.

190 **"Kill them all. God will recognise His own.":** Sumption, *The Albigensian Crusade,* 93, as quoted by Michael Baigent and Richard Leigh in *The Inquistion,* 12.

191 **"Islamic issue which brought about more bloodshed":** Philip K. Hitti, *History of the Arabs,* 139.

192 **"make raids on our neighbour":** Ibid, 25.

195 **"The mints of Granada":** William Prescott, *History of the Reign of Ferdinand and Isabella,* vol. 1, 317.

196 **"The ruins of Zahara":** Ibid, 318.

197 **the importance of Malaga:** William Prescott, *History of the Reign of Ferdinand and Isabella,* vol. 2, 25.

197 **"decreed the fall of Granada":** Ibid, 70.

198 **"Y weep like a woman":** Ibid, 99.

CHAPTER 10: BAGHDAD—ISLAM EMBRACES THE PERSIANS

199 **The Abbasid caliphs** based their claim to the caliphate on their descent from Abbas ibn Abd al-Mutalib (566–662), the youngest uncle of Prophet Muhammad, by virtue of which descent they regarded themselves as the rightful heirs of Muhammad as opposed to the Umayyads. The Umayyads were descended from Umayyah, and were a clan separate from Muhammad's in the Quraysh tribe.

200 **"largely of the old desert type.":** De Lacy O'Leary, *How Greek Science Passed to the Arabs,* 146.

201 **Abu Muslim** was the leader of the Abbasid revolt. Born in Balkh (now in Afghanistan) of Tajik ancestry, he established Abu al-Abbas as-Saffah as the head of the Abbasid family in 749 and subsequently as the caliph of Islam. He led the charge against Damascus and was instrumental in the defeat of the Ummayads. Abu Muslim later became governor of Khurasan, but because of his immense popularity and power, Caliph Mansoor had him murdered.

201 **no job more interesting and enjoyable:** Akbar Shah Najeebabadi, *The History of Islam,* vol. 2, 275.

203 **Anbar** is the province in Iraq where US troops faced large-scale resistance until the local sheikhs and tribal leaders were enlisted to fight the Al-Qaeda units.

206 **You have laid claim to this office:** Tabari, *The History of al-Tabari,* vol. 28, 167–69.

207 **"Muhammad was not the father of anyone":** Quran, 33:40.

207 **We, not you, are the heirs:** Tabari, *The History of al-Tabari,* vol. 28, 169–76.

208 **refuge and protection with a Hindu prince:** John Glubb, *The Empire of the Arabs,* 243.

209 **"This is a good place for an army camp.":** Tabari, *The History of al-Tabari,* vol. 28, 238.

211 **My good fortune:** John Glubb, *The Empire of the Arabs,* 262.

211 **smothered by two slaves.:** Hugh Kennedy, *The Court of the Caliphs,* 62.

213 **"Here I am":** Philip Kennedy, *Abu Nuwas,* 20–21.

213 **the most momentous intellectual awakening:** Philip Hitti, *History of the Arabs,* 306.

213 **Muhammad ibn Musa al-Khwarizmi** (780–850) was an Uzbek mathematician, astronomer, astrologer, and geographer. Born in Khiva, Uzbekistan, he worked most of his life as a scholar in the House of Wisdom in Baghdad. His *Algebra* was the first book on the systematic solution of linear and quadratic equations.

213 **Muhammad ibn Ibrahim al-Fazari** (d. 796) was a Persian philosopher, mathematician, and astronomer who is credited with building the first astrolabe instrument.

214 **adding his own contribution.:** Philip Hitti, *History of the Arabs,* 307.

218 **"For naphtha and shavings for burning the boy":** Robert Payne, *A History of Islam,* 168.

218 **when Harun Rashid died:** Tabari, *The History of al-Tabari,* vol. 30, 335.

222 **Harun Nasution begins his treatise:** Dwi S. Atmaja, Richard C. Martin, and Mark R. Woodward, *Defenders of Reason in Islam,* 9.

223 **"We confess that God has two eyes, without asking how":** Ian Almond, *Sufism and Deconstruction,* 11.

223 **"saved orthodoxy":** Quoted in Pervez Hoodbhoy, *Islam and Science,* 104.

223 **"reckon as unbelievers":** Hasan Dilshad, *Islam: Philosophy and Ideology,* 59.

224 **"there is no cause but God.":** Quoted by Averroes (Ibn-Rush) in *Tahafut al-Tahafut* (The Incoherence of the Incoherence), 316–17.

224 **"My teacher":** Mohamed Elmasry, *The Quran: 365 Selections for Daily Reading.*

226 **the right to the wealth** : "And those in whose wealth is a recognised right. For the (needy) who asks and him who is prevented (for some reason from asking)," Abdullah Yusuf Ali, *The Meaning of the Holy Qur'an.*

227 **rivers were clogged:** Philip Hitti, *History of the Arabs,* 468.

228 **Maalouf's account:** Amin Maalouf, *The Crusades through Arab Eyes,* 52.

229 **"How dare you slumber":** Ibid, xiii.

229 **"Man's meanest weapon,":** Amin Maalouf, *The Crusades Through Arab Eyes,* xiii.

230 **"death knell of Arab civilization?":** Ibid, 261.

230 **the Crusaders "exposed":** Ibid, 261.

230 **"Their leaders were all foreigners.":** Ibid, 261.

230 **"the Muslim world turned in on itself.":** Ibid, 264.

231 **"ruthlessly slaughtered.":** Philip Hitti, *History of the Arabs,* 486.

232   **They swept through the city like hungry falcons,:** Quoted in Edwin Black, *Banking on Baghdad*, 46.

233   **The river ran black with scholars' ink:** Ian Frazier, "Destroying Baghdad," *The New Yorker*, April 25, 2005.

234   **"home-grown religious orthodoxy.":** Pervez Hoodbhoy, *Islam and Science*, 109.

CHAPTER 11: SHARIA—GOD'S LAW OR MAN'S FLAW?

239   **Hasan Mahmud** is the author of *Islam and Sharia*. He is the director of sharia law on the board of the Muslim Canadian Congress, in which capacity he has been a thorn in the side of the Islamist establishment, successfully debating them in public forums including television.

240   *Ihya ulum al-din* (The Revival of the Religious Sciences) is a classic by Imam Ghazali, the 11th-century Persian philosopher. It's a work of Muslim spirituality, and has, for centuries, been the most widely read work after the Quran in the Muslim world.

241   **settle their affairs based on the laws revealed by Allah,:** Syed Wasi M. Nadvi, "Muslim Qawaneen aur Canadian Musalman," *Monthly Afaq*, Toronto, July 2003.

241   **far greater crime than a mere breach of contract:** Rabia Mills, "A Review of the Muslim Personal/Family Law Campaign," August 1995, www.muslim-canada.org/pfl. htm.

242   **The MCC** was founded by a handful of us in the aftermath of 9/11. The group seeks to promote the concept of a separation of religion and state, and an end to what it calls "gender apartheid." See www.MuslimCanadianCongress.org.

242   **ghettoizes the Muslim community:** Submissions by Muslim Canadian Congress. Review of Arbitration Process by Marion Boyd, August 26, 2004, www.muslimcanadiancongress. org/20040826.pdf.

242   **"Muslim principles":** Marion Boyd, "Dispute Resolution in Family Law: Protecting Choice, Promoting Inclusion," December 20, 2004.

243   **"the need to combat Pan-Islamism":** V.I. Lenin, *Lenin's Collected Works*, 2nd Eng. ed., vol. 31, 144–51.

243   **multi-tier legal system:** Omid Safi, "Progressive Muslims Oppose Introduction of Shariah Law in Canada," January 5, 2005, www.pmuna.org/archives/2005/01/ progressive_mus_2.php.

244   **a parallel private-sector judiciary:** Tarek Fatah, "Keep sharia law out of Canadian judicial system," *The Record*, August 12, 2005.

244   **the viability of their oppressive visions.:** Omid Safi, "Progressive Muslims Oppose Introduction of Shariah Law in Canada," January 5, 2005, www.pmuna. org/archives/2005/01/progressive_mus_2.php.

245   **"Is it possible to apply the sharia":** Estanislao Oziewicz, "Muslim Law Cleric Doubts Sharia Suitable for Canadian Society," *The Globe and Mail*, May 14, 2005.

245   **introduce Sharia with a different name.:** Taj Hashmi, "Sharia Is Neither Islamic, Nor Canadian," *Muslim Wakeup*, December 31, 2004, www.muslimwakeup.com/main/ archives/2004/12/sharia_is_neith.php#more.

246   **Council for American-Islamic Relations:** In July 2007, CAIR was named as an unindicted co-conspirator in a Texas case against a charity accused of ties to terrorists, which ended in a mistrial.

246   **"reviled" by many Muslims:** Haroon Siddiqui, "Sensationalism shrouds the debate on sharia," *The Toronto Star*, June 12, 2005.

246   **restored order:** Haroon Siddiqui, "Clash of Suspect Motives Clouds Controversy over Nigerian Lashing," *The Toronto Star,* January 21, 2001.

246   **no right to tell religious people:** "Muslim group opposes sharia law," *The Toronto Star,* August 28, 2004.

246   **outlawed all religious courts:** "McGuinty: No Sharia Law," *The Toronto Star,* September 12, 2005.

247   **strives to implement Islam:** Muslim Association of Canada, www.macnet.ca/national/modules/wfchannel/index.php?pagenum=7.

247   **"different but equal.":** "Debate Stirs Hatred, Sharia Activists Say," *The Globe and Mail,* September 15, 2005.

247   **"righteous change":** ISNA Canada website, www.isnacanada.com/isna/about.html.

248   **give us religious rights:** *The Times,* "If You Want Sharia Law, You Should Go and Live in Saudi," August 20, 2006, www.timesonline.co.uk/tol/news/article613976.ece.

248   **"go and live in Saudi Arabia.":** Ibid.

248   **a little honesty:** Ibid.

249   **Stockholm Syndrome,:** Hasan Mahmud's book *Islam and Sharia* is an impressive effort by the author, who delves deeply into sharia literature, from the most authentic Islamic sources, and dissects it in a scholarly way to prove his point that man-made sharia law is fundamentally flawed.

249   **immutable Basic Code:** Khan, Ali L., "The Second Era of Islamic Creativity," *University of St. Thomas Law Journal,* vol. 1, 2003, 341.

251   **"A Quranic injunction":** Hashim Kamali, *Principles of Islamic Jurisprudence,* 31.

252   **explicit command of God:** Syed Abul Ala Maudoodi, *Islamic Law and Constitution,* 140.

252   **"Islam wishes to destroy all States":** S. Abul Ala Maudoodi, *Jihad in Islam,* 6.

252   **integrated into the process of law:** Hashim Kamali, *Principles of Islamic Jurisprudence,* xiii.

253   **no longer capable:** Ibid, 50.

253   **cannot co-exist:** Abdullahi an-Na'im, *Toward an Islamic Reformation,* 8.

253   **"The legal theory of Usul":** Hashim Kamali, *Principles of Islamic Jurisprudence,* 502.

253   **historical necessities are used to justify:** Abdul-Aziz Sachedina, *Islamic Root, of Democratic Pluralism,* 57.

253   **"All human beings are born free":** Universal Declaration of Human Rights, adopted and proclaimed by the UN General Assembly on December 10, 1948, www.un.org/Overview/rights.html.

255   **You are not a watcher:** Chapter 6, Sura al-Anaam, verse 66, chapter 4, Sura al-Nisa, verse 83, chapter 6, Sura al-Anaam, verse 106–7, chapter 10, Sura Yunus, verse 108, chapter 17, Sura mal-Isra, verse 54, chapter 39, Sura al-Zumar, verse 41, chapter 42, al-Shura, verse 48, chapter 88, Sura al-Ghashiyah, verse 21–24.

256   **no dispute between scholars:** *Hadis al Kafi,* vol. 1. Similar information is also found in the website www.irib.ir/Special/imam%20ali/html/en/quran_compiled_by_imam_ali.htm.

257   **sharia laws:** Hasan Mahmud, *Islam and Sharia,* 24.

257   **left Islam:** A. Guillaume, in his translation of Ibn Ishaq's *Sirat rasul Allah* (The Life of Muhammad), has an account of the incident involving Abdulla Bin Saad as the Prophet entered Mecca after conquering it: "The Apostle had instructed his commanders when they entered Mecca, only to fight those who resisted them,

except a small number who were to be killed, among them Abdullah bin Saad who had been a Muslim and used to write down the revelations. Later he abandoned Islam and returned to Quraysh. Saad brought before the Apostle and asked that he might be granted immunity. Muhammad is said to have remained silent for a long time till finally he said Yes, and Saad's life was spared." (550)

258   **sharia-compliant mortgages:** Tavia Grant, "Sharia-Compliant Finance Is Increasingly Popular," *The Globe and Mail,* May 7, 2007.

259   **They all have little twists:** Ibid.

259   **five-thousand-person waiting list:** Ibid.

260   **watched, waited, and learned:** J. Millard Burr and Robert O. Collins, *Alms for Jihad,* 62.

262   **"a convenient pretext":** Timur Kuran, *Islam and Mammon: The Economic Predicaments of Islamism.*

262   **"dishonest banking practices.":** Muhammad Saleem, *Islamic Banking: A $300 Billion Deception,* back cover. 47. Ibid, 11.

262   **usury:** Timur Kuran, *Islam and Mammon: The Economic Predicaments of Islamism.*

262   **no distinctly Islamic way:** Ibid.

262   **"conducive to Islamist militancy.":** Muhammad Saleem, *Islamic Banking: A $300 Billion Deception,* 35.

263   **charging interest:** Ibid, 30–31.

263   **"praise each other":** Ibid, 32.

264   **he could not tell the difference:** Ibid, 31.

264   **Mecca Burger:** Ibid, 26.

265   **two types of Islam:** Ali Shariati, *Modernization and Islam: Refinement of Cultural Resources and from Where Should We Begin?* http://www.ghazali.net/book4/Appendix-I/appendix-i.html.

265   **Tomorrow's Islam:** Laleh Bakhtiar, *Shariati on Shariati and the Muslim Woman,* xxxviii.

Chapter 12: Jihad—Permanent War or Continuous Struggle?

267   **protection racket:** Not that this protection racket was exclusive to Muslim rulers. The Byzantines had imposed it on the Umayyads. In fact, in 1990 the Americans would run a similar protection racket, extracting from the Kuwaitis the cost of protecting it from Saddam Hussein's army.

267   **Muslim rulers had been running:** Many Muslim rulers throughout history have extracted tribute from weaker neighbouring non-Muslim states, but one of the earliest instances was in 782. The Abbasid army led by Haroon Rashid failed to conquer Constantinople, but was able to extract a humiliating peace treaty, signed near the Straits of Marmara, that forced Byzantine Queen Irene to pay a tribute of seventy thousand to ninety thousands dinars every year to the caliph's treasury as tribute.

267   **right and duty to make war:** Thomas Jefferson's communication to the Continental Congress, as reported in Michael B. Oren, *Power, Faith and Fantasy,* 27.

267   **Treaty of Tripoli:** The Treaty of Peace and Friendship between the United States and the Bey and Subjects of Tripoli of Barbary was authored by US diplomat Joel Barlow in 1796. Article 11 of the treaty read, "As the Government of the United States of America is not, in any sense, *founded on the Christian religion* [emphasis mine]; as it has in itself no character of enmity against the laws, religion, or tranquility, of Mussulmen; and, as

the said States never entered into any war, or act of hostility against any Mahometan nation, it is declared by the parties, that no pretext arising from religious opinions, shall ever produce an interruption of the harmony existing between the two countries." The treaty was first signed and sealed at Tripoli of Barbary in the year of the Hegira 1211—corresponding with November 4, 1796 CE. The treaty was sent to the floor of the Senate on June 7, 1797, where it was read aloud and unanimously approved. John Adams, having seen the treaty, signed it and proclaimed it to his country on June 10, 1797.

268   **"courses of action":** *Sahih Muslim* is one of the six major collections of the hadith (sayings) of Prophet Muhammad, collected by Imam Muslim. Although this ranks as the second most important hadith collection among Muslims, Shia Muslims dismiss it as inauthentic.

268   **The caliph makes war:** Ahmad ibn Naqib al-Misri, *Reliance of the Traveller*, 602–3.

269   *Sahih al-Bukhari* is considered the "reliable" book containing the "authentic" hadith (sayings) of Prophet Muhammad. They were compiled by Imam Bukhari of Khurasan about two hundred years after the Prophet's death. Bukhari collected 300,000 hadith, then rejected most as unreliable, choosing only 7,563 and saving them in hard copy. There is no record of the 293,000 rejected hadith.

269   **Jihad:** Muhammad Muhsin Khan, *Summarized Sahih al-Bukhari*, 1081.

269   **greater jihad:** Seyyed Hossein Nasr, *The Heart of Islam: Enduring Values for Humanity*, 260.

270   **slay The Pagans:** A. Yusuf Ali, trans., *The Holy Quran*, verse 5:9, 439.

270   **A promise binding on Him:** Ibid, verse 9:111, 474.

272   **"to establish the supremacy of Islam" worldwide.:** "Our Followers 'Must Live in Peace until Strong Enough to Wage Jihad,'" *The Times*, September 8, 2007, www.timesonline.co.uk/tol/comment/faith/article2409833.ece.

273   **"Your fight will prevail":** CNN: *Soldiers of God*, aired September 29, 2001. www.edition.cnn.com/SPECIALS/cold.war/episodes/20/script.html.

273   **"their blood.":** Ibid.

273   **"it's martyrdom.":** Dean Nielson, "Bin Laden's Deputy behind Red Mosque Bloodbath," *Sunday Times*, July 15, 2007, www.timesonline.co.uk/tol/news/world/asia/article2076013.ece.

274   **"jihad is obligatory":** Hassan al-Banna Shaheed, *Selected Writings of Hassan al-Banna Shaheed*, 31.

274   **supreme sacrifice:** Abul Ala Maudoodi, *Towards Understanding Islam*, 125.

274   **plainly a hypocrite:** Ibid, 125.

275   **to legitimize holy wars:** John L. Esposito, "Want to Understand Islam? Start Here," *The Washington Post*, July 22, 2007, www.washingtonpost.com/wpdyn/content/article/2007/07/20/AR2007072002137.html.

275   **negligent.:** Hassan al-Banna Shaheed, *Selected Writings of Hassan al-Banna Shaheed*, 52–53.

275   **It would be naïve to assume:** Seyyid Qutb, *Milestones*, 62.

276   **A Muslim has no country except:** Ibid, 118–19.

276   **no Islam in a land:** Ibid, 127.

276   **whenever an enemy attacks:** S. Abul Ala Maududi, *Call to Jihad*, 9.

277   **Jihad and Qetal:** Ibid, 34–35.

277   **specifically for war:** Seyyid Qutb, *Milestones*, 124.

277 **Jihad is as much a primary duty:** Ibid, 124.
278 **only one party of God:** Ibid, 117.
278 **accept the Shariah:** Ibid, 36.
278 **state of affairs in Britain:** Tarek Fatah, "Attack the ideology of Jihad: Tony Blair's strategy of cosying up to Islamists only helped to excuse those who condemn terror attacks but refuse to actually denounce jihad," *Ottawa Citizen,* July 4, 2007.
279 **doctrine of jihad:** Facebook Note. "The Glasgow Bombing: It's time to attack the ideology of Jihad," July 4, 2007. www.facebook.com/note.php?note_id=3449320246 &id=601700011&index=56#comments.
280 **no social vision:** Urooj Zia, "Learn from Latin America," *The Daily Times,* Lahore, September 5, 2007.

CHAPTER 13: HIJAB—ISLAMIC PIETY OR POLITICAL ISLAM?
281 **"a man's accusing finger":** Khaled Hosseini, *A Thousand Splendid Suns,* 7.
281 **"cut throats":** Ali Jaafar, "Islamist Group Threatens Female Journos," *Variety Weekly,* June 8, 2007, www.variety.com/article/VR1117966573.html?categoryId=2523&cs=1.
283 **"a useless reason.":** "Quebec martial arts team protests hijab ban," *The Toronto Star,* April 15, 2007, www.thestar.com/News/article/203338.
283 **"further their agenda in Canada.":** MCC, www.muslimcanadiancongress. org/20070417.html.
283 **illegitimate children:** "The Disadvantages of Discarding the Hijab," Centre Communautaire Musulman de Montreal, www.ccmmontreal.com/English%20page. htm.
284 **exposing her charms:** "Questions about Hijab," Centre Communautaire Musulman de Montreal.
285 **"destroy her future.":** Sarah Boesvald, "Muslim Woman Fears She Would Be Perceived as 'Not Clean,'" CanWest News Service, September 27, 2007.
286 **a huge distinction:** Unnati Gandi, "Concern for Reputation Leads Muslim Woman to Clarify Sex Assault," *The Globe and Mail,* September 27, 2007.
287 **"protect women's honour":** "Sheik apologises for sexist comments," *The Age,* October 27, 2006.
287 **uncovered meat:** Elsa McLaren, "Muslim Cleric Triggers Outrage by Blaming Women for Rape," *The Times,* London, October 26, 2006.
288 **Also (prohibited are) women already married,:** Abdullah Yusuf Ali, trans., 192, *Sura Nisa,* chapter 4, verse 24.
289 **female prisoner of war:** Abul Ala Maudoodi, *Tafhim-ul-Quran* (original Urdu edition), commentary on chapter 4, verse 24 of the Quran, 340. (Tarjumanul Quran Publishers, Lahore, 1951, www.tafheemulquran.org/Tafhim_u/004/surah_all.htm.
289 **proprietary rights:** Ibid, 341.
289 **"Our bookstore would not allow":** Leslie Scrivener, "Furor over a Five-Letter Word: A Translator of the Qur'an Doesn't Believe Muhammad Could Have Condoned Spousal Abuse," *The Toronto Star,* October 21, 2007.
291 **hijab:** Ibrahim B. Syed, "Women in Islam: Hijab," www.irfi.org/articles/women_in_ islam/women_in_islam_hijab.htm.
291 **asking women to cover their breasts:** *The Quran,* chapter 24, verse 31.
291 **khimar:** Muhammad Asad, *The Message of the Qur'an,* 538.
292 **"the women closest":** As quoted in Ibrahim B. Syed, "Women in Islam: Hijab."
292 **practice of power:** Fatima Mernissi, *The Veil and the Male Elite,* 9.

292 **deserving of death:** In March 2007, a man left the following phone message for the Muslim Canadian Congress: "This is a warning to Tarek Fatah and Farzana Hassan and to all the members of your munafiq [apostate] organization. Wa Allah al-azeem [In the name of God who is great], I swear . . . on all ninety-nine names of Allah, if you do not cease from your campaign of smearing Islam . . . Wa Allahi, wa Allahi, wa Allahi [by God, by God, by God], I will slaughter all of you."

292 **covering the bosom with a khimar:** Farzana Hassan, *Islam, Women and the Challenges of Today,* 156, 160.

293 **sexually corrupting:** Asma Barlas, *"Believing Women" in Islam,* 54.

293 **"hides God from men,":** *The Quran,* 42: 51.

293 **hijab:** Ibid., 41: 5.

293 **"negative significance.":** Fatima Mernissi, *The Veil and the Male Elite,* 96.

293 *Women Who Deserve to Go to Hell* caused an uproar in Britain when the *London Telegraph* revealed the book was being stocked in British libraries. "Report: Libraries stock Islamic terror books," *The Telegraph,* September 7, 2007.

294 **danger represented by change:** Fatima Mernissi, *The Veil and the Male Elite,* 97.

294 **protected from molestation:** Syed Osman Sher, *Religion, God and Islam,* 176.

295 **vague grasp of the Quranic verses:** Reem Meshal, "Banners of Faith and Identities in Construct: The Hijab in Canada," in Sultana Alvi, et al., *The Muslim Veil in North America,* 89.

296 **campus organizations,:** Ibid, 86.

296 **graduation ceremony:** Ibid, 34.

296 **"emotional distress.":** H.G. Raza, "Muslim Sues Orange County over Right to Wear Headscarf," *Los Angeles Times,* September 5, 2007.

298 **"Why was I born a girl?":** Mouna Naim, "Saudi women kept in the shadows," *Le Monde,* [Reproduced in the *Guardian Weekly*] December 28–29, 2003, www.guardian. co.uk/guardianweekly/story/0,12674,1117965,00.html.

299 **protest both sides of the problem.:** Quoted in Tarek Fatah, "French not only offenders on hijab. Anger against France is justified, but what about Iran and Saudi Arabia?" *The Toronto Star,* January 21, 2004.

300 **"male voices only,":** MuslimFest 2004, Call for Talent Information Package, Submission Guidelines.

300 **"narrow interpretation of Islamic culture":** Marina Jimenez, "Women Artists, Performers Criticize Muslim Festival Restrictions," *The Globe and Mail,* August 13, 2005.

301 **"discriminated against.":** Ibid.

301 **Ibn Khaldun:** Ibn Khaldun, *The Muqaddimah,* 331.

302 **moral values.:** Nawal Al-Saadawi, on *Al-Arabiya TV* on March 3, 2007.

CHAPTER 14: THE ISLAMIST AGENDA IN THE WEST

303 **WAMY,** a student group founded in 1972, is based in Saudi Arabia but maintains satellite chapters in fifty-five additional countries and is affiliated with some five hundred other Muslim youth groups on five continents. It is one of the vehicles through which Saudi Arabia's Wahhabis propagate Islamic extremism. WAMY was co-founded by Kamal Helwabi, a former senior member of the Egyptian Muslim Brotherhood, and by Abdullah bin Laden (Osama bin Laden's nephew), who served as WAMY's president through 2002 and is now its treasurer.

368 | Chasing a Mirage

303 **"Western civilization is rotten":** Catherine Porter, "Help Cure West's Ills," *The Toronto Star,* January 6, 2003.

304 **only Muslims will go to heaven:** Richard Gwyn, *The Toronto Star,* October 21, 2001.

304 **isolationist strain:** Ibid.

305 **Taliban's ban on women's education:** Jan Wong, *The Globe and Mail,* October 29, 2001, A14.

306 **financing from terror apologists:** Stephen Schwartz, "Hardliners in Costume as Moderate Muslims," January 3, 2007, www.islamicpluralism.org/articles/americanislam07.htm#Hardliners_in_Costume.

306 **"members of the U.S. Muslim Brotherhood.":** Josh Gerstein, "US Islamic Groups Named in Hamas Funding Case," *The New York Sun,* June 4, 2007.

306 **portrayal of Muslims:** Laurie Goodstein, "Stereotyping Rankles Silent, Secular Majority of American Muslims," *The New York Times,* December 23, 2001.

307 **effective coordination among Islamic organisations:** *Ain al Yaqeen,* July 12, 2002, www.ain-al-yaqeen.com/issues/20020712/feat10en.htm.

307 **defend Islam:** "Al-Walid Bin Talal Donates Half a Million for CAIR Campaign in the USA," *ArabicNews.Com,* Nov. 19, 2002, www.arabicnews.com/ansub/Daily/Day/021119/2002111910.html.

307 **"co-opt" Muslim organizations.:** "US Muslims Divided over Saudi Aid," *Los Angeles Times,* December 1, 2001.

307 **"demonise the Saudis.":** Ibid.

308 **property in the United States:** www.uaeinteract.com/news/default.asp?ID=178.

308 **Dubai is a mixture:** Sheema Khan, "Don't Be Fearful of Dubai," *The Globe and Mail,* March 22, 2007.

309 **average construction worker:** Pepe Escobar, "Dubai Lives the Post-Oil Arab Dream," *Asia Times,* June 7, 2006.

310 **terrorist financing:** Robert Fife, "Saudis Fund Radicals in Canada," *Ottawa Citizen,* July 4, 2004.

311 **IDB funding:** "Canadian Muslims Are Divided over Sharia, Funding from Overseas, and Religion's Role in a Secular Society," by Marina Jimenez and Omar El Akkad, *The Globe and Mail,* November 8, 2005.

311 **"a grant":** idb website, www.isdb.org/irj/portal/anonymous (accessed December 13, 2007).

311 **$270,000 grant:** Heba Aly, "Overseas Cash for Mosques Making Some Muslims Uneasy," *The Toronto Star,* October 19, 2006.

313 **Saudi-supported channels:** Hamid Algar, "Wahhabism: A Critical Essay," in Yvonne Yazbeck Haddad and Adair T. Lummis, eds., *Islamic Values in the United States,* 124.

314 **official approval of Wahhabism:** Ibid.

314 **"We will conquer Europe,":** John Mintz and Douglas Farah, "In Search of Friends among Foes," *The Washington Post,* September 11, 2004.

314 **"largest college groups.":** Ibid.

314 **Wahhabi control:** Stephen Schwartz, "Terrorism: Growing Wahhabi Influence in the United States," testimony before the U.S. Senate Committee on the Judiciary, June 26, 2003.

316 **censorship:** "Don't Be Silenced by Extremists," *The Toronto Star,* February 28, 2006.

318 **new friends:** Fred Halliday, "The Left and the Jihad," *Open Democracy,* September 7, 2006.

319 **"anvil":** Paige Austin, "Tariq Ali: Toward A New Radical Politics," *Mother Jones,* August 9, 2006, www.motherjones.com/interview/2006/08/tariq_ali.html.
319 **US foreign policy strategy:** Richard Dreyfuss, *The Devil's Game,* 265.
320 **channelled money:** Ibid, 288.
322 **keep their politics to themselves:** "Keep politics out of our mosques. Muslims cannot sit still while a fascist cult of Islamic supremacy takes over places of worship, says Tarek Fatah," *The Toronto Star,* June 7, 2006.
322 **arrests:** "Studio 2 with Paula Todd," TVO, Toronto, June 5, 2006.
323 **atheist:** Tariq Ali, *The Clash of Fundamentalisms,* 304.
323 **justified response:** Ibid, 304.
324 **What do the Islamists offer?:** Ibid, 304.
324 **Islamo-anarchism:** Alexander Cockburn, "Islamo-Anarchs or Islamo-Fascists?," *CounterPunch,* July 23, 2005; Tariq Ali, "London Bombings: Why they happened," *CounterPunch,* July 8, 2005.
324 **counterjihad against puritan heresy.:** Khaled Abou El-Fadl, *The Great Theft: Wrestling Islam from the Extremists,* 286.
325 **most dull:** Khaled Abou El-Fadl, "Reformation within Islam; Focus on Women," keynote speech at annual conference of the Canadian Council of Muslim Women (CCMW), September 14, 2002.
327 **victims of his own creation.:** *Crescent International,* "Lennon Killed by His Own Image," January 16, 1981.
328 **deliberately fed lies:** K.K. Aziz, *The Murder of History,* 175.
328 **struggle between the Muslim and the Jews should continue:** Nina Shea, "This Is a Saudi Textbook. (After the Intolerance was Removed.)," *The Washington Post,* May 21, 2006, B1.
329 **The apes are Jews:** Ibid.
329 **Whoever dies outside of Islam:** Ibid.
329 **Muslims will fight and kill Jews:** Valerie Strauss and Emily Wax, "Where Two Worlds Collide: Muslim Schools Face Tension of Islamic, U.S. Views," *The Washington Post,* February 25, 2002.
329 **emigrate:** "If You Hate The West, Emigrate to a Muslim Country," *The Guardian,* October 8, 2001.

CONCLUSION
332 **Fear:** Al Gore, *The Assault on Reason,* 23.
332 **"Both fear and reason are essential":** Ibid, 23.
332 **so effectually robs the mind:** Popular quote from Burke's *A Philosophical Enquiry into the Origin of Our Ideas of the Sublime and Beautiful* (1757).
332 **map of the Americas:** Abdullah Hakim Quick, *Deeper Roots: Muslims in the Americas and the Caribbean from Before Columbus to the Present,* 71.
333 **as early as 1885:** Philip Harsham, "Islam in Iowa," *Saudi Aramco World,* November/ December 1976, 30–36.
333 **Eqbal Ahmad:** From 1960 to 1963, Ahmad lived in North Africa, working primarily in Algeria, where he joined the National Liberation Front and worked with Frantz Fanon. He was a member of the Algerian delegation to peace talks at Evian. On returning to the United States in the 1960s after the liberation of Algeria, he plunged into the anti-war movement. In 1971, Ahmad was arrested, tried, and acquitted on a charge of attempting to kidnap Henry Kissinger. He was admired by De Gaulle, and

during these years became known as "one of the earliest and most vocal opponents of American policies in Vietnam and Cambodia."

AFTERWORD

342   no state, but only a ruler: Bernard Lewis, "Islam and Liberal Democracy," *The Atlantic,* February 1993.

Selected Bibliography

THIS LIST contains books referred to in the text. Full details of other sources appear in the Notes.

NB: The transliteration of Arabic names means that publishers listed below may have spelled names slightly differently from the style chosen for the chapter text of this book. Last names prefixed by "al-" or "el-" are listed under the first letter of the rest of the name.

Abbas, Hassan. *Pakistan's Drift into Extremism: Allah, the Army, and America's War on Terror.* New York: M.E. Sharpe, 2005.

Abu-Amr, Ziad. *Islamic Fundamentalism in the West Bank and Gaza: Muslim Brotherhood and Islamic Jihad.* Bloomington: Indiana University Press, 1994.

Abu-Sahlieh, Sami A. Aldeeb. *Muslims in the West: Redefining the Separation of Church and State.* Translated by Sheldon Lee Gosline. Warren Center, PA: Shangri-La Publications, 2002.

Afary, Janet, and Kevin b. Anderson. *Foucault and the Iranian Revolution: Gender and the Seductions of Islamism.* Chicago: University of Chicago Press, 2005.

Ahmad, Sayed Riaz. *Maulana Maududi and Islamic State.* Lahore: People's Publishing House, 1976.

Ahmed, Akbar S. *Jinnah, Pakistan and Islamic Identity: The Search for Saladin.* London: Routledge, 1997.

Ahmed, Ishtiaq. *The Concept of an Islamic State: An Analysis of the Ideological Controversy in Pakistan.* New York: St-Martin's Press, 1987.

Akhtar, Shabbir. *A Faith for All Seasons: Islam and the Challenge of the Modern World.* Chicago: Ivan R. Dee Publisher, 1990.

Alangari, Haifa. *The Struggle for Power in Arabia: Ibn Saud, Hussein and Great Britain, 1914–1924.* Reading, England: Ithaca Press, 1998.

Alfarabi, Alfarabi: *Philosophy of Plato and Aristotle.* Ithaca, NY: Cornell University Press, 2001.

Ali, Abdullah Yusuf. *The Meaning of The Holy Qur'an.* Beltsville, MD: Amana Publications, 2004.

Ali, Ahmed, trans. *Al-Qur'an.* Princeton, NJ: Princeton University Press, 1984.

Ali, Maulana Muhammad. *A Manual of Hadith.* Lahore: Anjuman Ishaat Islam, 1941.

Ali, Tariq. Bush in Babylon: *The Recolonisation of Iraq.* London: Verso, 2003.

———. *Shadows of the Pomegranate Tree.* London: Verso, 1993.

———. *The Clash of Fundamentalisms: Crusades, Jihads and Modernity.* London: Verso, 2002.

———. *The Leopard and the Fox: A Pakistani Tragedy.* London: Seagull Books, 2007.

Allen, Charles. *God's Terrorists: The Wahhabi Cult and the Hidden Roots of Modern Islam.* London: Abacus, 2007.

Almond, Ian. *Sufism and Deconstruction: A Comparative Study of Derrida and Ibn 'Arabi.* New York: Routledge, 2004.

Alvi, Sajida Sultana, Homa Hoodfar, and Sheila McDonough, eds. *The Muslim Veil in North America: Issues and Debate.* Toronto: Women's Press, 2003.

An-Na'im, Abdullahi Ahmed. *Toward an Islamic Reformation: Civil Liberties, Human Rights, and International Law.* Syracuse, NY: Syracuse University Press, 1996.

Arberry, A. J. *The Islamic Art of Persia.* New Delhi: Goodword Books, 2001.

Armstrong, Karen. *Holy War: The Crusades and their Impact on Today's World.* New York: Anchor Books, 2001.

———. *Muhammad: A Biography of the Prophet.* San Francisco: HarperSanFrancisco, 1992.

Arnold, Thomas W. *The Caliphate.* 1st ed. Delhi: Adam Publishers & Distributors, 1924.

———. *The Islamic Art and Architecture.* New Delhi: Goodword Books, 2001.

Asad, Muhammad. *The Principles of State and Government in Islam.* Kuala Lumpur, Malaysia: Islamic Book Trust, 1999.

———. *The Road to Mecca.* Gibraltar: Dar Al-Andalus, 1980.

———. *This Law of Ours and Other Essays.* Kuala Lumpur: Islamic Book Trust, 2000.

Atmaja, Dwi S., Richard C. Martin, and Mark R. Woodward. *Defenders of Reason in Islam: Mu'Tazilism from Medieval School to Modern Symbol.* Oxford, England: Oneworld Publications, 2003.

Averroës. *Averroes' Tahafut al-Tahafut* (The Incoherence of the Incoherence). Translated by Simon Van Den Bergh. Cambridge, England: E.J.W. Gibb Memorial, 1987.

——. *Decisive Treatise & Epistle Dedicatory*. Introduced and translated by Charles E. Butterworth. Provo, UT: Brigham Young University Press, 2001.

——. *Faith and Reason in Islam: Averroes' Exposition of Religious Arguments*. Oxford, England: Oneworld Publications, 2005.

Ayoub, Mahmoud M. *The Crisis of Muslim History: Religion and Politics in Early Islam*. Oxford, England: Oneworld Publications, 2005.

——. *The Qur'an and Its Interpreters*. Albany: State University of New York Press, 1984.

Aziz, K.K. *The Murder of History: A Critique of History Textbooks Used in Pakistan*. Lahore: Vanguard Books, 1993.

Badawi, Mostafa, al-. *Immam 'Abdallah ibn 'Alawi al-Haddad: Sufi Sage of Arabia*. Louisville, KY: Fons Vitae, 2005.

Bakhash Shaul. *The Reign of the Ayatollahs*. New York: Basic Books Inc., 1984.

Bakhtiar, Laleh. *Encyclopedia of Islamic Law: A Compendium of the Major Schools*. Chicago: ABC International Group, Inc., 1996.

——. *Shariati on Shariati and the Muslim Woman*. Chicago: ABC International Group, 1996.

—— , trans. *The Sublime Quran*. Chicago: Islamicworld.com (distributed by Kazi Publications), 2007.

Baladhuri, Al-, Abu-l Abbas, Ahmad ibn Jabir. *The Origins of the Islamic State*. Translated by Philip Khuri Hitti. New Jersey: Gorgias Press, 2002.

Balagha, Nahjul. *Peak of Eloquance: Sermons, Letters and Sayings of Imam Ali ibn Abu Talib*. Translated by Sayed Ali Reza. Elmhurst, NY: Tahrike Tarsile Qur'an, 1996.

Bamyeh, Mohammed A. *The Social Origins of Islam: Mind, Economy, Discourse*. Minneapolis: University of Minnesota Press, 1999.

Barber, Benjamin R. *Jihad vs McWorld: How Globalism and Tribalism are Reshaping the World*. New York: Ballantine Books, 1996.

Barlas, Asma. *"Believing Women" in Islam: Unreading Patriarchal Interpretations of the Qur'an*. Austin: University of Texas Press, 2002.

Beck, Lois, and Nikki Keddie, eds. *Women in the Muslim World*. Cambridge, MA: Harvard University Press, 1978.

Bell, Stewart. *Cold Terror: How Canada Nurtures and Exports Terrorism around the World*. Canada: John Wiley Canada, 2004.

Bewly, Aisha. *Muawiyah: Restorer of the Muslim Faith*. London: Dar Al Taqwa, 2002.

Bhutto, Benazir, *Daughter of Destiny*. New York: Simon and Schuster, 1989.

Bhutto, Zulfikar Ali, *If I am Assassinated*. New Delhi: Vikas Publishing House, 1979.

Bin Sayeed, Khalid. *Pakistan: The Formative Phase 1857-1948*. Lahore: Oxford University Press, 1969.

Biruni, Al. *Alberuni's India.* Translated by Edward C. Sachau. New York: W.W. Norton, 1971.

Black, Antony. *The History of Islamic Political Thought: From the Prophet to the Present.* New York: Routledge, 2001.

Black, Edwin. *Banking on Baghdad: Inside Iraq's 7,000-Year History of War, Profit, and Conflict.* New York: John Wiley, 2004.

Blankinship, Khalid Yahya. *The End of the Jihad State: The Reign of Hisham Ibn 'Abd al-Malik and the Collapse of the Umayyads.* Albany: State University of New York Press, 1994.

Bolitho, Hector. *Jinnah: Creator of Pakistan.* Westport, CT: Greenwood Press Publishers, 1981.

Bostom, Andrew G., ed. *The Legacy of Jihad: Islamic Holy War and the Fate of Non-Muslims.* Amherst, NY: Prometheus Books, 2005.

Bosworth, C.E., ed. *Iran and Islam.* Edinburgh: Edinburgh University Press, 1971.

Bosworth, C.E., and Joseph Schacht, eds. *The Legacy of Islam.* 2nd ed. Oxford, England: Oxford University Press, 1979.

Bowen, John R. *Religions in Practice: An Approach to the Anthropology of Religion.* Boston, MA: Allyn & Bacon, 1998.

Brown, Daniel. *Rethinking Tradition in Modern Islamic Thought.* Cambridge, England: Cambridge University Press, 1996.

Bucaille, Maurice. *The Bible, The Qur'an and Science.* Translated by Alastair D. Pannell and the Author. Indianapolis, IN: North American Trust Publication, 1978.

Burr, J. Millard, and Robert O. Collins. *Alms for Jihad: Charity and Terrorism in the Islamic World.* Cambridge, England: Cambridge University Press, 2006.

Charfi, Mohamed. *Islam and Liberty: The Historical Misunderstanding.* London: Zed Books, 2005.

Chejne, Anwar. *Succession to the Rule in Islam.* Lahore: Sh. Muhammad Ashraf, 1979.

Chowdhry, Shiv Rai. *Al-Hajjaj ibn Yusuf: An Examination of His Works and Personality.* Delhi: University of Delhi.

Cook, David. *Contemporary Muslim Apocalyptic Literature.* Syracuse, NY: Syracuse University Press, 2005.

——. *Understanding Jihad.* Berkeley: University of California Press, 2005.

Crone, Patricia. *God's Rule: Government and Islam.* New York: Columbia University Press, 2004.

Darussalam. *Mingling Between Men & Women Is Prohibited.* Riyadh: Darussalam Publishers & Distributors, 2002.

Davis, Gregory M. *Religion of Peace?: Islam's War Against the World.* Los Angeles: World Ahead Publishing, 2006.

Dashti, Ali. *Twenty-Three Years: A Study of the Prophetic Career of Mohammad.* Costa Mesa, CA: Mazda Publishers, 1984.

De Villiers, Marq, and Sheila Hirtle. *Timbuktu: The Sahara's Fabled City of Gold.* Toronto: McClelland & Stewart, 2007.

Dilshad, Hasan. *Islam: Philosophy and Ideology.* New Delhi: Anmol Publications, 2005.

Dozy, Reinhart. *Spanish Islam: A History of the Muslims in Spain.* Translated by Francis Griffin Stokes. New Delhi: Goodword Books, 2001.

Dreyfuss, Robert. *The Devil's Game: How the United States Helped Unleash Fundamentalist Islam.* New York: Metropolitan Books/Henry Holt, 2005.

Dunn, Ross E. *The Adventure of Ibn Battuta: A Muslim Traveler of the 14th Century.* Berkeley: University of California Press, 1986.

Elmasry, Mohamed. *The Quran: 365 Selections for Daily Reading.* Kitchener, ON: M.I. Elmasry, 2003.

Enayat, Hamid. *Modern Islamic Political Thought.* Austin: University of Texas Press, 1982.

Engineer, Asghar Ali. *The Origins and Development of Islam.* Kuala Lumpur: Ikraq, 1990.

Esposito, John L. *Islam: The Straight Path.* New York: Oxford University Press, 1988.

———. *The Oxford History of Islam.* Oxford, England: Oxford University Press, 1999.

Fadl, Khaled M. Abou el-. *Conference of the Books: The Search for Beauty in Islam.* Lanham, MD: University Press of America, 2001.

———. *The Great Theft: Wrestling Islam from the Extremists.* San Francisco: HarperSanFrancisco, 2005.

———. *Speaking in God's Name: Islamic Law, Authority and Women.* Oxford, England: Oneworld Publications, 2001.

Fakhry, Majid. *Averroes (Ibn Rushd): His Life, Works and Influence.* Oxford, England: Oneworld Publications, 2001.

———. *A History of Islamic Philosophy.* New York: Columbia University Press, 1983.

Fariborz, Janice. *The Role and Causes of Political Instability in the Fall of Muslim Granada 1461–1492.* Kalamazoo: Western Michigan University, 1968.

Fierro, Maribel. *Abd al-Rahman III: The First Cordoban Caliph.* Oxford, England: Oneworld Publications, 2005.

Frye, Richard N. *The Golden Age of Persia.* London: Phoenix Press, 2003.

Fyzee, Asaf A.A. *Outlines of Muhammadan Law.* New Delhi: Oxford University Press, 1964.

Gauhar, Altaf. *Ayub Khan: Pakistan's First Military Ruler.* Lahore: Sang-e-Meel Publications, 1993.

Ghazali, Al-. *Deliverance from Error: An Annotated Translation of al-Munqidh min al Dalal and Other Relevant Works of Al-Ghazali.* Translated by Richard Joseph McCarthy Louisville, KY: Fons Vitae, 1980.

——. *The Incoherence of the Philosophers.* Translated by Michael E. Marmura. Provo, UT: Brigham Young University Press, 2000.

——. *Ihya Ulum-id-din (Bengali translation).* 4 vols. Translated by M.N.M. Imdadullah. Dhaka: Taj Publishing House, 1994.

——. *Ihya Ulum-id-din (The Revivification of the Sciences of Religion).* 4 vols. Translated by Maulana Fazlul Karim. New Delhi: Kitab Bhavan, 1982.

Gilsenan, Michael. *Recognizing Islam: Religion and Society in the Modern Arab World.* New York: Pantheon Books, 1982.

Glubb, John. *The Life and Times of Muhammad.* Lanham, MD: Madison Books, 1998.

Glubb, John Bagot. *The Course of Empire: The Arabs and their Successors.* London: Hodder & Stoughton, 1965.

——. *The Empire of the Arabs.* London: Hodder & Stoughton, 1972.

——. *Haroon al Rasheed and the Great Abbasids.* London: Hodder & Stoughton, 1976.

——. *The Lost Centuries: From the Muslim Empires to the Renaissance of Europe 1145–1453.* London: Hodder & Stoughton, 1967.

Gore, Al. *The Assault on Reason.* New York: Penguin Press, 2007.

Gran, Peter. *Islamic Roots of Capitalism: Egypt, 1760–1840.* Syracuse, NY: Syracuse University Press, 1998.

Habeck, Mary. *Knowing the Enemy: Jihadist Ideology and the War on Terror.* New Haven, CT: Yale University Press, 2006.

Haddad, Gibril Fouad. *Albani & His Friends: A Concise Guide to the Salafi Movement.* UK: Aqsa Publications, 2004.

Haddad, Yvonne Yazbeck, and Adair T. Lummis, eds. *Islamic Values in the United States.* New York: Oxford University Press, 1987.

Hafiz, Ali. *Chapters from the History of Madina.* Jeddah, Saudi Arabia: Al Madina Printing and Publication, 1987.

Hamid, Tawfik. *The Roots of Jihad: An Insider's View of Islamic Violence.* US: Top Executive Media, 2005.

Hamidullah, Muhammad. *The First Written Constitution in the World: An Important Document of the Time of the Holy Prophet.* Lahore: Sh. Muhammad Ashraf, 1994.

——. *The Prophet's Establishing a State and His Succession.* New Delhi: Adam Publishers & Distributors, 2006.

Hamilton, Marci A. *God vs. the Gavel: Religion and the Rule of Law.* Cambridge, England: Cambridge University Press, 2005.

Hanbali, Ibn Rajab al-. *The Heirs of the Prophets*. Introduced and translated by Zaid Shakir. Chicago: Starlatch Press, 2001.

Haqqani, Husain. *Pakistan: Between Mosque and Military*. Washington, DC: Carnegie Endowment for International Peace, 2005.

Hassan, Farzana. *Islam, Women and the Challenges of Today*. Toronto: White Knight Books, 2006.

Hawting, Gerald R. *The First Dynasty of Islam: The Umayyad Caliphate AD 661–750*. London: Routledge, 2000.

Haykal, Muhammad Husayn. *The Life of Muhammad*. Translated by Isma'il Ragi A. al-Faruqi. US: North American Trust Publication, 1976.

Helminski, Camille Adams. Selected and introduced. *Women of Sufism: A Hidden Treasure*. Boston, MA: Shambhala Publications, 2003.

Hinds, Martin, and Patricia Crone. *God's Caliph: Religious Authority in the First Centuries of Islam*. Cambridge, England: Cambridge University Press, 2003.

Hitti, Philip K. *History of the Arabs: From the Earliest Times to the Present*. London: Macmillan, 1970.

Hodgson, Marshall G.S. *The Venture of Islam: Conscience and History in a World Civilization*. Chicago: University of Chicago Press, 1974.

Hoodbhoy, Pervez. *Islam and Science: Religious Orthodoxy and the Battle for Rationality*. London: Zed Books, 1991.

Hosseini, Khaled. *A Thousand Splendid Suns*. Toronto: Viking Canada, 2007.

Hourani, Albert. *A History of the Arab Peoples*. New York: Warner Books, 1992.

———. *Islam in European Thought*. Cambridge, England: Cambridge University Press, 1996.

Ibn 'Arabi al-Hatimi at-Ta'i, Hadrat Muhyiddin. *Divine Governance of the Human Kingdom*. Interpreted by Shaykh Tosun Bayrak al-Jerrahi al-Halveti. Louisville, KY: Fons Vitae, 1997.

Ibn Maja. *Sunan Ibn Maja*. 2 vols. Karachi: 1975.

Imran, Muhammad. *Ideal Woman in Islam*. Lahore: Islamic Publications, 1993.

Iqbal, Allama Muhamad. *The Reconstruction of Religious Thought in Islam*. Lahore: Institute of Islamic Culture, 1989.

Irving, Washington. *The Alhambra*. New Delhi: Goodword Books, 2006.

Ishaq, Ibn. *The Life of Muhammad*. Edited by Michael Edwardes. London: Folio Society, 2003.

———. *The Life of Muhammad*. Notes by A. Guillaume. Oxford, England: Oxford University Press, 2006.

Jafarzadeh, Alireza. *The Iran Threat: President Ahmadinejad and the Coming Nuclear Crisis*. New York: Palgrave Macmillan, 2007.

Jalalzai, Musa Khan. *Islamization and Minorities in Pakistan.* Lahore: Jumhoori Publications, 2005.

Jalbani, G.N. *Teachings of Shah Waliyullah.* Lahore: Sh. Muhammad Ashraf, 1979.

Kadri, Syed Shameem Hussain. *Creation of Pakistan.* Lahore: Wajidalis, 1982.

Kamali, Hashim. *Principles of Islamic Jurisprudence.* Cambridge, UK: Islamic Texts Society, 2006.

Kamil, Abd-al-'Aziz 'Abd-al-Qadir. *Islam and the Race Question.* Place de Fontenoy: UNESCO, 1970.

Kanwar, Mahfooz A. *The Sociology of Religion.* Calgary, AB: Mount Royal College Press, 1974.

Karamustafa, Ahmet T. *God's Unruly Friends: Dervish Groups in the Islamic Middle Period 1200–1550.* Oxford, England: Oneworld Publications, 2006.

Kathir, Ibn. *Tafsir Ibn Kathir.* 5 vols. Urdu translation by Muhammad Junagarhwi. Lahore: Maktab Qudoosia, 2003.

——. *Tafsir Ibn Kathir (Abridged).* 10 volumes. Riyadh: Maktaba Daru-us-Salam, 2000.

Kennedy, Hugh. *The Court of the Caliphs: The Rise and Fall of Islam's Greatest Dynasty.* London: Weidenfeld & Nicolson, 2004.

——. *Muslim Spain and Portugal: A Political History of al-Andalus.* Essex, England: Pearson Education, 1996.

Kennedy, Philip F. *Abu Nuwas: A Genius of Poetry.* Oxford, England: Oneworld Publications, 2005.

Kepel, Gilles. *The War for Muslim Minds: Islam and the West.* Translated by Pascale Ghazaleh. Cambridge, MA: Harvard University Press, Belknap Press, 2004.

Khaldun, Ibn. *The Muqaddimah: An Introduction to History.* Translated by Franz Rosenthal. Princeton, NJ: Bollingen Series, Princeton University Press, 1989.

Khan, Maulana Wahiduddin. *The True Jihad: The Concepts of Peace, Tolerance and Non-Violence in Islam.* New Delhi: Goodword Books, 2002.

Khan, Mohammad Asghar. *Generals in Politics: Pakistan 1958–1982.* New Delhi: Vikas Publishing House, 1983.

Khan, Muhammad Muhsin. *Summarized Sahih al-Bukhari.* Riyadh: Maktaba Dar-us-Salam, 1994.

——. *The Translation of the Meanings of Sahih al-Bukhari.* 9 vols. Riyadh: Maktaba Daru-us-Salam, 1997.

Khuri, Fuad I. *Imams and Emirs: State, Religion and Sects in Islam.* London: Saqi Books, 2006.

Kuran, Timur. *Islam and Mammon: The Economic Predicaments of Islamism.* Princeton, NJ: Princeton University Press, 2004.

Kurzman, Charles, ed., *Liberal Islam: A Sourcebook.* New York: Oxford University Press, 1998.

Lacoste, Yves. *Ibn Khaldun: The Birth of History and the Past of the Third World.* Translated by David Macey. London: Verso, 1984.

Lambrick, H.T. *Sind: Before the Muslim Conquest.* Hyderabad, Pakistan: Sindhi Adabi Board, 1973.

Lane-Poole, Stanley. *The Muslims in Spain.* New Delhi: Goodword Books, 2006.

Lapidus, Ira M. *A History of Islamic Societies.* Cambridge, England: Cambridge University Press, 2002.

Lea, Henry Charles. *The Moriscos of Spain.* New Delhi: Goodword Books, 2001.

Leigh, Richard, and Michael Baigent. *The Inquisition.* London: Penguin Books, 2000.

Lemu, B. Aisha, and Fatima Heeren. *Women in Islam.* Leicester, England: Islamic Council of Europe, 1978.

Lenin, V.I. *Lenin's Collected Works.* Volume 31, Moscow: Progress Publishers, 1965.

Levy, Reuben. *The Social Structure of Islam.* Cambridge: Cambridge University Press, 1957.

Lewis, Bernard. *The Crisis of Islam: Holy War and Unholy Terror.* New York: Random House, 2004.

——. *The Emergence of Modern Turkey.* New York: Oxford University Press, 2001.

——. *The Muslim Discovery of Europe.* New York: W.W. Norton, 1982.

——. *The Political Language of Islam.* Chicago: University of Chicago Press, 1988.

——. *What Went Wrong? Western Impact and Middle Eastern Response.* Oxford, England: Oxford University Press, 2002.

Lia, Brynjar. *The Society of the Muslim Brothers in Egypt: The Rise of an Islamic Mass Movement 1928–1942.* Reading, England: Ithaca Press, 1998.

Lings, Martin. *Muhammad: His Life Based on the Earliest Sources.* Rochester, VT: Inner Traditions International, 1983.

Maalouf, Amin. *The Crusades Through Arab Eyes.* New York: Schocken Books, 1984.

Madelung, Wilfred. *The Succession to Muhammad: A Study of the Early Caliphate.* Cambridge, England: Cambridge University Press, 1997.

Mahmoud, Mohamed A. *Quest for Divinity: A Critical Examination of the Thought of Muhammad Taha.* Syracuse, NY: Syracuse University Press, 2007.

Mahmud, Hasan. *Islam and Sharia.* Dhaka, Bangladesh, 2007.

Manji, Irshad. *The Trouble with Islam Today: A Muslim's Call for Reform in Her Faith.* New York: St. Martin's Press, 2003.

Manucci, Niccolao. *Memoirs of the Mogul Court.* Edited by Michael Edwardes. London: Folio Society, __.

Mas'udi. *From the Meadows of Gold.* Translated by Paul Lunde and Caroline Stone. London: Penguin Books, 2007.

Maudoodi, Sayyed Abul ala. *The Process of Islamic Revolution.* Lahore: Markazi Maktaba-E-Jama'at-e-Islami Pakistan, 1955.

Maudoodi, Syed Abul Ala. *Islamic Law and Constitution.* Karachi: Jamaat-e-Islami Publications, 1955.

——. *Tafhimaat.* 3 vols. Lahore: Islamic Publications, 2004.

Maududi, S. Abul Ala. *Call to Jihad.* Translated and edited by Misbahul Islam Faruqi. Lahore: Islamic Publications, 1980.

——. *Fundamentals of Islam.* Lahore: Islamic Publications, 1975.

——. *The Holy Quran.* 6th ed. Translated and commented by Abul Ala Maududi. Lahore: Islamic Publications, 1991.

——. *Jihad in Islam.* Lahore: Islamic Publications, 1991.

——. *The Meaning of the Quran (Tafhimul Quran).* 6 vols. Translated by Muhammad Akbar. Lahore: Islamic Publications, 2005.

——. *Political Theory of Islam.* Edited and translated by Khurshid Ahmad. Lahore: Islamic Publications, 1985.

——. *A Short History of the Revivalist Movement in Islam.* Lahore: Islamic Publications, 1986.

——. *The Sick Nations of the Modern Age.* Edited and translated by Khurshid Ahmad. Lahore: Islamic Publications, 1979.

——. *Unity of the Muslim World.* Edited and translated by Khurshid Ahmad. Lahore: Islamic Publications, 1982.

Mauwdudi, Abul Ala. *Human Rights in Islam.* Edited and translated by Khurshid Ahmad. Leicester England: Islamic Foundation, 1990.

——. *Towards Understanding Islam.* Edited and translated by Khurshid Ahmad. Leicester, England: Islamic Foundation, 2000.

Mawdudi, Sayyid Abul Ala. *The Islamic Movement: Dynamics of Values, Power and Change.* Edited by Khurram Murad. Leicester, England: Islamic Foundation, 1991.

McGrath, Allen. *The Destruction of Pakistan's Democracy.* Oxford, England: Oxford University Press, 1998.

McLeod, W.H. *Textual Sources for the Study of Sikhism.* Manchester, UK: Manchester University Press, 1984.

Meddeb, Abdelwahab. *The Malady of Islam.* Translated by Pierre Joris and Ann Reid. New York: Basic Books, 2003.

Mernissi, Fatima. *Dreams of Trespass: Tales of a Harem Girlhood.* Reading, MA: Perseus Books, 1994.

——. *The Forgotten Queens of Islam.* Minneapolis: University of Minnesota Press, 1997.

——. *The Veil and the Male Elite: A Feminist Interpretation of Women's Rights in Islam.* Translated by Mary Jo Lakeland. New York: Addison-Wesley Publishing, 1991.

Miller, Judith. *God Has Ninety-Nine Names.* New York: Simon & Schuster, 1996.

Milton, Giles. *White Gold: The Extraordinary Story of Thomas Pellow and North Africa's One Million European Slaves.* London: Hodder & Stoughton, 2005.

Misri, Ahmad ibn Naqib al-. *Reliance of the Traveller: A Classic Manual of Islamic Sacred Law.* Translated by Nuh Ha Mim Keller. Beltsville, MD: Amana Publications, 1994.

Moaddel, Mansoor. *Islamic Modernism, Nationalism and Fundamentalism: Episode and Discourse.* Chicago: University of Chicago Press, 2005.

Mohaddessin, Mohammad. *Enemies of the Ayatollahs: The Iranian Opposition's War on the Islamic Fundamentalism.* New York: Zed Books, 2004.

Morgan, Michael Hamilton. *Lost History: The Enduring Legacy of Muslim Scientists, Thinkers, and Artists.* Washington, DC: National Geographic Society, 2007.

Mottahedeh, Roy. *The Mantle of the Prophet: Religion and Politics in Iran.* New York: Pantheon Books, 1985.

Mubarakpuri, Safi-ur-Rahman al-. *Ar-Raheeq al-makhtum (The Sealed Nectar): Biography of the Noble Prophet.* Saudi Arabia: Maktaba Dar-us-Salam, 1979.

Murata, Sachiko. *The Tao of Islam: A Sourcebook on Gender Relationships in Islamic Thought.* Albany: State University of New York Press, 1992.

Najeebabadi, Akbar Shah. *The History of Islam.* 3 vols. Revised by Safi-ur-Rahman Mubarakpuri. Riyadh: Darussalam Publishers & Distributors, 2000.

Nasr, Seyyid Hossein. *The Heart of Islam: Enduring Values for Humanity.* New York: HarperCollins, 2004.

Nasr, Vali. *The Shia Revival: How Conflicts Within Islam Will Shape the Future.* New York: W.W. Norton, 2006.

National Council of Resistance of Iran Foreign Affairs Committee, The (NCRIFAC). *Democracy Betrayed: A Response to the U.S. State Department Report on the Mojahedin and the Iranian Resistance.* Auvers-sur-Oise, France: NCRIFAC, 1993.

———. *Women, Islam & Equality.* Auvers-sur-Oise, France: NCRIFAC, 1995.

Nomani, Asra Q. *Standing Alone in Mecca: An American Woman's Struggle for the Soul of Islam.* New York: HarperSanFrancisco, 2005.

Noorani, A.G. *Islam and Jihad: Prejudice Versus Reality.* London: Zed Books, 2002.

Norris, Pippa, and Ronald Inglehart. *Sacred and Secular: Religion and Politics Worldwide.* Cambridge, England: Cambridge University Press, 2004.

O'Leary, De Lacy. *How Greek Science Passed to the Arabs.* New Delhi: Goodword Books, 2001.

———. *Islamic Thought and Its Place in History.* New Delhi: Goodword Books, 2001.

Oren, Michael B. *Power, Faith and Fantasy: America in the Middle East 1776 to Present.* New York: W.W. Norton, 2007.

O'Shea, Stephen. *Sea of Faith: Islam and Christianity in the Medieval Mediterranean World.* Vancouver: Douglas & McIntyre, 2006.

Ostrovsky, Victor. *The Other Side of Deception: A Rogue Agent Exposes the Mossad's Secret Agenda.* New York: HarperCollins, 1995.

Paris, Erna. *The End of Days: A Story of Tolerance, Tyranny and the Expulsion of the Jews from Spain.* Amherst, NY: Prometheus Books, 1995.

Patai, Raphael. *The Seed of Abraham: Jews and Arabs in Contact and Conflict.* New York: Charles Scribner's Sons, 1987.

Payne, Robert. *A History of Islam.* New York: Dorset Press, 1990.

Peters, F.E. *A Reader on Classical Islam.* Princeton, NJ: Princeton University Press, 1994.

Petterson, Donald. *Inside Sudan: Political Islam, Conflict and Catastrophe.* Boulder, CO: Westview Press, 1999.

Phipps, William E. *Muhammad and Jesus: A Comparison of the Prophets and Their Teachings.* New York: Continuum, 1996.

Piscatori, James P, ed. *Islam in the Political Process.* Cambridge, England: Cambridge University Press, 1983.

Prescott, William H. *History of the Reign of Isabella, the Catholic.* Philadelphia, PA: J.B. Lippincott, 1863.

Quick, Abdullah Hakim. *Deeper Roots: Muslims in the Americas and the Caribbean from Before Columbus to the Present.* London: Ta-Ha Publishers, 1996.

Qureshi, Ishtiaq Husain. *Ulema in Politics.* Karachi: Ma'aref, 1974.

Qutb, Sayyid. *Social Justice in Islam.* Translated by John B. Hardie (trans. revised by Hamid Algar). New York: Islamic Publications International, 2000.

Rahman, Fazlur. *Islam.* 2nd ed. Chicago: University of Chicago Press, 1979.

Rahman, Syed Azizur. *The Story of Islamic Spain.* New Delhi: Goodword Books, 2001.

Rajavi, Maryam. *Islamic Fundamentalism and the Question of Women.* Auvers-sur-Oise, France: The Women's Committee of the National Council of Resistance of Iran, 2004.

Ramadan, Tariq. *Islam, the West and the Challenges of Modernity.* Translated by Saïd Amghar. Leicester, England: Islamic Foundation, 2001.

Rashid, Ahmed. *Taliban: Militant Islam, Oil & Fundamentalism in Central Asia.* New Haven, CT: Yale Nota Bene / Yale University Press, 2001.

Razik, Ali Abd al-. *Islam and the Fundamentals of Authority: A Study of Caliphate and Government in Islam.* Cairo: 1925.

Reilly, Bernard F. *The Contest of Christian and Muslim Spain 1031–1157.* Oxford, England: Blackwell Publishers, 1992.

Robinson, Chase F. *Makers of the Muslim World: Abd al-Malik*. Oxford, England: Oneworld Publications, 2005.

Rodinson, Maxime. *Islam and Capitalism*. Translated by Brian Pearce. New York: Pantheon Books, 1973.

———. *Muhammad*. Translated by Anne Carter. New York: New Press, 2002.

Rogerson, Barnaby. *The Heirs of Muhammad: Islam's First Century and the Origins of the Sunni-Shia Split*. Woodstock, NY: Overlook Press, 2007.

Rosen, Lawrence. *The Culture of Islam: Changing Aspects of Contemporary Muslim Life*. Chicago: University of Chicago Press, 2002.

Roy, Olivier. *The Failure of Political Islam*. Translated by Carol Volk. Cambridge, MA: Harvard University Press, 1996.

———. *Globalised Islam: The Search for a New Ummah*. London: Hurst, 2004.

Rumi. *The Essential Rumi*. Translated by Coleman Barks, with John Moyne, A.J. Arberry, and Reynold Nicholson. New York: HarperSanFrancisco, 2004.

Ruthven, Malise. *Islam in the World*. New York: Penguin Books, 1984.

Saadawi, Nawal el-. *Walking through Fire: A Life of Nawal el Saadawi*. Translated by Sherif Hetata. New York: Zed Books, 2002.

Sachedina, Abdul-Aziz. *The Islamic Roots of Democratic Pluralism*. New York: Oxford University Press, 2001.

Sa'd, Ibn. *Kitab al-Tabaqat al-Kabir*. 2 vols. Translated by S. Moinul Haq. New Delhi: Kitab Bhavan, 1944.

Safi, Omid, ed. *Progressive Muslims: On Justice, Gender, and Pluralism*. Oxford, England: Oneworld Publications, 2003.

Safran, Janina M. *The Second Umayyad Caliphate: The Articulation of Caliphal. Legitimacy in Al-Andalus*. Cambridge, MA: Harvard University Press, 2000.

Sakr, Ahmad H. *Muslims and Non-Muslims Face to Face*. Lombard, IL: Foundation for Islamic Knowledge, 1991.

Saleem, Muhammad. *Islamic Banking: A $300 Billion Deception*. US: Xlibris, 2005.

Samir, Amin. *Political Islam*. Translated by Gabi Christov. Washington, DC: Covert Action Publications, 2001.

Sells, Michael, trans. and intro. *Approaching the Qur'an: The Early Revelations*. Ashland, OR: White Cloud Press, 1999.

Shadid, Anthony. *Legacy of the Prophet: Despots, Democrats, and the New Politics of Islam*. Boulder, CO: Westview Press, 2001.

Shaheed, Hasan al-Banna. *Selected Writings of Hasan al-Banna Shaheed*. Translated by S.A. Qureshi. New Delhi: Millat Book Centre, 1999.

Sharif, M.M., ed. *A History of Muslim Philosophy*. 2 vols. Delhi: Low Price Publications, 2004.

Sharma, Shashi S. *Caliphs and Sultans: Religious Ideology and Political Praxis.* Daryaganj, New Dehli: Rupa, 2004.

Sher, Syed Osman. *Religion, God and Islam.* New Delhi: Regency Publications, 2006.

Siddiqa, Ayesha. *Military Inc: Inside Pakistan's Military Economy.* London: Pluto Press, 2007.

Siddiqui, Kalim, ed. *Issues in the Islamic Movement: 1980–81 (1400–1401).* London: Open Press, 1982.

——. *Issues in the Islamic Movement 1981–82 (1401–1402).* London: Open Press, 1983.

——. *Issues in the Islamic Movement: 1982–83 (1402–1403).* London: Open Press, 1984.

Siegel, Paul N. *The Meek & the Militant: Religion and Power Across the World.* Chicago: Haymarket Books, 2005.

Sifaoui, Mohamed. *Inside Al-Qaeda: How I Infiltrated the World's Deadliest Terrorist Organization.* Translated by George Miller. London: Granta Books, 2003.

Simon, Heinrich. *Ibn Khaldun's Science of Human Culture.* Translated by Fuad Baali. Lahore: Sh. Muhammad Ashraf, 1978.

Smith, Wilfred Cantwell. *Islam in Modern History.* Princeton, NJ: Princeton University Press, 1957.

Spray, Lisa. *Women's Rights, the Quran and Islam.* Tuscon, Arizona: BSM Press, 2002.

Tabari, al-. *The History of al-Tabari.* Vol. 5, *The Sasanids, the Byzantines, the Lakhmids, and Yemen.* Translated by C.E. Bosworth. Albany: State University of New York Press, 1999.

——. Vol. 8, *The Victory of Islam.* Translated by Michael Fishbein. Albany: State University of New York Press, 1997.

——. Vol. 9, *The Last Years of the Prophet.* Translated by Ismail K. Poonawala. Albany: State University of New York Press, 1990.

——. Vol. 10, *The Conquest of Arabia.* Translated by Fred M. Donner. Albany: State University of New York Press, 1993.

——. Vol. 11, *The Challenge to the Empires.* Translated by Khalid Yahya Blankinship. Albany: State University of New York Press, 1993.

——. Vol. 12: *The Battle of al-Qadisiyyah and the Conquest of Syria and Palestine.* Translated by Yohanan Friedmann. Albany: State University of New York Press, 1992.

——. Vol. 13, *The Conquest of Iraq, Southwestern Persia, and Egypt.* Translated by Gauthier H.A. Juynboll. Albany: State University of New York Press, 1989.

——. Vol. 14, *The Conquest of Iran.* Translated by G. Rex Smith. Albany: State University of New York Press, 1994.

——. Vol. 15, *The Crisis of the Early Caliphate*. Translated by R. Stephen Humphreys. Albany: State University of New York Press, 1990.

——. Vol. 16, *The Community Divided*. Translated by Adrian Brockett. Albany: State University of New York Press, 1997.

——. Vol. 17, *The First Civil War*. Translated by G.R. Hawting. Albany: State University of New York Press, 1996.

——. Vol. 18, *Between Civil Wars: The Caliphate of Mu'awiyah*. Translated by Michael G. Morony. Albany: State University of New York Press, 1987.

——. Vol. 19, *The Caliphate of Yazid b. Mu'awiyah*. Translated by I.K.A. Howard. Albany: State University of New York Press, 1990.

——. Vol. 20, *The Collapse of Sufyanid Authority and the Coming of the Marwanids*. Translated by G.R. Hawting. Albany: State University of New York Press, 1989.

——. Vol. 23, *The Zenith of the Marwanid House*. Translated by Martin Hinds. Albany: State University of New York Press, 1990.

——. Vol. 25, *The End of Expansion*. Translated by Khalid Yahya Blankinship. Albany: State University of New York Press, 1989.

——. Vol. 26, *The Waning of the Umayyad Caliphate*. Translated by Carole Hillenbrand. Albany: State University of New York Press, 1989.

——. Vol. 27, *The 'Abbasid Revolution*. Translated by John Alden Williams. Albany: State University of New York Press, 1985.

——. Vol. 28, *Abbasid Authority Affirmed*. Translated by Jane Dammen McAuliffe. Albany: State University of New York Press, 1995.

——. Vol. 29, *Al-Mansur and al-Mahdi*. Translated by Hugh Kennedy. Albany: State University of New York Press, 1990.

——. Vol. 30, *The 'Abbasid Caliphate in Equilibrium*. Translated by C.E. Bosworth. Albany: State University of New York Press, 1989.

——. Vol. 31, *The War between Brothers*. Translated by Michael Fishbein. Albany: State University of New York Press, 1992.

——. Vol. 32, *The Reunification of the 'Abbasid Caliphate*. Translated by C.E. Bosworth. Albany: State University of New York Press, 1987.

——. Vol. 34, *Incipient Decline*. Translated by Joel L. Kraemer. Albany: State University of New York Press, 1989.

——. Vol. 36, *The Revolt of the Zanj*. Translated by David Waines. Albany: State University of New York Press, 1992.

——. Vol. 37, *The 'Abbasid Recovery*. Translated by Philip M. Fields. Albany: State University of New York Press, 1987.

——. Vol. 38, *The Return of the Caliphate to Baghdad*. Translated by Franz Rosenthal. Albany: State University of New York Press, 1985.

——. Vol. 39, *Biographies of the Prophet's Companions and Their Successors*. Translated by Ella Landau-Tasseron. Albany: State University of New York Press, 1998.

Taha, Mahmoud Mohamed. *The Second Message of Islam.* Translated by Abdullahi Ahmed An-Na'im. Syracuse, NY: Syracuse University Press, 1987.

Taher, Mohamed, ed. *Encyclopaedic Survey of Islamic Culture.* 20 vols. New Delhi: Anmol Publications, 2003.

Takim, Liyakat N. *The Heirs of the Prophet: Charisma and Religious Authority in Shi'ite Islam.* Albany: State University of New York Press, 2006.

Turner, Howard R. *Science in Medieval Islam.* Austin: University of Texas Press, 1997.

Vassiliev, Alexei. *The History of Saudi Arabia.* New York: New York University Press, 2000.

Viorst, Milton. *In the Shadow of the Prophet: The Struggle for the Soul of Islam.* Boulder, CO: Westview Press, 2001.

Wadud, Amina. *Qur'an and Woman: Rereading the Sacred Text from a Woman's Perspective.* Oxford, England: Oxford University Press, 1999.

Watt, W. Montgomery. *Muhammad: Prophet and Statesman.* London: Oxford University Press, 1961.

Weaver, Mary Anne. *Pakistan: In the Shadow of Jihad and Afghanistan.* New York: Farrar, Straus & Giroux, 2002.

Wink, André. *Al-Hind: The Making of the Indo-Islamic World.* Vol. 1, *Early Medieval India and the Expansion of Islam.* Leiden, Netherlands: Brill, 1996.

———. Vol. 3, *Indo-Islamic Society 14th–15th Century.* Leiden, Netherlands: Brill, 2004.

Winkel, Eric. *Islam and the Living Law: The Ibn al-Arabi Approach.* Oxford, England: Oxford University Press, 1997.

Wolpert, Stanley. *Jinnah of Pakistan.* Delhi: Oxford University Press, 1984.

Wright, Lawrence. *The Looming Tower: Al-Qaeda and the Road to 9/11.* New York: Alfred A. Knopf, 2007.

Yaqubi, Al-. *Tareekh Al-Yaqubi* (The History of Al-Yaqubi). 2 vols. Beirut: Dar Sader.

Zadeh, Aghaye Falah. *Islamic Laws According to the Verdicts of the Imam Khomeni and Sayyid Ali Khamene'i.* Translated by Hamid Hussein Waqar. Lulu.com, 2005.

Zagzebski, Linda. *The Philosophy of Religion: An Historical Introduction.* New York: Wiley-Blackwell, 2007.

Zakaria, Fareed. *The Future of Freedom: Illiberal Democracy at Home and Abroad.* New York: W.W. Norton, 2004.

Zakaria, Rafiq. *Muhammad and the Quran.* London: Penguin Books, 1991.

Index